Just Wind

Just Wind

Tales Of Two Pilots Under Pressure

William G. Armstrong Jr.

iUniverse, Inc.
New York Lincoln Shanghai

Just Wind
Tales Of Two Pilots Under Pressure

All Rights Reserved © 2003 by William G. Armstrong Jr.

No part of this book may be reproduced or transmitted in any form or by any means, graphic, electronic, or mechanical, including photocopying, recording, taping, or by any information storage retrieval system, without the written permission of the publisher.

iUniverse, Inc.

For information address:
iUniverse, Inc.
2021 Pine Lake Road, Suite 100
Lincoln, NE 68512
www.iuniverse.com

ISBN: 0-595-28705-0

Printed in the United States of America

Contents

Introduction 1

Light Heart: The Trans-Atlantic Balloon Flight of Tom Gatch

Chapter 1	Night Launch 7
Chapter 2	Inheriting the Wind 31
Chapter 3	Morning Aloft 54
Chapter 4	A Mid-Ocean Mystery 59
Chapter 5	Search and Hope 62
Chapter 6	Reflections 74

The Earthwinds Chronicles

Chapter 1	The Flight to Hallelujah Junction 87
Chapter 2	Ben's Dream 109
Chapter 3	Building a Team 123
Chapter 4	Inside the Pressure Cooker 152
Chapter 5	Winter Worries 180
Chapter 6	In Search of Harmonic Convergence 207
Chapter 7	Slipping the Surly Bonds 235
Chapter 8	Sagebrush and Pogonip 245

Chapter 9	Analysis and Rebuilding	279
Chapter 10	Into Thin Air	310
Chapter 11	Around the World or Bust	334
Epilogue		355

Introduction

This book chronicles two seemingly disparate expeditions by balloon, placing in context the high-stakes competition to be first across the Atlantic, and then first around the world.

Two pioneer balloonists—Tom Gatch in 1974 and Larry Newman in the early 1990s—led projects that could have landed them in the record books. Both gained a huge amount of publicity in their day, and captured the imaginations of millions of followers.

From a historical perspective, the two stories have many parallels:

- Tom Gatch was trying to be the first to fly across the Atlantic Ocean by balloon. Larry Newman's team succeeded in doing so four years after Gatch failed. Newman was trying to be the first to circumnavigate the globe by balloon—a mission accomplished four years after he failed.

- Gatch and Newman as aviation pioneers explored and employed new technology in attempting to accomplish what no one had done.

- Gatch and Newman were the first—and so far the only—balloonists to use pressurized balloons in stratospheric flight.

- Gatch and Newman each employed an unusual array of multiple balloons in their systems. Gatch ascended under a cluster of 10 super-pressure helium balloons. Newman tried a unique double balloon system: a huge helium balloon above the capsule for lifting and a massive pressurized balloon suspended below, for creating ballast.

- Gatch and Newman, though possessed of sharply different personalities, each held close the vision of how they would conduct their flight.

- Gatch and Newman each flew inside sealed capsules into the stratosphere—seven miles high. Both pilots largely built and modified their own capsules.

- Each used balloons built by the same manufacturer, and each suffered a catastrophic failure while aloft.

Many differences distinguished the two men and their projects.

In the first book, a determined, self-financed and self-reliant Tom Gatch tries to conquer the Atlantic Ocean alone by balloon. He makes it halfway across before disappearing without a trace. The Department of Defense mounts a massive but futile search for him in mid-ocean. In the years since, people asked, "What happened to him? Why did he do it?"

In the second book, Larry Newman leads the most expensive and heavily marketed balloon expedition ever undertaken, attempting to become the first fly a balloon around the world non-stop. He tries three times, each time with a different crew.

- Tom Gatch spent about $60,000 of his own savings. On this shoestring budget, he neither sought nor accepted sponsorship, and he remained free of outside influence. Larry Newman raised more than $9 million from world-class corporate sponsors, using little of his own money.
- Gatch shied from publicity until his flight was ready to begin. Newman sought publicity for every event leading up to launch.
- Gatch relied on a tiny cadre of helpers and advisors, no more than five altogether, none paid. Newman recruited, used and dismissed hundreds of volunteers and paid staff.
- Gatch, an Army Reserve colonel, had little experience as an aviator, having logged only 23 hours as a balloonist. Newman, with no military experience, had been flying since he was seven years old, had logged thousands of hours in the air in dozens of different kinds of aircraft, and had already won a Congressional Gold Medal for Aviation.
- Gatch and Newman came from vastly different social settings and from different parts of the United States.

Gatch and Newman each believed that pressurized scientific balloons would stabilize their flights at a fixed height. By using so-called super-pressure balloons, each pilot hoped he could eliminate the traditional balloonist's challenge of balancing and managing ballast and gas resources.

Gatch and Newman artifacts remained in museum displays for a while—at the National Air & Space Museum of the Smithsonian Institute, for instance—but ultimately their names became only footnotes in aviation history.

Only by the most remarkable of coincidences did I come to know each man. Tom Gatch and Larry Newman each invited me to publicize their projects. During 1973–74, I worked as a volunteer media director for Gatch's Project *Light*

Heart. From 1990–93, I worked as the media director for Larry Newman's *Earthwinds* Transglobal Flight.

Tom Gatch was my friend, an intelligent, educated and gracious man who helped me earn my pilot license. He flew with me on his last flight before taking off across the ocean. Although I never flew with Larry Newman, we spent countless hours together over several years working as a team.

Over the years, many people have asked: What motivated these men? How did they carry out their work? What became of their efforts?

The stories here have been gathered first-hand through observation, interviews and published records. Both stories excite the imaginations of all adventurers.

William G. Armstrong Jr.
September 2003

Light Heart:
The Trans-Atlantic Balloon
Flight of Tom Gatch

1

Night Launch

Straight overhead, ten cone-shaped balloons illuminated by TV klieg lights glistened in the fading evening sky. They strained at the end of their nylon suspension lines like ten trained horses anxious to begin a long journey. I stood on the airport infield that cold Monday night in February 1974, serving as the volunteer director of press relations for a trans-Atlantic balloon flight. The gondola lashed to the balloons resembled an oversized golf ball. It contained Col. Thomas L. Gatch, Jr., my flight instructor and friend.

Only the fingertips of a dozen members of the ground crew restrained the gondola from flight. A few steps away, an official from the National Aeronautic Association held two blinking navigation lights suspended from the capsule. If the flight succeeded, Tom Gatch would break distance and duration records held by a Soviet balloonist and one for altitude, held by an American. To do so, he would have to travel 1,057 miles, stay aloft sixty-one and a half hours, and reach an altitude greater than 38,650 feet above sea level.

Frank C. White, a volunteer on leave from the Air Transport Association, earlier in the afternoon had filed a flight plan that showed *Light Heart* would be out over the Atlantic Ocean an hour and a half after takeoff—and would make landfall three days later—on Thursday, somewhere along the western coast of Portugal. That flight plan, while mandatory, was only a product of guesswork, since a balloon depends for its direction entirely upon the whim and mercy of the wind.

White had offered his services just six weeks earlier when Tom wrote to the ATA in Washington, D.C. seeking advice. White soon found himself as the Chief Tracker and Communications Director for Tom's project.

Gatch looks over the final preparations as he prepares to seal the Light Heart hatch just before takeoff on Feb. 18, 1974.

Launch director Dick Keuser asked me to move the reporters and television cameramen back so he could secure the last lines of the gondola. A tall, lean man who had launched many polyethylene balloons, Keuser had sent aloft and tracked a prototype balloon for Gatch five months earlier. He had worked closely with Raven Industries of Sioux Falls, South Dakota, who had designed and built Gatch's balloons. Wearing the red baseball cap that was his trademark, Keuser began calling out to members of the ground crew one at a time to release their grip on the gondola and step away.

The gondola stirred on its wooden dolly and the system's magical buoyancy soon became evident. Tom inserted the oval hatch into place overhead, below the rubber gasket, and fastened it in place with eight wing nuts. Strapping on his radio headset, he surveyed the cabin once more; its bulkhead literally twinkled from bright coating of aluminized Mylar he had applied to maintain moderate working temperatures as his craft soared into regions of unrelenting cold and penetrating solar heat.

◆ ◆ ◆

Television lights flashing around outside the gondola made round rainbow patterns on the three eighths-inch thick Plexiglas portholes.

Beyond the reflection, Tom could see his ground crew in last-minute preparation. Many of those helping him were names well known to the U.S. ballooning community: Bob Sparks, whose try at a trans-Atlantic balloon flight just six months earlier had ended with his rescue from the water near Newfoundland; Malcolm Forbes, the financial magazine publisher who would fail at a similar flight within a year; Bobby Berger, a novice who would die in a trans-Atlantic try six months later, and the Anthony Fairbanks family, the deans of gas ballooning in America who had taught Tom how to fly.

Standing nearby were Tom's closest relatives, sisters Nancy and Corki, two of Nancy's children, Kaia and Rick, Corki's daughter Jocklyn, the daughter of a naval aviator, cousin Robert Hatcher, a retired Navy commander, and his wife Eugenia. Hatcher's mother was there, too. The widow of a two-star Army general, this tiny and sprightly octogenarian had encouraged Tom as he planned his trip. As a sentimental gesture, Tom had installed in the capsule the old canvas cot that had been carried throughout World War One by her husband, Maj. Gen. Julian Hatcher.

Below it Tom had stored three 20-amp batteries; chemicals for purifying the air; ten pounds of liquid antifreeze he would use as ballast; an eleven-pound box of food and drinking water; and a meticulously packed Styrofoam suitcase containing a white shirt, tie, blue business suit, black shoes, blue socks and two sets of underwear that he would wear in Europe.

In a sealed plastic bag were the flags of ten European nations that had given "approval" to his flight; each country's flag represented a potential landing site, and Tom had boasted that he would be ready for their welcoming protocol. Nearby, his emergency kit contained an inflatable raft, flares, a flashing beacon light and other necessities. His tiny medical kit contained Dramamine for vertigo, lomotil for diarrhea, ephedrine spray for ear pressure, aspirin and Chap Stick.

Mounted just above the cot was a jerrybuilt life support device: an oxygen purification machine and a tray of chemicals to remove carbon dioxide. Only as a last resort did he carry bottled air and a facemask; he had confidence in his equipment, which had functioned properly in every test. He had built the carbon dioxide scrubber, or atmosphere purifier, in his living room, modeling it after the system used by NASA on early manned space flights. It consisted of a battery-powered fan blowing over a tray of lithium hydroxide crystals and silica gel. Tom figured it could keep him alive in his sealed chamber for as long as ten days.

He had never assembled all of the components of the *Light Heart* before arriving at Harrisburg; the actual flight would be the first comprehensive test.

Ten liters of liquid oxygen were stored in a LOX converter that Tom had borrowed from the Bendix Corp. He had written to many companies, universities and government agencies, explaining his project and asking for their help. Many cooperated by sharing technical data, yet not a single commercial sponsor was associated with *Light Heart*. That was the way Tom wanted it. He had paid for and assembled all the equipment; he had done the work; he had acted as his own chief of staff; he had recruited the volunteers. Tom was supremely confident that his three years of research would assure his success.

Now he was tucked neatly inside the six-foot sphere he had designed and crammed with equipment. This was to be his home for the next three days as he voyaged triumphantly nearly four thousand miles across the Atlantic Ocean. Glancing at his instruments, Tom, outwardly cool, decided that he was ready to fly. He signaled thumbs up to Keuser.

Police lines two hundred yards away held back a thousand well-wishers who awaited the beginning of the spectacular balloon flight they had read about in the newspapers and seen on television newscasts.

Crew Chief Keuser visually and manually checked the rigging once again. Satisfied, he then took half a step back and called out in a loud voice, "Okay. Everybody off!"

The gondola lurched away and began to trace a smooth white line upward as the brilliant television lights played on it. The craft was proudly buoyant and the helium tugged it swiftly into the sky.

All ten balloons in the *Light Heart* cluster huddled together, free at last from the unnatural constraints that had held them on earth. In the chilly, quiet night air, each balloon reflected red and white as the twinkling navigation lights bounced little sparks of light off the opaque bags. Members of the ground crew squinted as we got our last looks at the small white orb carrying our friend. Then, it began to seem that Tom Gatch had left us too abruptly standing on the cold tarmac in Harrisburg. When the sky absorbed him, it was as if he hadn't been there at all. Tom had taken off in perfect calm, just at dusk. It was 7:29 p.m., February 18, 1974.

◆ ◆ ◆

The flight was his first in a gas balloon, even though the Federal Aviation Administration licensed him for such flight. The agency's regulations then permitted pilots who had logged a minimum number of hours in hot air balloons and who passed a written examination, to pilot gas (helium or hydrogen) balloons, despite the fact that these operate much differently than hot air balloons.

Tom had made nineteen ascensions accumulating twenty-three hours and thirty-five minutes in hot air balloons, and earning at the same time his commercial pilot and instructor ratings.

His last flight had been three months earlier when, as my instructor, he flew with me over the lush hunt country of Fauquier County, Virginia. We had both come to appreciate the majesty of floating a balloon over backwater boroughs, of being a marvelous, monstrous spectacle in the sky, admired by little boys, chased by motorists and then sharing champagne with a farmer whose fence we might just have broken in tumbled landing.

That day, as we floated over the rich green fields and private estates, I found Tom an easy-going pilot, casual in his instructions. We shared a wry grin near the end of our flight when we were becalmed over a cattle watering hole, and had to wait for a breeze to push us toward the road and our waiting ground crew.

But I could not have guessed when we touched down in a pasture that cold November morning three months earlier that on his next flight, Tom would single-handedly excite the fantasies and imaginations of millions of people around the world as he prepared to fly farther and stay aloft longer than any balloonist before him.

Tom wanted to be the first to cross the Atlantic, and also wanted to prove the feasibility of a new type of manned balloon system that differed significantly from classic balloon systems. The development of modern plastics made possible the construction of internally pressurized plastic balloons sealed tightly to prevent the loss of gas.

Made of rugged, laminated polyester film, they are partially inflated prior to release. As the balloons ascend into the less dense upper atmosphere, the gas expands the balloons into their designated shapes. The strength of the fabric prevents the balloon from expanding further, and thus from rising. As a result, they float at a constant, level altitude.

Before Tom's flight, no one had ever ascended in a super-pressure balloon, although they had often carried scientific payloads to high altitudes and kept them there for weeks or months at a time. A few such balloons had carried instruments in orbit around the Southern Hemisphere.

◆   ◆   ◆

At the moment of takeoff, Tom sat crosswise on the canvas cot. With a battery-powered light shining on his script, he flicked on the radio and, using his registration numbers and the airmen's alphabet, he called to the controllers at Harrisburg's Olmstead Field:

> This is November Seven Tango Golf. I am airborne and request immediate clearance to Flight Level Three-Nine-Zero.

The two men in the control tower grimaced. Although they knew that Gatch was preparing to ascend momentarily, they were startled that he had not followed the customary procedure of requesting clearance first. Tom had feared, however, that clearance, had he asked for it, might have been denied. There were two reasons for this.

First, the FAA claimed that he had not met their requirements for an Experimental Airworthiness Certificate, and had failed to provide them sufficient engineering data on the design and operation of his aircraft.

Tom had tried for months to convince federal authorities that his aircraft was airworthy, and that he had assembled enough data for the flight. He even made some concessions that he soon came to regret. In November, at a meeting at the FAA offices at Jamaica, New York, they had forced Tom to change his planned flight level from 38,000 feet to 39,000 feet. Their purpose was to keep him well above the invisible traffic lanes used by jumbo jets laden with passengers.

This requirement, imposed after all the balloons and equipment had been ordered and the weights calculated, cost Tom a very precious fifty pounds of lift: in order to gain another one thousand feet of altitude, each balloon on the surface would have to be inflated a little less. Thus, instead of lifting seventy pounds, each balloon could lift only sixty-five pounds. This would have serious consequences, though Tom did not realize it at the time.

Second, Canadian air officials had steadfastly refused him permission to fly through their airspace, into which the flight path projected. In consciously ignoring this obstacle, Tom perhaps invited the wrath of U.S. officials who must work each day with controllers from Canada and many other nations. But he was exasperated with the bureaucracies he had fought for the last two years, and was anxious to begin his flight. The FAA man at Harrisburg made a note of his apparent nonchalance toward the regulations.

With the balloon cluster safely, if illegally, off the ground, and destined by its design to climb without stopping to thirty-nine thousand feet, Harrisburg controllers were obliged to support Gatch and protect other aircraft from him. They cleared a path for him. They assigned him a frequency for his radio and a squawk for his transponder, and instructed him to contact CapCity Airport, which serves commercial traffic in and out of Harrisburg.

As his balloon entered air traffic patterns, Tom became a very busy pilot. He was monitoring his rate of ascent on the variometer, listening to his headset for communication instructions, and trying to log everything into the spiral notebook on his lap. At the same time, he watched the instruments that were monitoring his oxygen converter and carbon dioxide remover.

Air traffic controllers who had been reading their teletypes that day were not surprised to pick up the signal from Balloon N7TG. Twice on Monday, NOTAMS (notices to airmen) had gone out across the eastern region of the United States advising that a high-altitude balloon flight from Harrisburg was imminent. The work of Frank White, they noted that the balloon would be in direct contact with Harrisburg departure control, with New York Air Traffic Control, and with Aeronautical Radio, Inc. (ARINC), the private communication system airliners use to talk with flight managers.

14   Just Wind

The balloons rose swiftly, though not as swiftly as Tom had planned; they were giving him a comfortable upward ride of about four hundred feet per minute. Although he had calculated a six hundred feet per minute ascent rate, this departure from the text did not trouble him; it was a steady ride into the dark. The craft began a slow, gentle rotation as it climbed, a rotation that would recur periodically as the balloon crossed through wind shears, horizontal winds of varying speeds and direction, on its way to the top.

The first contact with ARINC in New York took place just eight minutes after leaving the ground. Already Tom was more than three thousand feet high. The slightest breeze had carried him gently westward at first, then back on a path that took him over Harrisburg again.

In those early moments, a sense of isolation began to come over Pilot Gatch, a sense of the reality that he had sealed himself off indefinitely from the rest of the world in a manner that few others had ever attempted. This feeling of remoteness, described by some as euphoria, by others as lethargy, had been recorded by military balloonists who ascended to heights ranging from seventy thousand to one hundred ten thousand feet in a prelude to the U.S. manned space program.

They had proved that man could stay alive in the far reaches of the earth's atmosphere.

Below his gondola, as Tom took a moment to scan the view, flickered the dim lights of the Pennsylvania farm country, the home of the legendary Pennsylvania Dutch. A few moments later, a gentle breeze pushed *Light Heart* over Lancaster, where a monument in the center of town commemorates a local hero from the last century, the great American balloon pioneer John Wise.

Gatch knew from reading balloon lore that in 1835 Wise, at the age of 27, had made his first ascent from his farm near Lancaster. Wise quickly became enraptured by the notion of ballooning, and began barnstorming across the United States. Although more of a showman than Gatch, Wise had also been a trans-Atlantic pioneer. It was he who first advanced the theory that a constant stream of wind blows from the west to the east, and who first proposed to make use of that knowledge. To that end, Wise formed the Trans-Atlantic Balloon Company. Twice he prepared to take off on such a flight, first in his beloved Atlantic and later, in a balloon owned by the New York Daily Graphic. Both times he was forced to put off his plans. Wise was still dreaming of that adventure when he made a promotional ascent one night from St. Louis. Near midnight, the shadow of his balloon eclipsed the moon, and was seen by the operator of a train depot in Indiana. Nothing was ever again heard of Wise or his balloon, and it is believed that he disappeared into Lake Michigan.

The terrain below was familiar for another reason: Tom himself had completed his flight training near Coatesville, just thirty miles east of Lancaster, with Anthony Fairbanks and his family, who had been gas ballooning in the United States more than fifty years. Tom smiled as he recalled the hard work he had performed in exchange for his flight training, bartering his expertise in shingling roofs for theirs in keeping balloons buoyant. Long considered one of the patriarchs of American balloonists, Anthony Fairbanks had provided La Coquette, the beautiful gasbag used in the film classic Around *the World in Eighty Days*.

Tom gained nearly all of his balloon training with the family in southeastern Pennsylvania. They considered him a fascinating student and a quick learner, and encouraged him as he planned his trans-Atlantic flight. "He had a cool head, with nerves of steel," observed son Michael Fairbanks. "Nothing fazed him. And he was meticulous; he wrote down everything about every flight we made. He was very thorough." Mike, who openly admired Tom, murmured as *Light Heart* lifted away, "What guts. What courage!"

Perhaps Tom thought briefly about John Wise, or his friends the Fairbanks, as he gained altitude in the dark sky over the sloping countryside of the Susquehanna River Valley. But most of his attention was focused on his own wonderful *Light Heart*, what it was doing for him, and where it was taking him.

It was warm inside the cabin and he perspired. The restraining straps on his parachute increased the discomfort on his back and constrained his movement. He had been hot since he sealed himself in just before leaving the ground, but being airborne made him more aware of it and he was uncomfortable. He unhooked the chinstrap, then leaned forward and pulled off the protective helmet useful only for the critical moments of liftoff and landing. With his left hand, he wiped his forehead and pushed his thinning brown hair to the left side. Taking a deep breath, he unsnapped the jacket of his bright read flight suit. The padded arctic gear, stuffed with goose down, would give him warmth later on, but he wanted comfort just then. He picked up his microphone switch and resumed command of his balloon.

He studied the radar beacon transponder, whose blinking indicator lit up each time it was "interrogated" by various air traffic controllers. The blinking light assured him he was being monitored closely, and that airspace would be cleared for him so he would not be a hazard to other air traffic operating along the busy air corridors of the eastern United States.

At 7:51 p.m., twenty-two minutes into the flight, Harrisburg radar picked up N7TG's signal and Tom radioed back that he was climbing steadily through twelve thousand five hundred feet. The gray sky was getting black below him, and a deep dark blue above. Dusk had settled nearly an hour before, but a faint purple crescent on the southwestern horizon indicated the last whisper of a winter sunset. Tom busied himself with his notes and logged every contact with airports and other traffic in the sky.

At 8:02 p.m., he tapped his altimeter and the needle jumped: at eighteen thousand feet above sea level, he was entering the airspace known to pilots as the Positive Control Area. Tom picked up his microphone, clicked the frequency selector switch to 138.5 mHz, and called ARINC with his new altitude report. The men at ARINC recognized that they had a novice in the air, but they treated Tom with the same professional courtesy they give to all pilots.

"Roger, Tango Golf," the controller acknowledged, "Squawk ident."

Tom replaced his microphone on the hook, then pressed and released a small button on the front panel of the transponder, which initiated a special identification pulse that transmitted for twenty seconds. Tom watched as the ident lamp remained illuminated; that light was a constant and reassuring reminder that radar was picking up his track.

FAA officials later claimed that Gatch violated another regulation by entering the Positive Control Area without clearance. At this altitude, although nearly halfway to flight ceiling, he was only five miles east of Lancaster. Gaining the faster wind at that altitude, he began to move steadily eastward at about fifty knots.

The balloons expanded, pushing aside creases and slack in the fabric, rounding themselves into a spherical shape.

According to the flight plan, a critical moment was at hand. Tom had planned to pressurize his gondola at nineteen thousand feet, where atmospheric pressure is about seven pounds per square inch.

For this, Tom credited Auguste Piccard and Paul Kipfer, Belgian scientists who had made a series of stratospheric balloon flights in the 1930s. During one of those flights a mercury barometer was accidentally dropped on the floor of their sealed aluminum gondola. The corrosive liquid began eating a hole through the gondola. The pilots realized that they had to react quickly and imaginatively if they were to avoid a perilous death; they responded calmly by connecting a hose to the outside air, turning a valve and vacuuming away the danger.

For Gatch, however, forgetting to turn off the valve could be fatal. Hypoxia would set in, beginning with a tingling, a headache, numbness, possible nausea and unconsciousness. Tom was aware of the dangers that pilots before him had experienced. He leaned forward and turned off the spigot, sealing his cabin at seven psi and preventing his precious air from rushing out. From that point on, there would be no other air system but the one he had devised. He prayed that it would work flawlessly.

Oxygen continued seeping from the ten-liter LOX converter, and his instruments assured him that he was breathing the new mixture of forty percent oxygen and 60 percent nitrogen. It gave him another satisfactory sense of his independence to realize that he was sealed in an artificial chamber of his own making, in an increasingly hostile environment. Any leakage would mean certain death. Tom quickly reviewed the symptoms of hypoxia and decided that he felt fine.

He reported back to ARINC at 8:10 p.m. that he had passed through twenty-two thousand feet. By then he had covered only thirty nautical miles but was quickly picking up speed as he moved down range and continued to push upward into faster wind. Direction remained constant for a while, almost due east. At twenty-four thousand feet his ground speed increased to eighty knots. He made a slow smooth arc as he climbed out of Harrisburg. From the point of takeoff he imagined himself being lofted toward the Atlantic shoreline, where *Light Heart* would insert itself into the swift upper air currents. Tom had suspected that it would be a thoroughly gentle ride all the way up, but still he was fascinated by the sensation.

He noted the lack of turbulence that one sometimes feels in an airplane; there was only an occasional, ever-so-gentle sway as his balloons entered an air stream. As he peered through the two-inch window above, he could watch the reflection of the navigation lights on the translucent skin of his balloons, just as we had done at takeoff.

Soon he passed through twenty-five thousand feet, where he encountered a light haze. There moisture started to form over his ports; some of the droplets iced over and for the remainder of the night visibility would be obscured. The ice would dissipate in the morning, Tom thought, when the sun's radiation warmed the outside of his gondola; for the time being, he had to content himself with the ice on the windows.

By 8:15 p.m. the temperature outside was nearly minus seventy degrees. The cabin was starting to cool off. Gatch stayed busy on the headset, with the radio crackling in his ear; he was a star in the sky, and many pilots called him. He was instructed to switch frequencies as he entered a new control sector and crossed different radials on his high-altitude aeronautical charts. He watched the orange light of his transponder flash, indicating that radar screens were still picking up his location. As he reached thirty thousand feet, he was moving still faster, one hundred ten knots, and the wind was from two hundred eighty degrees. He was into the jet stream at last.

Varying in height between twenty-five thousand and forty thousand feet, the jet stream wind field can be as wide as three hundred to four hundred miles. It might resemble a horizontal hurricane stretching as much as three thousand miles in length. Like a meandering river of wind encircling the earth, the wind has been known to reach three hundred knots at the center of the stream. Usually the winds are one hundred to one hundred fifty knots, with a great swirling action moving outward from the core tunnel. Jet pilots routinely seek these winds in west-to-east flights to gain speed and save time; they avoid them when flying west. Commercial passengers may notice some choppy flying as aircraft enter or exit the pattern.

At 8:27 p.m., fifty-eight minutes after leaving the ground, Tom was in contact with the tower at Modena, and was told to change his frequency to 128.3 mHz. He radioed back that he was breaking through thirty-four thousand feet and climbing steadily. He watched the two arms move around the numbers on his altimeter. The variometer showed an even five hundred feet per minute climb.

The temperature reached forty degrees inside the cabin, making it harder to take notes, but Tom's body heat, contained by the Mylar-insulated capsule, kept him quite comfortable. Soon the needles on the altimeter and variometer slowed, and then stopped rotating altogether. Tom knew what this meant, and it was a moment he had been awaiting. He looked at his watch and made a note in his log: at 8:30 p.m., his balloons had reached their maximum volume and *Light Heart* was bobbing against the ceiling of the sky. A little more than an hour after takeoff, the critical ascent stage of the flight was over and it was successful. Tom breathed a sigh of relief. At nearby Millville Municipal Airport in New Jersey, a radar screen blipped at 8:33 p.m., and picked up the signal of N7TG. *Light Heart* was about six miles north of the airport and twenty-five miles west of the ocean.

◆ ◆ ◆

Back in Harrisburg, the ground crew was still ecstatic over the magnificent launch and the beauty of balloon flight generally. From the musty old one-room office of Stambaugh's Air Service in Hangar 133, I had been telephoning various news agencies to announce that the flight was underway. The office had served as flight preparation headquarters over the long weekend. Most of the crowd that had witnessed the ascent had departed. Members of the Gatch family were already enroute to Alexandria, Virginia, where they planned to maintain the vigil at Tom's home until he returned. Meanwhile, Frank White and I had uncorked a bottle of Beaujolais that I had been saving for after takeoff and we were celebrating with reporters for The Associated Press and Westinghouse Broadcasting.

White and I had spent three days in Harrisburg. It had been a thoroughly hectic and exasperating time for all of us, including Tom. The launch had been delayed a week due to a Teamsters' strike, which prevented delivery of the helium. When the tractor-trailer rig pulled into the hangar on Saturday morning, Tom let out a whoop of exuberance. When White arrived from Andrews Air Force Base with the liquid oxygen bottles, Tom announced that all components of *Light Heart* were finally assembled; he set the preliminary launch time for the next morning, Sunday.

Thus, hoping for calm wind at dawn, we began inflating the balloons late Saturday evening. As we cracked open each of the large wooden crates in which the balloons had been shipped from Sioux Falls, Tom noticed that one crate had a gouge big enough to put a hand through. Inspection of the balloon inside revealed no damage, however, and his anger subsided. The inflation proceeded.

There was a certain magic in that event as 2,600 cubic feet of helium hissed into each of the twenty-six foot tall balloons, and they took on a life of their own. Saturday night passed slowly after the inflation, as we waited for the wind to subside; if it were more than five miles per hour, the launch would be hazardous and the balloons would toss about in the wind; it would be difficult to hold the gondola in place before launch. Crew Chief Keuser and I made two middle-of-the-night forays to the local Flight Service Station to study weather maps, surface winds and conditions aloft.

Sunday, however, dawned cloudy and windy, stayed that way, and there was more of the same on Monday. Tension grew as press interest mounted. Crowds began visiting the hangar to inspect the gondola and the inflated balloons. Tom's family was concerned, although they maintained a placid exterior and tried to share his confidence. Meanwhile, he was presiding over a family reunion; trying to keep his volunteers happy, and was, of necessity, the center of press attention.

Late Monday afternoon it looked as though the wind would subside, and Keuser asked for help recruiting three dozen husky volunteers to move the balloons outside. A number of persons came forward who to our surprise, had balloon ground-crew experience. There was also a contingent of strong young men from a local college fraternity. Keuser briefed them on their tasks. Gradually, it began to look as if the perfect launch window would come along Monday evening.

Tom's family on Sunday night had ordered him to a nearby motel for some badly needed rest. For the previous three nights, in order to acclimate himself, he had slept inside his tiny capsule parked inside the hangar. Though he claimed to find this comfortable, it was obvious that he was fatigued; in addition, his two-week crash diet, during which his weight dropped from one hundred sixty to one hundred fifty pounds, did not help his appearance (although it made the balloon more buoyant).

When I arrived at the motel Monday afternoon to drive him to the field, Tom seemed relaxed but anxious to get underway. I did not know it then, but he had been visiting with his elderly Aunt Eleanor that afternoon. She later recalled that Tom appeared tired and depressed. To boost his spirits, she asked him,

> Tommy, why should you be so depressed? Look at all these wonderful people who have come from all over the country to help you. Look how they are paying attention to you!

When Tom looked up at her, tears streamed down his face.

I drive him to the airport about three o'clock. When we walked up to the hangar we could see extra airport police on patrol and a flurry of activity inside.

The national news media had their appetite whetted. Enthusiastic reporters who saw the balloons inflated all wanted to cover the start of the flight of "the Lindbergh of ballooning." The stories were already coming in nicely. National wire services had carried photos of Tom. An uncle called Tom from California to report that Tom's picture was on page one of the Los Angeles Times, and Tom turned to congratulate me, professing that he didn't understand how it was all possible. Many newsmen were waiting to interview him in the hangar. As Tom's publicist, I wanted each of them to have the chance to visit with him; as his friend, fellow balloonist and self-appointed aide, however, I also wanted him to have as much quiet time as possible so he could review the immediate weather data and communication procedures. I had to strike a balance between these conflicting demands.

The first priority was for Tom to think and relax. He closeted himself with cousin Robert Hatcher, Crew Chief Keuser and Communications Chief White. When he felt that he was comfortably briefed, we began a series of press interviews. Tom dressed in his flight suit for a network television crew; then again for still photographers; he took phone calls from key news agencies; he posed innumerable times for various pictures, and confidently answered all the familiar questions again and again.

Finally, he conducted a full-dress news conference for all the correspondents on the scene as he stood in the gondola. And, by early evening, he had successfully avoided the persistent barrage of telephone calls from FAA officials who sought to warn him again not to fly without a clearance. No clearance, of course, would be issued without an Airworthiness Certificate, which the FAA had denied him. At Harrisburg, with Tom's blessing, I had given the motel operator instructions to intercept all calls going to Tom's room, and route them to mine. Thus, I was the one stalling the FAA.

By 6:30 p.m. Monday, the ground crew had been positioned in the hangar: three persons were assigned to each balloon to hold the lines and sandbags as they

walked the balloons out of the hangar. When Keuser gave the signal, a buzzer sounded, and the giant metal hangar doors were rolled back on their tracks into recesses in the wall. Tom for the first time saw the huge throng that had come to watch him fly.

The launch procession of the *Light Heart* resembled a religious ceremony: the balloons inched forward from the hangar, bobbing like gangling acolytes, with the carriage bearing the high priest in the center. Tom stood chest-high in the open hatch, wearing vestments of bright red with the *Light Heart* patch and an American flag sewn on the right shoulder.

The procession moved cautiously to a corner of the runway and stopped. Under Keuser's careful supervision, volunteers unhooked the sandbags from each plastic balloon and winched the balloons up, hand-over-hand, to the end of their suspension lines. A slip by any one of them could have spelled disaster at the launch site, but none faltered. Magnificently, the balloons joined one another high overhead until all ten were assembled and rigged.

It was the kind of picture one never quite forgets. It already seemed like a dream Monday night as we reminisced about the launch and waited for an important phone call from ARINC in New York.

◆ ◆ ◆

Tom looked at his watch again. It was 8:45 p.m. as he studied his instruments and recorded their measurements as well as his own sensations. He had been leveled off in stable flight for fourteen minutes and was cruising effortlessly seven miles above the rest of the world, riding a good wind to Europe at a speed of one hundred twenty knots.

The *Light Heart* cluster was fully distended and all ten balloons strained at their twenty-four seams. Three balloons towered higher than the rest, giving the configuration a two-stage appearance. On lines leading to three of the lower seven balloons were black-and-red detonating wires that, when triggered from the gondola, would explode one balloon at a time.

Before activating any electrical explosive, the pilot would have to tug that balloon down and away from the cluster...pulling the equivalent of a sixty-five pound weight as much as one hundred twenty feet straight down. Tom had tried his strength with one of the inflated balloons in the hangar at Harrisburg found that with difficulty he could use the procedure to commence his descent over Europe when necessary.

The center balloon of the lower cluster was rigged with the U.S. flag, hanging perpendicular on its nylon line. At the topmost stripe of the flag was a sentimental and symbolic pennant: the commissioning pennant of the battleship *USS South Dakota*, which Gatch's father had skippered in the course of becoming a World War Two hero. Tom was enormously proud of that ribbon: it symbolized the memory of his father, who had been such a forceful influence over his life.

Both flags hung motionless in the stillness of flight as the huge balloons hovered near flight ceiling. Above them hung a brilliant orange streamer and a white silk banner with the aircraft registration letters N7TG. The six peripheral balloons nestled closely, straining and pressing against the center bag. In three places, frozen nylon lines an eighth of an inch in diameter rubbed against the balloon's .005-inch fabric.

Without warning, the center balloon exploded! Tom heard the loud report, then felt the limp fabric collapse onto the top of the gondola. A shock wave went through *Light Heart*, first shuddering down from the cluster, and then back up the lines again to the balloons, which banged together wildly to fill the void between them. There was an immediate danger that, in the bouncing free-for-all overhead, another of the balloons might shatter. Gatch knew almost at once what had happened. His eyes moved quickly toward his instruments. The variometer needle signaled a descent; the altimeter started a discouraging counter-clockwise motion. *Light Heart* began sinking slowly back toward the ground.

His data had predicted that the loss of one balloon would not bring him down. The flight could endure the loss of one balloon. In fact, that was why he had installed explosive squibs on three balloons. However, those careful calculations were just then being proved wrong, for he was quickly losing altitude. Collecting his thoughts, he recalled the advice he had received from Keuser, "If you start to lose altitude early at night and it looks like you will lose five thousand feet or more, ballast gently, not to regain all lost altitude, but only to stop or slow the descent."

Tom knew that this emergency threatened his life and that he had to act quickly. Thoughts of revenge against the manufacturer of the balloons flashed through his mind as he prepared his counter-attack. Reaching behind his seat, he pulled up a plastic bottle of liquid antifreeze, opened the container and inserted the long white hose into it. Then he reached for the spigot. As soon as he turned it, nature's vacuum began sucking blue liquid from the plastic container. He watched intently as the liquid level dropped to the halfway mark in a matter of seconds, and then began sucking air from the cabin with a loud swoosh.

The vacuum outside was stronger than he had suspected. Tom shut off the valve and watched his instruments. He remembered the admonitions of Anthony Fairbanks to his gas balloon students, "Ballast and wait. Ballast and wait." Still he descended.

He was frustrated. He knew that he had to lighten the load or give up the flight. In daylight, he might have considered landing. In darkness, there was no choice. The words of his advisers came wafting up to him then as Tom recalled that he had been urged to take off before dawn so that in an emergency he could descend in daylight. But those gusty early morning winds had postponed the flight two days; when the wind finally died Monday evening, Tom had overborne their advice and made the decision to take off. As a result, he faced this crisis in pitch-black uncertainty. Visibility was obscured, but he knew he was fast approaching the Atlantic coastline. Descent would be catastrophic, perhaps fatal.

He repeated the procedure with a second bottle of antifreeze. It, too, drained all the way to the bottom. He knew that the cluster of balloons at superpressure would hold him aloft if he were able to check the descent. He continued siphoning until he stabilized and the variometer showed neutral buoyancy. He had siphoned over all of his liquid ballast by the time he was in level flight again at thirty-five thousand five hundred feet. The lack of any ballast meant that, when he began the final descent, he would have to jettison some of the removable equipment on board. Meanwhile, there were more important concerns that demanded his attention.

The whole incident lasted less than five minutes. At 8:53 p.m., he reported his new altitude to ARINC, an altitude that put him eyeball-to-eyeball with commercial jet traffic. He also explained briefly the reason for his change in altitude. Tom had made a conscious decision to continue flying, and New York Air Traffic Control began re-routing traffic at Flight Level 355 to facilitate his safe passage. They "cleansed" the airways two thousand feet above and below *Light Heart* and gave the balloonist a wide lateral clearance. Even so, his position was probably better known than any aircraft in the sky at the time, since he was moving comparatively slowly and his aircraft was so unique.

Tom pushed the button on his transponder again, and within seconds, radar spotted N7TG near Sea Isle, New Jersey, soaring over the dark little beach communities that line the eastern shore of the United States. The balloon was being blown along at one hundred fifteen knots. A few minutes later, the steady westerly flow of the jet stream carried it directly into Warning Area 107, a zone used by the Twentieth Air Defense Command for maneuvers and testing. Gatch looked at his aeronautical chart and calculated that it would take thirty-four minutes to cross through this area; it was uneventful flying, since no tests were scheduled. The silent lighter-than-air leviathan passed overhead.

◆   ◆   ◆

In Harrisburg a few minutes before 9:00 p.m., the phone jangled at Stambaugh's Air Service. I picked it up with a triumphant "*Light Heart* Launch Control", and New York ARINC was on the line with a radio patch for us from November Seven Tango Golf. I signaled to the two reporters, who listened in on one extension as Frank White and I alternated on the other.

Tom did not sound his usual crisp self as he began talking; he was very serious and we immediately detected anxiety in his tone as we quizzed him on the flight's progress. It was the type of conversation one might have with a normally chipper friend who was suffering from a dull headache. Frank thought he was experiencing a case of "mike fright", common to those new to radio communications. Nevertheless, Tom was composed and businesslike as he began his startling transmission:

> This is Tango Golf. I have lost the lift of one balloon, but it's stabled off now. I'm at a steady thirty-five thousand, five hundred fifty. And it looks like I'm over a little stuff. It's holding steady now.

I repeated his announcement for the others in the room as I wrote down what he had said. Then we listened as Tom elaborated:

> The situation is stabilized now. There's no question about losing one balloon. It's draped over some of the...or at least one of the portholes. The situation is stabilized now. There's no reason why I shouldn't proceed. Over.

Tom sounded very reassuring on that point, and no one could dispute him. He was going to proceed. Partly for the benefit of the reporters, and partly because I wanted to know, I asked Tom to describe the ascent. I was hoping for quotable words of euphoria similar to those uttered by the early astronauts in describing the sensational thrust of a rocket, or the beauty of earth as seen from space. But Tom Gatch, who had worked as a novelist and a playwright, was not in a descriptive mood:

> I rose at a very even four-ten, and then it became five hundred. And then all of a sudden a loud noise. Tell Raven I want my money back on one balloon. I knew it would stabilize at a lower altitude, which it did quickly. I siphoned over the liquid I had and it's holding steady now.

Perhaps Tom had difficulty hearing some of our communications, because he asked that several question be repeated. Other questions he did not answer at all. I asked how much ballast he had dropped. He responded by giving the amount of altitude he had lost (fifteen hundred feet). Later, I would regret not following up on certain questions which might have given us more clues about his eventual disappearance. But then we were getting all the data Gatch wanted us to have.

We chatted for eight minutes. Frank advised Tom to turn off his transponder as soon as he was out of sight of land, or more than two hundred miles from the coast. The pilot appeared a little confused by what he was then seeing on the transponder:

> When I turn the dimmer up, I still get a bright flash, but I may be out of range by this time. I'm supposed to be in the jet stream going one hundred forty miles an hour. Just tell me if you think I should turn it off now.

Tom relayed various other factual information, such as the time the balloon broke, radio frequencies he was using, and so on. He also complained that his windows were "iced over" and that he believed he was over water as he spoke to us. "I don't see any lights at all", he said. Neither of us wanted to break the contact, but Tom did not sound as though he were in a talkative mood. He sounded frustrated when I said I was through. "Is that the end of your transmission?" he snapped. Suspecting that something else was causing this uneasiness, I asked whether his oxygen was okay.

> Yes, it's fine. Humidity's fine. It's cooling off in here, but I want it to. I find it's a very comfortable temperature.

Before signing off, White and I wished our friend Godspeed and promised that we would try another hook-up later in the flight using commercial air traffic, or maybe via a patch from some control tower in Europe.

◆   ◆   ◆

Two hours into the flight, N7TG entered New York Oceanic Airspace, and moved rapidly out over the Atlantic Ocean. At 10:30 p.m., after three hours in the air, radar tracked the balloon about two hundred miles southeast of New York City, traveling at one hundred thirty knots and still at thirty-six thousand feet.

Meanwhile, Tom continued receiving good radio communication throughout the night and into the early morning hours. While he was obviously worried about his broken balloon draped over the capsule, certainly he was relieved that he had survived this critical ordeal. He took solace in the fact that he was still progressing nicely toward his goal at an altitude and speed that seemed to guarantee his success. And, once over water, there was no longer any need for wearing the parachute. He punched the capewell, pulled the straps off, and relaxed.

It was a clear and still night below, perfect conditions for any aircraft and especially for one so fragile as a balloon. The only illumination came from the crescent of an old and disappearing moon. The *Light Heart* received a boost of extra buoyancy from the earth's radiation coming directly up to the balloons. If there had been a heavy cloud layer, the radiation would not have penetrated, and the *Light Heart* would have lost that much extra lift. For the time being, Tom was almost seven miles above the Atlantic Ocean and making good progress. As he moved farther from the heavily traveled air routes, his tiny VHF transmitter provided him less radio contact and there were long periods of silence. He sat on the canvas cot as the wind carried him ever eastward. At 11:29 p.m., he contacted Bermuda Air Traffic Control on 121 mHz.

A commercial flight in the vicinity, Pan American Flight 299, enroute from San Juan to New York City, overheard the contact and tried to work Tango Golf, but Tom was unable to hear the airliner's signals. An hour later, the captain of Eastern Air Lines Flight 928 reported contacting the balloon on 121 mHz. Tom told the Eastern captain that he estimated *Light Heart's* position approximately three hundred miles north of Bermuda, and that radar had clocked him at one hundred twenty knots.

He worked on his maps and charted his course with the information Bermuda ATC and other aircraft gave him. At 2:12 a.m., Gatch was in contact with another airliner: American Airlines Flight 676, enroute to Kennedy in New York with a planeload of San Juan passengers. Tom complained about his icing conditions and reported that it was affecting his navigation. He also indicated that he was trying to re-establish contact with Bermuda. He told the American pilot that he was at thirty-six thousand feet, but had slowed to about eighty knots.

◆   ◆   ◆

How different this was, Tom thought, from the trans-Atlantic attempts that had gone before his. They had all flown at low altitude, and had all come to grief in some form. No one had ever crossed so large a body of water in a balloon, though it had been man's dream for centuries. In fact, one of the tests of the early balloonists' fortitude had been crossing that formidable body of water, the English Channel. The first effort, financed by a wealthy American surgeon, was successful. Using a hydrogen balloon, Dr. John Jeffries and the French aeronaut Jean-Pierre Blanchard ascended in 1785 from Dover. Gas seeped from their balloon and they floated precariously low over the cold Channel. The pilots tossed overboard their shoes, most of their provisions, a mail sack, and then their clothing to keep from falling into the sea. They made it over the northwest coast of France and banged down to earth near Cape Boulogne.

When John Wise discovered the westerly wind that blows from North America to Europe, the dream of crossing the ocean was born. Several attempts in the mid-nineteenth century failed, and the dream was put aside for nearly one hundred years. Four Britons in a balloon called *Small World* tried an east-to-west crossing using the trade winds from the Canary Islands in 1958, but made it only halfway (they sailed to Barbados). Three pilots disappeared in 1970 after taking off from Long Island in *Free Life*. Bob Sparks lived to tell about the lightning storms that brought him down off Newfoundland during a 1973 attempt in his *Odyssey*. But Tom Gatch was making history by riding his balloon well above all the foul weather; he was confident of his success.

Tom was completely in character as he pursued his adventure, though few people understood his sensitive nature. Before Tom went to sleep on his cot high above the Atlantic that night, he removed from his wallet a well-worn folded paper containing a few lines of prose that he had adopted as his motto:

> You are as young as your faith, as old as your doubt;
> As young as your self-confidence, as old as your fear,
> As young as your hope, as old as your despair.
> Youth is not a time of life; it is a state of mind.
> Nobody grows old merely by living a number of years:
> People grow old only by deserting their ideals.
> Years wrinkle the skin, but to give up enthusiasm wrinkles the soul.

> Worry, doubt, self-distrust, fear and despair:
> These are the long, long years that bow the head and turn the spirit back to dust.
> Whether eighty or sixteen, there is in every being's heart the love of wonder, the sweet amazement at the stars and the starlight things and thoughts, the undaunted challenge of events, the unfailing child-like appetite for what next and the joy and the game of life.

Still dressed in his bright red suit, bending over his spiral notebook in the tiny cabin, Tom recorded his impressions of the long day's events, venting some frustration as well some exhilaration, before reaching for the light switch and trying to get some rest. After that, there were no more communications Monday night from *Light Heart*.

Although exhausted from the long ordeal of getting launched, Tom found sleep fitful. He awoke with a start several times to inspect his instruments and then, reassuring himself that all was well, dozed off again. While he rested, the wind did his work for him, pushing him east and southeast in the jet stream. Although he did not know it, the world had started to take note of this magnificent odyssey. Broadcast networks and wire services were already reporting his progress to the world.

It was Thomas L. Gatch's greatest moment, and just then he had every right to be proud.

2

Inheriting the Wind

After watching him spend the better part of his inheritance and almost three years planning his flight, Tom Gatch's closest friends still puzzled over this elaborate, life-risking challenge. Why, they would ask, was he doing this? Tom would reply that such as flight would prove the feasibility of superpressure balloons as stable, pollution-free cargo carriers; pioneer the use of high-altitude winds; establish balloon endurance records; contribute to international relations, and provide him with an adventure to write about in a new book.

In a deeply personal sense, however, Tom was driven by the momentum of several generations of an achievement-oriented family, and the realization, whether actual or perceived, that he was expected to prove himself in some important way. When he ascended in *Light Heart*, his fulfillment was within reach.

Tom's family claimed distinguished roots on both coasts of the United States. In the East, their colonial heritage ran deep into Maryland history. Among their ancestors, his mother's family traced its lineage from the family of President George Washington. Tom's maternal great-great-grandfather was John Ridout, a colonial administrator of Maryland before the American Revolution.

The Gatch family also claimed a stake in settling the Old West: on his father's side, Tom's grandfather had been mayor of Salem, Oregon. Great grandfather Thomas Milton Gatch was the first president of the University of Washington and, later, of Oregon State University. A strong sense of high purpose and good citizenship had been handed down almost as a family heirloom.

Tom was born September 13, 1925, the youngest of three children of Nancy Dashiell Gatch and Thomas Leigh Gatch. On the morning their brother was born, sisters Nancy, six, and Corki, four, were sent out on the front porch to kneel down and give thanks that a male child had been born and to pray that their new brother would proudly carry the mantle of his family.

The elder Gatch, away at sea when his son was born, had graduated from the Naval Academy in 1912. When Tom was born, Gatch was still mourning the loss of several classmates who had died ten days earlier when the Navy's only dirigible, *Shenandoah*, broke up and crashed in a storm over south-central Ohio. Gatch's Navy career often kept him away but when he was home, he tried to impart his collected wisdom and appreciation of life.

The stern-looking, mustached lieutenant commander delighted in reading to his children as they grew up. With Nancy, Corki and Tom at his feet, he would light a pipe, settle into a comfortable chair near the fireplace, and read aloud the heroic fiction that he cherished. Some of his favorites were Alfred Lord Tennyson's The Charge of the Light Brigade, and Sir Arthur Conan Doyle's The Hound of the Baskervilles. He also read and taught his children the works of Shakespeare, Rudyard Kipling and Edgar Allen Poe.

Perhaps he read them Poe's first published work, a hoax printed in a New York newspaper, suggesting that British Balloonist Monck Mason and his companions had crossed the Atlantic Ocean in a balloon and landed in South Carolina in 1844.

Gatch, of course, was especially fond of reciting sea adventures. In his long days at sea, he had memorized much poetry, and occasionally recited from memory the thumping, rhythmic lines from Vachel Lindsay's "The Congo". Gatch authored an unpublished textbook on celestial navigation, and bought his wife a fur coat with prize money from a Navy writing contest. An Episcopalian, Gatch assimilated theology and science, and conveyed his convictions to his children.

Tom's parents had married following a whirlwind romance in New York, just before the young Naval officer sailed for Europe in 1917. His mother recognized and accepted the responsibilities of an officer's wife. She established the standards by which the children should be raised.

Navy junior

Events in young Tom's boyhood revolved around his father's existence. The family would schedule outings on Chesapeake Bay, borrowing a twenty-foot motor launch, and set off to picnic and swim all day. Unfortunately, Tom developed an early aversion to water. He often grew seasick while everyone else was having a grand time, and felt too ill to swim. Gatch could not have his boy resisting the water, so he forced him to learn to swim. Tying a rope under Tom's armpits, Gatch would toss him in the water, pull him from behind the boat and shout encouragement—a brutal way to overcome a fear, perhaps, but Gatch believed that the way to overcome fear was to face up to it directly.

When Tom was eight and living near the Philadelphia Navy Yard while his father served as navigator on the battleship *USS New Mexico*, he entered public schools for the first time. Previously, two spinsters at a private school in Annapolis had tutored him. It was a traumatic transition from that tender situation into the rough-and-tumble Germantown section of Philadelphia. Maybe because he was new, or because they suspected his tenderness, the older neighborhood boys would taunt Tom and chase him home. Arriving winded and frightened, Tom would dash in the door to the comfort of his mother and sisters. This behavior, of course, infuriated his father. The remedy was to teach the boy how to defend himself, so Tom was enrolled in boxing lessons. Gradually, he learned that he was supposed to confront life's fears with action.

His mother chronicled Tom's formative years. She recorded that Tommy loved school (he twice skipped half a grade in elementary school), and craved attention, yet often preferred to be alone with his daydreams. ("Tommy just loves to patter down the street and sit and dream on the curb").

She once described him as

> violent in his affections and defiant as an imp…he is just thoroughly alive and never wants you to forget it. He is utterly impervious to any punishment. Whenever he does anything naughty he begins to question us each in turn: Mama, do you love me? Nancy, do you love me? etc, until his persistence finally makes us give in and say 'yes' for peace.

During Commander Gatch's tour with the Pacific Fleet, the Navy dirigible *Macon*, then the pride of naval aviation, crashed while conducting maneuvers off the coast of California. With it sank the Navy's future of rigid airship operations (the *Akron* had gone down in the Atlantic a year earlier). Gatch was appointed chief investigator for the Naval Court of Inquiry. When he came home late at night during the investigation, he and Tom would spread out the blueprints of the airship on the living room floor, as Gatch explained the airship's stresses, problems in trim, buoyancy and navigation, and tried to figure out why the 785-foot airship went down. Since that question was never fully answered, investigators were criticized in the press for failing to recommend how to prevent such disasters in the future. As a result, the *Macon* was the last rigid airship ever built in the United States.

Gatch was recalled to Washington in 1936 to work in the Navy's legal department. Tom, who by age eleven had developed a good soprano, applied for and won a scholarship to the prestigious St. Alban's School for Boys. Besides delighting his mother, who sang frequently at church and social gatherings, this afforded him the honor of singing in the famous men's and boys' choir at the Washington Cathedral. Four days a week, two dozen select boys would run over to the great Cathedral for the Four O'clock Evensong, and transform themselves into befrocked, innocent choir boys. Standing before the High Altar, they would lift their voices in liturgical hymns to the spires of the great church that towers over northwest Washington.

Tom constantly prodded himself to do better in school and worried about upcoming exams, though he usually received A's and B's. He taught himself to use the typewriter and thus turned in cleaner, neater papers. Ever pensive, he remained troubled by the loss of the *Macon*, and then by the fiery crash of the German dirigible *Hindenburg* at Lakehurst, New Jersey, in May of 1937.

He sketched designs in his diary of a new airship that he hoped would not fall from the sky; he built a seven-foot model dirigible in his bedroom and christened it Rio II. He was enthralled when Flossie Boswell, a distant cousin and pioneer aviatrix, visited the family and regaled him with her flying stories.

Perpetual motion marked Tommy Gatch's Washington life: besides his aggressive appetite for sports (especially soccer and baseball), he was an avid reader and movie goer, rating characters and plots as "excellent, swell, funny or boring".

This happy period in Tom's youth ended abruptly in the spring of 1938, when adolescence changed his voice. Without perfect control, he was unable to continue in the choir and despite his excellent grades the St. Alban's scholarship was withdrawn.

Tom moved back to his Grandmother Dashiell's house and enrolled at Annapolis High. Many of his classmates were Navy Juniors like himself, and frequently they toured ships that had arrived in port. Tom studied hard, and confided in his diary:

> Algebra has gotten to be the subject that I have to be able to get in order to get into the Naval Academy.

Cognizant of his father's increasing prominence (Gatch had been promoted to Captain) and the worsening world situation, Tom recorded world events as if they were happening to his own family. He filled his diary with references to Italy's invasion of Albania, an FDR speech, the election of Pius XII, the "continued crisis about Danzig", that "Germany now wants Danzig and the corridor" and finally, "England and France declared war against Germany today".

◆   ◆   ◆

Growing up, Tom was tugged emotionally between his mother, the de-facto family head, artist and teacher, and his father, the crisp, literary naval officer, the embodiment of virility and success. Tom internalized the tug-of-war, not understanding which example should dominate. Although he alternately manifested the traits of both, the two characters never quite reconciled themselves in him.

Mrs. Gatch and her son shared a clever, cynical sense of humor, "exquisite, sardonic sarcasm", as sister Nancy put it. No other family members could compete with their intense, personal humor; for that matter, no one wanted to.

Tom's diary reveals that he was saddled with the impression that he would never live up to his father's expectations or achievements. The senior Gatch occasionally fostered this impression by belittling his son's efforts. Left with the feeling that he was a disappointment to his father, Tom aimed at pleasing his mother by striving for better grades or higher achievement. Once, when his script for a school play was rejected, Tom wrote:

> I must think of something else. Mama so wants me to be in something.

Another time, when his grades were improving, he congratulated himself, boasting of "much good work for Mama." Other diary entries reveal a reflective young man, examining his relationship with God:

> Child of God, do your work.
>
> Are my talents or my body or my thoughts really mine? No! By the grace of God I possess them. Use them for His sake.

After graduation in 1942, Senator Millard E. Tydings of Maryland nominated Tom for the Naval Academy. When he reported for his medical examination, however, doctors discovered that Tom's eyesight was below Navy minimums, which made him not physically qualified for the Naval Academy.

His career aspirations were shattered. Stunned and depressed, Tom entered a dreary period before he regrouped his courage, rethought his plans, and decided to try for West Point. His mother scurried around, wrote letters and made numerous phone calls to secure him a nomination to West Point. By the time he passed the physical, however, it was too late for the fall term, so Tom enrolled in a "poop school" for orientation training, and then went on to Admiral Farragut Academy in New Jersey.

◆   ◆   ◆

In the winter of 1942, Tom's father took command of the new thirty-five thousand ton battleship *USS South Dakota*, which carried a crew of 2,200 men. Captain Gatch was anxious to test his own theories of extracting loyalty and professionalism from his fighting crew. As historian Samuel Elliott Morrison would write later in The Struggle for Guadalcanal, Gatch prepared his men well for battle:

> No ship more eager to fight ever entered the Pacific, for Captain Gatch, by constant target practice, neglecting the spit-and-polish things that vex bluejackets, and by exercising a natural gift for leadership, had welded his crew into a splendid fighting team.
>
> Gatch revived the old Navy practice of reading the Lesson at Divine services, and always urged his men to make their peace with God before going into action. He let the ship get abominably dirty and directed all his men's energies to perfecting their shooting. Whatever the reason, Gatch was adored by his men.

Tom went to Philadelphia in March 1942 to see the *South Dakota* commissioning ceremony, and spent a week with his father living aboard and inspecting the ship. He came back impressed:

> A grand week. I am more than lucky to have spent it and seen all that I did. A super-duper ship that the world will soon know as the greatest ship on the seven seas.

Tom's words were nearly prophetic. Shortly after *South Dakota* joined the Pacific Fleet, Bataan fell to the Japanese. On October 26, 1942, in the fierce battle of Santa Cruz, the crew of *South Dakota* performed heroically and was largely responsible for a decisive U.S. victory. On the first day of the battle, Captain Gatch maneuvered *South Dakota* into a position supporting the aircraft carrier Enterprise.

In thirty minutes, the crew of *USS South Dakota* shot down thirty-two Japanese aircraft. Severely wounded from shrapnel in the neck, Gatch found his left arm paralyzed. Three weeks later, with the arm in a sling, Gatch steamed his ship into the Battle of Guadalcanal, where he reversed a trap the Japanese had set for him; when the battle was over, three Japanese cruisers and a destroyer were sunk; *South Dakota* emerged without one new scratch.

When news of the engagement was released in the U.S. months later, Gatch became a national hero. He received public credit for the victory, was awarded the Navy Cross and a Gold Cross, and was featured in countless news articles. He wrote a lengthy account of the action for the Saturday Evening Post, and was heroically profiled in LIFE and Look Magazines.

Awaiting the start of his first year at West Point, Tom helped his father recuperate from injuries sustained in the Battle of Guadalcanal in 1942, where Gatch became a national hero.

Gatch spent months undergoing whirlpool bath treatments for his arm and shoulder injuries at Bethesda Naval Hospital. Tom, at home waiting to go to West Point, would drive his father each day to the hospital. As his father recovered, Tom helped him prepare speeches and sat with him during radio and newspaper interviews.

Later that spring, Miss Nellie christened destroyer *U.S.S. Dashiell* in the Brooklyn Navy Yard; the ship was named for her late husband, who had invented breech-block and turret control mechanisms for naval ordnance.

Tom entered West Point on the last day of June 1943, as the son of a contemporary war hero just named the Navy's Judge Advocate General. Although he encountered more than the usual amount of harassment, his spirit was not to be broken by the hazing. That did not stop him from a soldier's favorite pastime: complaining. One night, returning from a day of field maneuvers, he wrote to an aunt:

> I'm still homesick and all that, but I figure if I keep on the go I'll get into the swing of things here and I'll feel better, though I can't imagine myself very happy to be here. I'm really going to work hard when the studies come—I'll hit those books hard and heavy, cause if one sets his standard high at the offset, then the battle's half over.

Tom served in an accelerated three-year program because of the wartime demand for officers. During his second year, he entertained himself by writing plays. In his diary, he confidently counseled: "Be true to yourself: your own vast potential is more than sufficient for success." However, for the first time in his academic life, Tom experienced difficulty with some courses, especially physics. Coupled with the new academic straights was the embarrassing problem of getting numerous "gigs" and losing some weekend privileges.

Tom's heart was not always in his work, but the intense pressure upon the young cadets was relieved in August 1945 when the Japanese surrendered. On field maneuvers at West Point, Tom listened as President Truman announced the news on the radio; he noted the occasion in his diary, but added dryly: "We exist the same as ever up here at Pine Camp."

Although the final year at West Point went smoothly, Tom finished in the lower third of his class; the yearbook Howitzer noted that Tom's thoughts "were not confined to these gray walls."

When Tom graduated, his father was serving as Commanding Officer of the Atlantic Service Fleet. Vice Admiral Gatch sailed the Fleet's yacht up the Hudson River to West Point and personally commissioned his son. A photo of father and son appeared in the New York Daily News the day after graduation, next to a group photo of the other 874 Second Lieutenants in the class.

Korea and King Julian

His career at last underway, Tom completed Field Artillery School at Fort Sill, Oklahoma, then applied for a public information officer position. The Army instead sent him to Fort Bliss, Texas, to learn about missiles, and then to parachute school at Fort Benning, Georgia.

He complemented his military work with reading and creative writing. He read Somerset Maugham in search of plots for his own plays and short stories. He wrote one popular essay entitled, "Women of America, Arise!" Before leaving for Korea in September 1947, one of Tom's articles, "Light for America's Blindspot", was published in the prestigious Naval Institute magazine Proceedings.

His arrival overseas marked the beginning of an unofficial diplomatic career. A relative had given Tom a letter of introduction to Dr. Syngman Rhee, a Korean politician who later became president of South Korea. Gatch and Dr. Rhee struck up a friendship that lasted for many years. From Korea, Tom would write to his father, by then retired and making a nationwide lecture tour, of his strong anti-Communist views and his unabashed patriotism. Tom regarded himself as an advisor to his father, who was considering a political career (thoughts dispelled when he lost the Republican nomination for a state senate seat in Oregon).

Tom groped for fulfillment as a junior officer in a field artillery battery, but he found that life in a peacetime army consisted of passing long hours of boredom between relatively simple tasks. As a result, he sought more challenging assignments: he applied for and won a job as aide to Major General William F. Dean. He served the general four months, during which Tom moved gracefully amidst flag officers, official guests and Korean government officials. General Dean became Tom's patron, a surrogate father with whom he could discuss world politics, trade stamps, ski, play cribbage and relax. But when Tom returned to the field, he was frustrated. Farcical inspections and military classes consumed his time and bored him.

Tom recorded his dissatisfaction by scribbling in his Korea diary such notes as "dull damned life", "another lousy day of drill instruction", "dull bunch of officers to work with" and "present battery's not much to write home about, so I'm not." Finally, in frustration, Tom admitted, "Thank God I intend to resign in '50—the way I'm pushed around is a fright."

Yet he lived in relative comfort in Korea and Japan; he set up a beautiful hillside home with West Point classmate Larry Luettgren, who shared his cynical view of Army life. Luettgren, who later became a Jesuit priest, recalled that Tom was never much of a socializer. What we had in common was that neither of us wanted to make the kind of commitment the Army demanded. Tom was annoyed at the power struggle among the officers, didn't want to play that game, and it was apparent that he was not going to stay in the armed forces. He did find, though, that the Army was a convenient way to make a living. It supported him, and he was able to save money.

Also he had plenty of spare time to do his writing. Although I was a math teacher and had no idea how to help him write, I helped him edit some of his manuscripts. He was an atrocious speller, and I was pretty good at that. Tom was making out pretty well on the stock market, even though he was a real pinchpenny. He did his own laundry rather than send it out. And he made extra money by playing the Korean black market through our houseboy Kim.

Tom returned to the U.S. after a two-year tour and reported to Fort Campbell, Kentucky, in the fall of 1949 for additional parachute and artillery training. He studied for a law degree via a correspondence course, but failed the bar exam once and never took it again.

Meanwhile, back in Korea Tom's old friend Syngman Rhee was facing serious difficulties: In June of 1950, the North Korean Army had crossed the border into South Korea, and the country was plunged into war. The United Nations sent forces to stem the offensive, and within six months there were 365,000 troops, most of them American, massed near the 38th parallel. One early loss of the war was General Dean, who was captured and would spend three years as a POW in North Korean prisons.

In August 1952, after nearly all fighting had ceased, Tom received orders for Korea. Upon arrival, he expressed his shock at the site of the beautiful land where he had once served so peacefully:

> I saw Seoul again while passing through to the front. The city was a wreck. Invasion and counter-invasion had battered familiar landmarks into gutted hulks. The barracks in the compound where I lived were swept away. The comfortable brick house that was once mine had been leveled. The war became a deeply personal matter in my mind.

Tom spent the winter of 1952–53 with the Third Division Artillery. In March he was given command of Battery A, 59th Field Artillery Battalion—his first field command. The unit acquitted itself well along the jittery front and Tom was awarded a Bronze Star for ground operations against the enemy. In October, a few months after the truce, he returned to the U.S. and became advisor to an artillery unit of the California National Guard in East Pasadena. Fresh from combat and the intense daily discipline of a wartime Army, Tom had to make some adjustments. He found himself

> Charging about the battalion like a minor tempest. I would find something not to my liking, yell my objections, and then write a scathing letter about the situation. After completing a folder full of blistering reports I sat back waiting for the big reform to gain momentum. Somehow it never caught on. After a long wait I found myself doing most of the tasks I had expected others to accomplish.

It was frustrating, but after a trial period Tom decided that the time had come "to be a relaxed and friendly cuss and smile at the passing parade." He slowed down and the unit eventually found its pace.

In 1954, Tom published a novel on which he had been working for several years. After a number of publishers had rejected his manuscript, he contracted with a vanity publisher, who put the text into book form and for a fee promoted its sale. Although the book was not a commercial success, it merits attention because at age 29, Tom thought it important enough to spend several thousand dollars getting it printed. If nothing else, King Julian provides an insight into Tom's subliminal bitterness. Numerous clues attest to the novel's autobiographical flavor. A deeply personal sense of destiny and compelling duty mixes with love and compassion, all told with Tom's wistful humor, as if publication were cathartic for him.

The central figure of King Julian is a young prince, a mythical descendant of President George Washington who, it is explained, had accepted a crown as an American prince following his presidency. The Founding Fathers had decreed that Washington's heirs would be America's royal family and ceremonial heads of state. Young Julian stood in that line of succession. The tale is set in the present with King Mark as the reigning monarch, who had heroically distinguished himself in World War Two. The king was determined that his son should follow his footsteps into a military career. Julian, however, accepted with great reluctance the career his stern father had forced upon him:

> Julian never had much in common with his father, who typified the man who allows his wife to bring up their son during the difficult early years, then, when the son reaches the age when mutual interests are possible, the father finds too great a gulf of indifference or dissatisfaction to bother crossing.

As a young man, Julian pursued humanitarian and artistic causes, but lonely and bitter as a result of his inherited position. At times, he rebels. For instance, an entire chapter of King Julian describes the "beast barracks" at the Royal Military Academy, and Julian's distaste for military life. Another time, Julian disobeys orders from the Palace and goes off with the boys to enjoy himself as if he were a commoner. Julian's military assignment was as captain of an airborne field artillery battery. One day, word comes that King Mark has fallen from his horse and is near death; Julian hurries to Washington and arrives moments before his father dies.

Upon assuming the throne, Julian makes the customary call on the elected President of the United States (an imaginary figure who has held office for a record 21 years), and acquaints himself with the fixtures of the capital's political establishment. As King Julian begins grappling with issues of Cold War strategic planning, he emerges as a promising young leader. With Julian still a bachelor, much of the book is devoted to schemes among Washington's elite to find the king a bride. Finally, he meets the right woman, falls in love, and at a garden party during which he is introducing her, an assassin from within the palace court opens fire and kills the young king. End of story.

The book poses questions for those trying to understand Tom Gatch: did he foresee that he would be struck down one day, just as he was hitting his stride? Did he expect to go through life preoccupied with his father's prominence, and suffering the consequences of unrequited love?

The book did nothing to enhance Tom's Army career. And the blunt comparisons with reality did nothing to strengthen relations with his father.

Admiral Gatch and his wife had been "enduring" his retirement in Oregon. He traveled, lectured on public policy and dabbled in civic reform and politics, but these were secondary interests. Indeed, he had once mused to his daughter Nancy that he wished he had died in battle with his shipmates, for he truly believed that the most honorable way for a professional soldier to die was in his armor. Late in 1954, while Admiral Gatch and his wife were visiting friends in San Diego, he suffered a stroke and died. He was 63.

Suitable women

At age 30, Tom might have then felt freed from the compulsion to measure up to his father's inimitable standards, but by then the traits were ingrained and governed his life. Even after his father's death, Tom would often seem to be chasing a disapproving ghost. Now he only had his beloved mother, and vowed to take care of her.

When Tom's assignment with the California National Guard drew to a close in 1956, he was sent to Germany as a liaison officer on the staff of the 56th Field Artillery Battalion. He then arranged for his mother to join him. Her presence may have inhibited the lifestyle of a handsome, otherwise carefree and eligible bachelor officer, for it prevented any woman from getting too close to Tom. As sister Nancy explained: "It was essential that Tom marry well, and no one came along who was considered worthy." For a while, he dated a fraulein, but when he suspected that she only intended to marry a soldier so she could come to the U.S., he broke off the relationship.

Tom began to accumulate mediocre annual evaluations, and as a result, he remained in grade as a Captain, while others in his West Point class were receiving regular promotions. However, the enlisted men enjoyed working for him. Charles Amberger, his clerk and teletype operator, recalled Tom as:

> One of the finest men I ever met in the Service, but he was one of the most lax Army officers I ever came in contact with. He was not at all what you would call "gung-ho" and he was not strict as far as regulations were concerned.
>
> He put much more importance on getting the job done. He didn't care if your buttons were not all fastened, or your belt buckle shined or your boots were polished. He was strict, though, about being on time, being in the right place at the right time, and about getting the job done.

When it became obvious to Tom that he was not going to advance in the Army, he and three other officers pooled their assets and opened a chain of "Wash-a-rama Laundromats," which proved popular among the GI's and profitable for Tom. At the time, Laundromats were a new concept in Germany.

When they returned to the States in 1959, Tom and his mother settled back into the family home on Duke of Gloucester Street in Annapolis. One of the family members whom Tom anxiously awaited seeing was Darrin Robertson, the daughter of his first cousin. She was also the granddaughter of Tom's favorite uncle, Julian, the two-star general. Tom had been corresponding with Darrin while he was overseas, and she had blossomed into an animated, attractive 18-year-old. Although Tom was 32 by this time, he took a special liking to her, trying to ignore the fact that she was engaged to a midshipman. His strategy and his charm worked. Darrin soon broke her engagement and then, as she later recalled:

> We quickly became good pals; we did a lot of family things together. I found him a fascinating, dynamic personality, very keen and witty. Within a few months of his return from Germany, in fact, we were dating "hot and heavy."

Their relationship deepened. Darrin found herself flattered by Tom's attention, and she responded to it. The next year, having decided that it was time to settle down, Tom purchased a three-bedroom house in Alexandria, along the road to Mount Vernon. Darrin helped Tom select items to set up the home. Tom chose the smallest of the three bedrooms as his own, furnishing it in Spartan fashion with a simple bureau and a single bed. The master bedroom was for storage, and the third for his study, featuring a large portrait of his father, a painting of USS *South Dakota*, and books that had once been in his father's library.

Darrin didn't know what to expect of her cousin, but this didn't prevent her from spending many days and nights at his home. For by then, cousins Darrin and Tommy had become lovers.

"He treated me just like every other man who has been in love with me, including affection," she later recalled.

But Tom had more in mind than a simple fling. Playfully, he began calling her "Mrs. Gatch" around the house. It came as a complete surprise, however, when Tom actually proposed marriage to her in January of 1961. He was 35; she was 20. Darrin treated the suggestion lightly and reminded him of their blood relationship. Tom replied that he had already checked the laws in Virginia and found that marriage of first cousins was legal. Then he confessed that he had bought the house only to provide a permanent home for them. Awkwardly and after weeks of hesitation, Darrin had to explain to Tom that she simply didn't love him that way.

The night she formally refused his offer of marriage, Tom, who seldom cried, broke down and tears spurted from his eyes. Darin comforted him and asked, "Tommy, why are you crying?" He recovered just long enough to respond, "For what might have been!" Darrin, however, had no illusions about "what might have been":

> I liked Tom, but our marriage wouldn't have worked. From a woman's point of view, he wasn't an easy man to life with. For one thing, he had no idea what a father should be, no example of what a husband's role is. Also, Tom was a writer, and these artistic people need to get off in their own little world. He would want to be off somewhere writing plays when I would want to be going out.

Another thing troubled Darrin even more:

> I wanted to have children, but he hated kids and always referred to them as "brats." He was always making derogatory remarks about children and that kind of attitude was a real turn-off. I reminded him, "Tommy, you were a child one time" and he said, "Yes, but I got over it."

He found it difficult to get over his young cousin's rejection. The intensity of his love for her was a closely guarded family secret for years. He became distraught in 1963 when she married a graduate of the Naval Academy. About the time that Darrin was rejecting him, an Army officer selection board passed over Tom for the third time for promotion from captain to major, and he was forced to resign from active duty.

At age 35, Tom then enrolled in a master's degree program at Catholic University in Washington. He completed the coursework in a year and a half. After graduation, he affiliated with the Army Reserve, and took on special assignments for the Office of the Chief of Army Reserve at the Pentagon. Over the next 12 years, his service with the Army Reserve and his formal literary efforts gave Tom the most fulfillment and satisfaction of his career.

As a Reservist, he volunteered for extended periods of temporary active duty and carried out special projects. He was in a position to select the assignments when and where he wanted. He completed coursework at the War College and the Command and General Staff College, received the Legion of Merit, and won regular promotions. In 1972, he made full colonel.

The Army Reserve became his full-time profession, except for the money he made investing in the stock market. While he traveled (always in uniform, to take advantage of lower military fares), he consulted with his broker and built his investment portfolio. He counseled family and friends on taxes and estates. He lost money on an undeveloped land deal near Albuquerque, New Mexico, but more often than not, he came out ahead, and had a comfortable, suburban life.

After Darrin and her new husband left for California, Tom invited his mother to live with him in Alexandria. She took over the master bedroom. Once again, Tom had someone to believe in him, to restore his confidence and to build him up. One associate looked at this relationship later and said:

> Any mother can ruin a child by telling him he's too good when he's growing up. Tom's mother should have been building up his intellect, not his ego.

A year and a half after his mother settled in, she suffered a stroke, which left her left side paralyzed. Doctors advised that the damage was permanent, but for six months Tom devoted himself to her rehabilitation, much as he had helped his father recover from war wounds 20 years earlier. He took her to whirlpool bath treatments, and hired special nurses to sit with her. These nurses, listening at bedside to Mrs. Gatch's ramblings, would sometimes report to other members of the family how much Tom still cared for and talked about his cousin Darrin.

To relieve Tom of constant and expensive in-home care, his sisters and their husbands insisted on placing Mrs. Gatch in a nursing home, where all believed she would receive appropriate medical care. She certainly wouldn't get any better staying with Tom, they believed. Over Tom's objections, they moved her. The day after she moved in, Mrs. Gatch suffered a second stroke and died.

Plunged into bitter mourning, believing that he might have kept his mother alive, Tom would not be consoled. He arranged a funeral that further strained family emotions, insisting on a grueling three-day cross-country train trip from Washington to San Diego, where his mother was buried next to Admiral Gatch. Tom wept uncontrollably at the burial.

Alone again, Tom poured himself into his work at the Pentagon and into his writing. Now that he had the master's degree in drama, he decided that he would be a playwright. He wrote plays and short stories that he shared with a small circle of literary friends—and he sent many of them off to agents. Every publisher returned his manuscripts with a rejection letter, usually observing that although the characters were sharp and witty, they were inadequately developed. He continued hoping that agents for Broadway producers would look favorably upon his cynical plays. None did. They wrote back that the material was "in questionable taste," that the dialogue was "funny, but not funny enough," that the story was inconclusive, that scenes wee contrived, or that it was "better as writing than as drama on stage."

Wry social commentaries on life in the military, sprinkled with incidents of extramarital sex or homosexuality, dominated his themes. He had a single success when a one-act play, "Fraternal Feeling", about the integration of a college fraternity, was produced one summer weekend at Ford's Theater in Washington, D.C.

He remained in touch with Darrin, and was delighted when her marriage failed after two years. Tom made several trips to California to see her, but Darrin did not encourage him. She confessed:

> I didn't realize that he was carrying those feelings years later. I never thought I was the reason that Tom never got involved with anybody else, but I know I was the person Tom wanted to marry. He didn't really look for anyone before or after me, though. I guess I was the aberration from his pattern.

When Darrin married a second time, Tom avoided meeting her new husband. Instead, whenever he was on the west coast, he would surprise Darrin by showing up where she worked and taking her out to lunch.

Among Tom's literary friends, his favorite became Emma Cummings, an outspoken and brutally frank government attorney 15 years his senior. Tom escorted Emma casually and would call her often for dinner. An acute observer, Emma became aware of Tom's shortcomings. She made critical judgments—concluding once that he was "a precocious amateur, who had lots of natural talent that was not fully developed." Part of his downfall, Emma said, was that Tom really believed, as he had written in his diary as a boy, that "if one sets his standard high at the off-set, then the battle's half over," and that his own potential was enough to ensure his success. "It wasn't," Emma declared.

> He was a mama's boy. His mother told him how good he was all the time. She made him think he was smarter than he actually was. Tommy wanted to be a great hero like his father. The trouble was that he was limited by his mother's intellect. I think she was the ultimate cause of the poor guy's death.

A former nun, Emma was a "safe date" for Tom. Their friendship was unequivocally platonic. "He told me once that he would rather be alone with his thoughts than be aggravated by people," Emma recalled. But when he wanted company, he invited himself to dinner at Emma's house, and would show up with a lemon meringue pie. If they went to parties, Tom would stand by the piano singing popular songs, drinking a light bourbon and ginger and, if he danced, he would waltz, since "he couldn't do the jitterbug if he tried," Emma said.

Tom stayed healthy and trim, exercising every morning on weighted pulleys in the master bedroom, jogging around the Pentagon parking lots at noon wearing his purple knit ski cap and gray pullover, and playing tennis with fellow officers after work.

The things he had sought most in life, however, were slipping away from him. It must have dawned on Tom that he was falling short of his goals. The worthy things to which he had given his attention—passing the bar exam, publishing a book or writing a play, completing an Army career—became symptoms of self-deceit.

But if psychic conflict stormed within him, he masked it with an upbeat personality and a light-hearted self-confidence. Tom appeared happy; he was free of debt and responsibilities, successful as an investor (earning more than $100,000 in his portfolio one year) and perhaps reconciled to writing his clever little satires simply for amusement. Inside, though, he was searching for a worthy achievement.

Inheriting the wind

Tom received a windfall inheritance—$100,000—when an aunt died in 1970, leaving him as executor of the will and a major heir. He decided quickly that he would make that amount his budget as he formed in his mind a new goal: setting a record in ballooning.

That he had never ascended in a balloon or ever considered earning a pilot license did not deter him. But that he should be attracted to the adventurous aspect of long-distance balloon flight is not surprising, given the times.

There had been plenty of the publicity surrounding an attempt by three persons to cross the Atlantic Ocean by balloon. Their balloon, the Free Life, had taken off from East Hampton, Long Island, on September 20, 1970. Flying a helium balloon with a hot air burner to warm the gas, the crew kept the balloon in the air for 30 hours before going down in a storm. Despite a massive search and rescue effort, the crew was lost. That tragic flight triggered new interest in crossing the ocean by balloon. And once the imaginations of men were excited by such an adventure, it inevitably became a goal that had to be reached.

Tom Gatch chose to begin his pursuit early in 1971 by traveling to a balloon race and technical symposium at Valparaiso University in Indiana. There he met Karl Stefan, a scientific balloonist then on the staff of the National Center for Atmospheric Research in Boulder, Colorado. Stefan was lecturing about unmanned high altitude balloon-borne research. Newly developed super-strong synthetic fabric balloons had stayed aloft as long as 441 days and had orbited the earth. After listening to Stefan's lecture, Tom approached to discuss in confidence his trans-Atlantic aspirations. Stefan recalled:

> I was a little aghast at a complete novice planning such a major attempt. I urged him to get a lot of time in balloons before doing this.

Later that day, Stefan introduced Tom to Matt Wiederkehr, an industrial engineer from St. Paul, who was competing in the balloon race that weekend. "He said he was interested in buying a balloon, so I gave him a ride," recalled Wiederkehr, a distributor for Raven Industries hot air balloons.

> Tom asked a series of questions about how the balloon worked. He wanted to observe in flight—but he didn't want to take the controls, which was unusual. He seemed content to be studying the instruments, and referring to the ground. A month later, Tom telephoned me asking about high-altitude training, although he wouldn't say why. I had the impression he was going to try a high-altitude flight, perhaps going for a world record. But he was secretive, and I could only guess at his intentions.

Tom continued contacting various experts and refining his vision. In late spring, 1972, he visited Kurt Stehling, a balloonist by hobby and a government scientist by profession. A Washingtonian, Stehling had good political connections. Stehling later claimed in his book Bags Up that it was he who introduced Tom to the use of high-altitude super-pressure balloons, although reminding him that these were not man-rated and that because they were relatively small, they would have to be flown in a cluster—and the pilot would have to travel in a sealed cabin. Stehling, like Stefan, shared what he knew about government-sponsored superpressure balloons that had been aloft for as long as two years. However, as the conversation progressed:

> I learned that he had never piloted a balloon. I'm afraid I didn't realize then the full extent and firmness of his resolve. Describing previous unsuccessful Atlantic attempts, I tried in vain to dissuade him or postpone his ambitions until he got at least another $100,000 or so.

Stehling's last bit of advice was that Tom should design an electrical means for ripping apart at least one of the balloons to initiate a descent, an idea that Tom embraced.

> So Tom Gatch went away promising to get a balloon license, make flights, study his weather and navigation, and get a professionally built oxygen and carbon dioxide absorber system and a multi-channel radio transmitter-receiver so that radio amateurs and operators on ships and planes could talk with him. He would also try to build, or have built, a sealable cabin.

Upon verifying that he would need a license from the Federal Aviation Administration, Tom then contacted the Fairbanks family in Pennsylvania, and on January 13, 1973, began his flight training. The next month he joined the Fairbanks in Albuquerque, where they were competing in a major international hot air balloon fiesta. I was there, too, as a reporter, and that's where we met. After making a total of nine flights, including one thirty-minute solo, he earned his pilot license on June 23, 1973, missing only one question on the written exam—a question regarding the use of ballast in a gas balloon.

His closest friends were startled when Tom began divulging his plan to cross the Atlantic Ocean in a balloon. "This was a 180-degree turn-about for Tom," observed Maj. Gen. Milnor Roberts, his commanding officer at the Pentagon, "but he got all wrapped up in this adventure of his." Fortunately, his colleagues at the Pentagon were at least sympathetic to his cause. Col. Ed Canady, head of the State and Local Readiness Division of the Chief of the Army Reserve, recalled,

> Tom would spend three and a half days working like a herd of turtles for our command, then half a day working on his own project, using the toll-free phones to conduct his business.

He pursued this new goal devotedly, relentlessly and impatiently. Yearning for one big success, he saw the plan, which he christened Project *Light Heart*, as the major achievement of his life. The flight would earn Tom long-sought respect from his family. He would take his place in history as the Charles Lindbergh of ballooning. He would stand alongside his own father as an American hero.

Keenly aware of the significance of being first and wary of competition, he hurried his plans along. Some colleagues thought he was short-cutting on some vital areas, such as communications and tracking, testing, and physical and physiological preparedness. Friends who pointed out to Tom the dangers inherent in his haste found that he had developed a stubborn confidence in his plan. Suggestions of possible misfortune were brusquely turned aside.

Gatch and I had both been student pilots when we met in Albuquerque that February. We were helping the Fairbanks inflate their balloon when we discovered that we lived only a few miles from one another in suburban Washington, D.C. We agreed to meet there in a few weeks. After I had known Tom for several months, he disclosed his trans-Atlantic plans to me.

He sought no advance publicity, no funding, and no outside assistance. He asked if I would coordinate media coverage for his flight, which he knew would make news.

Tom conducted all the contractual arrangements himself. He retained Lunn Laminates, a firm in Port Washington, N.Y., to build the fiberglass gondola to his specifications, after Owens Corning backed out when they learned how Tom intended to use their product.

His cousin Robert Hatcher, a retired Navy Commander, made many physical calculations concerning pressure, stresses, oxygen requirements and so on. Hatcher insisted later:

> Tom did not approach the serious business of flying the Atlantic in a brash and amateurish manner. He spent months trying to collect 'expert' opinions from people concerned with high-altitude research, space flight, life-support systems, structures, insulation, coatings and a myriad of other pieces of information needed.

Hatcher's mother (Darrin's grandmother and the widow of Tom's boyhood hero, Major General Julian Hatcher) visited Tom often and encouraged him as he outfitted the gondola in his garage. Hilary Brandt, a neighbor who happened to be an aircraft mechanic, spent hours going over the flight plan, providing tools and advice on various fittings, and urging Tom to beef up his emergency gear.

Tom outfitted the capsule in the garage of his home in Alexandria, Virginia. He preferred operating alone.

Tom called me one day in October in my office at the Office of the Secretary of Interior, whose Bureau of Mines controlled the government supply of helium. Tom asked if I could investigate some inexpensive sources of supply. The best I could find Tom had already found—a private distributor in Amarillo, Texas, who was charging him $1,400 plus delivery charges for 35,000 cubic feet of gas.

On Nov. 13, Tom traveled to New York to brief the staff of the Eastern Region of the Federal Aviation Administration on his plans. During that meeting, they persuaded him that he must change his planned flight profile from an altitude of 38,000 feet to 39,000 feet above sea level. At the lower altitude, they explained, he would be on the same level as incoming international traffic as he left the east coast and floated through some of the most congested air space in the world.

This concession, to change his planned altitude in a superpressure balloon one thousand feet higher—would have serious consequences. It cost him a precious 50 pounds of carefully planned weight. It also meant that he would take off with his balloons less filled than planned.

In a paradox of ballooning, the physics are such that the less gas a balloon leaves the ground with, the higher it will fly. A balloon that is nearly completely inflated on the ground will climb only until its gas expands to fill out the balloon, then it can go no higher unless gas is released—and weight is dropped from the whole mass.

The result of Tom's agreeing to fly at a higher level was that he would be able to carry less weight. The only two places left to trim that much weight were from his ballast reserves and his personal body weight. He began dieting.

When Tom began the consuming process of planning the endless details of his transatlantic flight, he isolated himself from his friends and began putting his personal effects in order. He invited his sisters Nancy and Corki and Corki's daughter Jocklyn to witness the launch in Harrisburg, and then to house-sit in Alexandria until he returned.

Her second marriage having just ended in divorce, Darrin called Tom one week before he left for Harrisburg to wish him well. He told her that upon landing in Europe, he would tour for a while, and then would come out west to see her again.

Other old friends, meanwhile, had been feeling left out of Tom's life. Emma Cummings complained that she hadn't seen Tom for nearly two years. A few nights before he hitched the gondola-carrying trailer to his Mercedes for the trek to Harrisburg, Tom invited Emma over for dinner. She brought along Gina Barile, a State Department staffer with whom she had unsuccessfully been trying to fix Tom up. Emma recalled how gaunt and gray Tom looked that night. At less than 150 pounds, he had already shed 20 pounds to lighten the load his balloon would carry; wrinkles showed in his face, and he seemed distracted and withdrawn.

After dinner, Tom showed Emma the completed gondola, and explained his plan. Emma was skeptical and thought it looked amateurish; she asked questions about its durability. Tom by then had grown defensive. He had heard these questions before and was seeking praise and support from friends, not more challenges. Emma, practical and realistic, persisted. "Well, what if you don't make it?" she demanded.

Turning on the winning, boyish smile that had carried him through so much, the same smile that he had used as a child to win over his elders, Tom replied: "What a glorious way to go!"

3
Morning Aloft

His first realization of the new day aloft came when Tom saw hues of gray and orange light through the ice on the eight-inch porthole facing east. He sat up slowly on the canvas cot that had served as his bed. Although he was pale and on edge from the near miss of the night before, he spirits improved immediately as he watched the soft light of his first morning aloft.

As he awoke, his first wish was to ascertain his position and what progress he had made. Turning to his star chart and his watch—the time was 0900 Greenwich, or 5:00 a.m. Eastern—Tom placed his bubble sextant near the port facing easy and prepared to study the position of the familiar formations in the heavens.

Two lights stood out immediately, shining more brightly than any of the stars that morning. To the east the silver crescent of the old moon still hung in the sky. A little to the south of the moon was Venus. With a magnitude of minus 4.3, the Morning Star was putting on its most brilliant display of the celestial season. Together Venus and the old moon made a beautiful team. Tom paused in awe of this majestic view from his special platform before returning to the task of establishing his position.

Aiming the two and a half pound sextant slightly to the east and northeast, he sighted Vega, a bright and readily identifiable star commonly used by navigators. Vega was fixed about halfway between the horizon and the zenith of *Light Heart*. Almost directly east, in the direction he wished to travel, was Altair, about twenty degrees above the horizon. A little higher, but more southerly, was Antares, another bright star. Using these three stars and his carefully calibrated watch, he recorded his measurements and plotted his position in his notebook. Then Tom put down his pencil and turned to face the darker western sky; before him was an unobstructed view of the constellation Leo and its brightest star, Regulus.

He was pleased at what splendid work the wind was doing—although he was concerned that his cautious plans for a European landing might be jeopardized by the large, U-shaped trough of wind that *Light Heart* had overtaken. Tom had known when he took off that the trough was out there, and that it was moving eastward at about thirty knots along a north-south line about three hundred miles east of the U.S. coastline. A northwesterly flow of wind was behind it, and a southwesterly flow before it.

Flow charts showed that Gatch would ride its southern edge, bottom out, and be pushed back on course toward Europe, probably toward Spain. Unfortunately, once aloft he did not have the capability for receiving additional detailed weather information indicating the progress of the trough or any further deterioration that might occur in the high-level wind field.

Light Heart overtook the trough about fifteen hours after launch and by mid-morning Tuesday was near its southern edge. Before mid-day, the wind would change the *Light Heart*'s course and push it back toward southern Europe. Tom knew that as a result of this interruption in the anticipated flight path, he would fly for most of the day far south of the commercial air lanes, a circumstance permitting only intermittent air-to-air contact. Tom had been counting on airliners' messages to advise us as to his progress, but even if he veered off course, there was little to do but sigh and remind himself that "balloon navigation" is an oxymoron—and that he was the first aeronaut in history to fly for so long in the jet stream.

The sky became gradually, almost imperceptibly, brighter. As soon as the corona of the sun came over the horizon, light began reflecting on the Mylar inside the gondola, and the entire cabin took on a strange and brilliant illumination. This was the first time Tom had seen the inside of the gondola in daylight; his bright red flight suit reflected stunningly inside the sphere. Tom noted that his every movement was mimicked on the wrinkled Mylar, like the reflection from a thousand tiny mirrors. He wished that he had tinted the windows to shield some of the brightness.

Suddenly, Tom realized how hungry he was. His last full meal had been a fish dinner with his relatives two nights ago in Harrisburg. He opened the Styrofoam picnic basket and grabbed a handful of cashew nuts and some graham crackers, his favorite snack foods. He munched on this delightful breakfast and washed it down with a drink of cold water. Bobby Hatcher's wife Eugenia, a nutritionist, had prepared an assortment of low-residue, high-protein foods. Tom laughed aloud as he recalled how he had enjoyed the carefully assembled collection so much that he had eaten most of it before taking off. His teasing had confounded Eugenia. Consequently, the *Light Heart* galley was left stocked with only a few of the commercially available "space food" goodies she had prepared. There were some Slim-Jim beef sticks and some Up'N'At'em nutrition sticks, but mostly Tom had his cashews and graham crackers to keep him happy.

When he finished eating, Tom reached below the seat for a five-pound can of lithium hydroxide crystals. He opened the can and removed a polyethylene bag. To maintain oxygen purity, the chemicals in his life-support tray had to be changed every ten hours. The special grade of environmental lithium hydroxide would absorb carbon dioxide in the closed cabin. He took the used crystals from the plastic tray in front of the fan, and poured them into the metal can, and placed fresh crystals in the tray. Then Tom examined his carbon dioxide analyzer, which he had acquired from a mine safety firm and which would warn him should the air become poisoned. A glance at the instrument assured him that his air was pure. It would be good for ten more hours, he thought, and by then he would be on final approach to Europe.

Tuesday was a quiet morning up in *Light Heart*. Tom began signing some of the two hundred souvenir envelopes he was carrying. As a dedicated stamp collector, he well knew the value of limited-edition commemorative covers, and he hoped to make a profit auctioning these to philatelists. All the envelopes were addressed to Tom at his home in Virginia. He planned to have them postmarked and mailed from the postal station nearest his landing. He also carried on board a lead ingot, from which he hoped a mold would be made for special coins noting man's first ocean crossing by balloon. The Franklin Mint had rebuffed his initial request to mint the coins, but Tom believed that a successful flight would change their minds.

Despite his natural ebullience, Tom was troubled by the accident of the previous night. His confidence in the balloons had shattered when the first balloon did. He pondered the effect of the sun's heat on the remaining nine balloons. When the full effect of the sun's intense heat was felt, it would expand the helium and give the balloons a great test of strength. Any pinhole in the fabric would cause the helium slowly to seep out. The integrity test in the hangar at Harrisburg had not detected any leakage in the forty-two hours they had been inflated prior to liftoff.

Tom gazed through the two-inch observation port at the sight overhead: nine taut white suspension lines leading one hundred twenty feet straight up to the imposing opaque balloons outlined distinctly against the blue-black sky. It saddened him to discover that it was the center balloon of the cluster that had failed: with it had collapsed the U.S. flag and his father's pennant, both of which he had so proudly rigged. They no longer flew triumphantly over the gondola. Instead, they hung limply somewhere out of sight, while the lifeless balloon lay draped over one window.

The urge to do something about these banners was almost irresistible, but there was no way to do anything until he opened the hatch during descent and cut away the dead balloon, using that ninety pounds of ballast. Siphoning the liquid ballast had prevented him from falling into the sea Monday night, but he would need some ballast for his final descent. He was fortunate that the balloon had not shattered like glass when it broke. Raven executives had been unable to assure him that the balloons would not shatter when he destroyed them electrically to commence his descent, but they had assured him that the balloons were virtually break-proof and leak-proof.

The morning passed slowly. Exhausted and wistful, Tom surveyed the ocean rolling beneath. Off to the east, he studied the carpet of soft cotton clouds five miles below. He decided to cover some of the windows with the round Mylar shields he had designed. The capsule was becoming warm as the sunlight streamed in and beat down relentlessly upon the fiberglass skin of the gondola. Tom wished there were a way of bringing in some of the coolness outside, since the temperature just one-fifth of an inch away was minus sixty-seven degrees. Instead, Tom unsnapped and removed the Eddie Bauer cold-weather jacket he had been wearing; then, unhooking the suspenders and raising his legs, he squirmed out of the bulky pants. His new uniform of white cotton long johns gave him more flexibility of movement. Tom bundled together the flight suit and leaned back on it. The goose down made a good cushion for his aching muscles.

At 1520 Greenwich time (10:20 a.m. Eastern), the radio crackled. Air France Flight 227 was giving him a call. At that time, the Boeing 747 Jumbo Jet was midway on its flight from Paris to Point-a-Pitre, Guadeloupe. Tom reported that he was steady at thirty-six thousand feet, but did not know his precise position. Obligingly, the Air France captain advised the balloonist that he was approximately twenty-four degrees and eleven minutes North latitude and fifty-two degrees and forty-eight minutes West longitude, about halfway across the Atlantic Ocean.

Gradually, as he surveyed his position, he was struck by the realization that the *Light Heart* gondola in which he rode was the smallest, most fragile man-carrying craft ever to visit this part of the world. It was smaller than any passenger-carrying space capsule, tinier than the shortest sailboat. Tom continued peering out at the blue and green ocean and the immaculately beautiful horizon. There wasn't a sound anywhere. He noted a phenomenon: as the sun played on his balloons, *Light Heart* rotated completely around every hour or so. Occasionally, he burst into song, perhaps one of his own compositions. He discovered a strange echo and resonance inside the gondola as his baritone voice hit certain notes.

At 1535 Greenwich (11:35 a.m. Eastern), Tom heard a low rumbling and felt a vibration in the air. It was a sound familiar to him, but which seemed out of place in this isolated environment. It was, he thought, the roar of jet aircraft engines. He switched his radio to 121.5 mHz, and transmitted his identification, but there was no response. His heart raced a little faster as the roar became a shrill scream, and he strained at the window, looking for a source, but it passed within a few seconds.

Simultaneously, in the cockpit of Iberian Flight 989, a DC-8 air freighter bound for San Juan from Madrid, the co-pilot made an extraordinary discovery. He nudged the captain and the flight engineer. All three Spanish crewmen squinted at the sight as their huge aircraft overtook *Light Heart*. A few minutes later, the captain reported to ARINC that he had seen "what looks like a balloon. Its color is white, with something hanging at the bottom." Unaware that the balloon was manned, however, the Iberian captain did not attempt communication with it.

At 1605 Greenwich (12:05 p.m. Eastern), thirty minutes after the Iberian freighter flew past, British Airways Flight 683 contacted Tom on 126.7 mHz. They reported that he had a steady velocity of fifty-two knots in the jet stream at two hundred twenty degrees (toward the northeast) and that his position was approximately as given by the Air France flight an hour earlier. Tom responded that he was holding a nice altitude track of thirty-six thousand feet. He did not report any distress. He was more than one thousand eight hundred fifty miles from Harrisburg and had been aloft for sixteen and a half hours.

4

A Mid-Ocean Mystery

Thursday, February 21 dawned clear in the mid-Atlantic. Derek Posscher, first mate on the motor vessel Ore Meridian, stood on the bridge as the freighter steamed northeastward across the Tropic of Cancer. The seven hundred fifty-one foot ship, its cargo holds laden with iron ore loaded in Puerto Ordaz, Venezuela, was steaming toward Rotterdam. Below, Captain Franz Ringlemann was happy. The old German had skippered the Ore Meridian for more than fourteen years, and this morning was headed for home.

Posscher studied the sky. It was clear in every direction he looked, with a head wind of less than five knots from the northeast. The Ore Meridian slipped through the water at about fifteen knots as the Dutchman gripped the helm and guided fifty-one thousand tons of ship into the breeze. Then the first mate looked up, squinted, and came to attention. Almost as if it were coming off the horizon with the morning sun in pursuit, there appeared the oddest arrangement of clouds he had ever seen. Just as he called down to Captain Ringlemann, the old man raced up to the bridge for a better look at what he himself had seen out the galley port.

Together they studied the vision. This certainly was no cloud formation. But whatever it was, nothing in their seagoing days had prepared them for this.

"It was a fantastic picture", Ringlemann exclaimed later. The two officers called to the thirty-five other crewmen so they, too, could get a look at the mysterious image. In a short time they were all assembled on deck. Some brought binoculars; some began to wave. Unfortunately, as Ringlemann recalled, "nobody made a picture," even though there was a Polaroid camera on board.

Slowly *Light Heart* approached the ship. Captain Ringlemann stayed right on course, and the two ocean-going vessels from different lands came nearer. As the airborne apparition approached, the crew observed what looked like a long red banner hanging from a white capsule. They estimated the length as one hundred or one hundred fifty feet. It was the international orange streamer that had been rigged on the line of the fallen balloon. There was no sign of the American flag, *USS South Dakota* pennant or registration banner.

The crew of the motor vessel Ore Meridian made the last reported sighting of Light Heart, in the middle of the Atlantic Ocean, near dawn on February 21, two and a half days after takeoff.

The crew observed what appeared to be a "two-stage balloon" composed of about eight members, though some said it could have been seven or nine. Ringlemann noted, "Some of the balloons appeared a little slack." Nothing seemed to be out of order to the sailors, though Ringlemann admitted apologetically later, "I'm not experienced in ballooning, you know." He was far too captivated by this silent flying sight to blow the ship's whistle. One blast of the horn would have sounded a noise that would be heard for miles in the expanse of mid-ocean.

In thickly accented English, the captain explained:

> We did not suspect that nothing was inside. If a man should be in trouble in there, he would throw something down or send a smoke signal, you know? If I thought there was trouble, I would stop my ship and follow the balloon immediately. You see, that's my first duty as a captain at sea. We see so many little boats crossing the Atlantic, little yachts. Unless they give a distress signal, we don't bother, you know? We were just keeping our own course. But nobody suspected anything.

The *Light Heart* approached the freighter on the starboard side. When it was closest, one of the crews took an angle measurement. The *Light Heart* was sixty degrees above the horizon, at an altitude of an estimated one thousand feet. If accurate, that put the balloon within a few hundred yards of the ship.

The crew watched in fascination and in silence as the balloon passed almost directly overhead. It remained at a nearly constant altitude, and did not appear to be rising or falling. The crew continued to look back at the sight as it slowly disappeared in the southwest morning sky as mysteriously as it had appeared. The Ore Meridian continued her voyage. The strange encounter dominated conversation among the crew for a few days on the otherwise uneventful trip.

Later, Captain Ringlemann notified the U.S. Coast Guard and described what he had seen. His was the last authoritative report ever received about Thomas L. Gatch, Jr., and the *Light Heart*.

5

Search and Hope

On Wednesday, February 20, Frank White had sent a message asking that "watch supervisors" contact and brief all aircraft operating within one thousand miles of Gatch's last known position. Crews were asked to monitor 121.5 mHz, and if any signals were heard from *Light Heart*, pilots were asked to make minor course deviations and attempt a visual check of the balloon to establish its location and condition.

Because we had not heard from Tom, at first our concerns centered on whether the battery powering the transmitter might have become depleted. White had quizzed Gatch on the issue, but Tom had insisted that the batteries would be okay. Furthermore, the fact that he had drifted so far off course perhaps illustrated how little was known about the behavior of the jet stream bands. The *Light Heart* may have been pushed aside by the swirling winds and wound up on an extreme side of this conveyor belt of air, moving ever farther from the main wind field.

The last communication from Tom, twenty-four hours earlier, had come via the British Airways crew near noon on Tuesday. Under persistent encouragement from ARINC, many other aircraft tried to establish contact Tuesday and Wednesday.

Meanwhile, based upon the observed and radar-plotted positions, the *Light Heart* trajectory was being revised on our charts back in Washington. When our wind flow chart showed *Light Heart* headed more toward northern Africa than Europe, we advised the New York office of Gamma Press Images, a Paris-based agency doing comprehensive coverage of Gatch. They had sent the renowned award-winning photographer David Burnett to Harrisburg, where he took hundreds of frames of Tom relaxing and working in the days prior to lift-off. When we advised Gamma that *Light Heart* had changed course and might be destined for Africa, they put Burnett on a plane to record Gatch's landing and recovery.

The photographer sat in Dakar for more than two weeks hoping in vain that the balloon would come over the horizon.

On Thursday, February 21, the State Department cabled all U.S. embassies from Casablanca to Capetown, advising them that Gatch's arrival may be imminent, even though it could not be pinpointed. They passed the word to foreign governments that he was friendly, and should be accorded a hero's welcome. Messages were sent across the Atlantic to land-based tracking stations at Las Palmas, Lisbon and Dakar requesting they expedite any new information on the balloon. All reports came back negative. Ultimately, however, confusion erupted from all the signals flashing back and forth on a subject about which few of the messengers knew anything. This confusion led to a burst of hope for us early Friday morning when a message arrived from the Canary Islands:

> FOR YOUR INFORMATION, BALLOON N7TG TRIED CONTACT LAS PALMAS TOWER ON 121.5 AT 0415 AND 0530 WITH NEGATIVE RESULT. POSITION NOT KNOWN.

A sergeant on night duty at Dakar's Rogers Field transmitted the message. Had it been true, it would have meant that Gatch was less than two hundred miles from the Canary Islands and was eagerly trying to make contact as he approached land. A deluge of inquiries flooded the Las Palmas Tower. Regrettably, inspection of the log and a careful replaying of the tape recording in the tower determined that the sergeant had heard another station trying unsuccessfully to call the balloon. Embarrassed Las Palmas officials promised to "keep an extreme watch on 121.5 mHz." But for a while, that false report contributed to our confidence that Gatch would soon be over land.

Not until Friday morning, February 22 did we learn from the Coast Guard of the Ore Meridian sighting on the day before, hundreds of miles west of the Canary Islands. The reason for the delay in the report was never explained. Immediately, the Coast Guard began a series of messages to all ships in the vicinity of the Ore Meridian, and sent back to the freighter a series of questions that later helped to verify details of the sighting.

For the next few days the Coast Guard used its radio network extensively in the effort to find Gatch. Through its Automated Mutual Assistance Vessel Rescue (AMAVER) system, merchant vessels of every seafaring nation can be reached. In the Atlantic Ocean alone the Coast Guard made daily contact with more than nine hundred fifty ships.

Friday's new information, based on the confirmed sightings and description, altered our previous calculations about Gatch's progress. Frank White began plotting the last two confirmed positions (the British Airways flight and the Ore Meridian) and measured them at eight hundred fifty miles apart.

How had Tom traveled that distance from noon Tuesday to dawn Thursday? Had he been at thirty-six thousand feet the whole time, the wind would have carried him much farther. Had he stayed near sea level, not nearly that far, and perhaps in the opposite direction? White divided the distance by the number of hours between sightings, and studied the known wind at various elevations. He found a wind between ten and twenty thousand feet that would carry the craft at a speed of twenty-three knots, or the full eight hundred fifty miles.

Optimistically, we projected the winds from ten to twenty thousand feet and made a new chart that showed that *Light Heart*, staying within that range, would break land approximately over the Canary Islands by noon on Saturday.

All day Friday, dozens of efforts to contact the balloon on various frequencies proved negative. Finally, on Friday evening, after hearing nothing from the balloon, we began to discuss the painful possibility that N7TG might be down at sea.

White asked the watch supervisors to continue the visual search, and maintain a "listening watch" on 121.5 mHz or for the Emergency Locator Transmitter (ELT) that Gatch could activate from his life raft. Frank slept in his downtown Washington office on Friday night to be near the communications system he had set up, in case any word came. Saturday crept by and still there was no word.

On Saturday evening, February 23, Frank and I met with two associates at the Air Transport Association. White brought Bill Osmun, a technical information specialist for the ATA, and I brought Don Creed, a fellow government public information officer who had followed Gatch's flight preparations. We assessed the information we had and tried to draft some kind of press statement for the reporters who had been calling us. We had only a few facts:

- Five days after ascending, Gatch had failed to reach land.
- No one had made radio contact with him for four and a half days.
- A ship had sighted him one thousand feet above the water, when he was supposed to be at thirty-six thousand.

Our inevitable conclusion was that he was down at sea, at least at night, without communications. Yet we did not know why he had not used the radio. Perhaps he had become physically unable to operate it. Perhaps it had become damaged. Perhaps he had dropped it as ballast to check a descent on Tuesday or Wednesday. So much depended upon pilot judgment, yet we were frustrated in trying to offer an explanation for Gatch's disappearance, much less identify any likely search area. Our speculation necessarily made the assumption that he was alive, but our questions were endless:

Why had he descended? Did he come down in control? Had another balloon accidentally burst? Did the gondola decompress? Did Tom's atmosphere scrubber fail? Did he initiate the descent himself? If so, did he get down quickly enough to reach breathable air? Too quickly? Did the system encounter sudden turbulence that rocked it, knocked some equipment off-line, or injured the pilot? Was Tom asleep when the disruption occurred?

When the balloons hit the water, was he conscious and in control? Did he decide upon descending to ride out the night in the gondola, awaiting the sunrise and super-heating of the helium in the morning? Did he abandon the gondola and attempt to board a life raft? Was he successful in doing so? (There had been no rehearsal of this procedure).

If not Tuesday, did he come down on Wednesday? If he stayed with the gondola and rode the wind and the waves, did that make the pilot seasick? Was he asleep when the Ore Meridian saw him? Wounded? Sick? After the ship sighting, did he stay in the gondola, or subsequently try to board the life raft? Was he drifting with the wind or the current? Why didn't he activate the ELT once he was in the water?

Every question depended upon pilot judgment, and we had to continue assuming that the pilot was making decisions.

There was some basis for optimism, based on historical precedent. I thought back to the flight of *Small World*, an east-to-west trans-Atlantic balloon flight attempted in December 1958. Four Britons, flying a boat-like gondola beneath a large hydrogen balloon, had set off from Tenerife in the Canary Islands, planning to fly the trade winds to the New World. Although their plan was to fly no more than a few hundred feet above the waves, on the fourth day they were caught in a vicious thermal updraft. Valving gas to descend, they instead kept going up, topping out at 14,000 feet before stabilizing—and then began sinking rapidly. One of the first items they jettisoned when they ran out of ballast on the way down was their only link with the outside world, a heavy radio transmitter.

The *Small World* crew ditched the balloon during that storm, after one thousand two hundred miles of flying, but they heartily hoisted sail over their craft and scudded along for twenty more days until reaching Barbados. They arrived hungry and bedraggled, but the flight of *Small World* was at the time the only successful crossing of the Atlantic Ocean using any kind of free balloon. We hoped that Tom could use his resourcefulness to stay afloat and perhaps he, too, would appear on some shore within a few weeks—unless we could find him first.

Meanwhile, on Saturday night, February 23, we put out a statement to the inquisitive and sympathetic editors at the wire services and networks stating that we believed Gatch was down at sea somewhere in a thirty-two thousand square mile quadrant about nine hundred fifty miles west of Spanish Sahara. I also disclosed that Gatch's sisters had appealed to the Pentagon and the White House asking that an immediate air and sea search begin.

Just before we adjourned that night, Frank huddled the four of us together. With our arms around one another's shoulders, Frank White prayed aloud for Tom's safe recovery. It was a touching moment in our long ordeal.

Tom's family had sequestered themselves to his home in Alexandria since they had arrived there late on the evening he took off. They felt increasingly helpless and distraught since his disappearance. Their concern became greater as they settled in to Tom's house. Nancy and Corki found distressing evidence that Tom recognized that he might not return. For instance, they found two stacks of love letters, apparently from different women, upon which Tom had left a simple handwritten instruction: "Discard"—something he apparently lacked the heart to do himself. Another mysterious item they found in his house was a woman's nightgown, otherwise unidentified.

"I wonder if it was mine," Darrin mused when she learned of it months later. "What room was it in? What color was it?"

I spent most of Sunday on the telephone answering newsmen's questions. I also received a call from Congressman Albert Quie of Minnesota, who represented the district in which Gatch's two sisters lived. Rep. Quie and his staff would be most helpful during the coming weeks. The congressman told me he was telephoning various White House and Department of Defense officials and pressing them hard to conduct a military search and rescue mission. His staff took special interest in the Gatch case, with one aide assigned to work full time on it. Congressional interest in a matter always produces a quick military response; soon I was getting calls from generals and admirals.

On Monday, February 25, a week after the flight began, it seemed that the Pentagon was apparently considering a search, but officials said they were hindered by the same terribly real problem that I dealt with in my daily job at the Federal Energy Administration: a shortage of fuel in the midst of the Arab oil embargo. Committing the armed forces of the United States to a full-scale search and rescue mission for a six-foot gondola somewhere in the middle of the Atlantic Ocean would require a tremendous expenditure of fuel, the Pentagon had told Congressman Quie.

At noon I received a call from a Navy Commander asking that I report immediately to the Pentagon. I jumped in a taxi and took the short ride over the Fourteenth Street Bridge to the River Entrance of the Pentagon, following the signs to the Joint Chiefs of Staff and the National Military Command Center (NMCC), where I met Frank White. Stopping at two checkpoints for the proper credentials and an escort, we were ushered into what looked like the World Crisis Room. It was a place of subdued lighting, with maps of the world on paneled walls, thick carpeting and plush furnishings.

The NMCC had established a Balloon Task Force to gather first-hand data and consider a search for *Light Heart*. They had already assembled aeronautical and oceanographic charts, a thick file of data, messages and meteorological information. Navy Captain Edward R. Hallett, an aviator, who would brief the Joint Chiefs when the time came for a decision, chaired the Task Force. Both were glad to see me and Frank White arrive, armed with our own array of data and diagrams.

We spent five hours at the Command Center analyzing various contacts with the balloon, describing Gatch's survival and life-support equipment and explaining what little we then knew about super-pressure balloons. I had such a difficult time convincing the Navy officers that a super-pressure balloon behaves differently than the conventional old gas bags they knew in World War Two that we finally called Dr. Vincent Lally, the expert on super-pressure balloons at the National Center for Atmospheric Research in Boulder. Lally had advised Gatch on the performance characteristics of the balloons and had at first advised him not to attempt the flight. Later, however, he publicly praised Gatch's approach, predicted that he would be successful, and in a press release I prepared, allowed himself to be quoted that Gatch should go for an orbit of the earth once he was aloft.

After Lally explained "supers" to the Task Force, NMCC quartermasters and artists began mapping out two large search areas in the mid-Atlantic, one based on the theory that Gatch floated/sailed after the Ore Meridian sighting and the other on the theory that he remained down in the water after Thursday night. The two search areas each measured 120 by 180 nautical miles. Thus, more than 43,000 square miles had to be covered.

Further complicating matters, photos from the Nimbus weather satellite showed that a cloud cover and temperature inversion had moved in early Thursday near where the Ore Meridian had been. If *Light Heart* had been near neutral buoyancy, as seemed likely, this surely would have driven it back into the water.

Tuesday, February 26, the Commander-in-Chief, Atlantic Command (CIN-CLANT), began a tentative search for Gatch in the area the Task Force had outlined. A single P-3 Orion was sent over the area on a routine training mission, with instructions "to maintain both visual and radio alert for the balloon." The Orion is a low flying, radar-and-sonar equipped aircraft useful for spotting submarines, as well as search and rescue flying. Simultaneously, the Pentagon announced that all military and civilian ships and aircraft operating in the area between the Azores and the west coast of Africa have been requested to maintain both visual and radio alert for the balloon.

The Navy plane returned to Lajes Air Force Base in the Azores Tuesday night without any new information on the *Light Heart*. We all recognized the difficulty, if not the impossibility, of locating a small gondola or life raft in the broad expanse of the ocean.

Wednesday morning, February 27, at the regular 10:00 a.m. Pentagon press briefing, reporters quizzed Assistant Secretary of Defense for Public Affairs Jerry Freidheim about Gatch. Freidheim noted the Orion flight of the previous day, displayed an artist's sketch of the balloon cluster, and maps showing where Gatch had most recently been sighted. An aide said the Department of Defense had run a computer analysis, programming various wind speeds, altitudes and plausible flight paths. He said the computer came out with a total possible search area of six million square miles, including such remote sites as Hong Kong, where, they hypothesized, the balloon might have traveled had it stayed in the jet stream.

Also on that Wednesday, eight days after the flight began, far off in a town in the Valley of Oro Tava near Tenerife in the Canary Islands, a group of villagers, tourists and police reported seeing a blue balloon floating over a nearby volcano and drifting out toward sea. Someone reported to the Spanish news agency CIFRA that the balloon probably belonged to that missing American fellow, Tom Gatch. Soon after other news agencies read the report, they began repeating it. By mid-morning, AP, UPI and Reuters News Service were carrying around the world the report that villagers in the Canary Islands had reportedly seen the *Light Heart*.

When I was contacted for a comment, I could not verify or disprove the report until I had more information. It took several hours of telephoning foreign news agencies to assemble an accurate report of what the villagers had seen. By that time, most newspapers in the United States had printed the speculative report.

When we learned the facts, it turned out that what had been seen was "a blue globe, about six feet in diameter."

We scrutinized that report, and then came to the bitter realization that this had occurred on Ash Wednesday, the first day of Lent. What had been seen floating in the sky that morning was, no doubt, an escaping remnant from a Mardi Gras celebration the night before.

Nevertheless, the story badly damaged our credibility: we were trying to focus the search in the Atlantic Ocean. The Canary Islands caper had two expensive consequences. First, it convinced military authorities in Spanish Sahara that they should independently commence a search in the desert. Soon, they were dispatching dozens of jeeps and helicopters to sift through the sands in search of the balloonist we believed down at sea. The second consequence affected Tom's family.

Tom's sisters, watching and reading the news about him, sought relief from the tension that quite naturally had been building. The dispatch from the Canary Islands was the only one resembling a ray of hope. Nancy began believing the widely printed newspaper accounts of the "blue balloon", as well as following what she called her intuition, and made plans to fly to the Canary Islands herself.

Nancy and Corki, Gatch's sisters, were distraught. They believed that the Pentagon had not moved forward quickly enough to coordinate or carry out a search. Indeed, at that time, only one training plane had been diverted to look for the balloon. They felt that some dramatic action was needed to activate the search. We decided upon a press conference on Friday, March 1, at which Nancy and Corki and Corki's daughter Jocklyn would publicly appeal to the Pentagon.

Publicity had become a helpful tool for us, especially when we could control it. It was one device to keep pressure on public officials who could help. And there had been plenty of press attention around the country: Walter Cronkite mentioned Tom Gatch and his *Light Heart* balloon on four consecutive evenings on the CBS Evening News; round-the-clock phone calls from wire services, newspapers, photo agencies and networks poured into my office and my residence as the flight developed. Live all-night radio call-in show hosts had been rousing me from sleep for updates and to answer listeners' questions. Interest escalated dramatically.

In short, the news media were being very sympathetic to Gatch's cause. He was being portrayed as a great hero (if only he would return) at a time when the country desperately needed a hero.

I contacted those Washington newsmen who had been most helpful the previous two weeks and told them about our press conference. But the course of other events was far from our control. On that same day, Friday, March 1, a federal grand jury in Washington returned conspiracy and obstruction of justice indictments against six top presidential aides in conjunction with the Watergate political scandal (from a news standpoint, it was at that time the biggest break in the case).

The Gatch story was a good one, but it would have to wait for a slower news day. Nearly all general assignment reporters were at the courthouse. Tom was still missing, however, and we felt it was vital that a search begin at once. We went ahead with the news conference in Tom's backyard in suburban Alexandria. With half a dozen television and newspaper reporters gathered around them, the women calmly answered questions and displayed maps showing where they wanted the search conducted. The news conference was no sooner over than the Pentagon made this announcement:

> The Joint Staff has directed a second search of a broad area of the mid-Atlantic for missing balloonist Tom Gatch. Based on a computer run of the most recent information and the most logical assumptions, an area of 75,600 square miles, approximately 1,230 statute miles south-southwest of the Azores will be searched by aircraft of the Atlantic Command.

Perhaps the announcement was a coincidence, but the press conference seemed to be the catalyst that finally launched the Pentagon's search in earnest. The Department of Defense then did all that could reasonably be expected under the circumstances. During the next several days there were overflights conducted in the primary search areas. But on Wednesday, March 6, the news from the Pentagon briefing about Gatch was not good. In its final statement on the matter, Freidheim's office summarized:

> Efforts throughout have been adversely affected by the absence of concrete information and the wide scope of possibilities. Searches by aircraft were conducted in the areas considered most likely and will have covered more than 223,000 square miles of the Atlantic Ocean when completed. In each case, the effort combined visual, radar and communication methods and in some instances, the search was combined with other aircraft patrol missions. While active search will be terminated, military ships and aircraft will continue to be on the lookout for Gatch, particularly those transiting the general search area.

Termination of the Pentagon's search convinced Nancy to go to the Canary Islands and conduct her own search for her brother. It was hard to dissuade her. When she arrived in the Canaries, she chartered a small plane and directed its pilot to fly slowly and methodically over the remote areas of the island, particularly near the volcano where the blue balloon had been seen. After a week she returned, her hopes crushed.

Aside from those efforts, the emotional situation for Gatch's survivors was complicated by the intrusion of various clairvoyants who, I learned, often surface during such tragedies. Whatever sincere intentions these people harbored, it was difficult to give them much credence in this instance. There were three main instances.

The first took place as we were trying to commit the Pentagon to a search. A man named William Ritner called me from Harrisburg; he said he had witnessed the ascent and followed news accounts of Gatch's progress. He identified himself as author of a book titled, "Planned Reincarnation" and as a student of extra-sensory perception. He said he had been meditating about the fate of *Light Heart*, and called me after an all-night session with maps, a globe and a small flashlight with the conclusion that Gatch had already crossed the ocean, flown low over the Sahara Desert and kept flying. He "envisioned" Gatch aloft with four of the original ten balloons (a physical impossibility) flying somewhere south of Ceylon in the Indian Ocean. I thanked him for his call, but did not pass along his unrealistic revelation to the fellows at the National Military Command Center.

The National Inquirer, the weekly scandal-and-scare tabloid, instigated the second incident. Just after the Pentagon quit searching, the paper's editors proposed to me and then to Gatch's family a complicated scheme that, I believed, risked exposing the family's emotion and grief. They proposed to hire psychics in three cities to meditate on Gatch's whereabouts. If all agreed on one site, the *Inquirer* would absorb all costs of a special search in that place.

For this, the family would promise an "exclusive" on their reactions during the story, no matter what the results. If Gatch were found alive, the family would pledge its influence to have him sign a contract for his story with the National Inquirer. If the family rejected or altered these terms, there would be no search.

Their offer amounted to outrageous extortion, and I argued against it. Besides deploring the idea of dealing with cheap scandal sheets and phony mystics, I thought we had an obligation to protect Tom from having his story sold out from under him if he did return. In addition, I was trying to spare the family further embarrassment and exploitation. However, this proposal arrived after all formal search operations had ceased.

Corki and Jocklyn (Nancy was still in the Canary Islands) believed they had to grasp at any straw, and they thought there was a chance this might work. After consulting an attorney, they signed an agreement with the paper's representative, who served as an intermediary between the family and the mystics. Then Corki and Jocklyn went through Tom's bureaus and selected particular pieces of his clothing, which they shipped to the psychics. The psychics rubbed and fondled this clothing as they meditated.

On March 21, their collective report was relayed to the family: two of them agreed that Tom was stranded on an island off Portuguese Guinea on the west coast of Africa. A third said that he was in the middle of the Atlantic Ocean. As a result of this discrepancy, no story appeared and no search took place.

The third "supernatural" incident began on March 6, when Marcia Kuhn, a publicity-conscious housewife in suburban Laurel, Maryland, insisted that she had had a vision of Gatch. He was conscious, she said, but wounded and very weak, on Guadeloupe in the Caribbean. Mrs. Kuhn told her story first on a local radio talk show, then to newspapers, wire services and to whomever else would listen. She briefly had actually met Tom earlier in the year at a meeting of a local chapter of the Experimental Aircraft Association, to which her husband belonged. Gatch had been a guest at the meeting.

Mrs. Kuhn next thought about that encounter when her husband attended another meeting in March, at which Hilary Brandt appealed for help in finding Tom. Kuhn volunteered that his wife had psychic powers. She began meditating and claimed to have had several "visions" and received ESP messages from Gatch. She was convinced that he had ditched in the ocean, and then drifted to an obscure spot on Guadeloupe. She described some of the gear that Gatch had on board, but much of that could be ascribed to coincidence or published reports. Mrs. Kuhn provided authorities with exact coordinates, and apparently she persuaded some people.

As a result, by the end of March there was an unorchestrated worldwide circus taking place—with Nancy making low passes over Canary Islands' volcanoes, an army flaring out across the Sahara Desert, psychics calling for searches in the Indian Ocean, Portuguese Guinea and the Atlantic Ocean, the State Department flashing messages from Capetown to Casablanca, and the Pentagon projecting and computing a six-million square mile search area. To top it off, voodoo-worshipping Guadeloupean gendarmes on foot patrol, in helicopters, and private planes started searching through tall sugarcane fields based on latitude and longitude positions plotted by a Laurel, Maryland, housewife. Marcia Kuhn's story received a small boost of added publicity when an unidentified wood merchant reportedly told police he had seen "un ballon". They found nothing.

Hope for Tom's recovery continued receding after Nancy returned from the Canary Islands. She and Corki set up a $10,000 reward for information leading to their brother's recovery. Later, they added to that amount and established a perpetual scholarship at St. Alban's school for outstanding choir boys who wished to continue their education after losing their singing voice and thus, eligibility for a choir scholarship.

Periodically in the weeks that followed, reports appeared in the press postulating that various pieces of debris found in or near the ocean belonged to *Light Heart*. The U.S. embassy in Liberia reported a capsized lifeboat "believed belonging to Gatch" was spotted off the coast of that African nation. But Gatch was not carrying a lifeboat. Crewmen of the British freighter *Antilochus*, one hundred fifty miles off the coast of Liberia, reported seeing a large drifting object resembling a buoy, which they later thought might have been Gatch's gondola. A few days later, the Indian freighter Jag Vijay encountered an orange and white object about fifty miles south of the British ship's sighting. Neither item was recovered or examined.

Months later, the State Department passed along to me a report received from the U.S. consulate in the Canary Islands that the badly decomposed body of a Caucasian male, believed to be an American, had been brought ashore by a Korean fishing vessel on March 19, and buried. Although the description of the clothing on the body did not match what Gatch had been wearing, I asked the State Department whether the body could be exhumed for examination. They retrieved Gatch's medical and dental records from the Army, forwarded them to the consul in Tenerife, and the grave was opened. A three-man panel agreed that the remains were not those of Thomas L. Gatch, Jr.

It was the last lead that we ever pursued, for as time passed, the flight of *Light Heart* faded in the public memory, and no more clues to the disappearance of Tom Gatch ever came to light.

6

Reflections

Despite widespread publicity and official attention, no evidence ever came to light explaining when, where or how Tom Gatch disappeared. A number of technical and physical theories evolved, all impossible to prove or disprove without empirical data. More than a few persons even suggested that Gatch disappeared intentionally, that his voyage was an elaborate form of suicide. A close relative believes that he was fished from the water by a Soviet submarine and held as a spy.

Still others suggest that his disappearance fits a pattern of mysteries. Indeed, in his best-selling book, The Bermuda Triangle, author Charles Berlitz adds Gatch's balloon to the list of vessels afloat in the deadly calm waters of the Sargasso Sea, where lore holds that ships with no crews, or just bony skeletons, man the decks.

The crew of the M/V *Ore Meridian* no doubt contributes to those legends as they retell their mysterious sighting of *Light Heart*. Berlitz claims that since 1945 the Bermuda Triangle has claimed more than one hundred ships and aircraft. Usually these losses occurred in daylight, in clear weather, between November and February. In most instances, the pilot or captain had been reporting normal operations (as had been Gatch) immediately prior to the disappearance. Some of the explanations for the phenomena of the Bermuda Triangle include clear air turbulence, magnetic field variations, or in the cases of ships, sudden tidal waves, suction whirlpools or waterspout storms.

Leaving aside the mysteries of the Bermuda Triangle, however, theories concerning the loss of *Light Heart* fall into four plausible categories:

1. CO2 Poisoning. The function of the cabin atmosphere purification system was to remove poisonous quantities of exhaled carbon dioxide. The normal human intake of carbon dioxide at sea level is three-tenths of one percent. A fatal level is reached when consumption becomes one hundred times the normal, or about three percent of total atmosphere. If, for any one of several reasons, the home-built purifier failed, Tom would have endured a quiet, euphoric death, beginning with a calm sleep. Several causes of failure could be suggested:

a. failure of the battery-powered fan circulating air over the tray of lithium hydroxide crystals and silica gel;

b. inadequate purification action by the chemicals;

c. Tom's failure to replace the used chemicals once they were saturated with CO2, or

d. the inadequate design of the entire mechanism.

Any one of the first three events could have occurred while the pilot was resting or blissfully sleeping. About five and a half hours after a total failure of the scrubber, the fatal level of carbon dioxide would be reached.

2. *Depressurization.* The second theory suggests that the pressure which built up in the cabin by Tuesday afternoon, during the first rugged test of the capsule's strength, caused the skin to rupture, perhaps only slightly, and explode its purified air outward. With the seventy-below zero temperature outside, and heat inside approaching eighty or ninety degrees, the temperature difference alone could have generated significant stresses. This theory seems offset by the fact that the gondola had already flown successfully at high altitude for at least sixteen hours, and that it had been pressure-tested by Lunn Laminates, its manufacturer. But in order to avoid significant pressure build-up during the flight, Gatch would have had to periodically open the spigot to "vent" some of the accumulated pressure.

Launch director Dick Keuser had warned Tom to monitor pressure very carefully with instruments. Just as a pressure cooker on a stove needs a valve to blow off steam, the *Light Heart* needed a way to blow off its excesses. The cabin, however, was sealed tightly at seven psi when Tom closed the valve as he ascended through nineteen thousand feet on Monday night. The seal became tighter as the balloon rose into the less dense upper air. As the unfiltered noonday sun beat down, the pressure increased. Perhaps Gatch recognized the need to vent, but vented too much; perhaps he did not vent at all; perhaps the valve froze in an open (or closed) position.

Whatever the cause or the problem, Gatch might have had time to identify the problem, and realize that he was floating along helplessly at thirty-six thousand feet. No "mayday" call would bring help in time. Besides, he was probably poorly dressed for a sudden temperature change and perhaps had only enough time and strength to destroy one or two of the electronically squibbed balloons before commencing the hopelessly slow, fatal descent.

At the same time, one must recognize the severe psychological strain on Gatch at that time. In his isolated chamber, far from the reach of any human hand, and suffering from excessive fatigue, he perhaps endured the hallucinations of indifference symptomatic of the "breakaway experience" first observed by Air Force flight surgeons during the solo high altitude Man High balloon program.

Perhaps, after decompression, when he would have time for only one or two minutes of action, Tom opened the hatch and manually cut away one or more balloons, accelerating his descent into breathable air. He must have known, in those last moments, that the effects of superheat would keep his craft aloft during the increasingly warm hours of midday and that his chances for survival were rapidly decreasing. Cutting away too much lift would have caused the balloon to plummet toward the sea. In this scenario, the hatch would be open as *Light Heart* eventually came to rest on the surface. After tossing in the waves for a few days, water probably seeped into the gondola, causing it to sink.

3. *Incorrect Balloon Lift Calculations.* The third theory draws upon the fact that when *Light Heart* lifted off, it had a free lift capacity of 12.5 percent. With that margin, if all ten balloons remained intact, the superpressure balloons would stay aloft at thirty-nine thousand feet and would effect the crossing exactly as Gatch had planned it. However, the tragic flaw was the burst of one of the balloons, which upset that slim margin of free lift.

Donald E. Overs, a distinguished mechanical engineer at Westinghouse Electric Company, as well as a long-time leader of the American gas balloon community, prepared a formal analysis of the Light Heart flight. Overs, who had witnessed the launch and talked with Gatch in Harrisburg, observed that the Gatch flight "was unique in that it in addition to being the first manned superpressure balloon flight ever, it was the most likely to succeed." In a presentation to a conference of the American Institute of Aeronautics and Astronautics in San Diego in October 1981, Overs concluded:

> The crucial meeting with the FAA at Kennedy Airport in November 1973, after all of the components had been ordered, resulted in the directive that Gatch fly higher than he had previously planned. That decision cost him seventy-six pounds of ballast.
>
> The FAA was probably not aware of the 76-lb. impact upon Gatch's system, nor should they be expected to be since Gatch as pilot was responsible for his plans.

Gatch's fate seems to have been determined by his failure to allocate sufficient ballast to comfortably stabilize after a single balloon burst. Perhaps that could only be accomplished by adding an eleventh balloon and Gatch's financial and time constraints would not permit that.

Dr. Thomas F. Heinsheimer, a California aerospace scientist, studied Gatch's flight in anticipation of his own effort with Malcolm Forbes ten months later. He theorized that the balloon explosion occurred for one of four reasons:

1. a double fold in the envelope fabric, which ripped upon pressurization,
2. excess gas in one balloon, causing overpressurization,
3. buffeting of outer balloons on the center balloon, or
4. the outer balloons' seams rubbing the inner balloon's seams, causing seam tape degradation.

After the balloon broke, the balloon should have stabilized a few thousand feet lower, Gatch's feverish ballasting notwithstanding. Although the system never again would reach pressure height, it would remain at some safe, high altitude. And since one-tenth of the lift was lost, the nominal free lift margin was reduced to 2.5 percent. In fact, it might have been less. The flight continued in stable altitude because of the meteorological conditions below.

Satellite photos for Tuesday, Feb. 19, 1974, showed clear skies, enabling radiation from the earth to provide some artificial lift throughout the night. On Tuesday morning, heat from the sun light kept the balloon buoyant and aloft. By midday Tuesday, Gatch had been pushed far south of the commercial air lanes by the deteriorating jet stream, and out of radio range. He would pass the afternoon believing he was at superpressure and safely beyond the rain and thick cloud cover below.

With the approach of sunset and consequent loss of superheat late Tuesday, *Light Heart* slowly began losing altitude. Changing weather conditions below—a large low-pressure system accompanied by thick stratus clouds—cut off infrared radiation and caused the balloon cluster to begin sinking at an increasingly rapid rate. Gatch, who had no theoretical training in superpressure, may have been caught off guard by this slippage and begun broadcasting an alert, but could not have been heard because of his weak radio transmitter.

Had he understood the problem, said Heinsheimer, Gatch would have known that the proper response was to open the hatch at nineteen thousand feet and drop the exploded balloon. His free balloon system would then rise to some new stable height. On the other hand, by Tuesday evening, after a few hours of slowly but inevitably losing altitude, *Light Heart* passed through the cloud cover and into the rain, and touched down in the choppy mid-Atlantic under the most adverse circumstances.

On the way down, Gatch would have several options:

1. open the hatch and drop ballast to check his descent,
2. touch down and cut away the inflated balloons to remain on the surface in his gondola,
3. inflate and board his tiny raft, though this unrehearsed egress through the hatch would be hazardous in rough weather and nearly impossible at night, or
4. keep the balloons attached and ride out the night, hoping for sunny skies and more buoyancy from the sun's radiation in the morning, after enduring a rough and sickening ride on the swells of the ocean.

If Gatch descended on Tuesday evening, he probably opted for one of the latter two choices. Which election he made, of course, would affect where we would search for him. Heinsheimer postulated that to lift off in a windy condition, the whole system would have to be dramatically lightened, either by the egress of the pilot and his raft, or by disposing of some equipment during the night. The balloons would then dry and rise during the early morning hours. They would ascend all the way up again and arrive at ceiling altitude two or three hours after sunrise Wednesday morning, quickly exploding another balloon or two due to excessive overpressure. The system would then fall again on Wednesday night, after the storm front passed through, and reach the calm seas two or three hours after sunset. It would then bob along until sunrise when it would lift off (assuming very little wind) and ascend ever so slightly, when the crew of *Ore Meridian* would have seen a ghost ship.

If it was true that Gatch bailed out Tuesday night, then the entire search and rescue operation was conducted in the wrong area. Analysis of local meteorology using weather satellite photos and day/night temperature profiles of similar unmanned balloon flights, as well as a review of the weigh-off calculations, supports this contention, derived many months after Gatch's flight.

4. *Other factors.* Contributing to *Light Heart*'s disappearance undoubtedly were a combination of many other factors. Most aviation tragedies result not from a single cause or a single mistake, but from a pyramid of compounded errors. In Gatch's case, at least eleven significant shortcomings in the planning process can be identified. Those of us who conferred with Tom while he was planning his trip frankly share at least a portion of the responsibility for his loss. Had we been able to anticipate more of the potential problems, and prevail upon him to take more time to solve them, or had he delegated more authority to others to act on his behalf, the outcome might have been much different.

The eleven basic planning failures, as reconstructed by a variety of balloonists, communication consultants and scientists are as follows:

1. ***Staff chief.*** Gatch should have hired a chief of staff to make key decisions and take care of administrative details, especially during the critical final days of preparation. A chief of staff should monitor the flight's progress, maintain frequent communication with the pilot and, if necessary, decide when to initiate a search.

2. ***Pressure test.*** The gondola should have been pressure-tested again after the equipment holes were drilled and sealed. Although it had been shop-tested, Gatch's alterations necessitated a re-test.

3. ***Float test.*** The gondola should have been tested in water. As designed, it appeared more worthy of a soft landing in Lake Geneva than a rough ride in the ocean, yet Gatch never float-tested the capsule in any body of water.

4. ***Better radios.*** More powerful radios should have been on board, especially an HF unit. Gatch operated on a very low budget for a project of this magnitude, and was conscious of every additional nickel and every additional ounce of weight. His cousin Robert Hatcher, an amateur radio operator, might easily have installed a ham radio aboard *Light Heart* and alerted hams around the world to listen in, to assure continuous monitoring, but this was not done.

5. ***More lift.*** Because of the critical weight factors, the cluster should have consisted of more balloons, or larger balloons, and carried more ballast, at least part of which should have consisted of batteries rigged externally, to be jettisoned after use. At least this would have provided more free balloon maneuverability during descent or when flying out of superpressure.

6. ***Regulatory adherence.*** Gatch should have paid more attention to regulations, obtaining an Experimental Airworthiness Certificate, securing flight clearance and takeoff permission, and convincing Canadian air

officials to go along with his plans. FAA officials were so incensed at Gatch's arrogance in proceeding without complying with these three main areas that they had planned to revoke his pilot certificate if he had returned.

7. ***Practice emergencies.*** Gatch should have faced the possibility of a water landing, and practiced emerging from the capsule and boarding the inflatable life raft. However, he stubbornly refused to prepare for a water landing, and only upon the insistence of a neighbor did he carry the life raft.

8. ***Morning ascent.*** Gatch should have followed the advice to ascend at dawn in order to facilitate stabilization of the balloons and to conduct a thorough daytime check over land of on-board equipment and pressurization. Once aloft under a superpressure balloon system, it is relatively simple to remain aloft. A long test ride over land would not have cost more money, and it would have enhanced the opportunity for emergency recovery should that have become necessary.

9. ***Mental stress.*** Tom should have prepared himself psycho-physiologically for the stresses he would encounter. Yet he did not undergo even routine confinement tests such as those used in astronaut training or for pilots of the Air Force Man High project. He should have studied and known the effects on himself of fatigue, of silent isolation, of perhaps excessive heat inside a tiny, claustrophobic chamber, of hallucinations resulting from these stresses, and of his own efficiency and metal discipline under such conditions.

10. ***Dress rehearsal.*** He should have staged a full-dress rehearsal of all system components under simulated conditions before he arrived at the launch site. Though costly, this might have saved the flight. Instead, the first time all components were assembled was in the hangar on the day before takeoff, while waiting for weather to clear.

11. ***Failure effects model.*** He should have developed a "failure effects analysis" to which he might refer in the event of any particular failure. For instance, in the event of the loss of one balloon, the proper response would be to let the system descend to nineteen thousand feet (capsule pressurization altitude), re-open the hatch, and jettison the useless fabric.

Thus, Thomas L. Gatch, Jr. went to his rest somewhere deep in the waters of the Atlantic Ocean. He was granted the honorable wish that his heroic father had been denied: he died in his armor.

He came close to fulfilling himself and carrying out a personal dream—remarkably close, given his limited training and fiercely independent attitude. A few more hours or perhaps another day aloft, and *Light Heart* would have made landfall over the western coast of southern Europe or Africa.

Although it was not Tom Gatch's destiny to be the first to cross the Atlantic by balloon, his legacy is a tribute to the spirit of individual enterprise and freedom that have always characterized men and women of aviation. He had the makings of a hero.

◆   ◆   ◆

Tom's sisters and many friends and work colleagues from the Pentagon gathered at the Washington Cathedral later that spring to participate in a memorial service for him. At the event, Nancy and Corki announced creation of a special scholarship in Tom's name. It would be for young boys who had earned a singing scholarship to St. Alban's School for Boys, but whose voice had changed. The Gatch scholarship would let them continue their studies at the prestigious school, and not have to endure the loss of the choir scholarship as Tom had.

In its permanent exhibit on the history of ballooning, the Smithsonian Air & Space Museum included a huge poster-size photo of *Light Heart* ascending into the night sky.

In countless books about the successful crossing of the Atlantic, and ultimately, the trans-global balloon challenge, Tom Gatch and his achievement receive reverential mention.

◆   ◆   ◆

For all the years that followed, I thought often about those who died or risked death trying the Atlantic flight.

One night, years after Tom was gone, I visited a quiet beach along the New Jersey shoreline near the place where *Light Heart* had left dry land. I stood alone and looked out over the ocean. On that particular evening, the moon was in its final quarter and hundreds of stars lit the sky. Fluorescent lamps illuminated a cold and empty boardwalk. Just beyond, the beach was littered with the usual debris of the sea: shells, a few dead fish, and pieces of broken glass. A little further out, cold waves rolled in and crashed.

Theirs was the only sound. Strongly, incessantly, with a determination greater than the will of all mankind, the waves maintained their eternal motion. They spoke nothing about what happened to my friend. Once, though wracked by internal conflict, he had crossed this shoreline in glory, high above this point. Now, the water and the foam lapping at the sand gave no clues.

Somewhere out there he had struggled with those dark waters, and they had swallowed him. The bold challenge he had issued to the Atlantic had been answered swiftly, efficiently. For his boldness, the waters had extracted from him the maximum human price. They took him deep, silently, forever. His life and his flesh were gone, and his little round capsule, and all of its paraphernalia, and all trace of his balloons.

The waves lapped and licked at the shoreline, giving no clue.

The Earthwinds Chronicles

'All I want to do is just fly a balloon around the world,' said Larry Newman.

Slumped in his swivel chair, he looked pale, exhausted and besieged.

'Just fly a balloon around the world'—a simple thought—meant designing, building and managing the most complex privately funded aviation project ever to leave the ground.

On the afternoon of his complaint, he had encountered recalcitrant bureaucrats from the Federal Aviation Administration, faulty electrical wires in his capsule, a plumbing and exhaust system that leaked, belligerent faxes from his primary sponsor, and he suffered from terrible stomach acid and a nasty head cold. People were lined up outside the cold hangar door to discuss other problems. Time was running out. And this was just a normal day for Larry, leading the project to build an experimental, one-of-a-kind aircraft that was designed to fly only one time.

Before me was a complex, driven man whose public persona approached heroic proportions, but who freely acknowledged that his private personality induced angst within his support staff.

Larry had called months before and asked me to coordinate media relations for his project, Earthwinds. As the project unfolded, we were both going to have a lot of stories to tell...

1

The Flight to Hallelujah Junction

'The machine does not isolate man from the great problems of nature but plunges him more deeply into them.'
—Antoine de Saint Exupery, "Wind, Sand and Stars"

Plunging into nature

For the first time, *Earthwinds* stood at its full height: 354 feet from top to bottom. The restraining lines paid out slowly in a four-point tether as the crew looked directly down on the nearly pressurized, 100-foot diameter anchor balloon. The temperature on the field, 18 below zero a few hours ago, had warmed up…the dozens of workers were sure they could feel the difference: now it was only five degrees below zero.

Three feet of new snow, plowed only from the runway, gave the panorama a vast gray appearance that melted into the surrounding mountains.

Inside the capsule, Larry Newman, a slender, edgy airline pilot who led the project, glanced at a digital gauge on the instrument panel: the bottom load cell read 3,500 pounds: 2,500 pounds of anchor balloon and 1,000 pounds of free lift. It was exactly what he had ordered.

The combined noise from the engines below the floorboard and from the machines on the ground was distracting. In fact, an astonishing amount of noise had been roaring from the field most of the night.

Diesel-powered tractors and high-lift bucket trucks had raised workers and helium hoses high above the capsule to attach fittings and to reach the narrow inflation sleeves hanging from the balloon. The machines belched their acrid fumes into the dead-calm air, nearly choking the launch team.

Larry strained to hear launch director Tom Barrow and balloon designer Tim Lachenmeier on the hand-held radio. He wanted clarification on which cutter device was attached to which vehicle.

'I can't copy,' Larry said. 'What number are my cutters? Are we off the ground yet?'

'No,' Barrow replied, 'we're just holding on the bottom valve. I'd rather launch you now than try to float the balloon on the long tie-down.'

Larry leaned out the porthole, alarmed by what he saw. Directly south of the launch site—the direction he intended to go!—two vans were parked.

'We need to get rid of the vehicle to the south or we're gonna run right over it,' he shouted. 'And there's a Suburban in front of it, right in the way! The winch truck to the south is cutting into the anchor balloon. The vehicle needs to move forward.'

In a moment, the trucks in question started heading down the south runway.

'John,' he shouted to his chief engineer, 'have them back up! They're going the wrong way!'

◆ ◆ ◆

Bristling with antennas, exhaling helium vapor, laden with explosive gasoline, surging coolant through its labyrinthine heat exchangers, the 10,000-pound capsule hung suspended between a massive teardrop shaped polyethylene bag of helium and a 100-foot diameter globe filled with ordinary air. Built of polymers and resins, the capsule was made to withstand mountain rocks, ocean waves and thin air. It carried enough food and water to support three men for a month, and their suite of avionics, radios, cameras, computers, phones and faxes.

A microwave dish on top pointed toward invisible satellites. Through it, video cameras would beam live images of the crew throughout the globe. Sprouting from other penetrations were antennas for air-to-ground communication, and for the Global Positioning System that would track the flight. The GPS was linked to a laptop computer loaded with detailed maps of the world.

Inside, the peculiar resonance from the curved walls treated with sound-absorbent baffles gave the capsule an air of unreality.

Barron Hilton, the hotel magnate and principal sponsor, had named the capsule "the ultimate room with a view" and ordered his personal decorator to create a soft, relaxing interior. Fabric in shades of cameo rose, pink and sand covered the compartment, belying the harsh environment into which the machine would be lofted.

For the crew to survive exposure to stratospheric ozone, 70-below temperatures and the complex, dangerous machinery itself, everything would have to work precisely. In flight, the sensitive communication and navigation devices; the fuel gauges, electric fans, hydraulic pumps, pressure and temperature regulators; recording and transmitting devices, demanded continuous monitoring.

Besides the pilot, two other men were aboard. Don Moses, who had left his career as a boat builder and Hawaiian charter boat operator, was to keep the capsule's engine operating smoothly. Maj. Gen. Vladimir Dzhanibekov, a Soviet air force cosmonaut who had logged 145 days in space during five flights, served as the project's scientist and videographer to monitor atmospheric science experiments built by his countrymen.

The moment of truth was at hand for this difficult, complicated project that had run 500 percent over budget, taken two years longer than planned and chewed up scores of volunteers. The events of the past few years sometimes had seemed like episodes from a quirky sitcom, at other times like a faltering business enterprise, and rarely like the much-heralded "last great adventure in aviation."

◆   ◆   ◆

Tom Barrow tried to reassure the pilot:

'We've untwisted the anchor and as soon as it's clear we're gonna be ready to launch.'

Barrow began to recite the pre-arranged command sequence. 'Blow all four cutters. Blow all fo—.'

Larry flipped up the cover on the firing device he held in his hand, and pressed the button. The four tie-down lines dropped away cleanly. The balloon lurched upward.

It was 10:11 a.m., on January 12, 1993. The voyage of *Earthwinds* had begun at last!

◆   ◆   ◆

Media turned out to witness and report on the flight. ESPN broadcast the moment live in 28 countries around the world. Many of the 'big feet' media recorded the moment: Malcolm Browne of The New York Times, David Chandler of the Boston Globe, Jim Mitchell of the Los Angeles Times, Stuart Brown of Popular Science. Wire service reporters and photographers; many TV and radio network affiliates, and newspaper reporters trained their attention on the craft.

Lynne Newman, Larry's wife, joyously jumped up and down, then embraced the three men standing around her: Barron Hilton, whose hotel conglomerate shouldered primary financial support for the project; John Wilcox, who had inspired the project to make a TV adventure film, and former astronaut Gene Cernan, the last American to walk on the moon.

◆　　◆　　◆

The start was so gentle that Larry didn't know at first that the balloon had left the ground.

'Okay, is it going? Tom, are we going up?' he radioed to Barrow.

'All four cutters separated from all four launch points, Larry,' Tom replied. 'Have a nice flight!'

The rest of his transmission was drowned out by cheers from the crowd and by the triumphant whoops of sirens from emergency vehicles on the field.

Freed of the weight of its tie-down, the anchor balloon's digital load cell fluctuated a bit and then stabilized at just over 2,500 pounds.

The balloon climbed upward at a sluggish 400 feet per minute and began to drift away from the crowd of spectators.

The crew had been expecting the wind to carry them southeast, where there was a lot of low-level flying room, but now their craft was drifting northwest! And it stopped climbing almost at once.

Tim Lachenmeier, the designer on whose calculations Larry had staked the flight, took the radio and offered some last minute coaching.

'Larry, it looks like you encountered a bit of shear just above the inversion.'

Sitting near the open door, Don Moses felt the balloon's reversal of momentum.

'We're going down,' he reported to Larry as the balloon began a slow, gentle rotation.

Standing before a 10-foot long panel of gauges, Larry pursed his lips and glanced at the rate-of-climb indicator. He directed Don to spill out some of the lead shot bags.

'Here, grab this. You gotta throw some out. No, you gotta take the line, just take this off, take the top off! See how it unscrews? Hook the line around there so it doesn't fall on the anchor balloon. Chuck it as far as you can!'

Don, his bare fingers numb with cold, shook out a sackful of pelletized lead shot.

Larry saw that the anchor balloon reading was back at 3,500 pounds. What's wrong here? he wondered. At takeoff, the anchor balloon was only 95 percent full, its empty weight 2,500 pounds.

How could the load cell give this reading? He looked down at the anchor balloon. The pre-launch wrinkles had disappeared from the fabric below the sponsors' logos.

Larry flipped up the top switch below the anchor balloon's load cell panel. He hoped that would allow any pressurized air to escape.

'We're going down!' Larry shouted.

Lachenmeier tried calling him again. 'Larry, this is Tim. What is your bottom load cell reading?'

Don Moses urgently needed Larry to help him drop ballast.

'We need you right now!' he snapped.

'That inversion is really good,' Tim said over the radio. 'You know you're gonna have to ballast right through it.'

'We're going to start', Larry replied.

Larry opened a dump valve on the huge gasoline flask and let it run for a few seconds. It dumped 100 pounds of gasoline per minute.

He turned toward Don and told him how to drop the lead shot.

'Save the bag!' he said.

'I'm saving the bag,' Don answered.

'Hold it, hold it, hold it, hold it! Just dump that one bag!'

'Alright,' Don said.

'We're starting to go back up again,' Larry said, 'slowly, slowly.'

After six minutes at 1,000 feet, the balloon resumed a slow climb. At 2,000 feet, it leveled off again.

Oblivious to their troubles on board, Lynne took the hand-held radio from Lachenmeier and squeezed the push-to-talk button.

'I love you Larry!' she chirped.

'I love you, too,' he radioed back. 'We're pretty busy here.'

Lachenmeier took the radio back from Lynne. He and Barrow figured Larry would ballast whatever was necessary to restore a good rate of climb. They got in Tim's car and left the airport.

They wanted to get back to the Operations Center at the hotel as soon as possible.

'It looks like we're going to hit this mountain,' Larry radioed.

Lachenmeier mistook that transmission; surely Larry meant that it seemed as if they were going to hit, not that a hit was inevitable. He had just told Larry to ballast right up through the inversion.

The 13 mph wind pushed *Earthwinds* northwest and the towering craft rotated slowly. On every revolution, the crew could look out the port and see

Stead Airport and the city of Reno beyond; as the capsule revolved, they could see the craggy rocks that divide Nevada and California.

'We can't go through those mountains,' Don said.

'Which mountains?' Larry said.

'They're over that way now.'

'Shit!' Larry exclaimed.

'Get rid of another one, Larry. Let's get up!' Don said.

'Okay.'

'Get up Larry!' Don said again, now with a warning tone in his voice.

'Cut another one,' Larry ordered.

The terrain began to rise steeply on the east side of the range.

'We're going down or we're going into terrain,' Don yelled. 'We need to get up! Keep cutting!'

'Where is it? How close are we?' Larry asked.

'Getting close!'

They had been in level flight for 15 minutes now. Their altitude was 7,800 feet above sea level—about the same as the mountain peaks ahead of them—and about 2,800 feet higher than Stead Airport. Larry wanted more information on the obstacle ahead.

'Where is it? Which way is it?'

Don leaned out the open door.

'We're moving that way. You can see it right here. Take a look…'

They leaned out of the porthole together and watched as one peak slid right under the anchor balloon. Ahead was a wide canyon with only one peak in the center. *Earthwinds* was heading right for it.

They had been in the air for 25 minutes now, fighting for every foot of altitude the whole time.

The balloon drifted steadily northwest, stubbornly refusing to climb.

◆   ◆   ◆

The Operations Center staff back at the Reno Hilton watched the flight on television until ESPN signed off. Retired Vice Admiral Don Engen, an unflappable former FAA administrator presiding over the staff, waited for the first communication from the capsule. Hearing none, he reached for the red telephone on his desk.

He called the tower at Stead Airport. Did the balloon contact departure control? Had the balloon called the tower at all?

The tower operators had heard nothing, but had seen the take off.

The most sophisticated communications suite ever assembled in a balloon—Inmarsat satellite telephone, high frequency and very high frequency radios, amateur band—was not even turned on.

The men in the control tower saw on their screens five blips—indicating five transponders automatically squawking the default frequency, 1200, north of the airport. They came from the two Bell 206 helicopters with camera crews, the Lear 25 chase plane, the balloon, and another aircraft, Dick Rutan's long blue ultralight VeriEze, making loping passes around the balloon.

From their helicopter, photographer Bill Swersey and Carol Hart, Don Moses' girlfriend, watched the balloon track northward, now at about 25 miles an hour. Carol didn't like what she saw.

◆   ◆   ◆

Don Moses shook out the last bag of the 500 pounds of lead shot. His ballasting had no effect. Now the terrain was rising up to meet them. It was rocky and remote.

Larry tried adding helium to the upper balloon. He needed more lift. No other balloon had ever ascended with liquid helium, which enabled the balloonists to 'refuel' in flight. Here was state-of-the-art scientific ballooning. He stood before the console reading the checklist for the cryogenic helium panel.

To start the flow of helium, the instructions said,

'Switch Temp sensor panel to HX EXIT. Verify 24V power is on and all valves are closed. Open SV6 + SV7. Open SV3 to send ullage gas to balloon. Close SV3 valve when dewar pressure drops below 3 psig. Open SV1 (1/2 flow) or SV2 (full flow). To throttle flow: Open SV4 or SV5 (flash-pressure tank). Throttle flow by opening SV6 and/or SV7. Regulate pressure to psig by opening and closing SV4/SV5. Warning: Do not let temperature at HX EXIT drop below—110 F.'

It occurred to Don in a flash that this procedure should have been second nature to Larry. Why was he using the checklist? Don wondered. He asked how the flow of helium was going.

'Get any rate yet?'

'Barely,' came the answer. 'Just keep dropping 'em.'

Larry had forgotten that it would take almost an hour to add 1,000 pounds of lift to the polyethylene balloon. He left the cryo panel after three minutes and grabbed a 5-gallon plastic jug of water.

'Vladimir,' he shouted, 'help me get these back here, give them to Don!'

Don threw the jugs of water out the door. So far he had dropped 680 pounds of ballast in all. What Don did not know was that some of the jugs were becoming snared in the anchor balloon's load skirt, where they would be found after the flight. Larry couldn't understand why that ballast was having no effect.

'It's going down?' he asked Don incredulously.

The balloon drifted toward the Petersen Mountain Range. The two camera helicopters circled around the balloon.

Don saw the inevitable.

'Okay, brace yourselves!' Don shouted. 'Getting ready to hit right now! Brace yourselves!'

Larry knew the consequence of any contact with the ground.

'Shit, it'll blow that anchor balloon to pieces.'

The anchor balloon hit the rocks about 30 feet from the bottom, and split open. The whole system rocked gently and bounced up.

'It just did,' Don replied. 'Okay, we're hauling ass up now!'

Propelled up by the bounce off the rocks, *Earthwinds* now climbed quickly. Larry made his decision. He did not want to begin a long flight without a functioning anchor balloon. He flipped a switch that opened both electrically operated helium valves on top of the poly balloon. That slowed the rapid ascent.

'Wanna radio the mayday?' Don shouted.

Larry did not reply.

◆ ◆ ◆

'Let's go ahead and start getting down, Larry.'

'It's going down on its own, Don.'

The balloon descended until the ruptured anchor balloon dragged across the rocks and snow, scraping a trail of rope prints in its wake. Ahead was a small clearing.

'This valley would be beautiful if we could get down in it,' Don said. 'Can we vent down?'

'We're going down,' Larry answered.

One minute passed with no talk among the crew. As the anchor balloon dragged, it twisted the capsule with it. For five minutes the anchor balloon pulled through the snow. The capsule was still 100 feet off the ground.

Vladimir kept the videotape rolling.

Larry again opened the helium valves at the top of the balloon to bring the capsule down closer to the ground.

'Okay, we're heading back down into the valley now,' Don called.

'There's a little eddy. It'll bring us right into that spot. Let's set down right here.'

Don leaned out the hatch, evaluating the potential landing site.

Looking ahead to the landing, Larry feared that if he cut away the helium balloon, the heavy aluminum flight train fitting would crash right through the top of the capsule.

'I don't wanna cut the thing loose cause I don't want to punch a hole in the top of the capsule. So what we might do is get the manual rip line and just rip it out,' Larry said.

'Oh, okay,' Don said. 'Right.'

Seconds passed as the capsule came closer to the ground. Don realized he hadn't put on his helmet. He shouted:

'Hang on! Gimme my hat! Brace yourself! Here we go! We're gonna hit! Oh my god, we hit!'

Larry was standing at the console again. He had decided to activate the Holex fiber optic cable cutter after all. If they rid themselves of the helium balloon at just the right second, the capsule would come to rest. The helium balloon would fly away. He pulled two gold chains from the upper left side of the cutter panel, plugged them into the detonator outlets and armed the switch. As the capsule bounced in the snow, he pushed the red fire button.

'Okay, release!' he ordered Don.

The capsule rebounded up!

'Oh fuck! We're going back up! Did you cut it?'

'Yeah!' Larry answered.

'Okay. We still got the fucking helium balloon.'

Neither Larry nor Don had told Vladimir what they were doing.

'Did you cut the anchor balloon?' the cosmonaut asked. He assumed that Larry was dropping the useless lower balloon. The loss of that weight would offset the loss of lift encountered in the inversion. He knew there was enough helium to make a very long flight, maybe even as far as Russia.

'Just rip it out!' Don told Larry.

Larry scrambled toward the door.

'Don, get up. Here, look out.'

He pulled Don away from the hatch, crawled through it and swung up a ladder to the roof. Standing on top of the capsule, he grabbed the manual rip line. Pulling it would open a seam in the helium balloon and allow gas to escape.

Don leaned out the hatch again, looking at Larry on top, and glancing back to Vladimir.

'We're coming back down! Larry, let's just get out of it. Gimme that line, I'll help you rip out. Hang on! Hang on!'

'I can't drop it, I'm pulling it!' Larry shouted.

He was already trying to open the seam at the top of the balloon, but with 50 feet of slack in the manual destruct line, it took precious seconds to get enough tension on it.

'Okay, it's hooked up,' Larry reported.

The capsule struck the ground again. Don, perched on the step, tumbled out into the deep snow and fumbled for the rip line.

Relieved of Don's weight, the capsule bounded back up into the air, rising about 100 feet. That's when Larry saw a most frightening sight: the cables actually had been cut! The fiber optic cutter had worked after all! The capsule was now hanging from the balloon only because the terminant fitting hadn't slipped out of its restraint. It could give way at any moment! Larry scrambled back inside.

Don had expected Vladimir to jump, but the Russian was still aboard, crouched behind Larry.

'Hey, Vladimir!' Don cried.

Larry shouted desperately to Don.

'Don't pull any more! Don, no! Vladimir, get out! When we get down, you get out! Get ready!'

The capsule struck the ground again. Larry was standing in the hatchway. He jumped out and landed in knee-deep snow. Vladimir moved forward, banged his head on the ceiling and fell over backwards into the capsule with the camera.

The capsule with Vladimir still inside went back up in the air 40 feet. Don and Larry chased it through the deep snow, knowing that at any second it might fall from its fitting. If that happened, the drop would kill Vladimir.

'Vladimir, look out!' Larry shouted from the ground.

The cosmonaut regained his balance, and checked the camera. Oblivious to his immediate peril, he looked out at the two Americans thrashing about in the snow, and waited calmly for the balloon to settle again.

In another minute, the capsule plunked down in the snowy ravine for the last time. It had come to rest in a hamlet called Hallelujah Junction on the California side of the Nevada-California border.

♦ ♦ ♦

Three helicopters circled the ridge. Cameraman captured the "landing sequence" on videotape and still film. An Air National Guard helicopter carried Marilyn Newton, a photojournalist for the Reno Gazette-Journal. The other carried Bill Swersey and Carol Hart. A third machine carried John Wilcox's video crew. None of their pilots radioed *Earthwinds'* Operations Center to report what they had seen.

♦ ♦ ♦

From the launch field, *Earthwinds'* hourglass shape had become barely visible in the distant haze. Gene Cernan had stood there watching the balloon while reminiscing with his old friend, fellow astronaut Wally Schirra. Through the haze, Cernan's eagle eyes saw the anchor balloon hit the rock. He watched the balloon rise and then start down again. He hustled back toward the VIP tent, where Barron Hilton and the remaining guests and staff had taken refuge from the cold and had started celebrating.

Cernan's report was the first indication anyone back at Stead Airport had of trouble with the flight. As the media director, I immediately reached Don Engen on a cellular phone and told him what we had heard.

'What was the last radio contact the Operations Center had with the capsule?' I asked.

'We haven't had any contact,' Engen said, 'nothing at all. We are watching it on television.'

A crowd gathered as I talked with him, and Engen suggested I get to a secure phone. Barron Hilton's plush custom motor coach was nearby, and had a phone inside. Lynne, Cernan, Hilton, reporter Malcolm Browne and half a dozen others gathered in the bus to listen to our investigation-in-progress. The situation was bizarre! From the jubilation of the launch, Lynne sank into stunned disbelief. Her husband was down but wasn't communicating, and nobody could tell her what was going on!

Lachenmeier and Barrow arrived back at Ops in the midst of the confusion. They told Engen of their last exchange by hand-held radio. They couldn't shed any light on the crew's present whereabouts.

Engen began tracking down reports picked up via a police scanner that a sheriff's helicopter pilot had seen the balloon go down about five miles from Stead Airport.

Then Wilcox popped into the coach to say he had talked with the owner of the company from whom he had chartered his helicopters.

The helicopter pilot had reported that the balloon had landed, and that the crew was walking around outside, and safe.

Minutes later, the helicopter flying Carol Hart and Bill Swersey came back; they had seen the whole thing.

Now armed with eyewitness reports, I asked ESPN to go back on the air live with a bulletin about the landing—before rumors started. They reestablished the satellite link and set up for another broadcast.

◆ ◆ ◆

Just as ESPN was about to go to air, a helicopter from the 1255th Medical Company of the Nevada National Guard clattered over the hill and landed at the launch site.

No one on the ground knew who was inside.

When the machine touched down, Larry Newman stepped out, clutching two snowboot covers in his left hand. Lynne ran down the runway and embraced him. They walked arm-in-arm toward the cameras. Sharlene Hawkes, ESPN's *Earthwinds* correspondent (and a former Miss America), was cued as the cameras rolled live.

What happened out there, Hawkes asked.

'The upper balloon load cell said we had 22,000 pounds of lift, which should have taken us right to 35,000 feet, Larry replied, probably confusing the national television audience.

'As soon as we lifted off it looked good, then for some peculiar reason the balloon stopped climbing, so we threw off a thousand pounds of ballast and the balloon just continued coming down.

'So I'm baffled. I have no idea why it did that. We were down to 21,000 pounds total weight and we were still descending. We ran out of things to throw away.

'We thought about dumping fuel as an emergency. We realized that the balloon was still coming down, so we opened the fuel valve and started to dump, and then just closed it cause we realized we were gonna strike this mountain.

'When we hit the mountain it punctured the anchor balloon, and at that point the flight was over. We elected to land.

'I opened the helium valves to let helium escape and we made a smooth touch-down.'

Sharlene asked Larry about whether the temperature inversion might have been a problem.

'I'm somewhat skeptical about this inversion layer,' Larry answered. 'I've flown five flights with similar types of balloons, and I've never seen one do what this one did. It did not perform as expected.'

'Where are the other two crewmembers? What are they doing now?' she asked.

'Don is taking the antennas off the capsule, and Vladimir is filming Don taking the antennas off the capsule,' he replied.

◆ ◆ ◆

On Barron Hilton's luxury coach, Larry told his version of the flight. He couldn't imagine why the balloon didn't climb.

His patron leant a sympathetic ear, and assured him that he had done everything possible: dropped weight, added helium, landed safely.

We agreed on a 3:00 p.m. meeting in Barron's suite to prepare a message for a 4:00 p.m. press conference.

Mountaineers become mutineers

Having quickly dispatched Larry, Don and Vladimir remained on the mountain salvaging equipment from the capsule.

As they worked, the two crewmen compared notes on their long experience with the *Earthwinds* project. Neither thought the flight or the project had been well managed.

Soon, the chartered helicopter ferrying photographer Bill Swersey made a return trip, this time also carrying cinematographer Liesl Clark. They found Vladimir disassembling his scientific experiments, and finally persuaded him to fly back to Stead Airport. On the way, a heavy snow that had begun to fall obscured visibility, and the pilot had to fly low and follow the highway to the airfield. After one missed approach, he brought the machine down to the tarmac and landed right on the spot from which *Earthwinds* had ascended hours earlier. Vladimir, Swersey and Clark stepped off, and the helicopter took off again, faltered, and immediately crashed and rolled over right in front of them!

'It is not a good day to fly,' the cosmonaut observed wryly as the machine's three former passengers pulled the dazed pilot from the wreckage.

◆   ◆   ◆

Later that day, a National Guard medical helicopter flew Don off the mountain.

At the afternoon press conference at the hotel, the flight crew talked in general terms about the flight and their belief that the project should continue.

Larry said the problem with the balloon 'started right after takeoff. Its performance was sluggish. It was not climbing as scheduled. I am baffled why the balloon didn't climb as I expected it to.'

It was the crew's final public appearance together.

◆   ◆   ◆

Wednesday morning 40 staffers, who affectionately called themselves 'Earthworms,' crowded into a conference room at the Reno Hilton. Most had been with the project for nearly two years. Presiding over an all-hands debriefing, Larry was looking for reasons for the balloon's poor performance.

The restraint cables didn't snap back at takeoff when they were cut, Larry said, 'and that right there tells me there was a problem.' He thought it indicated less free lift than planned.

'No, negative,' Lachenmeier replied, 'those lines have very small elongation.'

Was the anchor balloon's empty weight calculated correctly when it was built?

Lachenmeier answered again. 'The unknown would be how much frost we picked up on it overnight. The anchor balloon could have had some condensation on it.'

Larry conceded that if condensation caused the bottom load cell to read 3,500 pounds, 'we essentially took off with no free lift.'

'The other factor to consider,' Larry continued, 'is the difference in the inversion layer temperature, because if you take this big cold helium balloon and you raise it into warm air, its relative density increases dramatically, and it loses its lift.

'We need to be sure we launch in warmer conditions, use considerably more free lift, and let the balloons climb at a much greater rate.'

Larry started describing how he had used the cryogenic helium to try to add lift.

Lachenmeier interrupted him:

'Larry, to put out 2,000 pounds of lift on that system is going to take two to three hours. So the cryo system probably wouldn't have the power to do any good.'

John Ackroyd, who had engineered the system, asked why more helium wasn't put in the lift balloon before takeoff.

'We were concerned about too rapid a rate of climb and there was that little hole in the side of the anchor balloon,' Larry explained. 'As you're climbing, say 1,500 feet per minute, you add pressure to the anchor balloon far greater than the valve will allow the air to escape, so you're now building up pressure at a tremendous rate.

'The logical thing to do is play conservative. Go with the minimum amount of free lift and climb out slowly. That was why the decision was made: fear of wind shear. It was a mistake.'

Ackroyd persisted: 'When it was obvious you were going to hit the mountain, why not drop fuel, or an entire fuel tank?'

'There are lots of scenarios, things we could have dropped,' Larry said. 'We could have dropped the fuel tank with the anchor balloon. I think landing where we did was a good move for us. Once things were going wrong and we had a serious problem, we put down where we were and saved what we could so we could do it again.

'Dropping a fuel tank could have had catastrophic effects on the anchor balloon. We didn't have time to drop it. There were just too many things to evaluate.'

Lachenmeier, reconsidering his calculations, admitted to the group:

'When you stop at that altitude, do not underplay the effects of that inversion. The inversion didn't affect our game plan. We talked about five percent free lift. We weren't even talking about an inversion…we didn't consider it because the winds were picking up. We didn't feed that ever into the lift equation. All we could see the inversion for was our surface winds. All the data feeding back to us was how much time we had. Those winds were going to make the launch difficult.'

The session lasted one hour. Barron Hilton appointed Don Engen to compile a written analysis of the balloon's performance. Most of the staff dispersed or gathered in small discussion groups.

◆ ◆ ◆

Don Moses had said little during the meeting. Now, his face was red with anger and he wasn't buying any more explanations or excuses. He had made up his mind, and he was painting Larry with all the blame.

'He doesn't know how to run that equipment,' Don fumed to a small group after the de-briefing. 'He is in so far over his head you wouldn't believe it. I don't think he knew how to fly the balloon.

'He never shared information with us. He was always saying things like: Tim will teach me how to fly this system, and I will teach you guys how to fly it; the same with the radios, the computer, the Inmarsat phone.

'He knows he's been an asshole. He knows everybody hates him and wants to replace him. As long as he keeps all the information close to his chest, he's secure because they can't replace him no matter how much they hate him. That's the bottom line: his insecurity, his ego. His reasons for doing this project are for money and for fame, not the same reasons the rest of us are here for.'

◆ ◆ ◆

They still had to get their debris off the mountain, and lifting the capsule would require a helicopter with a special crane. A commercial operator bid $15,000 for the job. Barron Hilton had another idea. He had announced recently that his company was spending $246 million to improve its five Nevada casino hotel properties, and Gov. Bob Miller had recently proclaimed Hilton Day. Now Barron Hilton called the governor to ask if the Nevada National Guard might do him a favor. Well, of course, Mr. Hilton, sure!

Only one kind of military helicopter, the Skycrane, had the lifting power for this kind of work. Unfortunately, the last of these workhorse aircraft had been de-commissioned from the Nevada National Guard in a big public ceremony just four days earlier. The machines were no longer part of the National Guard inventory and couldn't legally be used. Nevertheless, the governor directed his Adjutant General, Brig. Gen. Smith, to find a solution.

Gen. Smith bent the rules and authorized one more Skycrane 'training mission'. By Wednesday afternoon, the flight crew, Lachenmeier and Ackroyd and a handful of other helpers were back on Mt. Peterson preparing the capsule for extraction. Late that afternoon, the capsule was safely back in its hangar at Stead Airport.

The two balloons, thousands of square yards of polyethylene and white Spectra fabric, remained atop Mount Peterson, buried in new snow.

Don Moses left the airport as soon as the capsule returned. He had some macho partying and mutinous planning to do with Lachenmeier and Dzhanibekov. They stayed up late Wednesday night refining their plan and burnishing it with Jack Daniels.

Larry and Lynne took Malcolm Browne and me to dinner and a magic show. After the show, Browne encountered Don Moses in the casino lobby and learned that the crew was splitting up. Late that night, he tipped off Larry to Don's impending insurrection.

Suite 2714

It was no surprise, then, when Larry heard a knock on the door of his penthouse suite at 10 o'clock the next morning. Don Moses had come for his private meeting.

Having spent three years working on this project, Don told his old roommate, he hoped it would have succeeded by now. He just couldn't devote any more time, he said—so if Larry intended to fly again, he'd have to find another crewmember. Don wouldn't be able to come back.

Larry said he understood Don's commitments and his need to move on. If Don couldn't participate, Larry said, he understood, and it was all right. The meeting ended without rancor. They stood and shook hands, and Don was out of *Earthwinds*.

Larry was visibly relieved to be rid of Don. When he joined Lynne and me later at lunch, Larry unloaded on Don.

'Don complained that I never trained him, but he never took any initiative to learn things. He went off skiing instead of getting himself a balloon pilot license. He never read the manuals for our equipment; he would tell me to read them and then show him how this stuff worked. I am running this project. I didn't have time to show him everything. Don's problem was that he never took any initiative. Why did he wait until after the flight to say all this?'

Lynne started to relate details of her turbulent relationship with Carol Hart but Larry stopped her.

'That's not the issue anymore,' he said. 'The issue now is that I have to find someone to replace Don. I already have a list. I'm going to call Tim Lachenmeier first. If he can't fly with me and Vladimir, I'm going to call Richard Abruzzo...'

◆ ◆ ◆

At the same moment, Vladimir was huddled with Admiral Engen, who by then was trying to salvage as much of the project as possible for his friend Barron Hilton.

After lunch, Larry and Lynne returned to their suite. Within moments they heard another knock at the door. Vladimir wanted a private conference with Larry.

With cold candor, Vladimir unburdened himself.

'I will never again fly with you, Laddy,' he said, speaking slowly and deliberately through his accent. 'You have kept too many details to yourself. You have lied to the volunteers and to me about your health. You should have seen a doctor, and if you were not well enough to fly, you should wait until you are healthy.

'You never consulted me about designing the capsule. It is not a good design. You don't listen to my ideas. You panicked on our flight. You do not tell Don and me what you are doing and do not give us any training. I do not feel safe with you as the pilot.'

That Vladimir had harbored such deep bitterness shocked Larry. He was quiet and chagrined when Vladimir left.

Half an hour later, he was trying to put the best spin on Vladimir's departure, doubting that any other Russian, whether a balloonist or a cosmonaut, would take his place.

'I wouldn't have another Russian next time,' Larry told me. 'The language barrier and the cultural differences are too difficult. We only needed Vladimir in the beginning so the Soviets would let us fly through their airspace. That's all changed now.

'Vladimir never really grasped what was going on during the flight.'

But back in his penthouse suite with his wife, Larry must have heard the haunting voice of his mentor Ben Abruzzo, echoing back from 12 years earlier:

'Larry, they dealt you out,' Ben had said after back-to-back failures to launch a trans-Pacific balloon from Japan. 'They don't want you on the team because you're a Jeckyll and Hyde, you're hot and cold, you're abrasive, you're brash, you're not friendly to them and you insult them.'

The words remained chilling, and yet in an ironic way that experience vindicated him in the end. Hadn't that same crew reunited after splitting up? Didn't that expedition result in a great success the next season?

◆   ◆   ◆

The staff buzzed with rumors. The Earthworms met in small groups and whispered what they knew, what they were thinking. No one at this point knew who was in charge of the project, or to whom they should report. Was Larry still the leader? Where should they ship the files? Were Don and Vladimir in charge? Who did Barron Hilton support? Some of the staff stuck by Larry, but more sided with the mutinous Don and Vladimir. There was some kind of intrigue afoot with Tim Lachenmeier, they suspected.

◆   ◆   ◆

That night, Don and Vladimir secretly left the hotel and boarded the 6:45 Reno Air flight to Los Angeles, where they were met by a Hilton limousine that whisked them to the Beverly Hilton.

There they met with Mike Ribero, Hilton's senior vice president for public relations, and other top corporate officers, marketing staff and some Hilton Hotels Corp. board members, who had assembled to listen to their plan.

'The root cause of all the problems in this project is Larry Newman,' Don Moses told Ribero. 'He's very, very insecure. He does everything for the wrong reason. His reason for doing this project is money and fame; it has nothing to do with reality. He makes all his decisions from his ego; he fucks over peoples' lives. He's made everybody's lives miserable.

'He doesn't believe in harmony. He has catastrophes in his life every single day and he can't figure out why.

'He thought the capsule was his toy box. He had five GPSs (Global Positioning Systems). We didn't need five GPSs. We needed two. He brought all this shit aboard that isn't really proven and has no reliability...just because it's new and it's high tech.

'We knew days ahead that we were going to launch through an inversion. It's the best way to get no wind. But we also knew that we'd need extra lift to get through it. Any balloonist knows this.

'He's a salesman. He has created a giant illusion for everybody that he's a great balloonist, but he's never been in command of a gas balloon flight.'

'I will never ever associate with him again.'

'Now Tim Lachenmeier,' Don said, 'is the guy who built the whole balloon system. He's the best guy in the world to fly it.'

Don and Vladimir proposed dropping Larry from the project, and replacing him with Lachenmeier as pilot-in-command.

By noon of that day, they had persuaded Barron Hilton. Newman would have to go. They would have to find a graceful way of convincing Larry to withdraw, maybe allowing him to serve as Hilton's spokesman.

'He is so good with the media,' Hilton reminded them.

'Of course he is a good speaker; that was his job,' they responded. 'He used to earn his living as a motivational speaker, not as a balloonist.'

Lachenmeier set to work sketching out an idea for the new balloon, what he called a 'cocoon balloon'. It would consist of a polyethylene helium balloon with a pressurized helium vessel inside. Both NASA and the Russians had been experimenting with this balloon-inside-a-balloon design that avoided the dangling pressure partner underneath.

The reorganized team would have to build a new capsule and would need additional major funding. Don and Vladimir were confident of enlisting the support of most of the *Earthwinds* staff. Chief engineer John Ackroyd, having sensed the power shift, was sketching out plans for converting a military aircraft cockpit pod into the pressurized balloon capsule.

Don Moses declared himself the new project leader.

◆ ◆ ◆

Earthwinds' tangled web involving sponsorships, contracts, the ownership and disposition of physical assets, seemed almost endless. Millard Zimet, John Wilcox's attorney, was back and forth on the phone trying to untangle John from the original partnership with Larry. Wilcox and Newman had run up a $750,000 deficit in their American Soviet Balloon Venture, which they had hoped to erase through the sale of souvenir flight covers, movies and other peripheral products. In the limited partnership, each was responsible for half.

Wilcox still wanted to make the film about the global balloon flight, but not with Larry as the project leader. Wilcox and Zimet wanted to dissolve the partnership, and had to make Larry an offer he couldn't refuse.

In the meantime, Wilcox was obligated for a film within two weeks in fulfillment of his contract with Canon, sponsor of ESPN's 'Expedition Earth' adventure series. But the Canon executives in Tokyo quickly told him they were not about to end the TV series with a failed five-mile flight that crashed on a mountain. That invited ridicule. So this wouldn't count toward fulfillment of John's contract. The *Earthwinds* movie would have to find a new sponsor, and Wilcox had to deliver a new film. While he argued on the phone with Japan, his production staff worked round-the-clock making a 30-minute rough cut of a film to ship off to Tokyo by courier.

Unaware of the cabal about to overrun him, Larry was making plans to remain at the Reno Hilton throughout the year. He would take the time to work on the capsule, select and train new crewmembers, and rebuild his team.

Zimet and Mike Ribero were on the phone constantly that Thursday trying to find the crowbar or the carrot that would dislodge Larry Newman from his creation. In Beverly Hills, Ribero was getting just one message from the people he talked to: dump Newman.

'Larry's treatment of all these people was coming home to roost. They were coming back to repay him for having kicked them all in the balls so many times,' said one senior Hilton executive.

Ribero would propose to Barron Hilton that the company buy out Larry's share of the partnership. In return, Larry would lose his rights to the capsule and the other equipment, but walk away without a financial loss.

But Barron Hilton's job did not involve pulling triggers. He had marketed and promoted the name of Larry Newman for 18 months, housed him, fed him and clothed him, and made his name a household word in the science and aviation world; his hotels were showing continuous loop videotape about the *Earthwinds* Hilton project; stores were selling *Earthwinds* Hilton shirts, jackets, glasses, key rings, posters and teddy bears. Barron had personally befriended Larry, flown balloons and gliders with him, had him down to the ranch, introduced him to his friends, and still believed in him and his dream, despite all the backbiting he heard through the grapevine.

Most of all, Hilton wanted to avoid a monumental court battle with his contentious creation. If the sponsorship agreements unraveled, paper dust would swirl for years. *Earthwinds* would become a lawyer's golden retirement gift. He had to keep this out of court.

At the core of the project's web of complicated legal relationships was the original contract between Windward Ventures (Larry and Lynne's company) and Adventure World Productions (John Wilcox's company).

◆ ◆ ◆

John Wilcox would have to do it. He would be the one to tell Larry that the corporate sponsors had backed out, that the support team had abandoned him, that there might never be a movie, that they should dissolve their partnership and turn over all the assets to Hilton, that it was over...

Wilcox's wife was at the hotel but their three-day-old son (born hours before the launch) was back in the hospital with an infection, and John had been staying there with the baby, working the phone as often as possible. Zimet faxed him a draft of the dissolution papers. On Friday morning, Wilcox made an appointment to see Larry.

The two of them had started this whole project four years before.

What had they created in that first conversation? They had raised and spent more than five million dollars, hired and abandoned scores of staff members, excited the imagination of millions of school children and teachers, persuaded hundreds of volunteers in half a dozen states to devote tens of thousands of hours to make their dream come to life, enlisted the approval of 95 nations for over-flight clearance, appeared on all the network talk and news shows, broadcast three documentaries on international cable-TV about their project, been profiled in dozens of newspaper stories in big cities and small towns, moved governments of the two most powerful countries on earth to contribute their brightest talent, convinced corporations to offer their people and their facilities for free, and on and on.

Now it had to end.

John Wilcox wearily rode the elevator to the top floor and walked down the hall to Suite 2714. He carried a sheaf of dissolution papers in his hand.

◆   ◆   ◆

Larry wouldn't take the bait, of course. He *would not* agree to dissolve the partnership, even if his half of the debt was erased. As long as he had breath in his body, he would continue trying to fly a balloon around the world.

He needed to get a crew together, rebuild the support team and get the capsule ready for next year...

2

Ben's Dream

A movie to make

Perched above a ski slope overlooking the valley at Ashcroft near Aspen, Colorado, the Pine Creek Cookhouse is virtually inaccessible except by chairlift or cross-country skis. Its patrons find the prices of entrees as steep as the surrounding peaks that give the place its distinctive charm.

John Wilcox had opened it in the winter of 1989 to entertain clients of his adventure film production company, and keep up with a certain class of friends from the sports and entertainment communities who took their leisure in Aspen.

Wilcox had distinguished himself in journalism at age 25 by broadcasting live on ABC-TV from a hiding place the hostage drama involving Israeli athletes at the Munich Olympics Games in 1972.

Perceptive, peripatetic and driven, Wilcox stayed with ABC, winning a series of Emmy Awards for his work on The American Sportsman. He spent several years as the executive assistant to Roone Arledge, president of ABC Sports.

Among his special assignments was the network's documentary coverage of the first balloon crossing of the Atlantic Ocean. In 1978, ABC had paid $50,000 for rights to that flight. Wilcox outfitted the balloonists' gondola with cameras, and chased the five-day expedition across the ocean and into the European continent, where the three balloonists made a picture-perfect landing in a French barley field. His film subjects, Ben Abruzzo, Maxie Anderson and Larry Newman, became aviation heroes.

After that flight, Wilcox had featured Abruzzo in a balloon safari in East Africa (where actress Sally Field broke her ankle in a tumbled landing). Later, he produced a film about Abruzzo's four-man expedition across the Pacific Ocean by balloon, another first.

When his mentor Arledge moved on from ABC, Wilcox did, too, founding a small independent production company in Aspen.

◆ ◆ ◆

The son of an airline pilot from Greenwich, Connecticut, Wilcox loved flying and fast-paced adventure. He equipped himself with all the tools of an instant communicator. He spoke his thoughts into a dictabelt, always carried a cell phone in his hand, sent and received documents only by overnight mail, jammed letters into fax machines, then jumped in a taxi to catch the next jet out of town to the following day's urgent encounter.

Traveling constantly, he seldom spent more than one night in a place. On any given day, he might be found in editing studios in Los Angeles or New York, always finishing his workweek by Saturday morning so he could spend the day skiing in Aspen before presiding at his restaurant during the peak weekend evening meals.

He had a stream-of-consciousness way of trying out ideas, spewing phrases and words in sentence fragments that defied diagramming or transcription but that when coupled with body English somehow conveyed his thoughts.

He spent a great deal of his time on the phone, answering on a speaker box so his hands could continue gesturing while he paced and talked. Rarely did a conversation last more than two minutes.

His daily nourishment came from grazing, picking up random bites of food from desktops, candy jars and other people's plates.

This comical habit was so predictable that his small cadre of loyal assistants learned to order extra when they snacked.

He could not abide unfairness, and he could be tenacious and combative when it came to defending his interests against real or perceived threats.

◆ ◆ ◆

Good things were beginning to happen to the small production company he called Adventure World Productions, which had just signed an agreement to produce a 16-part series. It would be broadcast on ESPN, the sports network that was 80 percent owned by ABC's parent company.

By arranging sponsorships to produce television documentaries, Wilcox had developed a reputation for finding and funding characters no one else thought could succeed but who eventually did. Dealing with divergent personalities was an occupational hazard in the adventure business; Wilcox's faith and energy usually brought out the best in people.

For this adventure series, he had already lined up the Anchorage-to-Nome Iditerod dog sled race across Alaska; he would organize a team of sherpas and scale the Mt. Everest in the Himalayas; he would follow an acrobatic French parachutist out of a plane; he would kayak down a Soviet river; organize and direct the Trans-Antarctic Expedition (a 4,000-mile dogsled race), explore the jungles of New Guinea and save the giant pandas in China.

Wilcox had the business down to a science. He mixed the tightly edited action scenes and music with dramatic narration from a famous voice (Peter Benchley was a favorite) and the result was presto! his instant adventure film formula.

Now he needed a centerpiece adventure for the Expedition Earth series.

He thought about the round-the-world balloon flight his friend Ben Abruzzo had dreamed about.

It wasn't such a far-fetched dream. Why, in December of 1986, just three years ago, hadn't the Voyager experimental airplane completed a non-stop, unrefueled flight around the world in nine days? Hadn't that been a privately financed, grass roots project borne of aviation entrepreneurs?

And hadn't another miraculous craft, the Daedalus pedal-powered airplane, flown across the Aegean Sea from Crete to Santorini in April of 1988? Wasn't that built on a shoestring budget by a devoted band of grad students at MIT?

The idea of a global balloon flight compared favorably with those adventures. But few people knew how much anguish had gone into those successes.

Wilcox had been mulling the idea for years. It had started with Ben Abruzzo, one day after the Atlantic crossing in 1978. A reporter had asked Abruzzo whether the exhausted trio had just met the last challenge in ballooning.

'No,' Abruzzo said, astonishing reporters and crewmates with his answer, 'the ultimate challenge is a balloon flight around the world.'

The crew, Abruzzo said, should ride in a pressurized cabin under one big polyethylene balloon filled with helium. Jet stream wind of more than 100 miles per hour would carry the balloon around the world in ten days.

In time, Maxie Anderson, Abruzzo's partner on the Atlantic flight, had become a rival in the global flight sweepstakes. The aviators who had opened the golden era of long-distance ballooning had split up and become competitors. As each planned their earth-orbit flight, they encountered technological, physical and political barriers.

Abruzzo thought that the global flight, or a series of flights, would connect the work he had done on the Atlantic and Pacific flights. He talked about taking off from the west coast of the United States and flying across the continent, the

Atlantic, and then into Europe. He had sought permission to overfly the Soviet Union, but had been turned down every time.

Now, however, Abruzzo was gone, killed at the controls of his own twin-engine Cessna 421, taking out his wife and three other women at the start of a vacation to Aspen. He orphaned two sons, Louis and Richard, and a daughter, Mary Pat.

Anderson was gone, too. Having made flights over great distances attempting a global flight, he had fallen short. In 1983, he and his co-pilot were killed in a balloon accident in Germany. Anderson's business and flying fame was such that his death was reported on the front page of The New York Times and The Wall Street Journal.

Ben Abruzzo's dream, a global balloon flight, remained the last great adventure in aviation.

Wilcox had been in touch with the surviving third crewmember from the Atlantic flight, who had also made the Pacific flight with Abruzzo. Early in 1989, John Wilcox invited Larry Newman for dinner at his Pine Creek Cookhouse overlooking the valley near Aspen.

The heir to Ben's dream

Larry's reputation as a sometimes-cantankerous character preceded him, but it seemed to Wilcox that Larry had matured considerably. The brash rookie balloonist Wilcox knew in 1978 had now become a 757 captain for America West Airlines.

Wilcox knew from first-hand experience that Newman presented a study in contrasts. An accomplished aviator with multiple ratings, Larry had been lucky at age 30 to be invited by Ben Abruzzo into the Atlantic flight, on which he served as radio operator. A balloonist reluctantly, he acknowledged that he had made the flight to promote his hang-glider business. Abruzzo and Anderson had allowed Larry to sling a hang glider below the gondola, on which he hoped to glide into Europe. But when ballast was needed on the last night aloft, they jettisoned the hang-glider and Larry completed the flight as a balloonist.

The oldest of three children in a broken home, Larry had rejected the devout strictures of his Hungarian Jewish mother and disavowed any interest in religion; he had the ethnicity but not the practice of a faith. Larry once worshipped his father, who taught him to fly at age seven, to solo at eleven, and to become licensed at 17. He had given his father the trophies he won for the Atlantic flight. But father and son had become estranged in recent years.

From his father, Larry had inherited the technique of haggling, schmoosing and oozing sincerity when it suited his purpose. A knack for stories, jokes and persuasive explanations was as much a gift as the physical agility and keen eyesight that made him a good pilot.

While Larry appeared articulate and knowledgeable in public, he had done poorly in high school and barely started college. Yet with cocky self-confidence he had started manufacturing and selling hang-gliders, and then ultralight airplanes. Winning championships throughout the U.S. and Europe, he became one of the half-dozen best hang-glider pilots in the world.

Larry's company, Electra Flyer, sold hang gliders, parachutes and altimeters. When sales reached $1.5 million (two thousand gliders a year), Fortune magazine profiled him in a feature called 'How to make a million doing your own thing.' He began installing small gasoline engines on some models, and changed his business from hang gliders to ultralight aircraft.

Then he had lost it all when the business was consumed by insurance claims and patent litigation.

Larry's meteoric personality discouraged long-term trust. He could turn against patrons. Chuck Yeager could testify to that.

The man who broke the sound barrier the year Larry was born had been doing endorsements for Larry's ultralights, but midway through a four-day camping and fishing trip in the high Sierras, Larry had stomped out cursing Yeager, who for his part quickly disposed of the plane and the contract.

Wilcox remembered that the published records of the two great long-distance flights put Larry in a particularly bad light. On the Atlantic flight, the polished, refined Maxie Anderson had found Larry abrupt, coarse and impulsive. Larry, in turn, became bitterly inimical to Anderson.

'I rush so fast with people that I often seem abrasive,' Larry said of himself at the time. 'I am abrasive; I don't just seem that way.'

Others agreed. Larry 'said whatever came into his head almost as soon as it came into his head; sometimes the things he said in his candor were very rude indeed,' concluded Charles McCarry, who would write of their adventure in Double Eagle.

There had been worse trouble before the Pacific flight. The first launch attempt failed and tensions already had been roiling. Two of the crewmembers, Ron Clark and Rocky Aoki, wanted Larry out.

'He's not flying with us!' Clark said, 'He's impossible to work with. He's temperamental and if he says he doesn't want to fly with us, all the more so; we don't want to fly with him!'

Abruzzo, the expedition leader and Larry's friend, had abided by the crew vote, and Larry stepped aside. As time passed, Larry renewed his interest in making the flight.

He promised Abruzzo he would do a good job and that he would work hard not to upset people. Abruzzo persuaded the other two that they needed Larry. No one knew more about outfitting the gondola, or about radios. They had to operate as a team in order to succeed.

'The reunification of the crew' said Ray Nelson, who wrote a book about that flight, 'was one of the miracles of Double Eagle V. A potentially devastating obstacle was overcome quietly and privately, and few people ever knew about it.'

◆ ◆ ◆

The relationship between Larry Newman and Ben Abruzzo had been much stronger than that between flying partners. Abruzzo had financed his business, helped to make him famous, and had taught him valuable lessons about life and family. Abruzzo's death in 1985 left a void in Larry's life.

'Ben was like a father to me,' he said quietly and reverently, 'like the father I never had.'

Abruzzo's legacy was the unfulfilled dream of a global balloon flight. The unfinished work haunted Larry as much as Ben's death.

Larry didn't need Wilcox's coaching to think about what was already a personal goal. Although Larry in 1986 had attracted a little attention by announcing his plan for making a global flight, he had been unable to raise the funds or assemble a team.

Now Wilcox offered a new impetus.

◆ ◆ ◆

At their dinner meeting, Wilcox said he knew of no one else who could put together a global balloon voyage. He wanted to set things in motion now.

Wilcox explained that the story of the flight would become part of the Expedition Earth TV series, and marketed worldwide. If Larry put the flight together, John said he would raise the money. The Atlantic crossing 11 years earlier had cost less than $200,000; the Pacific flight had cost about half a million dollars. Larry guessed that a global flight might cost up to a million dollars.

Gesturing expansively and expressively, Wilcox said he would be a partner and raise the money for the flight; they would split the profit. And they would make a pile of money on the residuals and endorsements. But this time, having produced films about history's two greatest long distance balloon flights, John wanted more: he wanted to be aboard.

Neither one doubted that it would be a massive undertaking. For if Double Eagle's open baskets had been the refinement of 'balloon technology,' a sealed capsule flying in the jet stream would represent advanced commercial aerospace technology.

Larry and John spent four days mulling names for their project before deciding on one that had just the right mix of adventure and self-description in it. They would call it *'Earthwinds'*.

Larry knew from studying worldwide wind patterns that a global flight would have to take place in the winter months. Violent, high-reaching thunderstorms diminish in the northern hemisphere winter when the sun dips below the equator. Thus, the optimum weather would occur during a four-month winter launch window, roughly from the beginning of November through the end of February.

Wilcox contacted Bill Warner, an old friend from ABC days, who was now president of ESPN. With its reach into 53 million American homes and millions more throughout 14 European countries, ESPN had become the largest single network in the world. Warner agreed to contribute $50,000 to seed the project.

One of the sponsors of ESPN's Expedition Earth series was Canon, the camera company. The camera division of Canon USA, along with Canon Japan, decided to join in sponsoring *Earthwinds*. Canon would put in $100,000 up front, and another $100,000 when the flight took place. ESPN sold the Japanese broadcast rights of Expedition Earth to Sports TV in Japan, in which it had part interest, and the European rights to The Walt Disney Company. The balloon story would be marketed worldwide.

◆   ◆   ◆

Overflight permission from the Soviet Union had been one obstacle to a global flight. Covering 40 percent of the Eurasian landmass, the USSR spanned 11 time zones. It was the world's largest country, and a free-floating balloon in the northern hemisphere inevitably would drift over it.

Although permission to fly through Soviet airspace always had been denied, the winds of change had begun to blow across that land. The new leader, Mikhail Gorbachev, was loosening the reins of central government authority. Western investment was being encouraged. Economic overtures were being made to other nations.

The Iron Curtain was rusting away and by the end of the decade it was no longer fashionable to speak of the 'Evil Empire.'

Wilcox had made two films in the Soviet Union and had nurtured excellent high-level connections. His key contact there was Alexander Martinov, deputy director of PHOTON, a defense logistics agency. He believed Martinov could help him gain access to the official channels through which he and Larry could request permission for the balloon to overfly the USSR. Wilcox wrote to officials at Glavkosmos, the commercial arm of the Soviet space agency, emphasizing potential scientific gains, atmospheric research, and international cooperation.

The Soviet Government responded that a Soviet aviator should be on the mission. Glasnost was for real! Larry and John went to Moscow in April of 1989, where they presented their case and were given a list of five candidates. Examining the portfolio listing the credentials of Vladimir Alexandrevich Dzhanibekov, it was an easy choice.

'This guy is like their John Glenn and Neil Armstrong rolled into one!' Larry exclaimed.

Out of the dust of Tashkent

Five-year-old Volodya Krysn was face down in the dirt, sore from the latest beating, when he heard the noise. The other children stopped as they waited for it to pass. Another plane was landing at the airfield across from their school. They heard the whine of its engines before they saw the craft on final approach.

He felt humiliation and pain lying there on the playground. The schoolyard bullies had found this clumsy, chubby boy an easy mark. They made fun of his appearance, his name and his ethnic origins. A fat little Ukrainian boy in Uzbekistan! His family name meant 'rat'! Once again, he had wound up on the losing side of fisticuffs.

The plane's arrival gave him a chance to catch his breath.

Suddenly, an idea dawned on him: He could do that! He would learn to fly! He had seen the Soviet Air Force pilots as they walked around town in their smart uniforms. People admired them!

One day, he would get in shape and rise above these dusty, rough-and-tumble fields. He would be like those pilots he admired…he would go places.

When he told his parents of his plan, they objected. But if he didn't follow his own dream, he wondered, what might become of him?

His mother was a classic Russian from the banks of the River Volga, the life-giving mother of Russian agriculture. His father Alexander, a Cossack from the

Ukraine, was captain of a fire-fighting team consisting of a two-wagon team of four horses and a company of semi-invalids.

Life in the middle of the twentieth century in Central Asia began with a hardscrabble childhood. Summers were hot and dusty. Winters were harsh, dry and cold. Uzbekistan, producer of one of the largest cotton crops in the world, depended on the labor of children to prosper. Each day after school, Volodya and the other children of Iskandar would march into the fields to pick bolls off the cotton plants. It was slow work, hard on backs and hard on hands, and it was part of the culture.

At age 11, faithful to the promise he had made to himself, he applied to a military cadet school. It was a seven-year program, and most of the cadets were boys orphaned in the Second World War. The school had been founded specifically to care for such boys and provide them some military discipline. A few leftover spots were reserved for boys who actually wanted to join.

Vladimir, now using his formal name, was chosen and made it his duty to study hard. Ever conscious of his weight, Vladimir chose sports that enhanced his physique and grace. He became an expert fencer, attacking opponents with deft, aggressive lunges—and a prizefighter. Outdoors, he found the hunt with bow-and-arrow a satisfying discipline requiring physical agility and mental acuity.

He hadn't even been up in an airplane yet. The first ride came three years later, as a passenger in a noisy Ilyushin-14, when his family flew to the Caucasus for a vacation. His introduction to the world of flight consisted of a series of bumpy rides over 10 hours covering more than 1,000 miles. Vladimir found himself drafted into helping the cabin crew hush crying infants.

He was 15 when the Soviet Union launched Sputnik in 1957.

'Fortunately,' Vladimir recalls, 'I had a very nice teacher of physics who directed our attention to this new and interesting adventure. I always was dreaming about flying.'

Hoping to fly airplanes, and then to fly in space, Vladimir studied physics and mathematics at the Suvorov Military School. He enlisted in the Soviet Air Force in 1961, the year Yuri Gagarin made his single orbit of the world, and graduated from the Yeysk Higher Aviation School for Pilots in 1965, a three-year school later named for Vladimir M. Komarov, a cosmonaut killed in a space accident. Upon graduation, Vladimir Krysn received a commission in the Air Force, knowing that flying well could lead to selection as a cosmonaut.

Flight school consisted of mastering the usual military subjects such as mathematics, physics, electronics, tactics, navigation, topography, military regulations, and aerodynamics, as well as science of Communism, history of the Party, Marxist/Leninist philosophy.

Graduates of military aviation schools normally became fighter pilots in MiG-17 Fresco squadrons, but Communist Party leadership honored the best graduates by retaining them for instructor duty. Vladimir became a teacher, but kept his mind focused squarely on becoming a cosmonaut.

Finally, after five years, he was selected for training as a cosmonaut-pilot in May 1970.

When Vladimir married Lilia Dzhanibekov, he took her family name as his own, finally shedding the Ukrainian family surname that had caused him ridicule as a boy. Vladimir Dzhanibekov and Lilia moved into a one-bedroom apartment in Zvyozdny Gorodok, known in the West as Star City.

Vladimir wanted to become part of the Soviet moon exploration program, and then to lead an expedition to Mars. However, after a series of setbacks and the rapid progress of America's Apollo program, Soviet priorities had shifted to scientific exploration of the earth aboard permanently manned space stations.

At the beginning of the era of detente, he drew his first assignment: as the back-up commander for the Soyuz-Apollo Test Project. Vladimir trained with the Americans and learned the diplomatic niceties of the international aviation community. His crew studied the Apollo craft and practiced in simulators. As launch date approached, however, Vladimir was troubled by the distractions and temptations to which his junior partner succumbed. Asked by the training officers for a status report, he startled them by replying that they were not ready! He said he refused to fly with an unprepared partner, and withdrew as backup crew. This difficult and virtually unheard of admission took the 30-year-old cosmonaut out of flight rotation.

But by 1978, when Vladimir went to the Baikonour Cosmodrome, he was commanding Soyuz-27, aided by an engineer who already had two missions. As they rose away from the launch pad, computers guided them quickly into orbit and up to Salyut 6, the first permanently manned space station.

It became the first mission to link three spacecraft in orbit: their Soyuz, Salyut 6 and Soyuz 26. After five days in the space station, they switched their custom-made seats into the Soyuz 26, and returned to Earth. Landing in a Soyuz, thumping down to the ground in Kazakhstan, was always a jarring event. Oftentimes backs ached for days after a landing.

One of the rewards for success in space was a bigger apartment. Vladimir and Lilia moved into a two-bedroom suite with their two young daughters, Ina and Olga.

Vladimir returned to Salyut 6 for eight days with a Mongolian cosmonaut who became ill in space, leaving Vladimir to do the work of both.

A new space station, Salyut 7, was launched in April 1982. It had a more powerful computer and could dock with larger craft. Vladimir began training for a long-duration mission. But trouble developed with a forthcoming short-duration international mission. Cosmonaut Yuri Malyshev had a personality conflict with the French cosmonaut. Vladimir moved into the French flight.

Blasting off June 24, 1982, he commanded a three-person crew that was supposed to dock with Salyut 7. With him were fellow cosmonaut Alexander Ivanchenkov and France's first 'spacionaute', Colonel Jean-Loup Chretien. The spacecraft, as usual, was under automatic guidance from mission controllers in Kaliningrad; rarely did cosmonaut pilots take manual control of their craft before they came within two miles of rendezvous. But as Soyuz floated through space, its automatic guidance system suddenly went kaput. Three previous missions had been scrubbed because of guidance and docking mechanism failures. In this crisis, Vladimir knew what he had to do. He manually took control of the ship, guided it to a docking, and began the mission.

The crew performed a series of French experiments, working around the clock, enjoying Chretien's French cuisine, and having some fun. While a terribly constipated Chretien busied himself quietly in the toilet area, wearing his headsets, Vladimir quietly floated over to the volume control, and blasted his crewmate. Stunned, the Frenchman at first thought some tragedy had shaken the Salyut. As he flailed around and tried to pull himself together, Vladimir's technique worked: the constipation problem was solved all at once.

For saving the mission and conducting the French science experiments, French President Francois Mitterand presented Vladimir the medal of Commander of the Legion of Honor, the highest tribute given to a non-French citizen. From his own country, he received the star of the Hero of the Soviet Union, as did Chretien.

Four crews followed Dzhanibekov's to the Salyut 7 over the next two years, most conducting experiments during long stays ranging from four to eight months. Unfortunately, Salyut 7 was being plagued by a number of operational problems, including a propellant leak on one mission.

The Soviets, always wary of competition in space, knew that the Americans were about to claim the distinction of launching the first woman space walker, Shuttle astronaut Kathleen Sullivan.

Although only one Soviet woman had flown before, the Soviets hurriedly put together a flight. They named Dzhanibekov to command it.

The mission, his fourth, started July 17, 1984. Vladimir's first assignment was keeping peace between Cosmonauts Svetlana E. Savitskaya, the female, and Igor Volk, known as the 'wolf' of the cosmonaut corps. Vladimir pacified them and kept them focused on the mission. Svetlana, only the second female cosmonaut, became the first woman to perform an extra-vehicular walk when she and Vladimir floated outside Salyut for three and a half hours testing a welding device. The pictures of her floating in space were among the top propaganda prizes of the Soviet program. That crew logged eleven days in orbit.

A few months later, Salyut 7 went silent and ground controllers lost its signals. It was a national embarrassment: the Soviet Union's space station was tumbling out of control 230 miles above the earth.

Mission controllers debated the problem and whether it could be fixed. Significant risks attended any attempt to visit the station, even for a diagnosis: financial, scientific and human assets, not to mention national prestige, would be on the line. No one knew whether a Soyuz capsule could replicate the Salyut tumble for the purpose of inspecting it or docking with it. They had to find out. The pilot who had twice docked with the Salyut was chosen to conduct the mission.

During an intense three-month training period, Vladimir and Viktor Savinykh memorized every wire, switch and circuit onboard; they practiced rendezvous and docking procedures. Planning a short inspection trip, they lifted off June 6, 1985. Ground controllers led them to within a mile and a half of the space station, and then turned the craft over to Vladimir. He maneuvered up close. The solar panels were out of alignment; the slowly tumbling station obviously was frozen, quiet and dead.

'The station looks as if battered by savage storms,' he reported to the ground.

Vladimir slowed the rate of closure then locked on.

'Docking,' Vladimir would say later, 'is like driving a seven-ton truck with fragile freight on an icy road into a narrow gate at the end of this road.'

They sealed the two craft together, equalized the pressure, opened the hatch and floated into the dark, cold station. There was no sign of fire or collision, only an ominous silence; no switch responded to their touch. Mission controllers concluded that the space station was beyond repair, but Vladimir insisted on trying to bring up the systems.

In one 24-hour marathon workday, he and Savinykh hooked up a ventilation system, discovered a faulty switch that prevented the solar panels from recharging the batteries. The repairmen disconnected every switch and hooked up the good batteries directly to the solar panels, cobbling them together with miscellaneous parts found on board. They aligned the Salyut to find the sun's light, and waited.

The oxygen regeneration system was frozen, and the only heat available was from the pilots' bodies. The only way to save the station was to wrap their own bare skin around the pipes and breathe onto the pipes until the ice melted. That took 12 hours.

'It was so difficult to stay alive,' he reminisced later.

Eventually, some lights and ventilator fans came on and they restored radio contact. They rationed their drinking water, but the mental and physical strain took its toll on the two cosmonauts.

'The main thing in such operations is not to give way to nerves,' Vladimir said, 'although wariness gradually builds up into irritation, sometimes with yourself, sometimes with those trying to help you from the ground. You simply have to be able to pull yourself together in the face of setbacks and mishaps.'

During a spectacular space walk, they installed a third solar panel, and built structures to hold them. Soviet news media heralded their success, and when they returned to earth after 112 days, Vladimir and his partner became national heroes.

Laden with honors, he was promoted to Major General in the Soviet Air Force and elected a deputy in the Supreme Soviet, the country's governing body. Postage stamps with his likeness were issued. His exploits and picture appeared in a National Geographic cover story, and he authored a story for Parade magazine. His bust was installed on a pillar in the center of Tashkent, near his parents' home.

But his fellow cosmonauts made the gesture most meaningful to Vladimir. During his long stay in space, they built him a large country dacha, with an art studio on the second floor capped by a great cathedral ceiling. There, he would relax late into the night and paint, capturing from memory vivid space flight scenes as well as still life. As he traveled to other nations, Vladimir donated his oil paintings to museums and prominent friends.

The downside of his long flight in space was the problem common to all long-term zero gravity flyers: recurrent back pain due to lengthening of the spine in weightlessness.

Back at work in Star City, Vladimir was promoted to director of the cosmonaut training center. With a staff of 300, he was carrying out plans to train and put into flight cosmonauts from other nations including, he hoped, an American teacher.

Although retired from flying status, the spirit of adventure still moved him. When he learned that the Americans were planning a global balloon flight in the stratosphere, he applied for it right away.

So it was that one of the Soviet Union's premier cosmonauts, a stocky, serious-minded scientist who had performed flawlessly on five remarkable space flights, had logged 145 days in orbit, and who thoroughly enjoyed working on international projects, became a crewmember on the balloon flight around the world.

Wilcox, Newman and Dzhanibekov met and talked about the project. Larry and Vladimir discovered that in many ways they had shared experiences, noted important milestones together.

When Vladimir agreed to participate, John and Larry quickly organized themselves into the American Soviet Balloon Venture (ASBV) and agreed to donate $64,000 to a Soviet scientific agency, which would become an *Earthwinds* sponsor.

Larry and John rejoiced over this breakthrough! They had opened the skies over Russia!

3

Building a Team

Someone old, someone new

At the Western Reserve Club in Tempe, Arizona, Larry had been watching a tennis lesson when he met a pert, bouncy Irish Catholic divorcee from southside Cleveland. Lynne Rourk was an independent insurance agent working out of her own home in Scottsdale. Her youthful, radiant smile belied the fact that she was about the same age as Larry. They discovered a number of mutual interests and similarities, starting with sport fishing and a restless determination to attain the good life.

Immediately attracted to one another, they married in June 1989.

But beyond having a companion to provide moral support at home, Larry knew that substantial amounts of money and reliable skilled labor would be needed to make the project work.

He looked up his old friend Donald Lee Moses, a soft-spoken, muscular six-foot laborer about a year and a half Larry's senior. They had met while Larry spent a one-year sabbatical in Hawaii during his youth. Don worked harder and turned out more work in carpentry and construction than any two men. Although they had worked many jobs together on Kauai, Larry and Don differ in their recollections of those days. Larry says he was president of the construction company; Don says Larry tried passing himself off as a journeyman carpenter but the quality of his craftwork unveiled the ruse. When the business declined, Don got married, and Larry moved back to the mainland.

Don had not heard from Larry for several years, but they quickly recalled their fun days together on the beach, surfing the Na Pali coast below 4,000-foot tall cliffs. Don apparently had done well. In Kauai, he had founded a custom boat-building company, which produced 34- and 38-foot double-decker watercraft. With an ex-wife Don started Le' Ann Cruises, one of the largest fishing and sightseeing companies on Kauai. Tourists watched humpback whales or went snorkeling above the extraordinary white coral off the north shore.

After several marriages, Don had settled down with Carol Hart, an attractive red-haired oceanographer who had been research director for the Pacific Whale Foundation in Maui. She helped maintain Don's boats, and occasionally served as tour guide.

With Don's interest in two other tour companies, he had a steady income.

But in 1985 doctors found lung cancer. Don quit smoking, and was lucky. To relax, he sold his businesses and moved into a trailer parked next to his parents' house in Trona, Calif. He and Carol spent their time traveling, skiing and enjoying a good life.

Larry explained the round-the-world balloon expedition to Don. The closed capsule would need reliable electrical generators, he said.

Larry knew that when it came to fiberglass construction and power plants, Don knew what he was talking about. At first, Don was non-committal; he neglected to tell Larry about his recent bout with cancer, or that he had allowed his pilot license to lapse.

And he was wary of getting too closely involved with Larry.

'His social skills were just not there,' Don recalled, candidly assessing his friend, 'His greatest weakness is that he hates managing people.'

But the flight Larry described was intriguing, and Don still had a strong interest in aviation. Later, when Don visited Scottsdale, Larry pressed for his help. Don agreed to get involved if he had a chance of actually going on the flight. Larry said he'd consider that.

After Larry and John returned from the USSR, Don Moses joined the project as a back-up crewmember. He suspected that Wilcox's involvement in making the film and raising sponsorships would cause him to drop out as a flying crewmember. His instinct was right. In a short while, Wilcox withdrew as a would-be balloonist and Don Moses was added to the flight crew. The retired boat builder, now in his early 40s, couldn't have been happier.

Richard Branson and the Virgin people

Although ESPN had provided $50,000 seed money, and the documentaries would bring in more, Larry and John needed really big money. With a tentative budget of $1 million, they imposed some 'politically correct' limitations on themselves, vowing to refuse money from alcohol or tobacco companies. They circulated a loose-leaf kit to prospective corporate sponsors.

One found its way into the hands of Richard Branson, the British record tycoon, airline founder and free-spirited adventurer, whose personal empire Forbes Magazine estimated at more than $2 billion.

Branson caught wind of Newman's plan in April 1990, while he was inspecting a new airship at the Litchfield Park, Arizona, airship facility of Goodyear.

Tom Barrow, the aviation consultant who had helped Maxie Anderson and Don Ida on their last global attempt, now ran airship operations for Branson's company. Barrow knew his boss had talked of a transglobal balloon flight, so while they were in Phoenix, he arranged for Newman and Branson to meet.

Seeing the scale of the project, the Soviet cosmonaut's participation, and the opportunity of fostering environmental research while marketing his company's name around the world, Branson salivated. Larry told him that *Earthwinds* was preparing a formal announcement within a month at the National Press Club in Washington, and that the flight would begin near November 1990.

That night Branson signed on as the main underwriter and sponsor of *Earthwinds*. For his substantial contribution, whatever it would be, Branson wanted to be one of the crewmembers. They shook hands on the deal. The next morning, Irwin Russell, Larry's attorney, and Millard Zimmet, Wilcox's attorney, began drafting a contract.

Behind Richard Branson's mask of flamboyance, eccentricity and informality, his enormous toothy grin over a goatee, casual dress (open leather jacket and jeans), Branson was in fact a shrewd player of business hardball. He had an impeccable sense of timing, and a relentless curiosity. Reporters found his clever observations sprinkled with a light-hearted hint of mischief and adventure.

Having left boarding school at the age of 17, he founded Virgin Records as a mail-order house, and in quick succession opened a record shop in London, built a recording studio and started a production company. All this he parlayed into the Virgin Group, which included Virgin Atlantic Airways; SuperChannel Television reaching 25 million homes in Europe, and Virgin Megastores.

His airline, flying between London and six American cities, Moscow and Tokyo, was just then doubling the size of its fleet from eight to 16 aircraft, and adding service to other cities. Branson sometimes personally greeted passengers departing from London.

He had engaged in a series of colorful public adventures in recent years that made headlines and embellished his celebrity status. At first it was power boating. He tried twice before smashing the trans-Atlantic speedboat crossing record in 1986.

The next year, he formed a partnership with Swedish balloonist Per Lindstrand to attempt the first flight across the Atlantic by hot air balloon.

One of the indispensable keys to the Branson-Lindstrand success would become a key figure in *Earthwinds*. John Ackroyd was a rail-thin, 54-year old aeronautical engineer. He has designed the Branson-Lindstrand balloon capsule. A professional vagrant who seemed to favor project life, Ackroyd's wanderlust and enormous capacity for work had carried him from one project to another all over the world. Ackroyd's home on the Isle of Wight was more often than not unoccupied as he made a career of expedition life. He had designed and manufactured an electric car, and worked for such well-known British auto firms as Britten-Norman, Dornier and Porsche.

One of Ackrod's proudest accomplishments resulted from a three-year stint with Project Thrust, where he designed a four-ton twin-seat jet-powered race car. Running at the Black Rock Desert in Nevada, his car averaged 633.468 mph on October 4, 1983, to claim the world's land speed record. Ackroyd had engineered the car to attain a top speed of 650 mph; it had peaked at 650.88 mph. The introduction to ballooning came soon afterward when Lindstrand retained him as the aeronautical engineer on an altitude record balloon flight that reached 60,000 feet.

Barrow became project director for Branson's Atlantic flight, and brought in Bob Rice (a former Maxie Anderson ally) without whose advice no self-respecting long distance flyer would dare leave the ground. In the rarefied world of long-distance ballooning, Rice was the best interpreter of weather data affecting balloons.

The start of Branson and Lindstrand's trans-Atlantic from a ski resort in Maine was horrifying. Two huge propane tanks fell off just as the balloon ascended. The balloon entered the jet stream at 27,000 feet and dashed across the Atlantic at more than 100 knots. Over Ireland, the pilots tried landing but hit hard; two more tanks fell away, and up they went again. Lindstrand jumped from the balloon into the Irish Sea. Branson flew a few miles more before crashing into the water, from which he was rescued by a Royal Navy helicopter. In 34 hours, they had established a hot air balloon distance record of 3,075 miles. Branson told his wife and two children he would never again attempt such dangerous stunts.

Except that the Pacific challenge still beckoned. Ackroyd designed another pressurized capsule, replete with life support systems, internal and external cameras, and six huge propane tanks. Moments before takeoff in Japan in 1989, the balloon collapsed, and the attempt was abandoned. Or so most people thought.

Branson's family and business associates tried to dissuade him; he was, after all, the linchpin in the vast organization, their dinner ticket—but he couldn't resist Larry Newman's invitation to participate in the round-the-world balloon flight.

He had financed Lindstrand to do the preparatory work on his other flights; now he felt he was "hiring Larry Newman" to get the transglobal flight ready for him. Branson took the seat that had first been Wilcox's, and then Don Moses'.

Don returned to back-up status. If for any reason Branson decided not to fly, Larry assured him, you'll move back aboard.

A few weeks later, Branson was in Los Angeles on business and summoned Larry to a meeting. Learning this, John Wilcox asked Larry if he were going to talk money with Branson, meaning the specific amount and terms of the sponsorship. Larry said no.

Nevertheless, at the meeting in Los Angeles, Branson asked for an estimate of how much money they would need. Thinking quickly of a big gain, Larry said they would need $1.5 million (leaving him and Wilcox a profit of $500,000). Branson agreed, and Larry signed.

Any additional funds raised by the American Soviet Balloon Venture, the contract stipulated, would first reduce Virgin's commitment of $1.5 million. In effect, that pledge became the budget cap for the entire project, until and unless Branson were bought out.

The contract spelled out a performance schedule of incremental payments totaling $1.5 million. The final $150,000 would be paid on completion of the flight.

'I should never have missed that meeting,' Wilcox rued when he learned the terms of the deal.

Newman and Wilcox had envisioned a profit of well over $5 million from the project. They believed that the sale of residuals, product endorsements, book and movie rights would bring in more money than they could count. Branson was guaranteed one-third of the profits in excess of $5 million. Larry would draw $100,000 per year as project manager and his wife, as project administrator, would collect $36,000 per year.

Wilcox and Newman believed that Branson's involvement assured them access to the technical expertise he had gathered in his high-altitude hot air balloon crossing of the Atlantic and of the Pacific attempt. They counted on acquiring this basic research.

Branson, Newman, Wilcox and his film crew went to Russia to meet Dzhanibekov and shoot background scenes for Wilcox's one-hour movie.

Vladimir took them through mock-ups of his Soyuz capsule and at the Cosmonaut Training Center. Scientists at the Soviet institute of space engineering and at the Youth Scientific Technological Work Center were already selecting and designing ozone research and other packages being developed by Moscow State University. Larry and John then flew in a Soviet Air Force jet to Tashkent, the capital of Uzbekistan, where Vladimir was still hailed as a hometown hero.

NASA, NOAA, Weather and a Capsule

Back in the states, now leading an international crew and sporting significant financial sponsorship, Larry sought to borrow some government equipment and win an endorsement from NASA. Cunningly, he called Secretary of Defense Dick Cheney, whom he had recently met. Larry told Cheney about the Russian space agency's involvement in his project and complained that NASA wasn't cooperating. Could Cheney call NASA Administrator Richard Truly? Cheney did.

Acting as if he were Cheney's personal friend, Larry told the NASA chief what he wanted: communications and a NASA science package. Truly endorsed the request and turned *Earthwinds* over for staffing to a deputy. When Larry went to NASA's Godard Space Flight Center in Maryland, he sought access to high-quality communication systems through the Inmarsat satellite telephone network. He was willing to trade space on the capsule, where NASA could conduct experiments in the jet stream wind. NASA officials worked out the trade casually and quickly.

Dr. Erik Mollo-Christiansen, manager of the Earth Sciences Section at Godard, was there when NASA's science package was decided upon.

'One of the bigwigs popped his head into my office and asked if I could find a use for a free-floating manned balloon in the jet stream. I thought we could, and said that I would give it some thought. About an hour later, he came back and announced, 'Your proposal has been accepted!'

The Swedish-born scientist went to work developing a device that would measure minute changes in the jet stream wind flow, atmospheric temperature and pressure. It would be 'basic research in geophysical fluid dynamics,' gathering information about atmospheric turbulence by measuring the motion of the capsule and outside pressure and temperature.

'A free balloon can teach us something about high-altitude turbulence, and details on how the jet stream turns and bends,' he said. 'We will record *Earth-*

winds' trajectory with the Global Positioning System, the acceleration or deceleration of the capsule, and how it tilts when it goes through the jet stream.

'As the balloon enters the jet stream, the capsule will tilt and accelerate. Observing the tilt and acceleration will enable us to infer the wind shear, while temperature and pressure observations will give information about atmospheric density stratification,' he explained.

The meanders of the jet stream would be documented in more detail than could be obtained by routine weather observations, such as how the jet stream turns, and how that may relate to large scale weather systems. Because the core of the jet stream is so narrow, minute differences in speed and tilt of the capsule can be measured in movements so minute that the flight crew would not even be able to sense them.

'I came to see *Earthwinds* as a platform of opportunity unlike any other,' Dr. Mollo-Christiansen said, 'although I didn't claim that we would make any earth-shaking discoveries, we would learn something. This was basic research on the dynamics of the jet stream. We scientists lack data from the stratosphere. Airplanes don't float the same way a particle of air does; they crash through it at 500 miles per hour. With this experiment we would learn all about the history of an air particle.'

Instruments would record temperatures and altitude changes every five seconds, and store all data on a disk.

Because *Earthwinds* might fly over many of the world's mountain ranges—the Alps, the Urals, the Himalayas and the Rockies—'one of the other things we will look for is the wave off the mountain ranges, and of course, the lively convection in certain parts of the ocean, which can set up waves in certain parts of the atmosphere.'

With NASA's endorsement in hand, Larry went to the National Oceanic and Atmospheric Administration, to secure cooperation on world-wide weather forecasts and access to the banks of data crunched through their supercomputers. He approached Rockwell International about borrowing a satellite-based Global Positioning System (GPS).

There were fundamental decisions to make about the type of balloon to use. Should *Earthwinds* follow Ben Abruzzo's original idea: a massive polyethylene balloon, with a pressurized crew capsule, flying at high altitude, or should it be an open gondola, flying at a lower level? Should it be a gas balloon, or a hybrid gas and hot-air balloon?

He visited several balloon manufacturers. He traveled to Bristol, England, and visited with Don Cameron, whose firm proposed a 240,000 cubic-foot combination helium-and-hot air balloon, which would be flown in the lower atmosphere. Cameron's philosophy was driven by simplicity of design. In fact, Cameron himself had nearly succeeded at the Atlantic crossing two weeks before the Double Eagle flight in 1978; using a balloon of the type he described to Larry, he had landed 100 miles short of land off the coast of Portugal. But Larry was looking for new technology, not something that had been tried 12 years before.

Back in the U.S., Larry then inquired of Winzen Research, a balloon-building concern in Texas, about building a polyethylene balloon big enough to fly around the world. Winzen had built balloons for Maxie Anderson's three global balloon flight attempts in the early 1980s. Winzen declined to bid on the project, citing conservative management and concerns over product liability insurance.

He then went to Winzen's only competitor in the polyethylene balloon business, Raven Industries in Sioux Falls, S.D. Raven assigned the project to a young engineer on its staff, Tim Lachenmeier, and began a feasibility study.

Larry walked into an office in New York City to see Bernard L. Schwartz, the chairman of Loral Corp. Loral's acquisition of Goodyear Aerospace had bought with it the massive old Goodyear-Zeppelin hangar in Akron. That hangar was the only place big enough to house what Larry had in mind. It was the largest building in the world, and offered a good support community

Larry wanted the building because he recalled all too clearly how the fragile, massive polyethylene balloons had ruptured during Double Eagle V's attempts to launch from Japan. Larry wanted to inflate and inspect the balloon inside the old shed. Schwartz agreed to let him use it for a few weeks.

Finally, he went to Bedford, Mass. to discuss the flight with Bob Rice, who had done the weather forecasts for the Atlantic crossings, and whom Ben Abruzzo had called in a moment of crisis near the end of the Pacific flight.

Rice's meteorological education started during an eight-year hitch in the Air Force in the 1950s. He had been a member of a special upper air forecast team for the open-air nuclear tests in Nevada. Professionally, he specialized in forecasts for yacht races and long-distance ballooning. Twelve times he forecast for flights that covered more than 2,000 miles.

One of the first questions Rice asked was where the flight would start. Larry told him about the arrangements for the airdock. Despite Larry's concern for the balloon's integrity, Rice didn't like the choice of Akron.

'The latitude is no good, the longitude is no good, and the ground conditions are unstable,' he told Larry. 'Think about where else you could go, out west, maybe. But if you decide on Akron, I suppose that almost anyplace on earth can be made to work once in a while.'

It was the first time Rice had dealt directly with Larry.

Somewhere in the back of his head two voices popped up...the voices of Ben Abruzzo and Maxie Anderson.

'Don't ever trust Larry,' both men had whispered to Rice.

In spite of that, business was business, and Weather Services Corp. signed a $35,000 contract, due in three increments, to interpret weather data for *Earthwinds*.

Having secured his weatherman and the airdock, Larry now needed a capsule. He visited Burt Rutan's company, Scaled Composites in Mojave, Calif. Larry had known the Rutan brothers from the Voyager airplane project, as well as from his Experimental Aircraft Association days. He had even found for Dick Rutan and Jeanna Yeager a large sponsor, JVC Videotape of Japan, which had partly financed Double Eagle V. (Rutan and Yeager ultimately rejected the Japanese firm in favor of an all-American method, the VIP Club of small donors). At Mojave, Larry met a young engineer named Steve Ericson, who offered suggestions and began making blueprints of the capsule design early in May.

To get things started, artist Stan Stokes painted a rendering of the capsule flying high, with an American F-15 Eagle, a British Tornado, and a Soviet MIG-29 passing beneath the balloon in the corner. Three flags were painted on the capsule: the Stars and Stripes, the Hammer and Sickle and the Union Jack. On the landing skid below the capsule large block letters proclaimed a motto never used in real life, 'Save the Earth'.

Three brave lads

One year after making their deal, John Wilcox and Larry Newman evaluated their status: they had the project's flight crew selected, capsule construction planned, government and private sponsorship lined up. Things were falling into place, and it was time to go public. On May 9, 1990, Larry, Richard and Vladimir marched onto a stage at the National Press Club in Washington, D.C. to announce their ambitious intentions.

At the press conference the flyers and the filmmaker were joined by NASA Administrator Richard Truly, himself a former astronaut.

The room radiated an upbeat air of enthusiasm, anticipation and cooperation. This meeting had the flavor of the famous press conference that had taken place near there, three decades earlier, when the original seven Mercury astronauts were introduced to the media.

Here were the *new orbital adventurers!*...men from three countries planning a project with private funds!...and they would build the thing themselves! A Congressional Gold Medal recipient who had conquered both oceans and was the master of any machine that flew! A Hero of the Soviet Union who faced down demons in the voids of space! An eccentric Brit who dropped out of school, became a billionaire and conquered the Atlantic by sea and by air!

You could almost hear the trumpets coming up on Tom Wolfe's script. These brave lads—men of achievement, aviation record-holders all—had the new right stuff.

Branson was upbeat, flashing his ever-present smile. He played down questions about his near miss in 1987, when his trans-Atlantic balloon was rescued from the Irish Sea.

'You forget about the nasty moments in life,' he told reporters.

Asked why he was accepting this challenge, Branson said, 'Basically, I just couldn't resist it.'

Admiral Truly declared that his agency would provide instruments aboard the gondola to study atmospheric turbulence and ozone levels.

'The one cooperative part that I'm sorry NASA is not participating in,' Truly said, 'is for the NASA administrator to be a member of the crew.'

Nobody at that meeting could say much about the balloon itself (it was a 'secret-design balloon' gushed the Washington Times) other than to reveal that it would hold about one million cubic feet of helium and probably stand 300 feet tall.

After all, the balloon had not even been designed. The capsule itself was just then emerging from the drawing boards out in the high desert at Mojave. But it was coming together and they would launch that winter from Akron, Ohio, in a bold non-stop adventure that would keep them sealed up together for ten days, maybe as long as three weeks.

The press reception was enthusiastic, the play good.

'12 Days to Save the Planet!' screamed the front page of a London tabloid the next morning.

'Air We go! Branson takes on the world!' proclaimed another, 'Branson leads glasnost team in balloon trek to ozone layer.'

The American press—in Washington, in New York and around the country—gave Branson the lion's share of the attention, albeit in more restrained headlines.

Following the Washington press conference Larry, Vladimir and John Wilcox flew out to Rutan's desert workshop in California to inspect the design. A few days later, at the Newmans' home in Arizona, Larry told Vladimir in front of a visiting reporter, 'I grew up thinking that the Soviets were all criminals, our enemy.'

Vladimir looked at Larry and replied:

'Absolutely. We felt the same way about you.'

Both men laughed. They talked about the goodwill this venture would produce.

'It's good to work together,' said Vladimir. 'Such ventures someday could lead to a world in which 'we produce weapons for the hunters…but not for war.'

But with friends like these…

Misunderstandings almost immediately began creeping in to the relationship between Branson's people and the Wilcox-Newman side of the project. The Americans believed that one of the big benefits of having Branson on the flight (besides his money) was getting access to the data he had acquired in his stratospheric crossing of the Atlantic—especially the data about converting the thin air of high altitude into breathable air in the closed capsule. In the fall of 1990, one of Branson's deputies, Alex Ritchie, told Larry that he could not share any data with Larry regarding Richard's Atlantic balloon flight. He didn't say why.

It was essential to find a lightweight reliable air compressor powerful enough to bring into the capsule large amounts of thin air and compress it into breathable atmosphere. Branson and Lindstrand had used such a device on their trans-Atlantic flight.

It was a vital piece of technology that *Earthwinds* needed, but despite repeated requests for data and sources, Branson's people would not share the data.

'However,' as Wilcox later recalled, 'Alex Ritchie gave Larry the name of a company in England where he could purchase a screw compressor similar to the one used on the Atlantic flight. No technical information was revealed at that time. Richard Branson continued to assure us that he would get us the information that we requested.'

◆ ◆ ◆

Don Moses had been left behind at Mojave to help construct the capsule, which was taking shape under Burt Rutan's watchful eyes. Ericson had recommended an all-composite structure and an elongated egg shape to minimize stresses caused by natural atmospheric pressures. For a balloon capsule, it would be spacious: 24 feet long and 10 feet in diameter. Its weight was not to exceed 1,200 pounds.

Don loved being in the desert, only 80 miles from his trailer home in Trona. Just breathing the air in Rutan's factory gave him a thrill. Right under his nose, cutting-edge aviation technology leapt from the drawing board into the sky, and down the road at Edwards, Air Force pilots flight-tested the hottest jets.

He still had the capacity for hard work; in fact, looking at Don, one knew that it was for broad-shouldered guys like him that muscle shirts were invented.

Leading a team of volunteers at Scaled Composites, Don fashioned a wooden male mandrel, a revolving spindle in the shape of the capsule. In a single 24-hour marathon work session, he and a team of volunteers wrapped it in 10 layers of epoxy, fiber-reinforced foam. That formed the inner pressure vessel an eighth of an inch thick.

Around that they wrapped three inches of heavy Styrofoam and a layer of expanded polystyrene, topped with an outer layer of glass-reinforced polystyrene. In all, the capsule walls were little more than three and a quarter inches thick. It was cured as a single piece, resulting in a continuous, unidirectional 'fatigue-resistant' structure. By doing the work themselves, Don, Carol, Larry and Rutan's volunteers shaved nearly $100,000 off the original cost estimate of the capsule.

Ericson boasted that the finished product could withstand the low atmospheric pressures up to 50,000 feet, and rough landings on mountain tops or at sea.

Round doors for each end, 39 inches in diameter, were constructed inside. In flight, cabin pressure would hold them shut against soft rubber seals.

Ten circular window holes were cut, one through each port and eight through the capsule bulkhead. Three windows were arrayed port and starboard, one in the top (to view the helium balloon) and one on the floor (to look straight down). The 18-inch bubble windows were large enough to place one's head into for a look up, down or sideways. Ericson demonstrated the windows' strength by cold-soaking them on dry ice, pressurizing them to 25 psi, and then banging on them with a two-inch diameter steel rod.

But in making the capsule so durable, Rutan had erred on the side of caution: the finished shell weighed 2,000 pounds—800 pounds more than allowed! Larry worried that this 40 percent increase in weight could force redesign of other components.

'The overweight problem is a major one; it ripples through the whole design,' Larry lamented. 'Now we have to start deciding what we're not going to take with us.'

Every pound of excess weight could limit the flight's duration. Eight hundred extra pounds could shorten the flight by as much as one day.

While they pondered that, Larry, Don Moses and Steve Ericson began experimenting with ways of pressurizing, heating and ventilating the capsule and power its electrical systems and avionics.

They started with a kerosene-fueled auxiliary power unit made by Allied-Signal. The 125-pound unit, standard equipment in many small jets, puts out pressurized air and runs a generator. Larry thought he would be able to use it for an hour at a time then shut it off for four hours, allowing residual engine heat to warm water that would circulate inside the capsule.

'We started working on it,' he said, 'but it was just unacceptable. It used too much fuel, wasn't reliable enough, and it cost about $175,000.'

John Wilcox listened to the problem and suggested jokingly, 'Why don't you just put an engine inside like the Honda?'

They both laughed. About 10 minutes later, Larry's eyes lit up.

'Engine inside, Honda,' he said, 'Engine inside, Honda.' An idea was born.

A 12-horsepower generator like those used on recreational vehicles offered good fuel economy on regular gasoline. For a flight of uncertain duration, Larry wanted lots of capacity and redundancy. He decided on two 375-gallon external fuel tanks that would hang from a square load frame above the capsule.

Gravity would pull fuel into the capsule through a one-quarter-inch hose.

The only air pressurization pump that would work with the rest of the system was a modified, liquid-cooled helical screw compressor made in England by CompAir BroomWade. Unfortunately, the compressor made a deafening, high-pitched noise. An absorptive silencer on both intake and discharge only partly cancelled the sound.

Larry frumped that he still wasn't getting much help from Branson's people, despite what he thought was their agreement.

Two balloons, a bellows and a cock

At Raven Industries in South Dakota, Tim Lachenmeier had risen to the top of his profession: scientific high-altitude balloon design. Having grown up in Portland, Ore., he worked his way through college in eight years, finishing with an engineering degree from Portland State University. Along the way he fancied himself a cowboy: competing in his first rodeo at age 21, and winning a championship four years later. He entered the forest products industry, and watched it decline before he discovered the science of balloon engineering. Now in his mid-thirties, his regular clients were U.S. Government agencies, usually NASA and other research organizations.

Some of the balloons he built were orbiting in the Southern Hemisphere, high above the polar jet stream. Some had carried scientific payloads 30 miles high looking for cosmic radiation. He loved the occasional adventure of his new job. Once it had taken him to a Pakistan desert, where he tethered a balloon with a large antenna several miles up; a party of Saudi sheiks on a falcon hunting expedition needed the antenna to extend the range of their portable radios.

Lachenmeier was intrigued when Larry came to discuss a flight around the world; he had been thinking about such a flight himself.

The cowboy-turned engineer and the balloonist hit it off right away. On June 26, 1990, Raven signed an agreement with the Newman Wilcox partnership to produce a balloon.

Raven was introducing a new polyethylene for high-altitude research balloons, called AstroFilm 3. Thinner than ordinary sandwich bags, the film could be layered for strength.

Estimating the weight of the capsule and crew, ballast requirements and proposed duration of the flight—from 12 to 21 days—Lachenmeier proposed a one million cubic foot polyethylene balloon. He would use three thicknesses of AstroFilm; the finished balloon would be six-thousandths of an inch thick. Polyester vertical load tapes would hold together the 180 gores.

During a round-table discussion with five balloon-designing gurus, Lachenmeier grappled with the fundamental problem of long-distance ballooning: how to carry enough ballast to extend the duration of the flight, but keep the size manageable.

His group entertained revolutionary ideas. One was about to alter the course of the project. Much of a conventional balloon's gross lift is needed for carrying the ballast itself.

NASA had explored a solution called the Sky Anchor Balloon in the mid-1960s. It involved pressurizing a separate vessel with air, thus adding or subtracting weight as the balloon flew.

The object of the NASA's Sky Anchor had been to 'park' instrument packages at fixed altitudes by offsetting the day/night heating/cooling cycles with a variable ballast bag suspended from the lift balloon. Mylar, the toughest, lightest synthetic known in the 1960s, had been used for the 100-foot diameter Echo I and II satellite balloons, which reflected radio signals.

Unfortunately, Mylar burst when over pressurized, so the Sky Anchor hadn't worked as planned.

Yet the concept of recoverable ballast was as old as manned flight. A French theoretician named Jean-Louis Carra had described it in 1784:

> The balloon naturally ascends but this ascension ought of course to be bounded, and even managed in such a manner that we may be able to govern it.
>
> For this purpose, it is necessary to have a counterpoise susceptible of variation, and of such a modification that it may be diminished or augmented as necessity arises, at the will of the navigator...since we have the means of raising ourselves in the atmosphere by a light air, to descend requires no more than to imprison, or confine, a more heavy air in a separate vessel, in short, such air as surrounds us. It becomes necessary then to attach to the balloon which is filled with the gaz...another balloon, constructed of leather only, in which may be lodged a quantity of atmosphere air...
>
> It is also necessary that this latter balloon may be filled and emptied at the pleasure of the navigator, which may be easily done by the means of a pair of bellows and a cock. By means of the bellows the navigator can charge the balloon, and thereby descend at pleasure; and by means of the cock, he can empty it, and ascend when he thinks proper.'

It was basic Archimedean physics! All you needed was a second balloon (preferably made of leather), a bellows and a cock. As Tim's panel of advisers evaluated the intriguing idea, they concluded that they could apply new Space Age materials technology to a two-balloon system. The question on the table in Sioux Falls was: Could they find material of sufficient strength today? Was this the right place to try it?

The idea was intriguing. If they were correct, *Earthwinds* could fly virtually without ballast for weeks. Raven and the American-Soviet Balloon Venture signed an agreement shortly thereafter for construction of the two-balloon craft and for an engineering study.

Lachenmeier wanted empirical data. First, he needed to find a fabric strong enough to hold air under pressure.

Kevlar, a rugged duPont material in wide use, was rejected as not strong enough for this application. There was another option. In 1985 Allied-Signal Corp. had developed a new synthetic called Spectra, spun from a solution of ultra high molecular weight polyethylene. Spectra was strong, lightweight, easy to stitch together, and resisted ultraviolet light and water. As a bonus, it had low permeability, near-zero elasticity and did not conduct electricity.

Allied Signal marketed Spectra to makers of cut-resistant surgical gloves, sail cloth, bullet resistant vests, tennis rackets, artificial ligaments and other products. In rope form, Spectra was used in commercial fishing nets, rock climbing ropes, archery, competition kites and parachute lines. The company claimed Spectra was 10 times stronger than steel at one-seventh the weight.

Lachenmeier advised Allied-Signal of Spectra's proposed use. Larry knew one of the directors, former astronaut Gen. Tom Stafford. One afternoon while the Allied board met in Phoenix, Stafford brought them over to Scottsdale to see the capsule.

Larry and Lynne hosted a backyard cookout for the board, describing the project. They won the board's endorsement for a donation of all of the Spectra fabric they needed: 1,500 yards for experimentation and 3,500 yards for the actual flight. The gift was worth more than $200,000.

Lachenmeier tested a 10-foot scale model of the anchor on a hot air balloon flight. He found that the anchor balloon's weight could be increased at higher elevations, confirming both the theoretical data and the integrity of Spectra fabric.

But constructing and flying an anchor balloon would cost a great deal more money, and make the operation considerably more complicated.

Tim, Tillamook and the trial

Still, Lachenmeier insisted on a larger-scale test of the anchor balloon, a 'proof of concept' experiment. Although his company's responsibility usually ceased with the delivery of its products, Lachenmeier arranged to take personal leave to consult with Larry on *Earthwinds*. From the beginning, Lachenmeier devoted his vacation days to the project. As a result, his value as design engineer and unpaid consultant soared in Larry's eyes.

For the prototype flight, Raven built a 60-foot-diameter polyethylene balloon and a 50-foot-diameter anchor balloon lined with a plastic bladder. They budgeted $100,000.

The anchor balloon was fitted with electrical fans at the top and bottom, both supplied by a division of Allied Signal. In flight, the top fan would keep the balloon pressurized, and the bottom valve would vent air during depressurization. The capsule built by Rutan for the global flight was far too big and heavy for use on the small-scale prototype, so for a gondola, Larry and Don Moses mounted some aluminum poles on a plywood board, and laced red canvas between them. They side-mounted two Honda engines and a Bendix aircraft generator on one side of the open gondola. One engine would power the electric fans in the anchor balloon; the other would power the microwave oven and electrical equipment.

They wanted to inflate both balloons and inspect them before flight, so a blimp hangar was vital, preferably one on the West Coast. A two- or three-day test flight could carry them 2,000 miles, and they needed running room. Tim helped Larry secure the blimp hangar at Tillamook on the Oregon coast.

In mid-August, Vladimir met Larry in Phoenix. While they were flying a small Cessna to Tillamook, Larry became critical of Vladimir's flying skills. Unlike American astronauts, cosmonauts' flying days are virtually finished as soon as they are selected: there are no T-38 'personal jets' (or any airplanes) available to the cosmonauts. They focus only on spacecraft training. Larry later would tell people that Vladimir couldn't hold a heading—he had been away from the controls for more than two decades.

At one side of the old Tillamook hangar sat the Cyclocrane, an experimental airship used for logging in the Pacific Northwest.

At the other end was a blimp made for Richard Branson's Virgin Lightship Co. The day after painting the Virgin Lightship logo on the hull, an 11-man ground crew was walking the airship out of the shed. A severe side gust blew the blimp into a parked truck and destroyed the envelope. It was a lesson in handling buoyant aircraft around hangars.

Richard Branson was due to arrive from London for the prototype flight, but ballooning weather was not soon in coming, so they waited.

Branson had sent to the site one of his favorite photographers, Mark Greenberg, who had also covered the Voyager airplane project.

After three weeks, Bob Rice called and told them they had a green light: wind would be light from the west.

Since there was enough lift in the 125,000-cubic feet *Earthwinds* prototype balloon for a four-person crew—and it was apparent that Branson wasn't going to get there in time—Larry invited Don Moses to join Lachenmeier, Dzhanibekov and him on the test flight. Don appreciated the reward for his hard work:

'I waited for a long time to see if I was going to be on this flight,' he beamed.

The anchor balloon was inflated first and lightly pressurized. Larry and Tim supervised inflation of the polyethylene balloon in daylight inside the hangar. With all of its uncertainties, Larry said he felt more anxious about this test flight than he had before the Atlantic or Pacific attempts.

'It's pretty sophisticated. Everything has to work perfectly to get airborne. If the anchor balloon explodes, it could kill us.'

It was dangerous for other reasons, too. The crew knew that they could be carried well past the Rocky Mountains. Every landing in a balloon is a controlled crash, and this basket offered little protection from a tumbled landing. Not only did they need light wind for the ascent, but also for the descent.

In calm early morning winds, on Sept. 8, 1990, a volunteer ground party lifted the anchor balloon and carried it across the runway opposite the sliding hangar door. The 61-foot tall helium balloon appeared next, pulled from the hangar at the business end of a bright yellow tow truck. As the gondola was moved into position, wind began rustling the anchor balloon, which was held on ground by volunteers. It began rolling away like a beach ball.

Sixty spectators surged forward with open hands raised high and helped restrain the white Spectra balloon. They saved the big globe. A quick decision was made to retreat back into the hangar. The anchor balloon was proving that it could be a beast.

During the day, the makeshift basket was attached to the balloon inside the hangar. The wind settled at dusk and the team brought everything outside again. Winches slowly raised the gondola high over the huge anchor balloon. Triangulating cables held the gondola in place. In this awkward position, with the flight crew suspended from the balloon the aircraft radios failed. The flight crew could not communicate with the launch crew! They switched to simple citizens-band radios. The crew realized the balloon was not yet buoyant. They needed 4,200 pounds of lift, and were several hundred pounds short. Emergency sand ballast was dropped, the balloon stirred, the lines (weighing 250 pounds) were cut away, and *Earthwinds*' prototype double balloon slipped quietly into the cold night air.

The balloon stopped at 3,000 feet. The physics were such that in less dense upper air, the anchor balloon filled out and pressurized, essentially 'parking' the whole balloon at a fixed altitude. When Larry and Tim remembered to open the anchor balloon valve, the ascent continued.

They rose to 20,000 feet then dropped back to about 17,500 feet. There, they stabilized the altitude by closing the bottom valve on the anchor balloon and adding 300 pounds of pressurized air to it.

None of the exhausted crew had rested during the day. At high altitude, it was bitter cold. They drew every breath through canulas (nose oxygen), which dried out their nasal passages.

They waited out the night, all very uncomfortable in this flimsy, experimental craft.

At daybreak, the sun warmed the helium. Normally a gas balloon would then rise and vent excess helium out. On this experimental craft, Don turned on the engine; he and Larry pumped air into the anchor balloon, and then closed its valve. This was the critical test. The balloon drifted up a few hundred feet and then the ascent stopped. The *Earthwinds* prototype was successfully using its 'airbrakes'. Lachenmeier, who had busied himself measuring temperature and loads on the anchor balloon, calculated that based on overnight performance of the polyethylene-and-anchor-balloon combination, it had a theoretical duration of 10 days.

A chase plane with Jeana Yeager, Lynne Newman and the film crew came by in the morning. Jeana chatting with the balloonists as they passed Mt. Ranier made dramatic shots for Wilcox's movie.

Greenberg's spectacular pictures would symbolize the project for years afterward.

Don Moses, making his first balloon ascent, found that Larry's anxiety dissolved once airborne. He was surprised that Larry shared decision-making with Tim, Vladimir and himself, asking for their opinions and listening to them. In fact, Larry's whole conduct of the flight instilled renewed confidence in Don.

'He's good up there. That's his element,' Don said.

The balloon flew level all day at 18,000 feet, drifting slowly eastward. At darkness going into the second night, the crew opened the valve on anchor balloon a bit, eased out 475 pounds of compressed air, closed the valve again, and maintained altitude within 100 feet of 17,750 feet.

The experiment was proving its worth during the second night, but eastward progress was slow. The ground speed was less than five mph. But this was a physics test, not a distance contest. Having proved what they wanted to know—that they could maintain a fixed altitude—they decided to land in the morning.

Before daybreak, they began to unpressurize the anchor balloon and valve helium from the top balloon. Then the electrical cable connecting the anchor balloon fan to the balloon fell out! Suddenly, they couldn't operate the anchor balloon. The beast was three-fourths full. The plan had been to empty the anchor balloon and use its drawn-out shape as a conventional trail rope.

They had no choice but to descend 'as is' and let it bounce. If the sun came up with the lower balloon disabled, they would rise way up, and come down at sunset without ballast, completely out of control. They had to land before superheat acted on the helium—under the worst possible landing scenario, with the great beach ball dangling below them.

They drifted toward the ground in darkness, without emergency ballast for altitude control. The wind freshened to about 15 mph. The anchor balloon hit the ground with so much air trapped inside that it rebounded, then bounced up 100 feet, hop scotching two and a half miles.

Ahead in the darkness were power lines...the nemesis of every aviator. The anchor balloon hit the lines. Contact with the Spectra fabric, electrically non-conductive when dry, produced flames and sparks because the big balloon was moist in the morning air.

The basket tipped at a sharp angle, and Larry opened the helium valve, releasing gas. The anchor balloon dragged over the wires and the basket settled to the ground. After 31 hours in the air, they had landed in Omak, Washington, near Boeing's test airfield.

'It was the smoothest landing I've ever had in my entire flying career,' Larry told Wilcox's film crew.

'On this flight we didn't throw away anything, which is extraordinary; it's probably a revolution in ballooning,' he exuded. 'This balloon could have easily flown across the Atlantic, the continent and the Pacific all in one flight.'

A more reserved Lachenmeier said the test flight was 'proof of concept.' It stood on its own as a significant scientific achievement.

'I sure wish Ben could be here to see this,' Larry told Bob Rice. 'Hey, I'll bet even old Maxie Anderson would be proud of me now.'

Based on a lengthy Popular Science cover story published in November 1990, the *Earthwinds* prototype flight was named the 1990 award winner in category of Aviation and Space. ESPN broadcast Wilcox's 30-minute film about the test flight, and the project began to get some public attention.

The Gulf war and a gulf of misunderstanding

Larry still wanted to pressure- and temperature-check the capsule. Unfortunately, none of NASA's facilities would be available until after February. A launch in the target weather window of November-February was beginning to look unlikely.

On the other side of the world, Saddam Hussein had sent his army into Kuwait on August 2, 1990. Within weeks, it was clear that the region could be the site of a major battle, as a coalition of nations became arrayed against the Iraqi aggression. Seeing news reports of the streams of refugees coming out of Iraq and into neighboring Jordan, Richard Branson rushed a fleet of Virgin Atlantic jumbo jets with relief supplies. He administered a relief program personally while Larry Newman made the test flight in Oregon.

With the likelihood of war in the Persian Gulf, it became obvious that the safety of any free-floating balloon manned by representatives of the coalition nations could not be guaranteed over those hostile skies. Besides, the *Earthwinds* preparations were taking longer than anticipated. The capsule was not yet outfitted, the engine tests hadn't proved satisfactory, and there was much more to do.

In England, completely unbeknownst to Larry, Richard Branson and Per Lindstrand were quietly planning to renew their attempt at crossing the Pacific Ocean in a hot air balloon. Larry was angry when he learned that Branson was returning to Japan to try again the hot air balloon flight across the Pacific that had failed the previous year. Branson was supposed to be preparing to fly around the world with Larry's crew. Instead, he was off trying to break a world record that Larry had set.

Branson's Pacific Flyer was a hot air balloon whose volume of 2.6 million cubic feet was the largest ever built; 12 burners were fed by propane stored in six giant tanks mounted outside.

Branson and Lindstrand ascended on January 15, 1991, to a cruising level of 27,000 feet, dashing across the Pacific Ocean at speeds up to 200 mph. Forty-six hours after taking off, they crunched down on a frozen lake in the Northwest Territories—153 miles from the nearest road and 220 miles from Yellowknife, the nearest town.

Having survived the perilous flight, Branson and Lindstrand almost died on the lake awaiting rescue; the temperature was minus 40; they had no fresh water and had slept little for the past 48 hours. A massive snowstorm had grounded press and rescue helicopters. A bush pilot happened to be in the air so he could get better radio reception on news about the beginning of the air campaign against Iraq in the Gulf War, Jan. 16, 1991. He heard the balloonists' signal and finally directed rescue traffic inbound.

Branson and Lindstrand had flown 6,761 miles that by one measure (route flown) eclipsed the absolute distance record in ballooning set by Double Eagle V.

Larry Newman disputed the claim, asserting that the correct way to measure was point-to-point great circle distance. In his view, Branson had not broken Double Eagle's record.

Branson and Lindstrand found after landing that they still had 24 hours of fuel remaining; if they hadn't accidentally dropped the two full tanks over the ocean, Lindstrand said they could have flown 97 hours—enough, he said, 'to cover at least half of the Earth's circumference.'

It was a signal to Larry that Branson might try his own global flight.

The ultimate room with a view

Larry continued hauling passengers for America West while Don and Carol and the rest of the growing *Earthwinds* crew continued working on the capsule. One morning in April 1991, Larry was sitting in a coffee shop at the O'Hare Hilton Hotel during a layover in Chicago. Sniffling from a head cold, he looked up and recognized one of his flight attendants.

'I'm Erin Porter. I'm on your crew,' she said.

'Come over and sit with me,' he said, 'I am about to be interviewed.'

'Why would somebody interview you?' she asked.

'Well, I am going to fly a balloon around the world.'

Curious, Erin listened as Larry described his project to Norm Peterson of the Experimental Aircraft Association. The more she learned, the more enthusiastic she became. The spirit of aviation was in her blood.

Her father had owned a Beechcraft Bonanza executive airplane back in Grand Rapids, and she had worked as a research assistant for Harry Combs, a wealthy fixed-base operator from Denver, on his film about Wilbur and Orville Wright, 'How Strong is the Wind.'

She had worked for America West since early 1985, a little longer than Larry.

Larry mentioned the need for additional sponsorship—this venture was beginning to cost a great deal more than he and Wilcox had anticipated. Erin, bubbling with enthusiasm, knew plenty of people who were potential sponsors. Larry gave her a videotape of the test flight and the Popular Science magazine story. She discussed the project with her friend Combs, who soon thereafter invited her to lunch at the Barron Hilton Invitational Golf Tournament in Las Vegas. Combs knew someone who might help.

Barron Hilton, chairman of the Hilton Hotels Corp., was an aviator himself with glider and fixed-wing ratings. He had loved Combs' documentary film on the Wright brothers. Every two years Hilton threw a big party for hang glider enthusiasts at the Flying M, his Nevada ranch. In 1985, he had wanted to sponsor Voyager, the airplane that flew around the world, but Dick Rutan and Jeana Yeager decided not to relinquish control of the project, and they never came to terms. Later, at the suggestion of his friend Malcolm Forbes, Hilton had taken up ballooning.

Hilton had crisp command and chief executive written all over him. His powerful voice rang out with distinct long open vowels that sounded as if they had just rolled off a dry western prairie. His perpetual tan, silver hair, and a massive, ever-present cigar, punctuated his presence. He was host and friend to the famous—after all, Zsa-Zsa Gabor had been his stepmother and Elizabeth Taylor his sister-in-law. Trained to think on a global scale, the 64-year-old executive possessed a natural flair for marketing and promotion. His personal wealth of nearly one billion dollars—he controlled one-fourth of the stock of his company—facilitated a grand lifestyle.

Combs led Erin, the young flight attendant, into Hilton's office, and they got right down to business. To the right of Hilton's desk was a VCR, where he punched up the videotape of the *Earthwinds* prototype flight. After one minute, he stopped it.

'What does it take to be a sponsor?' he asked. 'These guys are away from home, they'll be sleeping in this thing, eating in it, communicating from it, but it's not their home. It's like a hotel room—so what's wrong with calling it the *Earthwinds* Hilton?'

Warming to the idea, Hilton called Larry a week later and peppered him with questions. At the end of the call, just to be sure, he asked, 'What was your name again?'

'He didn't even remember my name,' a dispirited Larry told Erin. He had lived through many of these disheartening pro-forma calls before.

They exchanged letters and set up a meeting, however, and Hilton soon agreed to a $500,000 sponsorship role. The capsule would become known as the *Earthwinds* Hilton. The deal's terms allowed Hilton to send $50,000 right away, but company lawyers insisted on a performance incentive clause: the remaining $450,000 would be released when the balloon reached 18,000 feet.

John Wilcox promised Erin a five percent finder's fee; her introduction would be worth $25,000. She agreed to help market the adventure.

Into a space chamber

By May 1991, after two years of work, Larry could assess his progress: he had a flight crew (despite his increasing unease with Branson), the valuable experience of a test flight with new technology and materials behind him, significant national publicity, two major sponsors and lots of in-kind equipment contributions. He still had to figure out how to run the mechanical system inside the capsule, but those solutions would come, he knew. The new launch window was the four-month cold period from November through February.

Don Moses was sanding, smoothing, rounding and outfitting the capsule, now parked in a hangar at Scottsdale Airpark. In the evenings and on his days off, Larry would join him. They attracted a string of visitors. Some, like Fred Gorrel, who ran a Phoenix hot air balloon ride business, wanted to be around to help with the launch. Others camped out at the Newmans' home. Steve Ericson, the brilliant bearded engineer from Rutan's factory, arrived for an extended stay, while he helped construct the engine compartment and outfit the capsule.

Several employees from Phoenix-area divisions of Allied-Signal donated time to help outfit the capsule. They built an instrument console to house all of the navigation and communication inside the capsule. Allied-Signal manufactured so many materials and instruments of value that the project became heavily dependent upon the firm: the Spectra fabric, Bendix-King radios, an ozone filter, pressurization fans, encoding altimeters; it was a long list.

Among those who stopped by for a look was Vern Rich, a transplanted Baton Rouge mechanical engineer who had earned a living building aircraft and automotive prototype parts. His specialty was restoring vintage racecars; he was proud of his role fabricating systems on a world speed record-setting Porsche 930 on the Bonneville Salt Flats. Rich himself once took a Porsche up to 220 miles per hour on a stretch of Arizona freeway.

'Aw...it was a limited access road,' he would shrug when asked about this bit of bravado. Larry and Don quickly discerned that his talent for building their engine derived naturally from such experience.

'The skills required in building a racing car,' Rich noted, 'are exactly the same as those needed in building the *Earthwinds* system. You just need high-performance, low-weight, fuel-efficient engines.'

He signed on as an *Earthwinds* employee and became devoted to fabricating engine parts, designing specialized components for the heat exchanger, working with Steve Ericson to bring the concept to reality, and then installing, testing and altering dozens of carefully machined parts.

Larry desperately wanted to conduct tests under simulated conditions to ensure that all the systems would perform as planned. Too much could go wrong in the air, and then there would be no turning back. He needed assurance that the Honda engines and the screw compressor would perform in both low pressure and low temperature environment.

How would he conduct floatation tests? Where was the vessel's waterline? How high would it ride in the sea? He had spent seven months negotiating with NASA about when he might slip into one of their test facilities, but still there was no time available.

By chance, he heard about the McDonnell Douglas Space Systems Center in Huntington Beach, California. He was amazed when company officials invited him to ship the capsule there right away. Without enthusiastic corporate contributions of people and facilities like this, *Earthwinds* would never have been able to go on. To lease the place and hire the staff, the McDonnell test facilities would have cost $600,000, he estimated.

So, early in June, Larry and Don found themselves trailering the capsule 400 miles west to the 246-acre McDonnell Douglas complex in Huntington Beach. Early one Saturday morning, a dozen engineers from the aerospace company showed up to conduct the tests.

But before they could begin the pressure test, they had to solve another problem: the Honda generators were cutting out. They traced the problem to two faulty spark plugs, and replaced them. The capsule was placed inside the 39-foot diameter space simulation chamber for the altitude tests. Larry, Don and the McDonnell Douglas aerospace scientists crowded into a control room next to the vacuum chamber. North Selvey served as test director; Norm Knobloch, who had helped build the facility, was among those who had volunteered off-work hours to the project.

Richard Branson had come over for his first look at the capsule in which he would ride.

Because no chamber could yet replicate both the extremes of temperature and the extremes of pressure, two tests had to be run: first for pressure, then for the minus-60-degree temperature. Selvey adjusted the instruments to simulate the atmospheric pressure in the jet stream. They turned on the engines, sealed the capsule by cranking the handles on the pressure doors, and waited. Nearly an hour later, the chamber's atmospheric pressure matched that of the earth's at seven miles high. The test showed that the capsule leaked and was far too noisy: the whining screw compressor would fatigue the crew in the short run and become intolerable in the long run.

After the altitude testing, the capsule was moved to the Underwater Test Facility, a 50-foot diameter, 35-foot deep pool. A crane lowered the capsule into the water. Larry and Don boarded and ran from one side of the capsule to the other trying to tilt it, but the capsule floated upright, high in the water. It satisfied them both.

Branson and two aides, his public relations director Wil Whitehorn and balloon director Michael Kendrick, joined Larry and John Wilcox in filming scenes at the McDonnell Douglas lab.

Afterward, Larry and John again pressed for technical assistance in light of Richard's Atlantic and Pacific flights. Kendrick then explained that the information Larry and John were requesting was proprietary to Lindstrand's company.

And Lindstrand had just been ousted as president, so there was no hope of ever getting that information.

Branson raised other issues. His logo wasn't visible enough on the capsule. He wanted signage prominently on the anchor balloon. Of course, there had been no anchor balloon when Branson and Newman signed the original terms of sponsorship. The contract with Virgin was renegotiated by mutual consent, providing additional exposure for Virgin.

As long as there was an anchor balloon, Virgin Atlantic Airways would appear prominently on the skirt.

Branson also suggested the addition of a fourth crewmember. He had met Japanese balloonist Sabu Ichiyoshi, Japan's leading hot air balloonist, while awaiting weather for his Pacific flight. Virgin Atlantic Airways flew scheduled service into Tokyo, and Canon expressed interest in having a Japanese pilot aboard; the addition of a Japanese pilot would excite the Japanese media. Virgin produced a Japanese-language *Earthwinds* brochure with profiles of Newman, Dzhanibekov, Branson and Ichiyoshi. But Larry had little interest in adding another crewmember—particularly Sabu, who had recently crash-landed a balloon in the Himalayas.

One reporter who knew Larry had seen the way other reporters swooned over Branson. It was clear that if Larry, Vladimir and John Wilcox were well known in their fields, Branson was regarded as a megastar.

'How are you going to handle Branson's ego,' asked Bob Downing, 'and the fact that wherever he goes Branson steals the spotlight?'

'I don't know how well I'm going to handle that,' Larry admitted. 'I know it's going to be a problem. I can see it coming. I'm worried about it.'

◆ ◆ ◆

The *Earthwinds* team returned to McDonnell Douglas in late July, for more temperature-altitude testing of the engine, air compressor, and heat exchangers. The space engineers donated their time after hours and on weekends. This was a unique challenge, and only their facility had the equipment to conduct tests that would enable the *Earthwinds* capsule to work as designed. A second test would verify the design changes under simulated flight environments.

In August 1991, John Ackroyd and Alex Ritchie traveled to Phoenix to review with Larry the changes made and the work scheduled. They reported positive progress to Branson, who promptly wrote a letter stating how pleased he was with the status of the project, and complimenting Larry on his excellent work.

Hummingbirds

Meanwhile, back at America West, things were not going well. The young airline was hemorrhaging money, having lost $75 million in the previous year. Routes were being eliminated and schedules cut back. The combined effects of price wars, higher fuel prices and a recession were squeezing the company. Late in June, America West filed for bankruptcy court protection. The stock that employees were required to buy fell overnight from $7.50 a share to 87 cents a share. Those thousands of shares Larry and other workers owned were the employees' personal retirement plan. Now Larry had to request an unpaid leave of absence from a company whose very existence was in jeopardy.

The Newmans' primary investment was their sprawling five-bedroom Spanish-style house in an upscale subdivision in the northeast corner of Scottsdale. They each had kept their own houses and bought a big one together. The house they loved, along with the Lincoln, the BMW and the lifestyle that came with these symbols was a far cry from Lynne's troubled girlhood in south Cleveland and Larry's broken family life in Fresno.

They upgraded the home and spent $80,000 on a patio and a 44-foot lap pool behind the house. Hummingbird feeders surrounded the idyllic patio—the honeysuckle, bottlebrush and cantanas were Lynne's favorites—and artificial rocks in which they stashed barbecue tongs, scuba gear, swimsuits and towels.

When they could get away, their favorite destination was a three-hour drive north to a 16-mile long stretch of cold rippling water just below the Glen Canyon Dam, where Larry and Lynne obsessed on fly-fishing for trout, the elite form of sport fishing.

Nary an ounce of fat grew on them. They stayed trim with an almost ascetic diet, a high rate of metabolism and plenty of outdoor activities.

But the balloon project crowded out their leisure time, and their personal relationship encountered serious newlywed strains. There was barely time to work things out. In the two years of their marriage, their house had become headquarters for a loose aggregation of 50 or so people working on the project. Strangers moved in. After Vladimir was recruited, the government of the Soviet Union sent a woman to live with the Newmans for two and a half months so she could teach them elementary Russian; Lynne complained that she refused to assume any household responsibilities like cooking or cleaning, choosing instead to spent a great deal of time at shopping malls and watching television.

The phones rang all day long, and then rang in the middle of the night with calls from London and from Moscow. Lynne was trying to manage her life insurance business from an office in the house by days—though, ironically, could find no policy that would insure her husband, given his impending adventure.

While flying for the airline 12 days a month, Larry spent virtually every spare day working on the capsule in the hangar over at Scottsdale Airpark.

Steve Ericson, who had designed the capsule at Scaled Composites, came to Scottsdale and occupied a spare bedroom.

Maj. Gen. Phil Conley, a retired Air Force officer who formerly commanded the Flight Test Center at Edwards Air Force Base, was serving as *Earthwinds'* program manager.

Conley, Vern Rich, Steve Ericson and a host of others were passing through the house at all hours. Don Moses and his bright-eyed companion Carol Hart had been living with them for seven months.

Carol and Lynne quickly found themselves at odds. Lynne believed that Carol crossed the line of decency when she contacted Larry's old girlfriend and invited her to the house for the weekend.

Lynne hit the roof! It further galled her not only that Carol wouldn't help with household chores, but also that Carol asked for overtime pay to help with dinner.

'I never had trouble being sociable with anyone,' Lynne would say. 'I like people. I was elected president of our homeowners association, and elected to local, regional and state office in Civitan. But I couldn't deal with a woman in my own home who was undermining everything I said or did.

'She would tell my husband lies about me. I had no doubt that she was jealous and was trying to break us up. Carol had no husband, no children, and no property. She just drifted, and lived in a trailer with Don, and he certainly wasn't going to marry her.'

At night, Carol and Don would come back to the house with Larry and eat a dinner Lynne had made; they would talk all evening about the project, about flying, things that excluded Lynne. These strangers, though friends of Larry, were free spirits, independent, carefree, unflappable. They talked easily about Don's past, and Lynne was appalled at the things she heard. She thought that Carol, who ignored her, was the root of much that had come between her and her new husband.

'Carol knew that if she got me out of the project, she would be the highest-ranking woman in *Earthwinds*!' Lynne recalled.

Lynne could stand it no more. Feeling that she was about to lose Larry, she was ready to pack her bags and leave. At the last moment, retired Air Force General Phil Conley, who had been serving as project manager, had a 'Dutch uncle' talk with Larry, and his intervention began the healing. Lynne gave Larry a choice of marriage counselors. Furthermore, she insisted that all these people had to get out of her house.

She and Larry began counseling sessions, which continued until late September, when the project schedule demanded that Larry, Don, Carol and Vern drive the capsule to Ohio. Lynne stayed behind to answer the phone and manage her insurance business.

4

Inside the Pressure Cooker

Keeping the lid on

Larry established a communication system resembling a bicycle wheel: he was the hub, and all the spokes of information ran to him.

Volunteers were summoned, worked their butts off, and disappeared into the ether when their portion was done, or when they had had enough.

Gen. Conley left the project when it moved to Ohio in the summer of 1991. He handed out bumper stickers to some of the volunteers reading, 'Have you flogged your crew today?'

Shortly after arriving in Cleveland, Larry told a group of reporters that he was adding Don Moses to the flight crew, a ploy aimed at forcing Branson's hand, Don had worked hard for more than two years, flown on the test flight, and had a crucial role maintaining the engines. Don was painfully reluctant to talk with reporters; media was a new realm for him.

Within a few days, Larry received an anonymous phone call. A voice told him to watch out for Moses…things in his background could be very embarrassing. Larry's heart leaped into his throat, but before confronting Don, he asked his lawyer to check on the information the anonymous caller had offered.

◆　　◆　　◆

NASA's Lewis Research Center, (later renamed the for John Glenn), was known for its work on advanced and exotic engines. NASA assigned engineers to help solve the festering engine cooling system problems. The four-month winter launch window would open in 30 days. Nearly everyone at the NASA center was eager to help; the agency's logo was painted on the hull, and Earthwinds had the official blessing of headquarters in Washington.

Right away, two serious problems were discovered: the capsule couldn't pass a pressure test, and the engines generated an excessive amount of heat. 600 cubic feet of air per minute seeped through equipment holes that had been hurriedly drilled through its shell and inadequately sealed. NASA's engineers supplied RTV, a silicon caulking compound.

The problem of diverting engine heat was more complicated. The capsule was insulated so well that the engines regularly overheated during the initial testing. Second, heat in a high-altitude engine creates special problems: fuel boils at only 150 degrees in the carburetor float bowls, and the engines run less efficiently, at 8 horsepower instead of 12. The engines gulped cabin air 'thickened' by the screw compressor. The screw compressor consumed so much air that the engines could barely keep up—and it, too, generated heat. As a result, there was barely enough air remaining in the cabin for three persons.

NASA recommended external heat exchangers. Air or liquid coolant could be piped outside, where the temperature was minus-60, and then recirculated into the engine. The heat exchangers would have to be custom-built.

Vern Rich designed a liquid coolant system to remove heat from the engine compartment. NASA engineers came up with a special glycol-and-water coolant suitable for use at high altitude.

The idea was that cool liquid running into the screw compressor would pull heat out through the exhaust manifolds.

The exhaust manifold heat was drawn off through a hose down to a plate on the capsule floor. The exhaust had a short retractable bellows with a valve on top. The coolant went through the valve hole, was forced around the exhaust pipes and into the radiator outside, where a thermostat governed the amount of air blowing it. The coolant then returned to the screw compressor.

'Through the testing we did at NASA,' Larry explained to visitors, 'we learned that air density has more potential for cooling, because of its mass, than temperature does. If you take the sea level pressure, which is 14.7 psi and reduce it to only 3.5 psi, it's gotten so thin that its ability to remove heat is diminished.

'For example, if you want to cool off a cup of hot water, blowing on it is not as effective as dropping a piece of ice in it. It doesn't have anything to do with the size of the ice versus how much air you can blow; it's the density of the medium. Density of altitude is our culprit. We learned that we can keep the engine compartment cool enough to keep running.'

From a Honda NSX racecar, Larry took an air conditioning fan to blow air into a second large heat exchanger mounted externally. That air came back into the capsule as cool air and circulated through the engine compartment for an alternative method of keeping the engine compartment cool.

The NASA chamber was only available after normal work hours. Larry, Don, Carol and Vern Rich would work all day to prepare the engines and capsule to run a single test. One evening, with the capsule sealed inside the chamber and the engine running, a hose clamp broke and sprayed hot engine coolant all over the entire inside of the capsule. The test was shut down. A day's work was lost.

Virgin Atlantic dispatched engineering consultants Alex Ritchie and John Ackroyd to attend some of the NASA testing sessions. They prepared a lengthy 'punch list' of problems that had to be solved before they would certify it for launch, and allow Branson to fly in it.

Among the changes they insisted upon was a second screw compressor. For one thing, it would increase the density of capsule air, increasing the margin of safety. If the single screw compressor onboard failed, the crew would die. Larry told them that he would study their suggestions. He already knew that there wasn't enough cool fresh air to support a second screw compressor in the cabin. Besides, he thought, it was too late to start changing the capsule around. Other suggestions Ackroyd and Ritchie made included the addition of quick shut-off valves for all fuel lines. Despite that, Ackroyd told Branson that the balloon was unsafe to fly, that it was 'a suicide mission' without many more changes.

The Ackroyd-Ritchie report created considerable bitterness. Larry certainly did not consider it a detailed analysis of the project's technology nor, as Kendrick called it, an 'independent consultant's report'.

Kendrick began pestering Wilcox and Newman about disallowing use of the Virgin name on the project. Virgin offered additional financing if Larry would wait a year and incorporate the changes that the analysts recommended. Branson hoped that would give Larry and John time to line up enough additional sponsors to buy out his portion of the project. But Larry and John suspected that Branson might be preparing his own around-the-world flight. Virgin threatened a court injunction to stop the flight.

Larry continued working on refinements that would keep the engine running, the temperatures down, and the capsule pressurized.

The long trial-and-error process was taking an emotional toll on Larry. Lynne was back at home; he was trying to build his team and assemble all the components. Don Moses, his acquaintance of more than 20 years, thought he knew how to deal with Larry's moods. Once in the middle of a design dispute, when Don knew he was right and Larry persisted, Don jabbed his finger into Larry's chest and said, 'Now shut up and sit down.' As he sank back into his chair, Larry listened to Don, and began crying.

Interacting

None of the engineering setbacks, commercial squabbles or emotional strains became public. There were appearances to maintain! John Wilcox had booked a live, one-hour, broadcast on ESPN with the flight crew for Nov. 1, the first day of the four-month launch window. ESPN would reach out to schoolchildren in six American cities linked via satellite. On the air, the three original *Earthwinds* aeronauts—Larry, Richard and Vladimir—along with Tim Lachenmeier and NASA's Erik Mollo-Christiansen, would answer the students' questions.

Wilcox invited a former Miss America, Sharlene Hawkes, to anchor the telecast and become ESPN's *Earthwinds* reporter and on-air talent.

ESPN donated $75,000 to print color brochures to thousands of school children. Kids who had studied ESPN's promotional literature could go on live TV and direct their questions to the *Earthwinds* team.

On the first day of November, Larry flew to Hartford with Vladimir, who had just arrived back in the U.S. Branson flew in from England, arriving moments before airtime with a trail of aides. He had little time to visit with Larry or Vladimir, although on the air he talked enthusiastically of his association with the project, the challenge and his humble place in it. After the broadcast, he exited as quickly as he had entered.

For Branson, *Earthwinds* was requiring an inordinate amount of time and attention, and was producing very little return. By now, he was hoping to get his money out with his company's reputation intact.

Alex Ritchie and John Ackroyd returned to England before the final weekend of testing at NASA, when the engine was finally performing at pressurization equal to that at 40,000 feet. Larry awaited word on whether Branson would still participate.

◆　　◆　　◆

In anticipation of hosting the project in Akron for its final pre-launch phase, Loral Defense Systems assigned Fred Nebiker, a vice president, to made arrangements. Nebiker's assistant Joan Reisig, a local balloonist who worked in the airship design department, identified a core group of 60 local volunteers, including retired Goodyear electricians and local balloonists with special skills.

My name had appeared on a volunteer list, too. Larry telephoned me at my office in New York City. At that time, we knew one another only by reputation: Larry as a pilot who had flown with men I admired, and I as a balloonist who had been a reporter and writer.

Larry described his project and asked if I would volunteer to handle his press relations and work with the sponsors. Then he made a startling admission.

'I am not an easy person to work with, so don't take things personally,' he said. I replied that I knew him by reputation and was prepared to deal with whatever came up.

Within days, I met John Wilcox in New York. As Larry's partner, he approved my assignment and my plan for marketing the project. I flew to Akron to meet Larry and become familiar with the project. I would take over full-time media duties during special events or in the weeks before launch, relieving Lynne of the burden of serving as both spokesperson and administrative director.

Reisig also recommended that Larry call Mike Emich, an Akron firefighter who was a life-long flying enthusiast. From boyhood, Emich had learned about gas ballooning from the legends of the sport, Goodyear's racing balloonists of the 30's. As a youth, Mike built model balloons and won trophies for their performance. He held fixed-wing aviation ratings for commercial multiengine land, instruments, as well as hot air and gas ballooning, and had more than a thousand parachute jumps to his credit.

I had known Emich for many years. We flew gas balloons together, and on one flight, we set a national distance record. Low-key and self-confident, Emich loved the air and everything that flew in it. When he started visiting the NASA facility in Cleveland, we began sharing all we knew about this project.

'When I first met Larry,' Emich recalled, 'I asked about engineering drawings, for documentation of the changes they were making. He said they had no time for drawings, but that they were videotaping every change made in the capsule.'

Emich was astonished at this procedure, which would haunt the team months later, but he was quickly hooked on *Earthwinds'* goal.

Another person on Reisig's list was Don Overs, the senior member of our gas balloon club. A mechanical engineer, Overs had written a book on balloon lifting gases and personally had flown in helium, hydrogen, coal gas and natural gas balloons. We regarded his aeronautical advice as gospel.

Overs met with Larry in Akron in October. He made a number of suggestions regarding launch procedures and equipment. His most emphatic suggestion in a memo to Newman was to use dehydrated air in the anchor balloon.

'Water in the form of vapor present in contained air cannot remain in that condition at higher altitudes,' Overs wrote. 'Some will condense within and on elements within the balloon (valves and balloon material) and freeze while some will be expelled with the expanding air and make its presence visible as fog or snow.'

Overs also recommended a launch procedure substantially different from the one used at Tillamook. Fill the anchor balloon with enough helium mixed with dry air to make it nearly buoyant, he said. That would simplify ground handling; the anchor balloon would ascend alongside the capsule until it began to gain altitude, and then assume a trailing position below the capsule.

The monolith on Shorty's field

The City of Akron was eager to host Larry Newman and his magnificent flying machine. Most everyone thought he had come to the right place, for the story of Akron was essentially America's story of lighter-than-air flight.

South of town lies a flat expanse within a 1,000-acre bowl where in the go-go years of the early twentieth century, barnstormers landed aeroplanes. B.F. 'Shorty' Fulton began landing there long before he became the city's airport commissioner.

But the focal point of these flat acres was a black steel monolith erected for a single purpose: to house massive lighter-than-air ships built for the Navy. Goodyear had purchased the Zeppelin company patent rights from Germany after World War I. When Congress authorized two 785-foot long prototype rigid airships, Goodyear-Zeppelin won the contract. But first the company needed a new hangar, which acquired the nautical nickname airdock.

The airdock became Akron's most visible symbol—the biggest structure in the world without internal supports. Its roof stood 211 feet above the floor; from stem to stern, it measured 1,175 feet long; from port to starboard, 325 feet; the floor covers eight and a half acres.

A great lore built up around the place. Ripley's 'Believe it or not' repeated the popular assertion that 'it rains inside this waterproof building!'

Construction of the airships introduced an amazing variety of skills to the Akron work force: riggers, riveters and stitchers took their place alongside electricians, aerodynamicists and theoreticians.

But the era of American-built rigid airships lasted only four years. Skeptical Navy fleet commanders were slow to employ the first prototype, USS Akron, or her sister ship USS Macon on long-range missions. On Apr. 3, 1933—19 months after her first flight, USS Akron left Lakehurst with Admiral William A. Moffett on board and headed out to sea. Tossed about in a storm, the dirigible hit the ocean and 73 men perished, including the admiral. Only three survived. The highest-ranking advocate of the rigid airship program was gone, and half his fleet. The second prototype, USS Macon, flew only 22 months. Struck by a heavy gust of wind off Point Sur, Calif., on Feb. 12, 1935, her upper fin was wrenched from the hull, fell into the sea and sank. This time, only two men perished.

Back in the airdock, where plans once called for a fleet of 10 rigid airships, dreams faded. Goodyear's hope for American passenger zeppelins also dissolved. The great airdock stood empty of purpose, her children gone and dead before maturity.

◆ ◆ ◆

At the beginning of the Second World War, needing airships that could hunt submarines, patrol coastal waterways, and escort sea-going convoys across the Atlantic, the Navy contracted Goodyear to build 178 new blimps.

After the Second World War, a few were built as platforms for testing airborne early warning systems and large-scale radar. Goodyear delivered its last naval blimp in 1960.

Akron and airshipping already were in demise. Manufacturing shifted away, following cheaper labor. By the mid-1980s no tires at all were made in Akron. The memory of the city's proud heritage remained, but the businesses formed to support the tire, rubber and automobile industries struggled for survival.

Secret military research took place in the old airdock. Barbed wire fences stood around the perimeter. On summer evenings, when one of Goodyear's commercial advertising airships landed at the airport to carry special customers, Akron families would gather at the fence, gaze nostalgically at the big ship, and tell their sons and daughters about the good old days.

On the streets of Akron, rumors and guesswork abounded concerning what took place inside the great hangar. Few knew.

For a fleeting period the glory nearly returned. Goodyear Aerospace bid for a new generation of naval airships. To remind the world of its pre-eminence in airship building, company executives held an open house. For the first time in 53 years, they would roll back the doors, and for a day anyone could come see the world's largest building. The public relations people quietly planned for about 25,000 guests…they brought in the Goodyear blimp America, the first blimp inside the airdock since 1960. On the appointed day, more than a quarter of a million people swarmed onto the property and streamed through the airdock to see this black womb from which fleets of Goodyear blimps and naval airships had come.

The pilgrims walked on the holy grail of America's lighter-than-air heritage, inhaled the musty atmosphere, nibbled the hors d'oeuvres and stood in awe. Visitors saw an enormous dark cavern, with walls arching up both sides to a curved ceiling. Blackened steel girders and framework laced the structure all the way up. Here and there across the top, light leaked in, evidence of corrosion on the vast metal roof.

At the end of the day, the great building was closed again, sealed up against those who might learn its secrets. The mystique was well preserved.

In 1987, Goodyear lost that naval airship contract to Westinghouse Airship Industries. It sold the airdock to the Loral Corporation of New York. Akron's days of large-scale blimp building were over, the spirit was gone and dust was collecting in the airdock.

Work in a cave, sleep in a silo

One November morning in 1991, the small *Earthwinds* staff moved into the four-room offices of Department 518, Airship Engineering, at the south end of the airdock. One large room already had been converted to a fully outfitted tool and machine shop, where Don, Vladimir and Vern Rich would spend most of their time; one was a luncheon and conference room; one was a drafting/design and reception area, and one became an office for Larry.

The shop doors opened to a temporary tent where the capsule was parked. Loral provided furniture and telephones. Nebiker had estimated that hosting the project would cost Loral about $3,000, mostly for security guards and a bit of overtime the night of the inflation and launch.

The airdock's orange-peel doors remained closed. Badges held at the plant gate tightly controlled access to the facility. Loral security police enforced the rules requiring escort badges for visitors.

Department of Defense regulations required that every foreign national not only have a badge and an escort, but also armed police nearby. Thus, when a two-star general arrived from the Soviet Union, Loral posted a security detail around the *Earthwinds* section of the airdock and staffed it all day. Fifteen federal inspectors were on site throughout the complex to ensure compliance with security procedures. Carol Hart began referring to the dimly lit old building as 'the bat cave'.

Lynne Newman flew to Akron to take up responsibilities as Project Administrator and Larry's alter ego, for better or for worse. Fred Nebiker loaned them a Cadillac Eldorado and arranged for the mayor of Akron to present them keys to the city. In a ceremony at the Quaker Square Hilton, Larry accepted on behalf of 'the four-man crew'—himself, Dzhanibekov, Branson and Don Moses.

Like the airdock, the hotel enjoyed landmark listing in the National Register of Historic Places. Built by the Quaker Oats Company in 1932 as a cluster of 36 grain silos, it was converted to an eight-story hotel in 1980. Each of the 196 rooms in the hotel measured 24 feet round: conference rooms, sleeping rooms, registration desk, lobbies and all.

The silo had once held grain and rice for the company. A restaurant now operated on the firing range where Quaker Puffed Rice was actually 'shot from guns.'

As long as the *Earthwinds* team remained in Akron, Hilton saw to it that the headquarters hotel was the Quaker Square Hilton, a local curiosity.

For the Earthwinds team, Hilton Hotels Corp. paid for the rooms; staff paid for their own meals. Larry and Lynne lived frugally. At breakfast tables, the hot water, lemon and honey were served free, so that's what they ordered. They shared a bowl of oatmeal. Snickering about their penny-pinching guests, the dining room staff soon learned the routine, and delivered the Newman Special Breakfast each morning.

Losing Virginity

John Wilcox spent a great deal of his time jawboning sponsors, searching for new sponsors, listening to Larry or Lynne, planning and arranging the video coverage of the flight.

He knew filming *Earthwinds*' flight would be 'the biggest fire drill of all time.' He would shoot, edit, and drop packages of videotape with couriers around the world, or have his production assistants hopscotch around the world to deliver completed packages. He would beam images via satellite to Bristol, Conn., for nightly use on ESPN and save some for his own one-hour special TV show. The details would stagger anyone with a doctorate in planning.

By mid-November, it was time to firm up Branson's intentions. Wilcox wrote in response to Kendrick's latest broadside:

> 'It is understandable that Alex and John would be extremely cautious and conservative in their approach to this flight. However, at the present time, Larry and his crew, now aided with technical assistance from Loral, are preparing the gondola for a final shakedown of the flight systems, which will include

continuous running of the systems for 15 days. Should Richard still be a candidate for the flight, he will have to make the decision to participate based on his own level of acceptable risk.

'We view Virgin as a participant in the project rather than a mere sponsor. It was our expectation at the outset of the project that our co-participant would certainly be able to share all of his know-how with us. It is patently absurd to suggest that Larry and I would enter into an agreement with Virgin if we knew at the time that Virgin would be unable to provide us with crucial information and expertise from past balloon flights.

'You certainly realize that there can be honest differences in opinion about the best way to solve certain problems; Larry has reviewed the list written by John and Alex and has made many of the changes suggested but does not concur with some of the others. In addition, Larry feels that certain suggestions, such as the addition of dual screw compressors, are simply not feasible.'

All through November, Michael Kendrick tried to extract Virgin from the project. He responded to Wilcox on November 21:

'Virgin Atlantic Airways Ltd does not consider the flight equipment as it now stands to be safe, and will not be prepared to associate itself with the project as its primary sponsor unless the safety measures outlined in the independent consultants report are complied with in order to make the flight safe and feasible.'

He restated the conclusions of the report:

'The workmanship quality was not sufficient given that lives will be at risk during the flight. {Ackroyd and Ritchie} thought it barely possible to launch before the end of February if their recommendations were to be implemented, and possible, only if you moved the technical qualified personnel into place immediately and committed the extra funding and testing.'

Kendrick began trying to stall the flight.

Since it was 'unlikely that all the work necessary to ensure that the equipment is as safe as possible will be completed by the end of the weather window in early March,' he wrote, 'the only logical route, in my view, is to postpone the launch. The flight will be a dangerous and risky undertaking at the best of times, without rushing it against the view of the acknowledged experts.'

Wilcox, already embittered at the Virgin organization for not sharing their technology, then suggested to Kendrick that in the event of an accident or loss of life, he would hold Virgin responsible 'morally or legally.'

Kendrick shot back his disagreement:

> 'Virgin is only a sponsor of the project, albeit its main sponsor, and has never been under any obligation to involve itself with the technical side of the project. Due to concern for Richard's safety during the flight, however, Virgin has so far done everything possible to assist with the project at its own cost. All technical information that has come to Virgin as a result of this has always been passed on to you immediately. Further, it is Virgin who has been prevailing upon you for the past month to take heed of John and Alex's report and recommendation. Our primary concern is for the safety of all involved with the project.
>
> 'Our proposal would be to postpone the project for one year. Virgin will consider underwriting the cost of this postponement in terms of Larry and Don's salary. I will not compromise Virgin's reputation by supporting a project we feel unsafe.'

It was becoming apparent that Richard Branson would not remain in the crew. However, Newman and Wilcox had spent more than a million of his dollars, and Branson wanted some return on his investment.

To pacify Virgin, they offered Branson a seat in the chase plane and a slot as the color commentator (along with Astronaut Gene Cernan) on the live ESPN broadcasts. Larry ordered that all the office phones in Akron should be answered by saying 'Virgin *Earthwinds*.' The project would be known as 'Virgin *Earthwinds*' in every mention.

Meanwhile, back in London, Branson found personal and professional reasons to disengage from the flight crew. From the outset, friends said he hated being around Larry; the thought of being cooped up with Newman for three weeks made his skin crawl. Secondly, he said he was reexamining his daredevil activities in light of family obligations: he had two young children at home. Thirdly, British Airways was engaged in a campaign of what Virgin called 'dirty tricks' aimed at taking business away from Virgin Atlantic. Fighting back required Branson's personal involvement.

The music goes round and round...

Back in America, the realities of building a complicated, experimental aircraft remained a difficult business. The amount of detail was staggering, and progress evolved by trial-and-error. Larry was under daunting time pressures, administering paperwork, receiving visitors, talking with reporters and sponsors, supervising every detail.

Inside the Pressure Cooker

Every morning at 9:00 a.m., Barron Hilton would call from Beverly Hills, seeking a status report and offering help. Usually Larry and Barron would talk for half an hour.

Back in the workroom, Don Moses, Vladimir and Vern Rich became buddies, working shoulder-to-shoulder tweaking up the generators and the attendant plumbing and piping.

Many parts of the engine were still being designed, machined, fitted or evaluated; the video and telecommunication package installed; the scientific experiments built and rigged; the capsule interior outfitted with its avionics and communication suites, wiring installed, and everything had yet to be tested.

The nerve center of the capsule, the engine palette, was mounted in a compartment under the floorboard. The engine would provide electrical current for the avionics and telecommunications, for the fan that pressured the anchor balloon, and for the screw compressor that condensed and converted thin outside air into denser breathable air.

The modified Honda engines offered several advantages: they were quiet, relatively inexpensive and easy to work on. The engines burned only .7 gallons per hour. With 750 gallons of gasoline in the fiberglass agricultural tanks suspended outside, the engines could run for more than 500 hours—or 20 days.

Flying at 35,000 feet, the cabin would be pressurized to the equivalent of 8,000 feet by the screw compressor. Aeronautical engineers called the difference between the outside air pressure at 3.5 psi and inside air pressure at 11 psi the Delta P. Compacting air generates extraordinary heat: air would rush through the screw compressor at minus 70 degrees and, joined by waste heat from the mechanical system, would come out at 300 degrees Fahrenheit.

The heated air screeching out of the screw compressor was conducted down through the floor of the capsule, through a long silencer under the capsule, through a large heat exchanger outside where it cooled the air. It came back into the capsule through a series of thin tubes at 50 degrees.

The engineers created a crude thermostat by mixing some of that hot air coming off the silencer with the 50-degree air. The crew would aim for a comfortable 70-degree cabin temperature.

But the powerful screw compressor created noise and poison. To deflect the screw compressor's high screech, Vladimir wrapped it with crumpled aluminum foil. But compressing air in the upper atmosphere also meant compressing ozone into lethal doses. A filter donated by Allied-Signal scrubbed the ozone out of the air.

Two 12-volt alternators charged all the batteries. Six batteries switched from 12 volt to 24 volt, providing two sources of power.

Crewmembers' exhaled air would be exhausted outside unless an engine stopped running for any reason, in which case the crew would have to descend quickly. Four bottles of emergency oxygen provided air for three hours.

Engine noise remained a major concern. With only the engines running, the sound level inside the capsule was 73 decibels—approximately the noise level of a busy freeway. The crew muffled some of the sound by wearing Bose noise cancellation headsets.

Larry and Don worried about the engines' durability. They scheduled a 225-hour duration test for early December. They would then remove the old engines and replace them with two new ones that would become the flight engines.

The engines had to work: they were essential for communication, life support and altitude control.

Tracking and communicating

Larry never forgot the failures that had plagued his first two great balloon flights. On the trans-Atlantic flight in 1978, the primary radios and the Omega navigational device inexplicably failed. They had been Larry's responsibility.

The aeronauts sailed on without the ability to fix their position, or to communicate directly with the operations center in Bedford, Mass., except by amateur radio and messages relayed via passing airliners. On the Pacific flight in 1981, there had been similar trouble. Larry never wanted to be out of touch with the ground again.

Fortunately, technology had solved old problems of communicating and pinpointing an aircraft's location.

Between the Inmarsat, high frequency (HF) and very high frequency (VHF) standard aircraft radio, he believed he would always be able to communicate, and to fix his exact position. Allied Signal's Bendix King division donated radios, VORs, Automatic Direction Finders (ADF)s, and a transponder whose signal could be read by the ARGOS satellite; it would broadcast the balloon's location to the operations center back in Akron.

Rockwell's Collins Radio division donated an $85,000 Politz 9000, the company's top-of-the-line HF radio. From the balloon, the crew could call Collins headquarters in Cedar Rapids, Iowa, where a phone patch could be made to any telephone in the world. The HF network had a range of up to 6,000 miles.

The Global Positioning System, linked electronically to a cluster of dedicated satellites, computed positions to within 50 feet. Rockwell International dispatched vice-president Loney Duncan, who had worked on the Project Mercury spacecraft for NASA. Duncan and a team of communication engineers installed the NAVCORE V GPS receiver in *Earthwinds*' flight console. The five-channel unit displayed longitude and latitude to within a few feet, as well as reporting direction of drift and velocity.

The GPS was linked to a unit that allowed the pilot to tune in any one of up to 250 waypoints, or intermediate known locations, and would display on the console the distance and bearing to that point, the ground speed and track angle, track deviation, estimated time to the waypoint, and other data. That unit also was programmed to provide data such as audible 'avoidance zone' warnings (such as military target practice areas), and status reports on the entire constellation of GPS satellites.

This device linked to an automatic message broadcasting on the amateur radio band. At thirty and fifty-five minutes past each hour, the recorded voice of Bill Brown, editor of the amateur radio magazine '73', would report latitude, longitude, altitude and speed. Hams all over the world would monitor the flight's progress.

Larry relished the gimmickry and gadgets of *Earthwinds*. With boyish enthusiasm, he boasted that he had tried to obtain every gadget he had ever seen; the result, as one reporter gushed, was that the capsule resembled 'a technological toy shop.'

Riches, dewars mist and suspense

Raven engineers claimed their polyethylene balloon could stay aloft for months, although they only warranted it for 20 days. With the anchor balloon keeping it in static equilibrium, *Earthwinds* would rise or fall only a few thousand feet each day. Once balanced, it would require little action by the crew to maintain level flight. In theory, it would float along in sunlight at 35,000 feet; descend at night to about 33,000 feet, and cycle back up the next day.

But Larry demanded redundancy. He wanted to carry liquid helium. Liquid helium could serve two purposes: it would replenish gaseous helium lost during normal day/night contractions, and it would be a form of disposable ballast. If *Earthwinds* were forced to descend to a lower altitude, for instance to repair an engine or wait for a change in weather, gasifying helium would allow the crew to return to altitude. No balloonist had ever done that.

A Colorado firm that built tanks for manned spacecraft built two 750-pound flasks, called dewars for *Earthwinds*. Lighter and thinner than the industry standard, *Earthwinds'* special dewars cost $250,000. They were constructed from three shells of aluminum blanketed with a 75-layer insulating sandwich of double-aluminized Mylar film and thin sheets of fiberglass. They looked like giant beer barrels.

Simple ambient-air exchangers on the tank exteriors and another exchanger atop the capsule would warm the helium enough to convert it to a gaseous state, Larry believed. One tank would hang on each side of the capsule.

Theoretically, in gaseous form, that would produce about 9,000 pounds of lift, or enough to replace more than one-third of the helium in the balloon. The two flasks would extend the potential duration by eight days, but added a dangerous complication. At minus 453 degrees Fahrenheit, any accident at launch involving a helium dewar or gasoline tank, or both, could have catastrophic consequences for onlookers and crew.

Vern Rich recruited his parents, Vern Sr. and Mary Sue, to pull a trailer from their home in Shreveport, La., pick up the flasks in Boulder, drive them to Middletown, Ohio, fill them, and deliver them to Akron.

But while trucking the fragile containers up the Interstate, something had jarred loose; when the trailer arrived in Akron, both flasks were gassing off about two percent of their capacity every day. And when a forklift operator set one down hard on the pavement, that shock doubled the previous leak. The helium flask sat there in the airdock, exhaling precious gas, 'an expensive way to clean the ceiling', as Mike Emich put it.

With considerable effort—pounding on the valves with wrenches—NASA technicians reduced the leakage to about one percent, or about $100 worth of helium per day.

◆   ◆   ◆

Don Overs reported for duty at the airdock early in December.

'Early the first day,' Overs recalled, 'Larry asked me to plan on meeting the next morning with him to discuss the new launch method. I explained the plan, and provided a sketch. It was quickly agreed that it would be done that way. The [crane operator] Keller-Hall people said that it was simple and solved all of their problems. It was all over in about 30 minutes.'

But back at the airdock office, Overs was surprised that key plans and components were missing.

'The major load suspension train was not complete or even designed. Larry asked me to work on the main suspension system. Two young volunteer engineers regularly came in about 5 p.m. after their regular workday at Babcock & Wilcox and were working on the helium balloon bottom load fitting design.'

The capsule was designed to hang from four suspension points: half-inch diameter holes built into the capsule. Each fitting of the two opposite pairs was connected by strands of Spectra rope passing down and under the capsule and epoxied in place.

> 'These were not well suited to resist the horizontal component of the suspension load,' Overs said. 'The anchor balloon was supposed to be suspended directly from the helium balloons using four Spectra ropes.
>
> 'I had a concern that the anchor balloon suspension ropes straddling the capsule could endanger the side window ports and thus the capsule integrity.
>
> 'My plan was to use steel cables for all connections between the helium balloon and the capsule. A new fitting would be pinned to each of the four half-inch fittings at the top of the capsule, and a metal tube placed between the fittings would relieve the original gondola fittings of the horizontal loads.'

Overs redesigned the suspension system. The weight of the capsule would be shared redundantly by the new and existing suspension points. Although it would add a few pounds, it had the unique advantage of being adjustable in place.

Overs wanted to use adjustable steel cables to suspend the dewars and fuel tanks, and spent nearly a week designing the suspension system.

He satisfied himself that he had solved several of *Earthwinds*' most vexing problems by strengthening the capsule suspension system and simplifying the launch procedure. Then he presented his plan.

'Larry stated that he wasn't interested in doing any of this,' Overs said.

> 'Rejecting my suspension system additions also included rejecting my launch scheme, which he had previously bought into. I told him I didn't think I could be of any further value to the project.'

Overs withdrew as a volunteer, checked out of the Quaker Square Hilton and returned home to Pittsburgh. He would watch in the years ahead the consequences of failing to implement his specific suggestions.

◆   ◆   ◆

John Ackroyd had arrived in Akron in November, and took over the job of designing the flight train and suspension system—literally to figure out how everything would hang together. Every part still had to be built. All the components—the capsule, the two gasoline tanks, the two helium dewars and the anchor balloon—would hang from a single piece of alloy at the base of the polyethylene balloon, like the limbs of a marionette.

For this formidable challenge he called upon his aviation engineering and metallurgical experience. Standing at a drawing board in the reception bay, Ackroyd designed a 'spider' of a hi-strength alloy, with six holes drilled through a half-round bottom hemisphere. It would be held in place by a large cotter pin. When an Akron metalworking shop made the fitting and smaller 'bits', they etched their names and 'Good luck *Earthwinds*' onto the main bit.

The components would all hang by Spectra rope, since that material was being donated.

Every suspended piece was fitted with a load cell, which would electronically display in the capsule the exact weight carried below that point. These crucial devices had to function electrically as well as mechanically, providing readings on a digital display, as well as bearing weight. Revere Transducers, Inc., a California firm, supplied six specially modified load cells. The main cell measured lift; it was fitted between the poly balloon and the main bit. Another load cell measured the anchor balloon's weight.

Four smaller load cells weighed the two dewars and two tanks. As the engine consumed gasoline, the weight of the gas tank would decrease; the weight would be calculated to gallons of fuel remaining, and the pilots could calculate the rate of fuel consumption.

Just above each load cell was a Holex fiber optics laser cutter, which could be triggered from inside the capsule. Both fuel tanks could be instantly cut away by plugging a jack to the appropriate detonator receptacles and pushing a red button.

Allied-Signal loaned more than $200,000 worth of Spectra material for the anchor balloon. Raven's engineers cut the pieces and sewed them together. A polyethylene 'bladder' inside the anchor ensured airtight integrity. The 100-foot diameter globe weighed 2,500 pounds, although its skin was only 15-thousandths of an inch thick.

A truck delivered the anchor balloon in early December, and Tim Lachenmeier spread out the huge beach ball on a ground cloth and with a large industrial fan inflated it in the airdock. When pressurized, the anchor balloon became solid as a rock. It would loom massively over every act of preparation.

High anxiety

With so much remaining to be done, the tension around the airdock was palpable. Larry made himself the focal point for every decision, every detail, and found himself utterly unable to delegate. He and Lynne controlled every detail, even to the point of interrogating volunteers who would call one another to talk about the project. He began immersing himself in endlessly inconsequential trivia; questioning motives; correcting grammar; directing craftsmen how to do their jobs; summarily rejecting plans and advice brought forth by well-meaning volunteer engineers; changing his mind on components; fighting off Branson; working from 9 a.m. to 9 p.m., and finding it impossible to relax or let go. The project was running behind, many components had yet to be designed, built or tested, and money was tight.

But if Larry was difficult to live with, everyone recognized that there was no project without him, and he had the final word on every decision. Among all those who had dreamed of the global flight, he alone had the chutzpa and the drive to have come this far. He was driving *Earthwinds*, however slowly, to the point where it might really be ready to fly. Whatever the difficulty of style, his leadership was keeping it on track, and so far there had been no major derailments.

Under constant stress, Larry said whatever came into his mind, without pausing to consider the effect of his words on others. His orders were sometimes crisp; opinions to the contrary discouraged. He found the new experience of being in command a burden. He had spawned an enterprise that was now bigger than any one man, and struggled continually to control every aspect of it.

In early December, he had caught a cold. Coupled with his recurring pain from stomach acid (the result of a hole in his duodenum) he was in physical distress. He gulped Tums. When he suffered a long spout of diarrhea, Lynne revealed that Larry was unable to sleep more than an hour a night. Nothing helped, not even the wave machine that produced soothing sounds of the sea, on which he had grown dependent at home.

Every morning, he'd get to his desk and find more technical reports to read, more calls to answer or to make, bigger problems to solve, taller mountains to climb. Film crews and news reporters would come in to see him; there were demands on his time. When he got this way, he would often be either unresponsive, hostile, or would just stare with wide unbelieving eyes, a caricature of himself. The staff found avoided him while they worked on their aspect of the project; if they came near him, they approached tentatively.

One morning in early December, sauntering into Schumacher's for breakfast, Larry crumpled into a booth, and began shaking and sobbing uncontrollably. Lynne summoned Vern Rich and Don Moses to come over to the table; they propped him up and escorted him out quickly. They put Larry in the back of a car and took him to the hospital. He was diagnosed with a bad case of flu and a stomach virus exacerbated by nervous tension. He was given a prescription for Flexerol, a stomach muscle relaxant, in addition to the usual dose of Prozac, the antidepressant he and Lynne both took.

A grand opening: 'Earthwinds Hilton'

Barron Hilton thought of the capsule as a hotel room—'the only one in the Hilton chain that changed time zones', he would say. He wanted a Grand Opening ceremony akin to that for his hotels, and instructed his California pr firm to set it up, no matter what the cost. Early in November a date had been selected: the Capsule Christening Ceremony would take place December 17, Wright Brothers Day. Following weeks of advance work, Hilton's entourage descended on Akron in a completely repainted corporate BAC 1-11 aircraft—the official *Earthwinds* Hilton chase plane! They parked it inside the airdock near the capsule.

Hilton presided over an elaborate private dinner party at the Quaker Hotel that evening, toasting the world adventurers and comparing them with Wilbur and Orville Wright. Burt and Dick Rutan were there. So were Phil Harris, the old vaudeville comedian, Gene Cernan, the Apollo astronaut, and Akron's Congressman Tom Sawyer.

It was a heady evening spent pondering the grand dream, saluting the heroes, drinking the finest brandy and smoking premium cigars.

Vladimir used the occasion to speak grandly about his dream for joint U.S.-Soviet missions, and about what this flight meant to him personally.

'I dreamed of a flight to the Moon, or to Mars, but now I have this adventure,' he said, placing *Earthwinds* on a par with the ultimate space adventures. Eloquently and extemporaneously, he spoke about life without political boundaries, 'breathing the same air, drinking the same water', and reiterated his nation's call for a joint mission to Mars. He toasted the spirit of friendship made possible through aviation.

People left the dinner believing they had witnessed the beginning of one of the most magnificent and memorable aviation achievements imaginable.

In addition to lavishing money on Earthwinds, Barron Hilton spent lots of time with pilots Vladimir, Larry and Don.

The ceremony the next day inside the dark, frigid airdock took place under a huge heated tent erected for the occasion. One hundred fifty guests walked to the ceremony across a red carpet that stretched the width of the airdock, lined by rows of poinsettia plants and Christmas trees. Visitors enjoyed a catered champagne brunch, a ceremony emceed by Cernan, speeches by local politicians, blessings by a rabbi and a priest (full redundancy again), a ribbon cutting ceremony and an elaborate parting of a curtain that revealed the capsule.

The three pilots were each invited to speak. Larry, who had yet to learn about sound bytes, droned on for 45 minutes explaining the minutia of the project; by the time he finished, all the bubbles had risen from the bottom of the champagne glasses. So full of medicine, he acknowledged later that he couldn't remember anything he had said.

Don Moses followed Larry to the podium, but could only choke out in an emotional voice, 'We'll take all of you with us in our hearts'.

The Hilton pr staff videotaped the ceremony, beamed excerpts by satellite to TV news stations all over the country, and arranged for express delivery of still photos to the major wire services.

Barron Hilton had pledged to equip the 'ultimate room with a view' with all of the amenities available in luxury hotel rooms. That's why he had sent Jeraldine Canon, the interior decorator of all Hilton properties, to design the capsule interior. Vladimir selected the subdued colors; the artist in him understood what would show well on television and in photographs. Hilton also arranged for a newspaper to fax a daily summary to the capsule. The Hilton school of hotel management would furnish all of the meals.

For in-flight entertainment Hilton gave a case full of Hi-8 movies. In addition to the inevitable 'Around the World in Eighty Days,' however, the case included such interesting titles as 'Dead Again', 'Shattered', 'Ricochet', 'The Doctor', 'Double Impact' and 'The Terminator'.

Hilton spent more than $125,000 on the grand opening.

Finishing touches

When the guests, sponsor representatives and news media went home, hundreds of time-consuming little tasks remained. The capsule had arrived in Akron looking like a smooth egg with ten bulging Lexan eyes. Somehow the two large liquid helium dewars and two gasoline tanks would have to be nestled alongside.

Inside the Pressure Cooker 173

Carol Hart and Don Moses, despite their problems with Larry and Lynne, led the team in building the capsule and maintaining relations with the volunteer work force.

The fiberglass team, Don Moses and Carol Hart, built arms to hold the tanks in place. They custom-cut lightweight blue foam and coated it with fiberglass.

Don's big blackened hands revealed the kind of work he did. Each day, they would be covered anew in grime, lubricant and grease from the engine compartment. He spent endless hours crouched in the bottom of the capsule, finding and sealing leaks, replacing drive belts, wrenching, tightening, aligning, adjusting. He and Larry were building a one-of-a-kind craft without blueprints, and it necessarily involved lots of TLAR (that looks about right) engineering.

◆　　◆　　◆

Sporting a narrow beard from jaw to jaw and a round face that smiled in repose, Vern Rich was usually was visible only through a welder's face shield. He toiled quietly in his corner of the workshop, and talked slowly with a patient, confident Louisiana drawl. It was a comfortable environment, with his father and mother on the team running odd jobs and errands. His trim blonde wife Darlene joined them all after quitting her job in Arizona.

Vern was not just a professional fabricator; he was a perfectionist. He spent weeks constructing three external heat exchangers, which resembled old-fashioned steam radiators. He took aluminum pipes, heated one section at a time over a gas torch until it was hot enough to bend, then doubled it over, measured and started the next bend. The rooftop heat exchanger, an intricate series of turns through which liquid helium would convert into gaseous form, consisted of 10 parallel lengths of pipe each about 12 feet long, running along the capsule on the port side.

One heat exchanger converted 300-degree air to 50-degree air, for the screw compressor and cabin air. The other, mounted on the opposite undercarriage, carried hot liquid coolant from the engines outside and back in again. Fluid going into the heat exchanger would exit the capsule at a high temperature, and immediately begin to chill as it entered the cold metal pipes in the outside air, which would be about 70 degrees below. The pipes were bent in such a way as to follow the vertical contour of the capsule. Both consisted of seven parallel tubes that followed the curve of the capsule exterior.

After the heat exchangers were installed, a visitor came to the airdock one day and insisted that Larry demonstrate the machine used for pipe bending. Of course, there was no machine; it had all been bent in Vern's stout hands.

Across from Vern's workbench, Vladimir stood constructing 15-foot a movable arm to be fitted outside the capsule, at the end of which would be a small video camera. The robotic device would be controlled from a knob inside the capsule, rotating in a vertical axis and permitting the video camera to look at the top of the capsule, then swing down and look at the area below the capsule.

Besides being of considerable help to the flight crew in observing external conditions, the camera would provide spectacular video for John Wilcox's film and for ESPN's worldwide television audience. Vladimir took long narrow-gauge aluminum angles, welded them together into a rectangle pole, and placed a wheel and steering wheel cable control in the center and a counterweight on one side.

The 'lipstick' video camera at the end of the pole was just five inches long and an inch wide. John Wilcox had adapted these wide-angle surveillance cameras for remote videos, such as on racecars and on America's Cup yachts. He permanently mounted three more of the tiny cameras inside the capsule, and another, with a rotating knob, directly atop the capsule. There would be more video coverage inside the *Earthwinds* capsule than in a New York bank lobby.

Vladimir Dzhanibekov at his worktable in Akron's airdock.

Plotting every day's upper air currents on a polar projection chart, and building his ozone detection device, Vladimir carried other burdens on his shoulders. Enormous political changes were sweeping across his homeland as President Mikhail Gorbachev's power ebbed and decades of Communist Party rule crumbled. His leave from the Cosmonaut Training Center was about to expire, and he was due back at Star City in January; he wrote to his old hunting partner, Gen. Yevgeny I. Shaposhnikov, interim head of the defense ministry, and received a two-month extension of his orders enabling him to continue work on *Earthwinds*.

The end of the Soviet Union came on Dec. 24, 1991, when Gorbachev resigned. The Supreme Soviet was dissolved and Vladimir was out of politics. His native Uzbekistan had declared independence in August.

In the midst of the political turmoil, his wife Lilia joined him—her first trip outside of the USSR. She carried with her all the way from Moscow a cake made by their daughter Olga, which she shared with the *Earthwinds* crew at the airdock. Lilia had never seen Vladimir begin any of his five space flights, and she longed to see him begin this voyage.

After launch Lilia hoped to follow the flight on Hilton's chase plane.

Speaking minimal English, she communicated using sign language and some essential words. She sat next to Vladimir at the airdock everyday, knitting green sweaters for the flight crew, or reading newspaper clippings about her husband's space exploits.

Sometimes, Carol Hart, Mary Sue Rich or Erin Porter would take her shopping—but at the cash register she would be embarrassed by the high cost of goods (at K-Mart!), and would put everything back on the shelves. Later, the women would retrieve the goods, buy them for her and make a present of them. But Lilia wanted to do more that knit and sightsee. She wanted to help.

'Geev me jobe!' she would say, stomping her foot. Finally, Lynne gave her an assignment: she could inventory the souvenir T-shirts. When she was through with that, she could mop the floor.

And so every evening before leaving the airdock to return to the hotel, the general's wife would go to the utility closet, take out a mop and bucket, and wash all the floors in the workspace. The sight of this smiling little babushka working her way around the floor captured everyone's heart.

Holiday tension

The project's money was running out. The first monthly phone bill came in; with virtually every call long-distance, it was staggering.

Fred Nebiker checked on his tenant daily, offering help. He quietly made the phone bill disappear. Whenever he could, he treated Lynne and Larry to a quiet dinner in Akron's better restaurants. A former combat pilot, Nebiker was sympathetic to the pressures that Larry was under, and admired Larry's stamina and energy.

'He's indefatigable,' Fred would say. 'He walks through doors without opening them!'

But the money pressure was serious and Larry had to begin slashing expenses. He couldn't fund a trip for one of Vladimir's colleagues working on the ozone experiment. He couldn't pay the airfare for the wife of Doc Wiley, a key senior volunteer. Don Moses, Carol Hart and others who had been on the payroll became volunteers. Only Vern Rich remained as a paid worker.

One day the FAA called with the news that Canadian Air Traffic controllers had refused clearance to *Earthwinds*. Long known for being obstinate bureaucrats, they just didn't want to be bothered with it. When Canada refused, all the dominos began to fall—controllers around the world rejected the entire flight plan.

Barron Hilton gave Larry the name of an old friend he could call upon in Washington to solve aviation problems, former FAA Administrator Donald D. Engen, who had an international aviation consultancy. Larry made a one-day excursion to FAA headquarters, where he and Engen secured international airspace clearance for the balloon.

Throughout December, Larry kept changing specifications on the helium balloon that Raven was making for him. Lachenmeier was trying to procure a helium valve and Larry pushed him hard to get it. He told Lachenmeier to deliver the balloon by early January.

With so much going on around him, Larry acted impulsively, ignoring the consequences of his actions. Mistakes were inevitable. Searching one afternoon for a piece of stainless steel tubing to use for an engine part, he grabbed the first piece he found and hack sawed the section he wanted, inadvertently destroying the specially engineered square load frame from which the gasoline tanks, helium dewars and capsule were to have hung. Don Moses bellowed furiously, but it was too late. Loss of the load frame prompted a redesign of the entire flight train, and added two weeks to the schedule.

A few days later, the screw compressor ran low on lubricating oil during a test, and froze up. It was a one-of-a-kind item, and no parts were available in the U.S., so Ackroyd packed it up and hand-carried the piece back to England where it was rebuilt. That took a week.

Larry's edginess was palpable. On Christmas Eve, he called Len Laiden, president of Loral Defense Systems, at home and began in a hostile voice:

'Len, if you have got a problem with my project, let me know. I heard from Barron Hilton that you told Congressman Tom Sawyer at the christening ceremony that Gene Cernan said *Earthwinds* has less than a 50 percent chance of success and that I have a death wish.'

Laiden, surprised that Larry was so sensitive to casual chat among fellow aviators, started to defend what he had actually said. They got into a shouting match. Laiden hung up and immediately called Fred Nebiker at home, ordering him to get rid of Newman and *Earthwinds*.

'If you want me to do that, I will,' said Nebiker, who knew both men well. 'Just tell me when. Now? Christmas morning? How long should I give them to clear out their equipment? Shall I kick him out right now?'

Laiden calmed down, knowing that the decision to allow Larry to use the airdock had been made in New York by his chairman, Bernard Schwartz.

The day after Christmas, the 225-hour endurance test began. Volunteers formed teams to sleep on cots inside or next to the capsule in the airdock and monitor engine performance. Security people had to remain in the airdock, too, so Loral's overtime charges began to accumulate. The engines ran flat out for 10 days and checked out okay, with only a few adjustments.

It was time to start thinking about how to launch this complex craft. Larry called Tom Barrow, who negotiated a contract that included a large payment for a successful launch. He arrived in Akron two days after Christmas to take charge of the procedure. The 47-year-old former architect and structural engineer, having launched Maxie Anderson and Richard Branson on epic flights, had the diplomatic skills to deal with massive egos, the management skills to organize a project, and the technical knowledge to understand the complex physics of ballooning.

Barrow's full salt-and-pepper beard, twinkling eyes and careful eloquence enhanced his expertise. His deep voice uttered the exact words that conveyed his meaning in thoughtful, measured sentences. His manner of presentation was matter-of-fact and serious, and no occasion called for raising one's voice above conversational tones.

He carried unique credentials, having launched two global balloon attempts and a flight across the Atlantic. In addition, he was a fairly accomplished hot air balloon pilot himself. He drew great pleasure from simple flights over his Montana countryside, but was equally at ease training students such as King Hussein and Queen Noor of Jordan. Barrow's friendship with Richard Branson had led him to this project. His professional training as an architect and engineer gave him the enviable talent of being able to sketch and describe exactly what he wanted to do.

He took a long look at the proposed launch site—directly outside the south side airdock doors—and moved it half a mile north. Barrow then wrote the overall goals for the project on brown wrapping paper, and posted them in the lunch room:

1. To achieve the earliest possible launch-ready date. To take advantage of the first good flight opportunity we are presented with.

2. A clean and safe balloon launch with no significant balloon or equipment damage and no injuries on the ground.

3. A high, fast, long and successful flight with the most reliable equipment and systems possible, good tracking and recovery and emergency procedures.

4. Safe landing, clean disconnects, crew protection, emergency contingencies well covered, every one walks away smiling.
5. Total success. Pride in achieving 'the impossible', friendship and camaraderie that comes when the strength of the group brings out the best in all of us.
6. To sleep in, take the month of February off and go lie on the beach somewhere!

5

Winter Worries

Computing the jet

With half the launch period gone, the capsule incomplete, the balloon still on the table in Sioux Falls, the flight crew not trained, the first two months of 1972 promised a frantic race against the clock—or more precisely, a race against the sun, as it made its way north.

Each day the sun moved north, it brought with it the increased likelihood of disturbances in the upper atmosphere, the disappearance of the sub-tropical jet stream flow, and the end of the *Earthwinds* launch window.

Bob Rice, the weather guru, set up camp in one of the old cereal factory's conference rooms early in January, a room that inevitably became known as the Rice Bowl.

Beginning his workday ritual at 3:30 each morning, Rice would stuff his pipe with Black-and-Tan (his exclusive private brand), ignite the tobacco and proceed to incense the room like the high priest of forecasting before celebrating the weather mass.

He would spool up three computers, download synchronized satellite photos of the North American continent, tap into reams of variables moving across the map, examine data from around the world that skittered across the modems from the supercomputers at the National Oceanic and Atmospheric Administration (NOAA) and isolate the factors that would influence weather, especially wind, in any one spot on earth.

From this, he would prepare his daily interpretive product: a 10-day flight chart, and a two-page written narrative.

He had confirmed with Larry and with Tom Barrow the twin patterns that *Earthwinds* needed. First, near-calm had to prevail at the surface for six or eight hours—it would take Barrow's crew that long to move the balloons out of the airdock, raise the helium balloon, connect the capsule, board the crew, attach the anchor balloon, raise the system and release it.

Ideally, the pattern would occur on a typical northeast Ohio hard-frozen day in the midst of a slow moving high-pressure system with clear skies. To be even more perfect, a three-inch ground cover of snow would evenly distribute surface heat. But no local condition had value unless it coincided with an acceptable jet stream windflow.

The acceptable upper air pattern would blow approximately from the 35th to the 55th parallels to carry *Earthwinds* into Europe somewhere between Gibraltar and the Baltic Sea. The forces and pressures that would act on the balloon complicated the enroute forecast considerably: the jet stream was a turbulent, narrow-minded, unreliable friend. It could take a turn north, and begin a loop, and keep looping, or go farther north, or turn sharply south. Usually in long-distance flying, speed of the upper atmosphere wind was the essential element for success because most balloons were limited in duration by the amount of ballast they started out with. Rice knew he could seek something different this time.

'The greatest difference between this forecast and others' he would say, 'is the vastly superior theoretical duration of the system. Previously, we would inevitably look for speed because of the limitations of the system's duration capabilities.

In this case, that's not necessarily true—you have enough duration to allow for some slow flight.

'I would personally not want to see this balloon in strong jets, because of the height of the balloon. I'd much sooner have it at a lesser wind speed, into a zonal flow.'

In the winter months, two jet stream patterns form in the northern hemisphere, a polar jet and a sub-tropical jet. The polar jet yields slower, more stable wind, with fewer oscillations, or north-south wave patterns. The sub-tropical jet, considerably faster and closer to the equator, traverses more miles, and not incidentally, blows over less politically stable nations. In the summertime, the sub-tropical pattern virtually disappears as the sun moves north across the equator.

Insertion into a slow, steady, polar jet stream flow would mean a 20,000 mile flight in 75 knot winds—or a journey that would last about 12 days. Before that could begin, however, Akron's winter wind needed to settle down for a few hours so that the helium balloon could be inflated—outside the airdock—and then taken back in for evaluation.

CBS This Morning

The need to protect the flight crew from external intrusions clashed with the sponsors' agenda. Barron Hilton pushed his pr firm to get some national TV exposure, even more than the christening ceremony had harvested in December.

Responding to this pressure, Neil Cohen, one of the account executives, called all the morning talk show producers and succeeded in convincing CBS This Morning to do a live segment. He booked it right away for Friday morning, January 17 and then called Lynne Newman to tell her. Lynne published it in the weekly sponsor bulletin and soon all the sponsors knew a week or two in advance that the crew would be on live TV.

That set off a great circus among them to get the crew to utter the sponsors' names on national TV. It also greatly upset John Wilcox, who because of his alumni relationship strongly preferred ABC, whose ratings were better. Wilcox reached Cohen on the phone, shouting at him and calling him unprofessional and incompetent; that got Barron Hilton boiling mad at Wilcox, and Hilton called Newman, who got caught up in the middle of this imbroglio, not knowing which way to turn.

This intrusion came at the worst possible time. Communication technicians from NASA had been running system checks since Monday, and were all over the capsule from early morning to 9 o'clock at night. Nonetheless, Larry recognized that nothing would fly without the sponsors, and urged everyone to cooperate.

The CBS Morning News stayed on the schedule.

Late that week, engineers from Rockwell International arrived to install and test the Global Positioning System and the Inmarsat satellite telephone. To hit the satellite and ensure that GPS/Inmarsat worked correctly, the capsule had been wheeled outside. The air was raw and the wind-chill way below zero. Loney Duncan and his Rockwell crew were in the midst of their tests when the CBS crew showed up and announced that they had to get access to the capsule so they could wire it for sound and light. They had to test transmit at 5 a.m.

The capsule decor had been removed (it was held in place by Velcro) so the work on the radios could take place; it would take hours to stick it all back in place for the TV shot. Carol Hart agreed to work late that night to re-decorate, and to hang the sleeping compartment curtain that bore the legend '*Earthwinds Hilton.*' Larry agreed to come in early the next morning to unlock the department and open up the capsule. His rule was that one member of the flight crew always had to be present whenever someone else was inside the capsule.

Complicating this picture, Patricia Godefroy came in from the Los Angeles pr firm to ensure that Hilton received its money's worth. Just mention the words *Earthwinds* Hilton'...say the H-word, Larry!

But it wasn't that simple. Allied-Signal's pr firm also sent a publicist in from New York to make sure that Larry said the words 'Allied Signal Spectra fabric' on national TV. Allied's publicist literally shadowed CBS producer Carol Story, following her from room to room, feeding her questions that Paula Zahn and Harry Smith should ask the flight crew. He pressed fabric into her hands, showed her the Spectra bullet proof vest and press kits, and had a supply of Allied Signal hats ready to pop on the crew members' heads just at show time.

Before leaving the airdock the night prior to the interview, Vladimir was introduced to the CBS producer, who suggested maybe they could review some questions he'd especially like to answer.

'What television?' he asked, 'Does this mean I have to come in early tomorrow?'

Larry had not bothered to tell Vladimir that he was going to be on live network television the next morning.

Early the next morning, the CBS crew made up 'the set'. Thirty minutes before airtime, Larry, Don and Vladimir dressed in their light cotton flight suits. The Allied Signal ball caps went on their heads and promptly came right off again. Pat Godefroy's anxiety level went north because Larry had not rehearsed what he was going to say, and nobody seemed in charge of telling the crew what their 'message' should be. Certainly nobody had trained them in the advantages of live TV, where skilled talkers can control an interview by giving only prepared answers.

As the magic moment of 8:36 a.m. approached, observers, sponsor representatives and the CBS producer gathered in the small video truck outside the air dock. A stiff wind kept rattling the satellite dish, and the signal to New York kept going fuzzy. It was unclear if they could even do the shot. Then it was on!

Paula Zahn did a brief intro, and Harry Smith asked Larry what records might be broken on the flight. He answered the question (distance and duration). He asked Vladimir how this compared to space flight (it doesn't). He asked Don what the capsule looked like (football shaped). Smith thanked the crew and it was over.

No sponsor got mentioned. Pat Godefroy thought she'd lose her job.

Watching the whole thing on television at home in California, Barron Hilton was thrilled because the sleeping curtain just had one word on it: the H-word.

Plastic, pigeons and wooden owls

Worries began to crop up concerning potential damage to the poly balloon from birds in the hangar, especially pigeons and owls. No one knew for sure if pigeons that flew in and out of the airdock would try to land on the delicate polyethylene balloon once it got inflated. Could a simple pigeon's claws—or pigeon drippings—cripple a fragile $3.5-million project?

Years ago the classic problem of mice in the hangar had been solved by bringing in owls, which feast on little rodents. Would the owls come out at night and fly into the balloon? Would bats? Nothing so delicate as the *Earthwinds* balloon had ever stood in the hangar. The answer, someone said, was to erect wooden owls near the balloon to scare off the pigeons. The answer, someone else said, was to forget about it because birds don't collide with balloons.

But small puddles of water on the floor evidenced a more real threat: the airdock leaked after every rain. Drip spots containing rusty flakes of metal appeared just where the helium balloon was supposed to stand. If rusty water accumulated on top of the balloon, it could damage the fragile plastic and the valve plate at the crown. The water could also freeze. Mike Emich envisioned a pool of ice forming on the valve, rendering it useless.

The solution was to hang plastic sheets from the ceiling of the airdock rafters. Barrow okayed the plan, and they told Larry about it. Unconvinced, Larry replied that there was no money in the budget for anything unnecessary like that. Emich believed he could get some Akron fire fighters to suspend fabric from the ceiling.

John Wilcox agreed and said that if it protected the poly balloon, Emich should do whatever was necessary to get the covering up there. Wilcox authorized a donation of up to $2,000 to the Akron fire department's favorite charity, the Burn Center at Akron Children's Hospital. Emich got his fire chief to okay the plan, Loral supplied the poly sheets, and it looked like a no-cost operation.

The day scheduled for the work, Sunday morning, January 19, the thermometer stood at zero. Twelve firemen, under Emich's enthusiastic leadership, having just finished a 24-hour shift at 8 a.m., went straight to the airdock. Under Emich's direction, they cut and assembled the plastic on the airdock floor, climbed 20 stories of stairs to the top, and crawled along the wooden catwalk.

They worked for eight hours straight, without breaking for lunch or coffee, raising by pulleys a 100-by-100-foot section of plastic and securing it to the ceiling girders. Occasionally, Larry came out of his office and glanced up. He did not offer them a souvenir pin, patch, t-shirt or hat. When the work was done, Mike thanked his buddies and they went home to get warm, eat and go to sleep. Mike was chagrined that Larry hadn't met with them, but was satisfied that he had done the right thing to protect the balloon.

The next morning, Larry drove in to the airdock, looked at the fabric on the ceiling, and ordered Mike to take it down. Flabbergasted, Mike asked why.

'Because you didn't sweep the floor first,' Larry said. 'Those plastic sheets you used act like a magnet for dust, and surely are covered with dust on the side facing down. If that dust gets on the balloon, it will draw sunlight to it, the polyethylene near the spots will heat up, holes will melt in it, and the balloon will leak. Now take it down.'

Mike started to protest, but Larry cut him off.

'How many poly balloons have you flown? How many have you even inflated?'

'None,' Mike said.

'Well, I want mine to be perfect,' Larry shot back. 'Maxie Anderson's balloon Jules Verne had a black spot on it when he flew it out of Egypt, and the sun melted a hole in it. Maxie was forced to land after a day and a half. When my balloon comes out of the shipping crate it will be in pristine condition and I want it to stay that way.'

[Anderson's balloon had developed a leak, but for a different reason. The manufacturer had applied large black registration numbers to the plastic, big enough to read from another aircraft. When ultraviolet rays acted on those block letters, the fabric melted. It was not from dust particles.]

A few days later, Emich and some others climbed the stairs again, and using some dust-free towels from the Hilton Hotel and gently rubbed the bottom of the plastic shield. In the weeks following, the plastic sheets caught rain and held it, and protected the balloon. Larry never thanked the firemen.

The remarkable Inmarsat

If a device was on the cutting edge of technology, Larry wanted it for *Earthwinds*. One such device was the International Maritime Satellite Telephone, known as Inmarsat.

In its simplest form, it allowed a user to make a phone call from virtually anywhere on earth. Sailor/commentator William F. Buckley had used a prototype on his Sealestial voyage across the Atlantic in 1991. Battlefield commanders relied on it during Operation Desert Storm. Four geosynchronous satellites provided continuous coverage over 97 percent of the earth; each could simultaneously process thousands of individual calls.

Since whatever was put through a phone line could be put through an Inmarsat transceiver, Inmarsat became *Earthwinds'* primary and indispensable communication method.

To start a call, one referred to the Global Positioning System for latitude and longitude, tapped a button to target one of the four Inmarsat satellites, and then entered the exact latitude and longitude on the numeric keypad. The unit calculated the azimuth and elevation of the chosen satellite and rotated the antenna toward the right direction. Once aligned correctly, calling any phone number in the world was simply a matter of punching in the numbers.

The engineers from Canon had built six prototype transceivers that could process digitized video imagery. Four were in Japan, and two were dedicated to *Earthwinds*: one installed in the capsule, the other at ESPN headquarters.

Vladimir, the on-board cameraman, would be able to take a snapshot or a moving picture and feed the digitized image into the Still-Video Transceiver linked to the Inmarsat Control Unit.

The digital data would be fed to a satellite, and downlinked to the COMSAT Earth Station in Southbury, Conn., where a dedicated line retransmitted the data to ESPN headquarters in Bristol, Conn., and fed into a high-speed Canon A-200-SV personal computer. Custom software re-constituted the data and exported it into one of several formats: a hi-quality still video image on the computer terminal, or a live on-air broadcast.

The whole process would take four seconds!

The same system allowed compressed motion video to be transmitted. Vladimir could plug a camcorder into a device that compressed motion video. The result was a low-quality video—like a videophone—that yielded fuzzy but recognizable images. John Wilcox referred to those images as 'Max Headroom', for the robotic TV character.

Larry and John had a lot riding on the operation of that equipment. The public image of the flight and the success of ESPN's film and daily updates depended upon successful operation of all the equipment.

One morning, Larry sat quietly reading the Inmarsat operating manual at breakfast. Every once in a while he looked up and recited a fact or two expressing his amazement at the unit's capability. Then, holding up the manual to Lynne, he mused:

'The guys I'm flying with don't have the foggiest idea about how to navigate or communicate. 'I've thought about leaving them a note while we're flying saying, if there's a problem, wake me up, but they don't even know enough to know if there is a problem.'

'Couldn't you give the manual to Vladimir and have him study it?' Lynne asked, 'He must know something about it from his flying with the Russian air force. And Don is a pilot, isn't he?'

'Honey,' Larry said, his drop-dead look freezing her in mid-thought, 'I can barely understand this and I'm a commercial airline pilot. There isn't any way Don or Vladimir will understand GPS or Inmarsat by reading books. The Soviet Air Force's best equipment dates back to what we had in the 1960s. Loney Duncan from Rockwell is coming in this weekend to train me. I'll be the operator.'

The Russian science package

Vladimir had come to the United States expecting to focus on environmental studies and work with NASA. He spent much of his time assembling, constructing and fitting to the exterior of the capsule three instruments that he had brought from Soviet agencies. Part of his work was being sponsored by the Youth Scientific Technological Work Center, known as FOTON, to which Wilcox had agreed to donate $64,000. The Russian scientists sent experiments to measure the ozone layer in the stratosphere, measure aerosol particles, and gauge the intensity of cosmic rays. They envisioned a long-term program of stratospheric and tropospheric explorations using manned balloons, and disclose results of their *Earthwinds*-based studies at the Earth Summit in Rio de Janeiro, scheduled for June 1992.

The Central Research Institute of Machine Building (CRIMB), the Russian institute of space engineering, selected experiments, one of which would explore the stratospheric ozone layer.

The Russian experiments would measure both chlofluorocarbons and ozone, providing baseline data for scientists. The experiment called Obzor was designed by two scientists from the CRIMB spectroscopic laboratory to measure ozone layer thickness along the balloon track, identify penetrations of the lower atmosphere by ultraviolet light, explore the upper troposphere illumination intensity, and test new ecological research instruments. The instrument detected separate UV radiation photons; a six-channel photometer installed on the outside of the capsule was connected to a control panel inside the capsule.

Vladimir would measure and manually record the intensity of solar UV radiation penetrating the ozone layer. Data would be compared with data the Soviets were collecting from the orbiting Mir station as well as from ground stations.

A second Russian experiment would measure the aerosol particles that change the optical and thermodynamic properties of the atmosphere and distort ozone-content measuring results. An aerosol detector mounted outside the capsule would suck in atmospheric air and direct it to substrate holes on a rotating disk. Vladimir would collect 36 samples during the flight. Each substrate sample would be examined by an electron microscope to reveal the presence and density of aerosol particles.

The third experiment, from the Nuclear Physics Research Institute at Moscow State University, would measure radiation in the jet stream. These measurements would help scientists study abnormal nuclei in galactic cosmic rays, and the impact of space radiation on the operation of optical-electronic hardware.

Vladimir had seen complicated projects emerge into a solid plan. One day, he sketched an elephant with three men riding in the howdah on top. The elephant's body consisted of a jigsaw puzzle of little pieces, all labeled with *Earthwinds* components.

'We are going to eat the elephant one bite at a time,' the cosmonaut said.

Frustrations in the Rice Bowl

In meetings every morning, Bob Rice reviewed the charts with Larry. It was proving a challenge to find one good calm period in which to inflate the balloon. Finding a second one for launch would take a miracle.

Locally produced wind created a paradox both inside and outside the airdock. Tom Barrow put up a string of pilot balloons, called pibals, with telltale streamers at 50-foot intervals in the airdock with the doors partially open. While the wind outside blew slightly, the lower tell-tales blew straight into the hangar, the middle streamer fluttered, and the top streamer (150 feet over the floor) stiffly blew straight out of the hangar. With warm air at the top, the temperature differential between inside and outside the hangar created a ferris wheel windflow at the doors.

Barrow theorized that leaving the hangar doors open at both ends, with a breeze blowing through the hangar, could neutralize the temperature differential.

Old-time airshipmen began stopping by the weather center to recall that the great rigids and non-rigids built for the Navy always went out the north side of the hangar, where one door's track was now blocked by a building. No, sir, we never took airships out the south doors. Too windy.

Finally, Rice predicted that conditions would settle down after midnight one Saturday. Inflation would take place outside, and then they'd try to bring the balloon inside. Nobody knew if this plan would work.

Although it had been standard practice in long-distance ballooning to build two balloons for every attempt, here there was only one balloon. Nobody had to remind Tom Barrow that if he broke it and left it draped on the doors of the airdock, there would be no flight this year. What's more, he wouldn't collect his fee.

The launch procedure was complicated by Larry's insistence on a 48-hour static test inside the hangar after inflation. He wanted Raven to prove that the *Earthwinds* balloon was absolutely gas-tight.

Rice knew that most plastic balloon pilots believed that their balloon leaked, but was mystified as to why Larry wanted to put his balloon back in the hangar. That was pointless, Rice said: there's nothing you could do except use that balloon, or throw away $140,000 worth of material. Even if there were a small leak in this one, he said, so what? *Earthwinds* had redundant duration and range, with the liquid helium flasks, and an extra large envelope.

Larry told Tom Barrow he would rather wait until the following year than go without the leak test—which none of the battle-weary staff wanted to consider.

Rice rumbled that he was getting the feeling that Larry 'doesn't really want to fly this balloon, or isn't ready to.'

Lynne

Lynne Newman clung to her husband's side. Now that they had patched things up, they were inseparable. They ate breakfast with one another, usually alone. They commuted together in the big white El Dorado from the hotel to the airdock, where they shared the large back-corner office. She served as his executive secretary, household manager, treasurer, receptionist, nutritionist, laundress and alter ego. And she learned from Larry to oversee every detail, however inconsequential.

If they had to be in different parts of the hangar, Larry carried a walkie-talkie in his jacket so she could always reach him. After each stressful 12-hour day in the cave, they would return to the hotel together and share dinner, often arriving in the dining room minutes before the kitchen closed.

The deep chill that lingered between Lynne and Carol Hart affected Lynne the most. As a result, Lynne and Carol now rarely spoke to one another, and that affected the dynamics of how Don Moses and Lynne got along, and Larry and

Carol, and Don and Larry...the four of them weren't friends anymore, but work associates.

Geographically, Lynne was back on home turf. She had been raised just half-an-hour away, in the south Cleveland suburb of Garfield Heights. She visited her mother Bernice and her sisters once in a while; her father was gravely ill in a Cleveland hospital.

She remembered a turbulent home life influenced by her father's alcohol abuse. It was a lonely childhood—no date for the senior prom!—in which she followed in the shadow of older twin sisters. Classmates teased 'Skinny Minnie' mercilessly about her slight build. She married at age 19 and had gone to work in the personnel department of an insurance company.

Moving to Phoenix, she divorced in 1980 and busied herself by raising money for the handicapped through a charitable foundation. She formed her own insurance agency and purchased a home before she met Larry. But a visit with her family in Cleveland was still a rarity: Lynne and Larry spent only 30 minutes at the Thanksgiving dinner table with her family before his restlessness and illness at ease convinced Lynne that they should leave.

Then, on a bittersweet day just before Christmas, Lynne's father passed away. His funeral Mass took place on a day when Larry needed her, too. The new stresses won out over the old stresses; after starting out for the church, she turned around and went back to the airdock, skipping her father's funeral altogether.

Lynne talked openly about her marriage, as if public disclosure were a form of cathartic therapy. If she and Larry weren't having sex during their time in Akron, she would say, it was because the project drained them of their energy.

In public, she openly admired her husband. Her smile radiated and her eyes sparkled whenever Larry appeared on television or spoke from a podium. But during technical discussions of the dangerous aspects of the flight, Lynne's lips would purse and her eyes would moisten.

'I just don't want to lose my husband,' she would say.

Her world revolved entirely around his.

Dances with sponsors

Helping sponsors calculate how they would capitalize on their investment demanded an inordinate amount of time and attention.

Larry had soured on Virgin Atlantic and all of Branson's people, and was openly antagonistic toward them. He was high on Barron Hilton.

As January wore on, major sponsors decided to meet in Akron. They would try to agree on a publicity plan and a theme. But they still hadn't come to terms even about basic things like letterhead; Virgin already had rejected two designs. Representatives came from Virgin, Hilton, Canon and ESPN, all anxious about signage and getting their corporate name used as often as possible. From London's Virgin Group came Wil Whitehorn, the London-based publicity coordinator, Michael Kendrick, and Lori Levin, Virgin Atlantic's New York pr director. From Hilton came Mike Ribero, the senior public affairs executive; Doug Buemi and Neil Cohen from the pr firm, and Pat Barry, an independent pr counsel for Barron Hilton. John Wilcox presided and Lynne represented Larry.

At this crucial meeting the two major sponsors were to decide on a message and how to display it. Hilton's people were eager to produce basic materials such as stationery, signage and jackets.

Five minutes into the meeting, Kendrick turned ashen and excused himself, ill from a tomato juice allergy.

The committee finally designed a logo for news release letterhead, with the two big sponsors at the top and minor sponsors at the bottom. It would appear on the windbreakers the launch crew would wear for the benefit of the TV crews.

Virgin then insisted on adding its logo to the curtain in the capsule, so both sponsors would have visibility during live interviews from the capsule. Hilton's people objected: the capsule was named *Earthwinds* Hilton. And so it went, back and forth.

When Wilcox announced that an additional sponsor had been added—the Swiss sports watchmaker Sector had pledged $50,000—Virgin demanded that Sector's $50,000 be wired to them to help buy back Branson's seat. Such a diversion of cash would cripple the project. Anticipating this, Wilcox had structured the deal so that Sector's money would be wired into an *Earthwinds* account ten minutes after launch.

Whitehorn stayed an extra day so he could get a look at the airdock, the capsule and the press viewing area. (It took an extra day for Loral to prepare credentials for a 'foreign national.')

In the morning, Larry called me and instructed sternly, 'don't let him get inside the capsule unless I'm there.'

Whitehorn gaped at the cavernous old hangar and walked through the offices and machine shop and reviewed the launch site.

The minute he left for England later that day, Larry called me aside.

'You do understand, don't you, that Wil Whitehorn is the lowest form of snake there is?' Larry's eyes widened as he spoke, 'and that he's here as Richard's spy? He goes around and looks at things on our desks and reports right back to Richard. Don't tell him anything. He's just here to try to get information on *Earthwinds*.'

Stick it to 'em

'Don't tell Larry about the shot!' Lynne warned Mike Emich one morning.

Larry could not bear the sight of blood—anyone's.

Watching him pad around the airdock in his two flannel Penningtons and designer jeans, leading a bold project on the cutting edge of technology, one would never guess that his knees quivered in the presence of doctors. Emich, a trained paramedic, had come in one day with tetanus booster shots, and quickly administered them to Don and Vladimir.

But Lynne's warning left him perplexed about how to get the shot into Larry's arm. After considerable scheming, they sat him down, held his hand, talked soothingly and distracted him as Mike needled him from the blind side.

But when his health and attitude were good, Larry enjoyed moments of playful banter. He would sit in the lunchroom and recount his fly-fishing trips in the Glen Canyon Dam, the dream vacation he and Lynne had in New Zealand, his experiences in the Double Eagle V crew, where he had mercilessly teased Ron Clark for rejecting sushi in favor of steak and potatoes.

Summoning his years of experience as the class clown in high school, he would hang a spoon from his nose, or imitate voices. Occasionally, he called the media center posing as a foreign correspondent: in heavily accented Japanese one time, in German another. Late one afternoon at the airdock, he picked up one of the incessantly ringing phones and answered simply '*Earthwinds*'—after he had issued the edict that all phones must be answered 'Virgin *Earthwinds*'. At the other end was one of Richard Branson's top people, whose voice Larry recognized. He quickly switched to Eastern European ethnic and pretended to be a Loral maintenance man, throwing the call to Lynne until he could recover.

But his favorite imitation was doing 'the Branson wave.' During a videotaped interview, Branson had acknowledged a host's introduction with his white-picket-fence smile, a palm-out dipsy-doodle salute from the temple with a concurrent lift of the eyebrows. The more the tape was played in the airdock's lunchroom, the funnier it looked. Larry had it down cold, and offered instructions to others on the right moves.

How not to enjoy the Super Bowl

Huddled in the morning's usual thick vapor of pipe smoke in the Rice Bowl, Barrow and Lachenmeier examined an after-midnight wind forecast on Saturday, Jan. 25. The pattern was moving a little more slowly than anticipated, so a few hours after midnight might be the right time to bring the balloon out and inflate it. The ground crews were alerted.

With the prospect of inflation so near, Tom Barrow requested another numbers check. Tim Lachenmeier began reviewing the balloon's size and shape, and came up with revised numbers. Eventually, he concluded that he would need two tuber trucks of helium to fatten the balloon enough to get it inside the hangar. Barrow called for another truck of helium. Taking an extra 50,000 cubic feet of helium would make handling easier, make the balloon more stable, fatter, and thus shorter, making the risky job of putting it back in the airdock easier.

He wanted to finish work that night with 230,000 cubic feet in the poly balloon.

However, every decision had a consequence. Adding more gas would make the balloon lighter, but also could exacerbate the 'creep' factor in the polyethylene. Over time, especially in warmer weather, stretching can add up to seven percent of the balloon's size. But by putting the balloon back in the airdock with less gas inside, temperature and pressure changes could, under certain conditions, also make the balloon grow taller. In a high-pressure, low temperature condition, for example, the helium contracts, and the partially inflated balloon would grow—by how much, no one knew.

'What we don't want is to find ourselves coming in some morning with the zero pressure balloon scraping against the ceiling,' Barrow mused.

With the clock running, Barrow decided to shoot for inflation.

The volunteers were poised. The air mass carrying this light wind was moving slowly. It looked as though the wind would abate about 3 a.m. and remain calm through dawn. Volunteers were asked to report to the airdock at 2:30 a.m. on Super Bowl Sunday.

Thirty did, along with a retinue of camera crews, Loral security and crane operators. Larry stayed at the hotel. Barrow pre-positioned two helium tanker trucks on the apron in front of the clamshell doors on the south side, and the crate containing the balloon was loaded onto a trailer.

Helium-filled yellow pibals were raised on tethers. The dampness made the 20-degree night air seem colder. The volunteers sipped coffee as the hangar doors rolled open, but the wind remained stubbornly at 5–8 mph overnight from the west-northwest.

Accentuated by the angle at which it intersected the north side of the airdock, it created a swirling wind near the entrance well in excess of tolerable conditions.

Barrow waited, then at 5 a.m. announced to the shivering group that the operation would stand down for the night. The exercise increased anxiety about finding an available moment for inflation, and then another one for launch.

So dig a trench!

With the disappointment and fatigue resulting from the intense drill on Sunday morning, the anxiety level was ratcheted up another notch. The balloon was too tall to inflate inside, but getting the wind to calm down, and then getting the balloon back inside for its endurance test seemed a formidable challenge. With increasing pessimism that the wind would ever stop blowing long enough to inflate the poly balloon outside, some of the old hands at the airdock came up with a suggestion. They remembered that beneath the railroad tracks running down the center of the airdock floor—the tracks that once guided the mobile masts of the Akron and Macon—was a 15-foot deep utility trench.

'We can dig up those tracks in a couple of hours with jackhammers,' they said, 'and you can lay the balloon out flat in the tunnel. It'll give you enough clearance topside so you won't hit the ceiling.'

Barrow considered the idea, but demurred. Someday, the balloon would have to go outside and in again. And he wasn't yet up against the weather window.

Back in the Rice Bow, Bob Rice listened to the way Larry treated people trying to help him. After another of Larry's sniping lectures about sponsors—especially Richard Branson—he remarked: 'He treats Branson with contempt,' Bob said, 'but Branson is the one who is financing his dream.'

Sometimes Larry asserted totalitarian control over matters that seemed to others completely inconsequential. Bob Rice needed Global Navigation Charts to post on the walls of the place where senior decision-makers would gather during the flight. Larry had told Lynne to resist ordering a set for Rice, hoping instead for a donation.

'The GNC charts', Rice told Larry, 'that we need in the command center haven't—' '—This is not a command center,' Larry interrupted him. 'That implies that decisions will be made here. I'm in command in the balloon. You can call it the weather center or the operations center.'

'Well,' Rice said, 'in my weather centers I've used GNC maps for 12 long-distance balloon flights. Don't tell me that I don't need them,' Rice fumed.

Lynne wasn't allowed to buy the maps that Rice needed to track the flight!

Rice began to think that Larry kept getting in the way, and he told a group of staffers:

> 'This project should have been thought of, financed and flown in one year. Here we were, two and a half years into this thing, and they were still building it and changing things. They can't even get maps for me. This would still be just his wet dream if it weren't for Tom Barrow and John Ackroyd.'

Larry's insistence on calling himself The Captain (the others were untitled) resulted in Rice, Barrow, and number of staff members mockingly whispering 'Oh Captain, My Captain,' whenever he left the room, a play on Robin Williams' Dead Poets Society. Some would even stand up on chairs and say it.

It was all in good fun, and it broke the tension.

The Times makes the man

Shortly after Christmas, I had visited Malcolm Browne, The New York Times' senior science correspondent, in New York, and invited him to do a story. I knew that Browne had a long-standing interest in lighter-than-air matters, a contrast to his days as a Pulitzer-prize winning correspondent who covered the Vietnam war and who snapped the famous photo of the self-immolating Buddhist priest in Saigon in 1963—a photo that became an icon of the war.

My overture to Browne now paid off. The project scored a giant publicity coup in The New York Times when a two-page spread appeared on the front of the Science News section on Tuesday, January 28. Browne's story, with graphics and a photo of the flight crew with Barron Hilton in front of the capsule, described the balloon in its entirety.

The dollar value of the publicity for Hilton was almost incalculable. I knew that this excellent report would produce worldwide media attention that would rocket *Earthwinds* to center stage. A big friendly story in The Times legitimized any project. Now, news organizations from around the world began calling our Virgin *Earthwinds* Media Information Center requesting interviews with the flight crew, or fact sheets, or additional story angles.

Just as importantly, Malcolm Browne believed he had discovered the story, and would report on its progress to conclusion.

Larry decided to capitalize on the growing public interest by installing a 900-number. Callers would be charged $2 for information on *Earthwinds*' position; Larry would update it himself.

I also persuaded the Beacon Journal to activate a hotline. Reporter Bob Downing would record a new announcement every day and publish the number. By noon the next day the recorded message line at the Beacon Journal had logged 277 calls, a pace that continued for weeks.

Under the big top

The publicity intensified the sense of urgency. Bob Rice was forecasting an inflatable condition for Tuesday night. He predicted light wind from sunset until midnight.

The daytime weather was cold, freezing rain and snow, but low-level clouds would seal in the surface conditions long enough to try the six- hour inflation sequence. A message was passed throughout the project, phone trees were activated, extra helium ordered, and Tim Lachenmeier went to work on his calculations again.

Getting this beast inflated and then back into the garage was going to be his challenge. The margins were close. Although the airdock was the only building large enough to hold the balloons, its ceiling was too low to permit inflation inside. The poly balloon stretched out flat measured 202 feet long. Two 270-foot-long inflation sleeves hung from the 'shoulder' of the balloon 30 feet from the top. When enough gas was pumped through the sleeves and into the balloon, the top bubble of gas would pop up. The balloon gradually would be 'winched up' hand-over-hand, until it stood up straight and skinny. Then it would fatten out, with the bulge increasing in size, and gas added until the balloon became rounder and shorter.

With the ground crew reporting for duty at six p.m., and flags barely fluttering, Barrow made his decision. He opened the shipping crate and began to lay out the balloon. Tim Lachenmeier installed the valve, checked the internal electrical rigging, and then tucked the helium diffusers inside the inflation sleeves.

The bottom fitting of the balloon, a 12-inch wedge-and-collar device from which hung a large eyebolt, was secured to the lip of a heavy-duty front-end loader. Inside the cab sat a gregariously friendly bear of a man, Mike Osborne of Keller-Hall crane operators. Osborne, who had limped around the airdock for the last month building and planning, was a multiple recipient of the Purple Heart for combat wounds in Vietnam. With an uncanny confidence in his own abilities, he reacted to any problem with a scowl, a scratch of his beard, and a great gap-toothed grin; there was no problem he couldn't solve. He typified *Earthwinds* volunteers and the spirit needed for any such enterprise to succeed.

Since the balloon would have more than seven tons of lift, Osborne had loaded seven tons of weight—scrap steel beams and reinforced concrete blocks—into the bucket. The elegance and sleek lines of the clean plastic balloon and the mechanized power of the front-end loader contrasted with the rusty metal and concrete chunks in the bucket between.

Bob Rice had come out to the field and looked worried as a cold puff of wind touched his face, and a piball swayed on its tether.

'It's as quiet as you can get this place,' he muttered, glaring at the sky 'and we've still got air motion. All of the things around here…the construction, the air mass itself, and the air dock…create air motion. It's thermally inspired. It's an urban environment, unlike your open countryside. In most launch sites, you take a marginal weather environment and improve upon it. But this place is not conducive to light air. It sucks, actually.'

He stared for a moment at the old airdock.

'That place is alive. The son-of-a-bitch is breathing. It's up there laughing at us.'

Despite Rice's pessimism, launch master Tom Barrow assembled the inflation crew at the base of the balloon near the front-end loader. He identified the four individuals who would be allowed to touch the delicate polyethylene film. Then he spoke calmly, 'We are going to move slowly and deliberately through the inflation process.'

Helium inflation started at 7:41 p.m. when Barrow raised his index finger and moved it in rotor fashion. Lachenmeier turned to his Raven Industries colleague Ray Ramstead.

'Go ahead and crack the diffuser, Ray,' Tim ordered.

With that, Ramstead turned the handle on the helium nozzle and gas whistled into the long plastic tube. Another pair of workers held a nozzle inside the second inflation sleeve opposite the helium truck. Both tubes filled with gas and arched over the pavement, terminating nearly at the other end of the balloon.

It happened slowly. Releasing 220,000 cubic feet of helium from a pressurized tuber truck into a fragile plastic bag required a dozen helpers. When the top of the balloon had enough helium, it popped up off the ground, to the delight of the workers. As gas streamed in, the bubble fattened slowly. Finally, having been winched up by those careful hands, the giant polyethylene bag stood straight up. People groped for words to describe the sight.

'It's the world's largest Trojan,' smirked Don Moses.

About 9:30 p.m., Barrow pulled a finger across his throat to stop the helium flow. A kink had developed in one of the two inflation tubes, choking off one fill line. The balloon had sipped only three-fifths of the night's load, and was still far too tall to take inside. Sometimes such wrinkles came out, sometimes they didn't. A twisted tube could mean a balloon had to be scrapped!

Looking at it from a different perspective, the always relaxed British wit John Ackroyd cracked, 'It looks a lot like a womb, actually. One of the fallopian tubes is blocked, you see. A lot of things in science are replicated in nature.'

After 30 anxious moments of gently tugging, bending and squirting helium into the twisted tube, it righted itself and soon both 'fallopian tubes' were taking gas again.

Mike Emich, perched on a catwalk at the top of the airdock, was giving visual and measured assessments of whether the top of the balloon could clear the inside of the airdock. Crouched on the narrow wooden planks 160 feet above the floor, he placed a self-leveling laser device on catwalk number 5, aimed the level laser and waited. When the poly balloon rose up, he trained the red dot on it. When the dot disappeared, the balloon would fit below the ceiling, and might be walked in. He knew it would be close.

'There was no way we could do this visually,' Mike said.

Larry remained in his office inside the airdock. He busied himself by removing 50 pounds of margarine and spices from the food kits to reduce capsule weight and save space. He and Lynne sent made up a hand-lettered sign reminding visitors and volunteers to wipe their feet before entering his office spaces.

Outside, his entire project hinged on inflating this balloon correctly, but he ignored it. He would return to the hotel before there was even talk of moving the balloon back in the hangar. Ironically, he had done the same thing—ignored the balloon inflation—in Japan before the Pacific flight, and in Maine before the Atlantic flight. For the rest of his team, the mystery and miracle of erecting the fantastic monster helium balloon was spellbinding. Either Larry had nerves of steel, or couldn't stand to watch.

One thing Larry did care about was who would be allowed to take pictures of the inflation. After weeks of weighing offers from various photo agencies, he and Wilcox had signed a contract with Gamma Liaison photo agency. They would make money from every photo Gamma sold. Nobody else would be allowed to carry a camera within the restricted area of the airdock, the capsule or the chase plane, except Bill Swersey, the Gamma photographer. Apparently, the New York

AP Photo desk hadn't gotten the word. Somebody from Loral had let in an AP stringer, to cover the inflation, and Larry was beside himself.

'Get him out of here right now,' he said to me.

I knew we would have had PR disaster on our hands if he had thrown out the AP. The question was whose picture would be used on the AP wire: Gamma's or the stringer's. After a number of phone calls, I arranged for the AP stringer to process Gamma's film and move Gamma's picture from the Beacon Journal darkroom.

Back on the inflation field, the kink had just straightened itself out when a real disaster struck. Without warning, the helium balloon jerked upward and actually lifted up the bucket of the front-end loader, over-riding the truck's hydraulic system.

The bucket already had 15,000 pounds of weight in it. Mike Osborne strained to get the bucket down again, then left the cab to search for more weight. He found another 5,000 pounds of steel beams, and loaded them into the bucket. Still, the balloon went up and the bucket with it. All the careful measuring of the inside height of the airdock and the length of the balloon was about to be wasted. If the balloon went up another five feet, it wouldn't clear the airdock ceiling and the project would be lost. Osborne proposed a dramatic solution.

The bucket truck operates like an extension of a human arm, with a wrist, forearm, elbow and arm. Osborne sent for some 8-foot lengths of steel I-beam. He welded 5,000 pounds of steel ballast on the I-beam next to the base of the balloon. Then he welded one side onto the bucket and the other side onto the movable arm, to keep the bucket extended down, three inches off pavement. He attacked the job as if it were something he did every day. The angle iron was welded from the hand to the forearm, to prevent the wrist from bending upward. The welding took place only three feet below the delicate balloon.

'When they started welding, and sparks started flying within inches of that poly balloon, I had to walk away,' said Lachenmeier.

Vern Rich held a blanket and a piece of plywood between the welder's torch and the fragile balloon that only four people were allowed to touch. The welding job held. The bucket stayed down.

Barrow's crew milked the last of the helium from the two tankers, and when they were finished, the load cell showed that the helium was tugging upward 15,540 pounds of weight.

Bob Rice was still nervous.

He characterized each moment of weather as if it had its own life. He looked around the sky, and said 'I wouldn't trust this son-of-a-bitch after midnight.'

Barrow and the rest of the crew couldn't tell if Bob knew that something would change or whether his forecast was only valid until midnight. He wore a fearful, skeptical, look, as if he were the only sane person watching asylum inmates perform some meaningless bizarre midnight ritual in bitter cold. Muttering ominously to no one in particular, he scanned the heavens, watched tell-tale streamers jump around, looked over his shoulder and kept repeating, 'I wouldn't trust this son-of-a-bitch after midnight.'

Tim Lachenmeier stood in the cold, having re-run his calculations again, and knowing that colder night air was causing the helium to contract, which made the balloon taller.

'This will be very close,' he said.

Up in the Green Machine, Mike Osborne faced the task of driving the big bucket truck and its unusual cargo back into the airdock. Well after midnight, Barrow stood next to the truck and motioned forward. The balloon swayed.

Osborne aligned his cab with the center of the airdock and drove. The giant plastic bag shrugged as if it longed for the sky. It was made to fly, not to be garaged. Nobody knew for sure whether it would fit, or if the wind around the hangar would surge and a rough edge would gash the plastic bag. Osborne stopped at the door of the airdock while Barrow radioed Emich.

'Will it fit?'

'I think so,' replied Mike, 'but I'm not sure.'

Barrow then asked Lachenmeier, 'Whaddya think?'

The balloon builder paused and quietly said, 'I have no idea.'

Out of helium, out of time and with Rice's words echoing in his ears, there was only one way to find out.

Tom took a deep breath and waived Osborne ahead.

Aloft on his perch at the lip of the clamshell doors, Emich prepared for a catastrophe. If the balloon had ruptured on a girder, he might have been engulfed in helium. He carried a self-contained breathing apparatus on loan from the fire department.

The diesel growled again and Osborne threaded the needle without hesitation, a steady push straight into the hangar. The fragile balloon nudged under the plastic on the ceiling with a clearance of only 10 inches.

'You didn't really have any goddam idea how big that balloon was did you?' Barrow prodded, jousting with Tim Lachenmeier at 1:30 a.m. in Schumacher's bar. Recalling Vladimir's sketch of the elephant puzzle, the launch master summarized the day:

'If we're eating the elephant one bite at a time, tonight we swallowed the butt.'

But his sober assessment was that there could be just as many surprises on launch night. If inflation took twice as long as planned, launch could be a bitch.

Getting the helium balloon inflated and then back inside the huge airdock in Akron was a major achievement.

Wired

By the next morning, most newspapers had run the dramatic wire service picture of the inflation outside the airdock, showing the anchor balloon waiting inside. Larry and Lynne drove out to the airdock early. From his desk drawer, he took a red marker pen and walked across the hangar to the polyethylene balloon.

'Designed and manufactured by Larry Newman, Scottsdale, Arizona,' he wrote on the collar at the throat of the balloon. It was his.

He commissioned a sign painter to add in plain block letters on the capsule:

'Larry Newman, Pilot-in-Command. Don Moses, Crew. Vladimir Dzhanibekov, Crew.'

Lynne called the media center to say Larry wanted all the television stations and newspapers there at 2 p.m. When everybody was escorted into the airdock,

Larry and Lynne were casually standing behind the red picket fence in front of the helium balloon tied to the Green Machine. I asked Larry if he could send out Don and Vladimir.

'No,' he said, 'just tell these reporters that the other crewmembers are busy. Every hour we waste talking to the press means we start flying an hour later.'

He went into his office, changed into his cotton flight suit with the patches all over it, and came out to greet the press. The tape rolled, cameras clicked, and reporters scribbled. Two wire services, five TV stations, and three newspapers—about 20 journalists altogether—hung on Larry's every word. The other two pilots were nowhere to be seen.

Larry told the reporters that the wind direction was unfavorable for at least the next five days.

'Operationally, we have just a few small details to finish up. We are waiting for weather. That's the big issue.'

But what he did not disclose was that troubles plaguing the capsule presented a more serious impediment.

While work had continued on the capsule, various workmen installed and connected electrical systems. As days passed, it became apparent that the electrical wiring had become a rat's nest, an unfathomable maze. Every contractor or contributor, including Larry and Don, who had installed equipment had simply used their own wires or whatever was handy.

Two employees of a local ignition firm installed new 12-volt alternators. All of a sudden, one of them burned out. They were putting out too many volts, threatening to short out vital equipment, melt wires and overcharge the batteries.

Larry turned to three retired Goodyear Aerospace workers, Gene Kemmerline, E. J. Hendrix and Dick Paige, to work on the problem. Complex electronics was nothing new to them. They had spent their careers developing guidance systems for air-launched missiles like the Mace, Maverick and Pershing. Oftentimes, they'd be on a military project for months at a time; they knew all about project life.

One day in November, they had taken a look at the *Earthwinds* capsule and began rewiring every instrument with a craftsman's care. They installed circuit breakers to protect the power source. They reduced the fire hazard. Larry loved them and he gave them a collective nickname. They became the Three Amigos.

The day after the inflation was marked with confusion, fatigue and emotion. Erin Porter burst into tears and almost went home after Lynne yelled at her for giving a Fact Sheets to a cameraman who was to ride the chase plane.

'That fact sheet is none of his business. He's not a reporter,' Lynne screamed through the phone. 'I'm warning you: those are only for reporters. You don't have any business giving him one of our Fact Sheets. We can't just hand them out to anybody.'

Erin recounted the incident, again in tears, to Rice and Barrow, who just shook their heads. Barrow gave Erin a hug and restored her equilibrium.

'I have never met two people,' Bob Rice said, 'who were so intent on controlling so much minutia.'

Tom Barrow shook his head in wonderment.

'How can you yell at volunteers who are doing so much for you?' he asked.

In a few moments, though, Tom found out. He telephoned out to the airdock to ask Vern Rich, Sr., to carefully haul down the pilot balloons used in and around the airdock.

'We can use them again when we launch,' he said. 'Just pull down all the helium balloons in the airdock, untie the strings and let the helium out. That way, we won't have to go out and buy more weather balloons.'

Vern sounded confused.

'I'm not sure I understand what you want,' he told Tom. 'Am I supposed to take down all the balloons?'

'Yes,' said Tom, 'we just put them up for practice last night, and when we are ready for the flight, we can inflate them again.'

'Okay,' said Vern, 'even the one on the truck, the big one?'

'No', shouted Barrow, 'don't touch that one. Don't let the gas out of the big plastic one, just the little yellow ones with the strings on them!'

Larry's attitude had by this time become a great unifying force within the project. People would rally around the one who received the latest chewing out and pull one another through the dark moments. The joke around the airdock became that *Earthwinds* had the makings of a great Agatha Christie murder mystery...no one would know who had 'done him in.'

Wilcox's crew continued filming for the TV special, and doing hometown videos of the volunteers and staff. These packages would be sent to hometown TV stations. I prepared the same types of releases for newspaper use. Vern Rich Jr. was being outfitted with a microphone at the airdock as Wilcox's crew prepared to film and interview him. Larry went over to the workbench, pulled off Vern's microphone and shooed away the camera crew.

'Vernon is being paid to work,' Larry said, 'not to do interviews.'

This happened in full sight of Vern's parents. Humiliated, Mary Sue broke down and cried all the way home from work, as did Vern's wife Darlene. That night in hotel lobby there was a near-mutiny. Vern was waiting for Larry to come back from the airdock; when Larry walked in, Vern collared him, led him off to a corner and pushed Larry into a couch. They sat frozen and talked quietly for nearly an hour.

'You can mess with me, boy,' Vern told Larry, 'but don't you ever make my momma cry!'

◆ ◆ ◆

Bob Rice's 240-hour charts showed no usable weather for the foreseeable future. Rice saw a local-condition window that might have been promising on Sunday, Feb. 2, if the capsule had been ready. But it wasn't. We were in for a long wait.

Polar bears, a broken watch and dog tails

The probability that *Earthwinds* could blow off course was real; the remote possibility existed that the polar jet stream could spin the balloon off beyond the Arctic Circle, where a forced landing would make recovery hazardous and time-consuming, as Branson and Lindstrand had found at Yellowknife the year before.

Landing in the polar region was one of Ben Abruzzo's recurring nightmares, and Larry found that fear in the attic along with the rest of the round-the-world dream.

Specifically, Abruzzo was terrified about being attacked and eaten by polar bears.

To be certain that he had a large enough weapon to ward off the polar bears, Larry dispatched Fred Nebiker to the Tallmadge Rod and Gun Shop. The senior vice president of this big aerospace corporation walked in wearing a suit and explained the problem cold—that he had a friend who was going on a long trip with a boat builder and a Russian cosmonaut and they wanted to defend themselves against attacks by polar bears. Yup, seriously! After a couple of tries, Nebiker persuaded the owner to donate a 30.06-gauge shotgun to *Earthwinds*. A gun rack was mounted inside the capsule.

◆ ◆ ◆

Dick Rutan, the global aviator, felt a fraternal closeness to the project. Besides having watched the capsule come alive at Mojave, he had made two trips to

Akron to see it, and checked in periodically for status reports. He called one day and said he was overnighting a gift to the crew: the official timepiece and calculator carried on Voyager. It was Dick's good luck charm.

Even though the watch no longer worked, he asked if I would I put it into the hands of one of the crewmembers so they could carry it on *Earthwinds*' trip. The next day the carefully wrapped timepiece arrived complete with a certificate of authenticity.

When Larry came by the Media Bowl, I mentioned Rutan's bequest.

'Send it back to him,' Larry answered slowly and irritably, 'Tell Dick that if he wants his watch to go around the world again he should build himself another airplane.'

Later, Don Moses gladly agreed to hide it in the pocket of his flight suit and sign the statement of authenticity.

◆ ◆ ◆

By late January, the phones were ringing constantly in the Media Bowl; up to 100 calls a day each required an explanation or follow-up. With stories appearing every day, Larry would sometimes get questions about items that had been in the paper. We tried to make sure that he saw everything that was printed, but sometimes we let him down. One morning, he came in to the Media Bowl and scooped up the Akron Beacon Journal, the Cleveland Plain Dealer and The New York Times.

'Um, I think Bill bought those papers, Larry,' Erin said.

Her comment started him simmering, and then boiling. Within a few minutes, Larry called from his desk at the airdock, speaking sternly.

'When I want something out of the media center,' he told Erin, 'I will take it. Is that understood? You remember this: I am the dog and you are the tail.'

His dead serious manner overwhelmed Erin's frayed nerves. In a moment he called me back and repeated what he had told Erin, explaining that if she didn't understand the policy, she could go home. Only with the perspective of time and retelling did his self-description as a dog wagging us tails strike everyone as ludicrous.

The Swat Team

Nobody knew how many people might show up for the launch. Crowd estimates, originating in the Beacon-Journal, were soon ranging up to 200,000. People remembered Goodyear's big open house at the airdock a few years earlier. The Newmans, the Akron police department and the Department of Defense security people at Loral were very nervous.

Larry wondered how he would get to the launch site with those kinds of crowds. The Akron police decided to escort him in a motorcade. His biggest concern, though, was that some crackpot would try to shoot him down as he ascended. Even if they missed, a hole in the anchor balloon would render it completely ineffective.

At a meeting with city officials Lynne and Larry conveyed their fear about the impending attack, and Larry's fear of crowds. Some city officials had already sensed this, and thought that he might actually try to launch in secret some night, without telling anyone.

'If Larry Newman tries to slip out of town unnoticed,' an official in the mayor's office told me, 'there will be a lot of very pissed off people in the city of Akron.'

To help assuage Larry's concerns, the police chief decided to offer the same protection to the *Earthwinds* crew that they provide visiting heads of state. On launch night they would treat Larry Newman like a Secret Service protectee, or a visiting head of state.

One element of this treatment involved deploying the city's 40-member SWAT team into the woods within a two-mile radius from the launch site. Twenty marksmen would be stationed inside the security perimeter, and 20 outside. They identified sites in wooded areas in which the SWAT team members would take up positions after midnight on the proposed launch day.

In addition, the city would deploy 40 traffic cops for their own internal estimate of 10,000 spectators around the airport. The cop count would go up linearly with each group of 10,000 spectators. Lots of city police and firemen volunteered for this duty. They wanted the honor of watching, as well as the overtime. Still, city officials feared they wouldn't have enough advance notice to call out the forces they might need.

6

In Search of Harmonic Convergence

Bucks, young bucks...and Buck's

Money was tight. And Larry was embarrassed when The New York Times called him a millionaire; he had a few investments and the equity in his houses, but was not wealthy. He had put a lot into this project, sacrificed to keep it going, and hoped to become wealthy by succeeding at it. After the flight there would be product endorsements and lucrative speaking engagements; Hilton had guaranteed Larry 10 appearances at $25,000 apiece.

Don had a similar contract. Canon was wooing Vladimir as a spokesman for its camera products. He would also work the lecture circuit, as he had done after his space flights.

But that was the future. In January 1992 *Earthwinds* was down to its last $19,000.

Branson had been eyeing Hilton's pending balance of $450,000 to help buy back his share. Wilcox asked Hilton to defer its payment lest that money go right to Virgin Atlantic.

The Lighter-Than-Air Society set up tables in the lobby of the hotel every weekend to sell pins, patches, T-shirts and videotapes of the test flight. Sales quickened in direct correlation with how much *Earthwinds* was in the news. Annie Pryne, a spirited, sixtiesh aviatrix who loved ballooning projects, took in tens of thousands of dollars in cash sales of *Earthwinds* souvenirs, turning over every penny to the Newmans.

Larry told the Beacon Journal that the T-shirt money would pay for the helium. At fifteen dollars per shirt, there were no freebies for the staff or for key volunteers. Those who gave up a paying job to go to Akron still had to fork over $12.50 for a patch, or $7.50 for a souvenir button.

A big mystery developed over a carton of sports watches from Sector, a minor sponsor. When John Wilcox signed up this Swiss firm for $50,000, the company shipped 25 of its expensive watches to *Earthwinds*, but Larry only found 19 of them, which he distributed to the senior staff. He made a point of calling others to say that since some had been stolen, he didn't have enough to go around. At various times, they were said to have been held up at Customs, stolen by Federal Express, and taken from a desk drawer.

After months of togetherness in this campaign atmosphere, working long hours, rarely seeing daylight, feeling constant tension, waiting long weeks for weather, staff morale was sagging. Many people had left families behind, and put other plans on hold, just to be part of *Earthwinds*. Yet the aircraft wasn't even finished—and after it took off, the support staff would still be needed for the flight itself.

John Wilcox decreed that it was party time. He directed his production assistant Liesl Clark, Erin Porter and me to set up an *Earthwinds* family bash for the following Thursday evening. Spend up to $20 per head, he said; get food, beer and wine and music.

ESPN would be the official host, and it would be a surprise party for Larry. They'd give him an award, and an opportunity to thank all his volunteers.

But even without an organized party, the *Earthwinds* group had begun to travel in a pack each night, taking over a favorite restaurant in groups ranging from 10 to 40 at a time. Some nights a single word would be passed: Mexican, Chinese, or Italian, or Buck's, and everyone would know where to report. The traveling troupe expanded and contracted depending on who was in town, but usually included NASA scientists, sponsor representatives, sound and light technicians, local volunteers, the launch crew, the press center crew, and the core group consisting of both Vern Rich families, John Ackroyd, Tom Barrow, Carol and Don, and Vladimir.

The surging entourage sensed its uniqueness, knowing that every once in a while some among them would be interviewed; their names would appear in wire service dispatches and newspapers around the world. Some found their pictures syndicated worldwide, and got their Warhol-guaranteed 15 minutes of fame.

Above all, there was the sense of participating in an adventure that would capture the world's imagination. When the flight began, they knew it would be covered live on all the networks. Soon enough they'd put down their tools, wash their hands, burst forth from the cold dark cave they called the airdock, and dance on the world's stage.

In fact, some of them already were bursting forth on stage. One of the most popular gathering places was a noisy tavern called Buck's, adjoining the Quaker Square Hilton.

Thursday night was karaoke night. Setting up a long table with pitchers of beer and plates of nachos, they would sing, mimic, joke, drink, and bond. There was a happy blend of play-acting, shoptalk, future plans, and the vibrant excitement of getting acquainted. These high tech gypsies had come together from a variety of unconnected disciplines to breathe life into *Earthwinds*. Each night, everybody would be out there, except Lynne and Larry.

Choreography

Tom Barrow spent weeks writing the launch sequence libretto and ordering the heavy machinery he would need. In Larry Newman, Barrow knew he was up against an inveterate tinkerer. One day, he would say, he would have to take the capsule away from Larry, and declare it ready to fly; otherwise, modifications and refinements would never cease.

Eighteen hours before liftoff, he would park the capsule on the ramp, half a mile from the airdock at the edge of the concrete.

Staging the two balloons and the capsule would require about six hours of work, he figured—if all went well.

Barrow's playbook called for three tow trucks and two high-reach winch trucks. The helium balloon, still tied to the Green Machine, and the anchor balloon, tied down to its 60-foot wide pallet, would roll out to the staging area.

Barrow feared that a breeze would roll the anchor off the pallet, and that the ground crew would be unable to restrain it merely by holding its three restraining ropes.

At the staging area, the helium balloon's bottom fitting would be attached to Spectra ropes coiled on two diesel-powered winches and raised about 60 feet off the ground. The capsule would then be attached to the flight train, and the load cell at the top of the capsule connected mechanically and electrically.

At that point, launch crewmembers on three high-reach cherry-pickers would transfer the balloon and capsule to three smaller winches, and the pilots would board the capsule.

The next step involved raising the whole system more than 120 feet—the capsule dangling below the helium balloon. A tractor would pull the anchor balloon into place underneath, and the restraint lines would be paid out until the configuration stood 400 feet in the air. Larry would push a button to sever the restraint ropes and start the flight.

Some engineers scoffed at this plan. It was needlessly complicated, said Don Overs, whose advice Larry had rejected.

'Techniques such as tying a balloon down to a heavy transporter…were given up perhaps a century or more ago,' he argued.

Overs' alternative was much simpler. He would have inflated the anchor balloon with about 10 percent helium, making it slightly buoyant.

'Filling the anchor balloon totally with air prior to launch only causes ground handling and launch problems, not to mention the sacrifice of the extra payload that a buoyant anchor balloon would provide.

'Any argument that an initially buoyant anchor balloon would not function the same as an air-filled balloon as a stabilizer at cruise altitude is not to understand the physics involved. The stabilizing effect is dependent only on the volume of the anchor balloon and the density of the displaced air.'

He would have connected the helium balloon to the capsule and then to the anchor balloon, which would be nearly lifting its own weight because of the helium content. A single restraint below the capsule would then be cut and the flight would launch.

Such a procedure would permit a greater tolerance for higher wind, and at no time would the crew face the danger of being suspended high above the ground while the anchor balloon was raised into a vertical position.

Volunteers

Earthwinds' complexity stunned people. Invariably, skilled craftsmen came to the airdock to look at the project. The more they learned, the more they wanted to do, like moths drawn to a flame. A Goodyear retiree walked in to the lunchroom one afternoon and said, 'Ah, excuse me, I heard you needed some help machining some threaded fittings.'

'Great!' someone called out to him, 'Now you're the cryogenic helium suspension expert.'

Local businesses built parts on short notice. A family-owned metal fabricating shop, FM Machine Co., made two vital parts. First was aluminum 'gate valve' installed between the screw compressor and the heat exchanger. Second was a spider suspension bit, a crucial component of the flight train.

Thrilled at the chance to fabricate parts for this soon-to-be-famous aviation project, they machined the pieces smoothly. The result looked like a piece of sculpture. They felt that their work was good enough to sign, and proudly stamped in 1/8-inch letters the message 'Good luck *Earthwinds*' and each of their names—Dad, Mom and four children—on the side of the gate valve and on the spider bit.

But when Larry saw their names, he personally milled them off, ostensibly to save weight by grinding away excess metal. In his haste, he ground right through the gate valve, which cracked and buckled, and had to be remade.

◆　　◆　　◆

Entering the final two months of the launch window, Mike Emich volunteered whole workdays. Emich spent every day away from the Fire Department at the airdock. Steeped in the rich heritage of Akron's lighter-than-air history, he had learned about flying at the feet of masters, and wanted this piece of history to reflect well on his hometown.

Emich observed extraordinary turbulence around the south end of the airdock. A six-knot wind turned into 12-knots whipping around the building. To test a balloon's handling, he had inflated his 70-foot-tall hot air balloon in the hangar. With Larry, Don and Vladimir standing in his basket, the airdock doors were opened. Although restrained by tether lines, his balloon was blown dangerously close to the doors.

Emich introduced Don Moses and Vern Rich to skydiving. He flew them up to 12,500 feet in his club's jump plane and, strapped to an instructor, they made tandem free-falls. It was one part of Don's training that everybody hoped he wouldn't need.

He prepared a five-pound medical kit, and then through his connections in the skydiving trade, he arranged for a donation of $10,000 worth of the flight crew's personal parachutes and bailout altimeters.

Larry asked Emich to serve as the directing official for the National Aeronautic Association, the agency in the U.S. that maintains aviation records. Mike spent dozens of hours on the phone arranging this at his own expense, completing the paperwork to certify the record attempt.

Barrow made Emich assistant launch master. One part of the launch procedure gave him nightmares. For an hour during the staging, the flight crew would be hanging in a 'dead-man zone' more than 120 feet over the tarmac. In an emergency, such as an on-board fire, sudden wind or catastrophic failure of the poly balloon, they would have no escape route.

Emich and Barrow rigged a climber's clip-on buckle to each pilot's chest pack. They hooked one end of a 200-foot coil of half-inch Spectra rope on to the capsule. In such an emergency, the crew would exit and slide down the rope to safety. They delayed telling Larry about it for fear that he would reject the idea.

Mike worried about establishing reliable communications with the flight crew in the event that they went down and became separated—or if they lost their primary communications.

◆ ◆ ◆

Doc Wiley, a friend of Larry's father who had first been brought into ballooning projects by Maxie Anderson, shared his concern. A retired Air Force colonel, Wiley had joined with Bob Rice in coordinating the search-and-rescue procedures for long distance balloonists. Wiley was now ensconced in the Rice Bowl, sweating the details.

Wiley remembered that when the radios failed as Double Eagle V began its flight across the Pacific, the crew communicated through an Emergency Locator Transmitter (ELT) equipped with a voice device.

Wiley thought that each *Earthwinds* crewmember should carry a standard ELT. Instead, each pilot had acquired a different device, none of which allowed voice communication with search-and-rescue teams. NASA had given Larry a compact, hand-held unit about the size of a small cassette tape player, identical to those carried by Shuttle astronauts. Vladimir brought a heavy device from the Soviet space program that was about the size of a big-city phone book. Don Moses had picked up an Emergency Position Indicator Radio Beacon, known as an EPIRB, from a nautical shop. All three devices, once manually deployed and turned on, would beam a radio signal to an orbiting satellite.

◆ ◆ ◆

John Ackroyd had designed the flight train for use with Spectra rope. Every component that would hang from his spider bit at the bottom of the poly balloon depended on the strength of spliced Spectra cord. Upon testing it, Ackroyd found that the spliced Spectra ropes failed at the exact juncture of the eyesplice—at 40 percent of the design load. Friction and heat were Spectra's enemies. Ackroyd then insisted on using steel cables for the flight train suspension (the idea first proposed by Don Overs).

A staple of ballooning

Larry occasionally offered reporters an opportunity to work on the capsule. Bob Downing of the Akron Beacon Journal received the surprise offer and laughed.

'Larry, I am not the least bit mechanically inclined,' he said. 'I hardly know more than how to check the oil in my car engine. I wouldn't feel right working on something where three people's lives were potentially in my hands.'

Malcolm Browne, on the other hand, accepted Larry's offer enthusiastically. A chemist and scientist by training, The Timesman had spent months on assignment in the Antarctic, and maintained his own cabin in the woods in Vermont. Always eager to get his boots muddy, as Browne put it, he agreed to spend a few 'hands-on' days working on the capsule. On his first day, he found himself involved in a pressurization test on the capsule. With the engines running, the capsule's internal pressure was increased to simulate the atmospheric pressure difference at 8,000 feet.

As it 'climbed', a loud hissing sound emanated from points where fire-resistant Teflon coated wire had been pushed through the wall of the capsule. The wire coating separated from the sealant and popped the wires right out. The capsule had been pressure-tested at NASA, and eventually the leaks were sealed there. But after work began in Akron, dozens of additional holes were bored through the skin of the capsule for electrical cables, linking the scientific instruments outside with controls and monitors inside. Each hole had been sealed with RTV caulking. Just as Mike Emich had feared, nobody had maintained engineering diagrams of where each hole had been drilled, or for what purpose. There were about 30 such penetrations. No one knew exactly how many; drilling had been indiscriminate to suit the purpose of the day.

It turned out that the coating on the Teflon did not grip the silicone caulk. After the pressure test failure, the problem had to be solved by pulling each of the Teflon wires through the holes, roughing them up, and coating them with a substance to which the caulk adhered. Cornstarch dusted on the sealed penetrations prevented anything else from adhering to the caulk. (Additional pounds of cornstarch were used for dusting off the plastic between the anchor balloon dolly and the anchor balloon itself). After his day in the hands-on mode, Browne walked into the Media Bowl grinning and covered in cornstarch. 'This is obviously a staple of ballooning' he punned.

John Ackroyd knew that the capsule should have been engineered instead of evolving.

'It's colossally sound', he said one day, 'but they keep punching holes in it to run wires through. The correct way to have done this would have been to put up an aluminum bulkhead and go through that, but not to keep punching holes in the capsule, and blotting them with caulk, which should only be used as a last resort.

'But this is just today's crisis,' he shined cheerfully, 'and tomorrow there will be another one.'

Don Moses was equally philosophical, telling Browne 'problems like this have arisen at every stage of this project, and there'll always be more of them. But at a certain point you just have to decide you can cope with any new ones and start flying.'

A cement that could have been used that day to coat the wires was available at a specialized aviation/electrical shop right down the road at Akron-Canton Airport. However, in December Larry had stiffed the supplier for $1,000 worth of electrical wire, and the vendor refused to do further business with him.

Well into February, word came from the Rice Bowl to expect launchable weather soon, on one of two dates, one Sunday/Monday, the other Monday/Tuesday, which were flip sides of the same weather system. The only limitation seemed to be a high amplitude pattern in the jet stream that flows up to the GIUK (Greenland, Iceland and United Kingdom) Gap, then south and north again crossing 'every country in Europe,' Rice said.

Larry rejected the scenario that Rice presented. But Rice refused to state that the jet stream pattern was the reason.

'The last thing I want is to have in print,' Rice said, 'is a statement that we can't launch into a high amplitude pattern...then a week later we do, and they wind up in the Congo. Then you've got still another law suit.'

An impromptu social

The 'captain' found out about Wilcox's surprise party two days before it was scheduled—and cancelled it. The beer, wine and champagne had already been donated, a menu selected, and word was being passed to the volunteers—including the 12 cold firemen. What Wilcox had intended as a morale booster now reduced morale to a new low.

The 40 or so regulars on the *Earthwinds* team began wondering whether this monster was launchable at all. Larry seemed determined either to blame his unpreparedness on the weather or to believe that perfect weather would form when he was actually ready to fly. Waiting was tough on everyone.

'We are more patient than anxious', he told Malcolm Browne.

Thursday passed without a party or prospect for launching; just more long days in the cave and in the cereal factory, and more tension as the Newmans arbitrarily snapped at people.

But if it was hard to wait for suitable weather, it was easy to dispose of the wine and champagne that had been donated. On Friday night, there was a spontaneous gathering in the Media Bowl. It started when, at the end of his 15-hour workday, Bob Rice stopped by to visit, looking tired. We opened a bottle of wine and unwrapped a big fruit basket. Others drifted and more corks came off. With the appropriate lubrication, the senior staff again began to sound off about Our Captain.

Rice and Barrow, working the champagne to its best loquacious advantage, declaimed sternly that they viewed this extraordinary flight as a very dangerous mission—especially the landing.

Rice and Barrow had tried to envision what would happen when *Earthwinds'* capsule contacted the ground. Now they recited again to one another and to a growing huddle of others their familiar litany of concerns: that there were no crew restraint devices in the capsule, that in a tumbled landing the batteries would overturn and become projectiles, that nothing will prevent the capsule from rolling down a hill, that a windy landing would be more like a bus crash than a balloon landing. Things would be flying through the cabin—every loose item becoming a weapon.

Rice knew the first priority in the event of any water landing should be getting out of the capsule, and into a floatation device or raft.

Ten-, twenty- or thirty-foot swells in the ocean would quickly kill the crew who remained aboard. Despite the capsule's stability and buoyancy in the McDonnell Douglas pool, Rice believed that ocean waves would quickly invert it. There were no personal crew floatation devices, no raft, no sea anchor, no crew restraints and no helmets on board. Rice could not understand Larry's refusal to acknowledge or plan for that kind of emergency.

What's more, time for a launch itself was running out.

'You've got a four-month window,' Rice said, 'and we're down to the last two weeks of it. Our Captain has dicked around for a year and three months, but the status of the machine itself is still in question.

'If there were something really fat', Bob said, reverting to weather slang, 'then you could work 24 hours around the clock to get ready to fly.'

No such extraordinary effort was being made, however, and as things stood this night, the launch-ready signal seemed many days away.

And Larry's lack of technical knowledge about weather mystified Rice: 'For a guy who flies commercial airliners for a living, he knows less about weather than anybody I've ever met.'

Rice was still pissed off about the charts, and a dozen other professional slights he had endured. Then, in a subtle statement of his powers, he summed up his feelings.

'If this kind of thing keeps up,' Rice deadpanned, 'I'll be tempted to launch Our Captain into the biggest goddamned thunderstorm I can find,' convulsing the party into laughter.

He and Tom Barrow continued pouring out their concerns and pouring out the contents of the wine and champagne bottles as the party in the Media Bowl grew to two dozen people. These proud professionals were hired to make *Earthwinds* work, and to ensure the survival of the crew. They continued discussing these deficiencies even after Malcolm Browne and his wife Lelieu joined the gathering. Reporters don't always take notes when they're doing a story, but surely Browne was picking up on the general theme of diminishing confidence in Larry Newman's judgment and his ability to survive. To our relief, none of the frank talk from that party appeared in print.

Standing alone

The next morning, Larry called Tim Lachenmeier.

'I need you come here on Tuesday and spend some time with me so I can understand how this balloon works,' Larry told him. Rice had reported that a big dome of very promising high pressure was due in by Thursday evening (for a Friday morning launch).

'I can do that in about an hour, Larry,' replied Tim.

'Well, I want to take a whole day to do it,' Larry answered.

Lachenmeier made plans to fly back to Akron.

After his Atlantic flight, when Larry, Maxie Anderson and Ben Abruzzo were awarded the Congressional Gold Medal, he was looked upon by the general public as a man who belonged to an elite fraternity. At home in Albuquerque, however, the ballooning fraternity disdained him—why, he had only logged 15 minutes in a balloon when he took off across the Atlantic, and he couldn't be one of them! He was an interloper...an outsider? Their lack of acceptance embittered him.

As a result, Larry was reluctant to associate with any balloonists, fearing that they would treat him the same way the Albuquerque pilots treated him.

Larry seemed to pride himself on the fact that he was not a practicing balloonist and that there were very few balloonists actually in his inner circle...in the greatest ballooning adventure of all time!

Larry had refused to join the Balloon Federation of America, the national pilots' organization. So it was a surprise that he agreed to speak with a group of their board members who were meeting in Akron.

When the group walked in to the hangar one afternoon and gazed at the enormous plastic balloon the anchor balloon and the capsule bristling with antennas and satellite dishes, helium vapor drifting toward the ceiling, the sight of it took their breath away. The scene resembled a fantastic science fiction adventure.

'Hardly anyone involved in *Earthwinds* is a gas balloonist,' Larry told them. 'Don Moses is not a balloonist. Vladimir is not a balloonist.'

He mentioned the names of the few record-holding gas balloonists who were helping him: 'Fred Gorrel and John Shoecraft, Bill Armstrong, who's helping with PR. That's all.'

I reminded him of Mike Emich.

'Oh yes, how could I forget Mike? If for some reason Don Moses couldn't fly, the person I would choose to replace him would be Mike Emich.'

Later that day Vladimir quietly called me aside.

'Bill, when we start, it is important that you call my embassy science officer in Washington and tell them they are invited, and the reporters from Isvestia and Trud and television, too. That they should come here and see the start. If the story does not get in the papers,' Vladimir said, thinking of his post-flight speech circuit, 'people back home will not know what I am talking about.'

Neither Vladimir nor Don was receiving weather briefings from Larry. I wondered whether he was sharing any information with them. What other information had he compartmentalized? I resolved to get Vladimir get as much Russian media attention as possible. Soon, he was getting more attention than he ever wanted.

Periodically, Vladimir would slip out a side door of the airdock. He had modified a Bendix hand-held VHF transceiver and tweaked up the frequency so he could talk with the two Soviet cosmonauts orbiting in the Mir space station. He carried a schedule of the nine-minute periods 18 times a day when Mir would be 'visible'—that is, in direct line of site for HF radio over Akron on a given day. For instance, during orbit number 2,220 on Feb. 9, Mir would be visible beginning at 3:18 p.m. Vladimir planned to continue those contacts with Sergei Krikalev and Alexander Volkov while he himself was orbiting the globe in *Earthwinds*.

Krikalev, one of his star pupils, had been reported complaining to ground controllers because his mission was lasting much longer than anticipated, and there had been western press speculation about whether there was enough money to bring him home. He had been in orbit nearly 300 days. The media made a big deal of the 'stranded cosmonaut' story.

Russia had skipped one crew rotation, when the country changed from the Soviet Union to Russia, prompting questions about who—if anyone!—had assumed the financial responsibility for this flight and for the Mir station. Vladimir didn't feel like commenting about this while he was away from Moscow. He had trained these cosmonauts, and felt a deep kinship with them.

Suddenly, Wilcox's office called me to say that ABC-TV wanted to interview Vladimir. Nightline was rushing a crew to Akron and said Ted Koppel would talk to the cosmonauts aboard Mir while Vladimir, their teacher, joined in from Akron.

But that's not what happened. A cameraman showed up, lit up the Media Bowl like high noon, set up a single chair, and arranged a speaker box next to the chair. Vladimir came in, the cameraman showed him to the chair, began rolling tape, and the voice of the network's science correspondent, Michael Guillan, came over the speaker box.

'Would you rather be stuck in space or standing in a bread line in Moscow?' he asked, pausing for reaction. 'Do you think Krikalev deserves a medal for panicking in space? What kind of man is he? What are his weaknesses? Is it true the Mir station is for sale?'

It was an ambush! Vladimir handled the interrogation with the coldest not-ready-for-prime-time Communist-revulsion-of-decadent-West stone-faced stare he could muster.

Wilcox and I called Guillan's producers and complained. Not one second of the interview ever aired.

◆ ◆ ◆

Vladimir was under tremendous pressure and relished his occasional free time. One of his great delights was walking across the campus of the University of Akron, just roaming around. He loved shopping in the Radio Shacks, hardware stores and computer shops around Akron. He would buy various tools and gadgets, then wink and say, 'not for project, for Russia.'

One day Vladimir the hunter noticed that Allied Signal's Spectra catalogue offered very fine chord. His eyes lit up. Allied gave him a huge spool containing line that could spring-load the arch of the toughest bow in the Rodina.

Alone in this country, he read and heard about political turmoil and fears of civil war at home. He saw the value of the ruble drop from an equivalent of nearly $2 to a few pennies, and wondered about the effect of that on his wife and two daughters.

Most of all, there was Vladimir's silent problem with Larry.

Often, Larry would 'forget', or hold back, Vladimir's cash allotment. Yet he was dependent upon Larry for money, for favors, and for travel. Often, he would tuck himself in his room at night and painted out his frustration.

Vladimir understood the risks perhaps better than anyone else. When Larry answered a reporter's inevitable question about danger, 'What do you think your chances are?' he might say, 'Oh, about fifty-fifty.' Vladimir would put a different spin on it. He would say, 'It's about Point Five livability.' He believed there was half a chance they would all die trying this flight!

One morning he brightened the Media Bowl by presenting three oil paintings of *Earthwinds* in flight. His impressionistic interpretations of scientific subjects belonged in an art gallery. He had finished a four-by-three foot canvas at 4 a.m. the night of the inflation on an easel set up in his bathtub, his adrenaline pumping as he saw the actualization of the flight within reach. He filled another canvas with splashes of color amidst the twin balloons peacefully making their way.

He had formed a perspective on his junior crewmate. 'Larry,' he confided to me one night, is 'psychologically invalid.' It wasn't clear whether he meant that Larry was a psychological invalid, or that he was psychologically invalid. But the resentment that lingered longer than any other was that the Newmans carelessly and without apology had allowed Lilia's visa to lapse without raising a finger to renew it. She had returned to Russia at the end of January, and the cosmonaut missed her.

But by his own admission, he sometimes overdid the vodka, his only resident Russian friend

Barron Hilton and the hounds

Whenever talk of a launch date intensified, a group of men in Beverly Hills would pack their bags and head for Akron: the chase crew.

The concept of a chase crew for a balloon grew out of the custom of driving a pickup truck into a farmer's field, retrieving the balloonists and their equipment at the end of a flight, and returning them home, perhaps with a stop at the nearest pub.

But this chase team would also provide an aerial platform for John Wilcox's crew, and provide occasional voice and visual contact with the crew. The chief hound was Barron Hilton himself, Innkeeper to the World Flight. His heavily loaded aircraft was supposed to roar into the sky after *Earthwinds* ascended.

Hilton's staff would watch Bob Rice's weather and then call ahead and try to iron out landing and flyover clearances, secure visas and prepare a flight plan.

Nobody in corporate America believed more in any cause than Barron Hilton believed in the global balloon flight. Whenever he got going on the subject, the possibilities of this thing, well…they were just endless, and you couldn't stop him. The cigar would come out of his mouth, and he would start his campaign speech.

'God dammit!' Hilton would bark out in a take-command baritone. 'This project is gonna' bring the people of the world together! America needs something like this! People gotta' have faith in something wonderful. This is BIG! This is gonna' CHANGE THE ECONOMY!'

The proper senior minion response was a straight-faced affirmative nod. Nobody on the corporate staff had ever seen their chairman act this way. *Earthwinds* had become for him a positive, uplifting distraction that took his mind away from the progressive illness of his beloved wife, Marilyn, who suffered at home from multiple sclerosis. The mother of his eight children, she had once served as his intuitive companion, his sixth sense, his eyes and ears in sizing up business companions. Now she was confined to their residence in the Holmby Hills section of Bel Air, Calif. The balloon project absolutely had rejuvenated him.

Hilton insisted that flying the plane around the world would be a public relations coup. He had his people pumping out pictures of the plane, stories about the plane. He knew that, on the ground at least, his specially painted plane would be the only visible sign of a balloon circumnavigating the earth. The press oughta' see who's up there following the adventure!

Since the 24-seat aircraft was limited to a range of 3,000 miles, the idea was to use key cities around the world as hubs. There would be stops in, say, London, Brussels and Moscow to do press conferences in conjunction with the new Conrad Hotels. The Conrad side of the business—Hilton's international hotels—was opening 28 hotels in the next five years, mostly in European capitals and Pacific Rim countries.

Neither the plane nor the crew had ever flown outside the U.S. Pilot Tom Hartman was not even sure whether he could make a phone call from the plane to Europe.

As the apparent launch window narrowed, more attention focused on the plane, how its passengers would communicate with the balloon, drop off film, and make all the stops that Barron Hilton wanted to make. Some of those might coincide with the balloon's trajectory, but all landings would be in big media markets.

The manifest included Gene Cernan, who would provide ESPN's color commentary, Richard Branson if he wanted to come along, and Bill Black, a Hilton friend and former diplomat. Hilton couldn't wait to get going.

'Every day will be a different adventure,' he said. 'We must be ready to depart at a moment's notice to capture footage of the balloon over dramatic landscapes. We also need to be flexible since accommodations may vary from our Conrad Hotels in Europe to army barracks in Siberia. It's not for the faint of heart, but we will be privileged to watch aviation history.'

Nobody in the *Earthwinds* support crew envied the plane's passengers. Theirs would be a far more exhausting trip than the balloon flight itself. The plane's limited range, and the daily out-and-back trips to intercept the balloon at sunrise or sunset (the most favorable camera times) meant trip segments of at least 1,500 miles. If the wind in the jet stream were blowing at 100 knots, the balloon would cover 2,500 miles in a day.

Between intercepts, the airplane pilots needed eight hours rest, they had to find hotels for the passengers, stock up on food, call the weather/operations center, ship the video footage to ESPN, file a new flight plan, make arrangements for the next night, and take off again. In the air, once the plane pilots found the balloon, an intercept at slowest speeds would mean a pass at perhaps 300 knots, which left very little time for taking pictures.

There was the other problem of finding jet aviation fuel in Russia. Newspapers were reporting half of the former Soviet airports closed because of a lack of fuel. Others thought that what was lacking was hard currency, so a little purse with $100,000 in American cash was loaded on the chase plane. John Wilcox would carry a canvas bag containing $25,000 in hundred dollar bills.

Splitting airs

Bob Rice identified a pattern early in the second week of February.

He alerted Tom Barrow that Thursday evening held some promise for a launch Friday morning.

Work was expedited on the capsule; food and water were loaded aboard. Imminence of launch drove many last-minute details, such as modifying and filing the flight plan for the chase plane, arranging helicopters to chase in the first few hours of the balloon flight, getting the Keller-Hall crane people on site, relocating a perimeter security fence, alerting media, etc.

Everybody worked from checklists.

Larry kept the most important checklist, a pencil tally showing the exact weight of each item.

By Thursday afternoon, 18 hours before the proposed launch time, Akron was socked in. It was hard to see the tethered pilot balloons around the airdock.

The close-in forecast indicated light wind through sunrise.

Although drizzle and freezing rain fell all day, and freezing temperatures were expected, the wind would fall off to near calm.

Rice remarked that it was easy enough to forecast 'light and variable' winds—that means wind of less than ten mph. But the critical difference between wind of three or four mph and six or seven mph was like splitting hairs. At some point, he warned, his forecast would become a now-cast. When you open the airdock doors, what you see is what you'll get.

Mike Emich couldn't believe it. No local balloonist would even consider going for a walk in such slop. The good news was that a thin, low cloud cover would remain, and an inversion below the cloud deck would keep surface winds light. As a result, the weather as forecast would present no operational hazard to the balloon system, but the launch crew might have to work throughout the night in drizzle or light snow flurries.

Perfect calm was needed. A slight breeze would create havoc. In the first few moments after release, *Earthwinds* would skim the surface, Barrow calculated. It would take about 10 seconds to climb the first 60 feet and another 30 seconds to climb the first 200 feet. The tallest obstacle on the field was the 211-foot-tall airdock. Even with a one-knot wind, it would take 10 or 11 seconds to attain a 45-degree climb-out angle.

A more rapid rate of climb would stress the envelope, and invite catastrophic rupture.

Thursday's bleak weather produced slippery, icy roads, the most dangerous driving day of the winter. Three tow trucks from Rivers Towing in Ravenna sat on the runway waiting for *Earthwinds*, while cars around the county were sliding into ditches and waiting to be pulled out; it would have been Rivers' busiest and most profitable day, but their trucks were committed free-of-charge to the balloon flight.

Barron Hilton was flying east. Media were alerted: Stuart Brown from Popular Science in California, Dave Chandler from the Boston Globe, Malcolm Browne from The Times, television and radio from all over. A Russian TV crew secured emergency clearance from the State Department to drive from Washington to Akron to interview Vladimir; they traversed the Pennsylvania Turnpike in an icy blizzard. It was a classic winter storm, with hundreds of car, truck and bus accidents.

Barrow slipped the schedule back two hours as wind persisted.

Don and Vladimir attended to last-minute things at the airdock, spending nervous energy. Larry and Lynne relaxed over dinner with Fred Nebiker at Schumacher's Restaurant, then retired for the night. Barrow would call them when he had the capsule ready.

The ground crew assembled inside the airdock about 6 p.m. The media set up camp; television crews did live broadcasts; wire services moved stories about the imminence of the dramatic voyage.

Television networks readied microwave trucks to send to broadcast the launch live in the morning. ESPN was ready to go live at a moment's notice. Sharlene Hawkes, the former Miss America trying to break into broadcasting, flew in from Salt Lake City to anchor the ESPN coverage of the launch and flight.

Balloon designer Tim Lachenmeier of Raven Industries confers with New York Times science correspondent Malcolm Browne while waiting for inflation to begin in February 1992.

Inside the airdock about 9:30, Tom gave the signal to pull the capsule trailer toward the door. But it was wedged between the anchor balloon and the sheltering structure; precious time was lost backing and turning before the capsule was aligned and aimed at the doors. Attached port and starboard were the two giant gasoline tanks and the huge flasks of liquid helium. The capsule and its attachments, weighing more than seven and a half tons, finally rolled out of the airdock to the staging area about 10:20 p.m. passing in review in front of the correspondents.

Police, launch officials, volunteers, official photographers and video camera crew escorted it. The helium balloon was supposed to come out at midnight.

Virgin Atlantic's press people had convinced Richard Branson that he should be there for the launch. He caught a flight from London to JFK, chartered in to Akron-Canton Regional Airport, and rushed to the launch field. He walked alone onto the runway in his unassuming get-up: jeans, leather jacket and open shirt.

Although we had scheduled him for three live shots on the 11 o'clock news, he had not seen the capsule since it was in California eight months earlier.

I showed him around the capsule, and then took him inside the airdock for a quick look at the huge poly balloon. He paused at the door, speechless for a moment, walked toward the towering craft, and then said quietly 'Shit!'—a statement clearly open to interpretation, but the consensus translation was along the lines of 'Oh my god, this guy Newman has taken my money and my dream and made something of it, and now this thing is flight ready and I'm not going to be on it! What have I missed?'

Branson, having seen the system, albeit briefly, could now talk about it. He scurried across the field to do the stand-up interviews. His comments, intended as realistic, came across as negative when he put the project in perspective. The dangerous flight had only a 50 percent chance for success, he said. He told the TV crews that although business commitments prevented him from flying this time, if there should be a postponement, he was looking forward to being part of the flight crew again next fall.

The night air was bitter, cold and damp. Wind from the northwest, aiming right for the airdock, tipped the pibals a 70 degree angle and back up again. Bob Rice reported that wind was dying off in all the surrounding reporting stations. At the *Earthwinds* corner of Akron Fulton Airport, however, it was gusting eight to 10 mph. We gave the restless media updates every 30 minutes. Barrow walked around the field, and then discussed the options with Fred Gorrel, Tim Lachenmeier, Don Campbell and Mike Emich. It wouldn't work tonight, they decided.

They checked again with Rice and Wiley back at the hotel, then made the call to Larry's room: keep sleeping.

It was 1 a.m., and 60 news reporters and TV crews were still faithfully waiting to record the liftoff. This night's operation, I told them, would have to stand down. One had to be philosophical; sometimes the weather just didn't cooperate.

There were still two weeks left in the launch window. But it was clear to everyone that if things didn't let up soon, the monster in the airdock would become the biggest hangar queen of all time.

In the mean time, Barron Hilton and his party were heading back to California early the next morning. He saw the wariness on the Newmans' faces.

'Come with me,' he said to Larry and Lynne, 'and I'll drop you off in Phoenix.'

The Newmans had not had a day to themselves for almost a year. Lynne jumped at the chance to get Larry back to Scottsdale, and show him the new furniture and improvements she had made in their house. They were in the air half an hour later.

Within minutes of their departure, Richard Branson showed up in the lobby, greeted people, visited with Don Moses and Carol, then joined Vladimir and me for lunch. Larry had neither called nor seen his million-dollar sponsor during his whirlwind stop in Akron. Neither expressed regrets. Branson returned to London that afternoon.

It was fortunate that the flight did not start on that Friday morning. During a test running of the engine a few days later, a rubber coupling which connected the engine to the alternator had failed. The other would have failed shortly thereafter. There were no spares aboard. If this had happened in flight, there would have been no way to run the engines.

The Earthworms and a touch of poetry

Following the first launch attempt, the peripatetic John Wilcox left $500 for the staff to lavish on themselves. On short notice, we restored the dinner party, booked a banquet hall, invited 70 guests, and planned to relax on Saturday night.

Bill Swersey wanted to do something special. He had been humming the tune to The Addams Family theme song, and so that afternoon as Erin Porter, Bill and I shut the door to the media center, we wrote words to go with his tune, and took them to the party. The hall was filled; the pitchers of beer were filled and drained. After dinner, with everyone standing in a circle, we handed out our song sheet

226   Just Wind

and the whole team heartily belted out what became the *Earthwinds* family theme song:

> The *Earthwinds* project started / To fly a course uncharted / They still have not departed…The *Earthwinds* Family.
> Akron we call home base / The airdock is our workspace / Launch soon or egg on our face…The *Earthwinds* Family.
> Hot air…Quaker Square / Jet Stream…Bad Dream
> Around the world in Eighty / The anchor makes it weighty / They could end up in Haiti…The *Earthwinds* Family.
> The Rice Bowl we check in with / To calculate the wind drift / The Newmans they are spendthrift…The *Earthwinds* Family.
> Round rooms…pushing brooms / Two balloons…plastic spoons
> Though he can't part the water / Don Moses built crew quarters / Last week we met his daughter…The *Earthwinds* Family.
> When wires crossed we panicked / Amigos (not Hispanic) / Saved us from being manic…The *Earthwinds* Family.
> Freezing rain…chase plane / Wipe your feet…keep it neat!
> Tom Barrow is Launchmeister / Let's buy him a de-icer / He couldn't be much nicer…The *Earthwinds* Family.
> Lights, cameras and action / John Wilcox came from Aspen / We'll be the main attraction…The *Earthwinds* Family.
> Virgin…Buy a pin / Load skirt…Buy a shirt
> We started out romancin' / With British mogul Branson / But will we keep on dancin'?…The *Earthwinds* Family.
> Some big bucks came from Barron / Whose pins we're all a wearin' / Was introduced by Erin…The *Earthwinds* Family.
> INMARSAT…Buy a hat / Cosmonaut…Aeroflot
> His upper lip unshaven / Young Tim came in from Raven / Balloon-designing maven…The *Earthwinds* Family.
> Engineering scholar / Rich junior makes the dollar / Held Larry by the collar…The *Earthwinds* Family.
> Sector Watch…Spectra swatch / Free beer…not here!
> We left our jobs at big firms / to call ourselves the Earthworms / At this rate we'll not return…The *Earthwinds* Family.
> This party it was postponed / 'Til certain people went home / That's off the record, Malcolm…The *Earthwinds* Fam-i-leee!

◆ ◆ ◆

Solemn toasts followed. Don Moses choked up as he thanked everyone for their generosity and said we'd all be with him in his heart when he flew around the world; Chuck Slusczarcyk, a former competitor of Larry in the ultralight airplane business, told of his exploits flying across Lake Erie; several Loral executives brought their families and laughed with us. Then Malcolm Browne, the Timesman, stood up on a chair and began a speech:

> 'The readers of my paper, and the papers that subscribe to our news service, are treated to a daily diet of a miserable economy, civil wars in Yugoslavia, a famine in Ethiopia, of the decay of the Soviet Union and possible famine there and just about every goddamned horrible thing you could possibly imagine.
>
> 'Here, I've been privileged to share for a couple of weeks in what I think is a great dream and I think that the readers of our paper and people everywhere have been, too. Somehow this has given them something that's a little different from the horrors they read about every day—because what, after all, is better than a dream? A dream that's going to be realized.
>
> Gilbert and Sullivan had a line: "What after all is life without a touch of poetry in it?" You people—all of you—have given the world a touch of poetry and for this I think the whole world, and I in particular, owe you a tremendous debt of gratitude. Thank you all.'

Vladimir, bringing a hush to the room, spoke of the kindness all had shown to Lilia, and of the broader meaning of the project:

> My dear friends…all the people supporting us and here together with us: thank you very much for your activity, for your hospitality. I will be missing all my life you and Loral and our workshop. Everything was so nice for me and I am so lucky in my life that I had the occasion to work here for 100 days.
>
> In three months and a half I learned a lot of very important things about American character. I learned that you are absolutely the same sort of people as Russian people. We do not fight and you do not fight. We want to be friends with you.

We had bonded.

Well, it's not the Spirit of St. Louis

On Sunday, the wind was light and variable, less than five mph. It looked like it might be possible to launch that night. The upper wind, however, tracked north of the Arctic Circle, then turned sharply toward the Mediterranean Sea. Tom Barrow raised the possibility that by using the 'hand brake', as he described the anchor balloon, *Earthwinds* could ascend slowly, then "park" at 18,000 feet or so for 48 hours waiting for the jet stream to straighten out.

Rice, Barrow and Wiley operated without Newman's input. They couldn't find him. He had left Scottsdale early Sunday morning without contacting anybody in Akron. Messages left in America West's paging/check-in system did not reach him. There were decisions to make and maybe things to set in motion, but here was his exasperated senior staff sitting in Akron playing Find Waldo!

This inability to communicate caused considerable anxiety in the Weather/Operations Center; the staff was reluctant to pass up this window without Newman's concurrence. Doc Wiley opposed a launch that might lead the flight toward the polar region because it would put the crew far from any military search-and-rescue.

If they crashed on pack ice, Wiley would have no way to bring them out. Bob Rice—for once—wished that his client were there, for without Larry's input, no launch sequence would start.

So nothing happened.

Larry returned from Scottsdale Sunday night to find the Quaker Square virtually deserted. The Media Bowl was open, as usual, but the staff had followed Larry's example and scattered for a few days to catch their breath; many had been working non-stop since November. Don Moses and Carol Hart had flown to Aspen for skiing, and dinner at Wilcox's Pine Creek Cookhouse.

Ultimately, when he learned the facts, Larry agreed with the decision not to start the launch procedure. He wanted no part of landing near polar bears.

But Larry was steaming mad about something else that had happened over the weekend. The launch crew who had stood in the cold for more than seven hours the previous Thursday night had truly believed that they were about to put the balloon in the air. Many of the regulars and the volunteers signed their names on the capsule or the undercarriage, along with brief epithets like, 'Good luck' or 'godspeed'. When Larry saw the capsule with this graffiti on it, he made a list of every person who had scribbled on it, and pointedly reminded them that they had 'desecrated' his capsule. Mike Emich pointed out that Charles Lindbergh had actually invited the people at Ryan Aircraft in San Diego, where The Spirit of St. Louis was built, to write their names under the wing. Even the Double Eagle gondola, hanging in the Smithsonian, still bore the names of those who had written goodwill messages on its hull. Nothing mollified Larry. It was desecration!

Monday afternoon, Larry conducted a dry run and demonstration of the capsule systems for four of us. He wanted to be certain that we would understand exactly how all of *Earthwinds* components interacted. Bob Rice, Tom Barrow and Doc Wiley and I listened as Larry made a brilliant, enthusiastic and thorough presentation, talking virtually non-stop. He didn't need a flight manual; he seemed to know every instrument's position by heart.

Want to know the temperature in the anchor balloon?—black digital panel on the right side; turn it to the number eight position. What's that alarm sound?—Voltage is exceeding 13.5.

Want to open the bottom valve on the anchor?—Flip up the bottom switch below the load cell panel. To verify cabin pressure?—Read the left-side indicator. How much liquid helium in Tank Number Two?—Read the right cryogenic panel for percent remaining. Why did the thermocouple digital display go down?—It was linked to the microphone and to the amateur radio experiment; only one could be used at a time. He went on for three hours.

This clearly was no 'Lone Eagle' adventure; nobody could fly this system alone, but Larry was in charge. Don and Vladimir would receive on-the-job training; there was no flight manual, no engineering diagrams, and no paperwork or emergency procedures guide.

The next night, at a quiet dinner with him and Lynne, I found Larry relaxed, still studying the Inmarsat operating manual.

Carpe diem

At Bob Rice's morning briefing on Thursday, February 20, the prognosis for Friday night/Saturday morning showed a weak high pressure system over Toronto, moving at one or two knots. The rotation around the system was good, and Rice expected wind of less than five knots between 7 p.m. and 7 a.m. His computer indicated that the boundary winds at 2,000 feet would stay down, too, bringing cooler but relatively warm air.

Rice called this 'well worth playing with'...as close as he ever came to sounding the clarion call. He also pointed out another window just behind that one, for a possible Saturday night/Sunday morning launch, and recommended taking advantage of these circumstances.

'Everything after that,' he said, 'looks like dog shit. It's fairly clear that spring is coming.'

The Friday/Saturday window looked 'marginal,' he said, 'but we're operating in desperation. We have to look with eagle-eyed alertness at every opportunity.'

The one thing causing concern was what he called a split-flow situation across the top and bottom of the jet stream. The projected flight path formed a positive

'Y' in the track over the eastern Atlantic. It was unclear which way the balloon would go.

One track had it going north over the U.K. and the other over North Africa.

'Meteorologically, this is not significant,' Rice said, 'but politically, you start to visit some strange places...Libya, Iran, Iraq, Vietnam.'

Doc Wiley noted that these include four of the five places his State Department contacts told him to avoid. The plan for overflying those countries: power down the radios and hope for the best.

A festive atmosphere pervaded the camp. The work had been done, and the long wait was about to end. Erin Porter helped Lynne pack her clothes, and ship back to Scottsdale cartons of paperwork. Barron Hilton and his entourage spooled up the chase plane and headed east for the second time in eight days, while the Quaker Square hotel staff once again reported to battle stations.

A spontaneous, tumultuous party erupted again at Buck's—Thursday was karaoke night—and the vodka, whiskey, beer and wine flowed freely. After the long adventure down the yellow brick road, Dorothy was going back to Kansas.

As we said our goodbyes to the travelers, Vladimir brought out the tears in the girls who hugged him; Don and Carol sashayed around the floor arm-in-arm; Barron Hilton led his band of merry men in the raucous celebration. Even Larry and Lynne came by for a few minutes. Tom Barrow warned the workers that the next day would be a long one, but hardly anyone listened; they might face the morning with a hammering hang-over, but this was their last party, and they would be damned if they'd miss it.

In other parts of the world, officials swung into action. In Japan, Dr. Keizo Yamaji, president of Canon, Inc., studied the latest trajectory charts. Every day for weeks he had been analyzing Bob Rice's plots, and imagining where the balloon would go. If the present course held, *Earthwinds* would fly right over Japan on the last leg home. Yamaji took a great deal of personal interest in his company's sponsorship of *Earthwinds*.

In Russia, Vladimir Korsakov, deputy director of the Soviet space agency Glavkosmos, completed the communication and tracking methods his agency would use.

Korsakov was normally occupied with the reentry and landing of Soyuz vehicles. Now he faxed to his comrade position reports on the Mir station, and tested the codes that we would use to report *Earthwinds*' position.

Early Friday morning, with launch staring him straight in the face, Larry called a briefing session in the Rice Bowl.

Lachenmeier went through the ascent sequence, so the flight crew, as well as Rice, Wiley and Barrow, could understand it clearly.

He also reviewed the sunrise/sunset scenarios, to pressurize and unpressurize the anchor balloon. Doc Wiley reviewed the communications procedures, and set up a preliminary schedule of when Larry should call the Weather/Operations Center.

Rice wanted Larry to level off about halfway up to altitude to allow time for the jet stream overhead to arch a bit more northerly. But during that intensive operational briefing, Larry told him that the balloon would not be able to level off, contradicting Rice's previous understanding. Wind speed through the lower atmosphere during climb out on Saturday morning would be about 55 knots, increasing to 90 at flight altitude and maintaining that speed at least until reaching the Azores.

The moment everyone had awaited for two and a half years was approaching. I taped a sign to my desk with the exhortation, 'carpe diem'.

At 1:30 p.m. on Friday, Emich called Rice and reported that the pibals were straight up. There wasn't a breath of wind.

'They'd better get their asses out there,' Rice replied. 'This system is breaking down faster than I thought.'

Barrow directed that helium truck come alongside the poly balloon inside the airdock. He inserted the diffuser valve into the inflation sleeve, charging the balloon with another 100,000 cubic feet of gas.

The load cell read steady at 19,910 pounds of lift. Adding the 2,434-pound weight of the balloon itself, the all-up load was 22,344 pounds. The capsule and anchor balloon weighed in at 20,325, leaving a free lift of 2,019 pounds, or more than nine percent. That was 1,400 pounds over the nominal payload of the balloon, but still 768 pounds under the maximum allowed.

At Barrow's command, the airdock doors were rolled partially open at 4 p.m., and a truck pulled the capsule out, the trailer so heavily loaded that Tom worried about blowing a tire.

At 6:30 p.m. with the hangar doors open completely, the balloon floated lightly in the zephyrs inside the airdock. Barrow was determined to step right through this process without delay. Now he expedited it. He ordered Mike Osborne into the Green Machine. Two minutes later, Tom was standing in front of the truck, walking backward, thumbs gesturing over his shoulders.

The balloon turned, twisted slightly, and exited the airdock.

After clearing the building, the procession paused on the apron in front of the south doors.

The balloon rolled to and fro on its vertical axis. Slowly, it completed one revolution and began another. It was swiveling on the load cell making a full revolution every 20 seconds. Barrow decided to move it to the launch site, away from the effects of the airdock's self-generating wind. Barrow decided to keep the anchor balloon in the airdock until well after darkness.

John Wilcox reviewed the shooting schedule with video camera crews and work out who would go in which chase aircraft in the moments after liftoff. He invited Malcolm Browne to fly with him in one chase plane. Wilcox continued trying to persuade the FAA to impose restrictions around the balloon as well as around the airport, partly for safety reasons and partly to protect the exclusivity of in-flight photography. A midnight launch looked possible.

Carol Hart prepared to fly to Newark, board a Virgin Atlantic flight to London, and then connect with another Virgin flight to Tokyo. Virgin's Operations Center authorized minor route deviations to intercept the balloon. On each flight, Carol planned to photograph the balloon and talk with Don.

The weather was perfect. Larry and Lynne finished a quiet dinner with Fred Nebiker, and then went to their room. Don and Vladimir were also supposed to be sleeping. Barrow would wake them up and a police escort would whisk the Newmans, Don and Vladimir to the airport.

Prompted by radio and TV news reports and daily coverage in the Akron Beacon Journal, thousands of Akronites began camping out in cars around the airport. The SWAT team quietly took up its positions; one of them intercepted a youth who was about to climb a tree for a better look. From the lip of the bowl around the airport, the balloon was plainly visible; giant klieg lights glistened on it, and twinkling reflections bounced off all 180 gores, forming a sparkling crown.

Down on the field at 7:45 p.m., the balloon swiveled again, the load cell twisting and torquing. Barrow began to wonder about the integrity of the load cell attached to the bottom fitting of the poly balloon. It wasn't intended for such abuse.

Rice reaffirmed his forecast for light wind, though on the open airfield there were now gusts of four to seven mph. Barrow assured the launch crew and reporters that 'we are going to ride it out,' but there was still too much air movement to try ground-handling the anchor balloon. It was also a bit too windy to consider the next step in the staging process: coupling the capsule to the poly balloon. Barrow waited for the wind to settle.

An hour later, the launch was still on hold.

Mike Schein, the NASA cryogenic helium expert, took portable 120-gallon tanks via forklift truck out to the capsule, and drained the liquid helium into the big beer barrels.

At 9:30 p.m. Barrow was alarmed to discover that the load cell showed signs of failing due to the continuous torque action. He knew that if it failed, it would explode quickly, and the balloon would rocket away. He asked Ackroyd to rig some restraining chains to the bottom fitting of the balloon. Precious minutes passed. When the chains were attached, two trucks backed into place facing opposite directions and the chains were attached to the tow trucks. With pressure on the front end loader eased, the rear axles of both trucks slowly lifted up off the ground, startling the launch team. Barrow then rigged the balloon's destruct line to the front-end loader. That wouldn't save an escaping balloon, but it would prevent an uncontrollable, radar-invisible monster from obstructing air traffic if it floated away.

There was no choice but to wait for dead calm. Synoptically, Bob Rice reported, this continued to be a good night. At reporting stations from Indiana eastward, the wind dropped off to zero. It was supposed to happen on the field at Akron, too.

Even four or five mph might be acceptable, but the present seven or eight mph presented an unacceptable handling risk. If the wind increased, the situation would be considered dangerous, Barrow said. Anticipating the worst, he speculated that the first failure might be the temporary restraints. As he said that, the load cell blinked, and failed electrically. Although it was still intact structurally, the launch master could no longer use it to read lift. The ground crew shuffled around, drank coffee and stamped their feet to stay warm. The wind fluctuated between six, seven and eight mph. The balloon pirouetted on the load cell, tugging at the bottom fitting. Lachenmeier examined the fitting as the wind tugged and spun his balloon. The buffeting was gradually causing the balloon to slip its collar, like a head coming out of a shirt.

'The difference between seven and eight knots and three and four knots is subtle but significant,' Barrow told the growing gaggle of media, yet the launch schedule remained plausible. 'We built a fair bit of contingency into it,' he said confidently.

At 11:45 p.m., Barrow directed the crew to re-rig the restraining devices, and add shackling chains. He warned spectators to stand back, but dozens of curious ground crew and selected media crowded in to look and listen. They heard the popping noises coming from the load cell as the balloon rotated.

Seven VIP buses arrived, filled with Loral guests, city officials and family of the crew. A catering truck from the Akron Hilton delivered hot coffee and sandwiches. Two postal workers camped out on the floor of Larry's office, awaiting word on when to begin affixing the special cancellation to 1,000 souvenir caches Larry was planning to sign and carry on the flight.

The phone at the airdock office rang incessantly with calls from people anxious for word on the start. Media called. City officials called. And then the Vice President of the United States called—it was Dan Quayle, the voice said, up late, listening to the news—yes, it was the Vice President!—and a buzz of excitement arose...until somebody deciphered Larry's imitation.

At 1:00 a.m. Barrow made the long walk from the airdock out to the end of the ramp for another look at the base of the balloon.

Even if he decided to start the sequence now, five hours of hard work would take the launch right past sunrise, with the possibility of thermals and more wind. As he came up close, the balloon swiveled overhead. The crackling sound repeated as the base fitting turned the load cell until it looked like a discarded beer can. The sound became more intense.

'Remember, face down and away if it lets loose,' Barrow cautioned me as we crawled up next to the failing device. He was issuing survival instructions! 'If the load cell goes, it will explode outward in all directions like shrapnel, and all hell will break loose.'

Barrow returned to the airdock office after his examination, and telephoned Rice and Wiley, still maintaining their quiet vigil back at the Operations Center in the hotel. Rice, who had been up for nearly 22 hours by this time, told the launch master that wind was calm everywhere but on Shorty Fulton's old field. Their short conference produced the inevitable decision.

Barrow woke up Larry Newman and told him to keep sleeping. Then he asked Mike Osborne to do what he had said could not be done: drive the balloon back inside the airdock.

As the Green Machine slowly began rolling on its return trip, I told the media briefing that we were standing down for the night.

The second launch attempt had been aborted and *Earthwinds* was finished for the season. The launch master sounded completely discouraged.

7

Slipping the Surly Bonds

You gotta know when to hold 'em, know when to fold 'em

In the wee hours of Saturday morning, Tim Lachenmeier stood inside the airdock examining his poly balloon. He was alarmed to see that it had slipped about half an inch in its base collar. He didn't know how much more slippage it could take without degrading its structural integrity. He left the airdock and returned to the hotel.

In the media bowl, sipping champagne, he joked that he would not let his children go up in that balloon—only his ex-wife. His bosses at Raven already had wired a formal notice concerning expiration of the 20-day warranty, absolving themselves of liability for the helium balloon, which by then had stood inflated in the hangar for 26 days.

Bob Rice was tired. He and Doc Wiley, now nearly 70 years old, had kept their vigil for nearly 24 hours in the Weather/Operations Center. Barrow had been working under stress straight through Friday and through Friday night; he was losing some feeling in his fingers, and had trouble remembering and formulating some words.

The Newmans and Barron Hilton's traveling entourage had awakened well rested. At a mid-morning meeting in the Rice Bowl, cigar clamped between his fingers, Barron Hilton thumped the fist of his free hand on Bob Rice's desk and veritably shouted encouragement.

'This is not a failure,' he commanded, 'this is a process. This project will continue, and we will be back to do it next season.'

He vowed to stand behind Larry.

At a Saturday afternoon news conference, Larry told the media that the weather had been the culprit all along. He attributed this to a warmer-than-usual northeast Ohio winter, and the fact that Lake Erie 25 miles to the north had not even frozen. Warm air rising from the lake created continuous thermal activity throughout the region. Larry said the crew would prepare for next fall. Asked about Branson's participation, he replied that the present crew was trained and compatible, and that he saw no reason to make changes.

Vladimir seemed sanguine. He knew a good party line when he heard one: 'This is absolutely normal in these kinds of flights,' he said.

When I returned to the media bowl, someone had changed the slogan on my desk from 'Carpe diem' to 'Seize next November.'

Larry Newman and his wife Lynne in a rare moment of relaxation—at the end of the winter flying season in Akron.

Larry and Lynne joined the pack for our final dinner that night. Boyish, relaxed and enthusiastic again, Larry wanted to discuss how we could keep the family together. Neil Cohen talked about writing a business plan for the next eight months with milestones such as fundraising, a newsletter, media appearances, equipment tests and shipping.

Looking at the long table of aerospace experts, welders, phone answerers, engineers and marketers, who had been drawn to *Earthwinds* like moths to a fire, Larry sighed and said he felt badly that he had disrupted all their lives without a result. Now he mused that he was tempted to drop the project altogether—except that he felt an obligation to these people. He was being driven by his creation.

Scraps for the homeless

The next day, the balloon stood motionless in the airdock. The staff discussed how to dispose of it. To push it out the doors and release it would pose a serious threat for air traffic. To wait for the wind to calm again and valve it down outside might take weeks. To push it outside and break it would be bad form, maybe even dangerous. To deflate the balloon slowly inside the airdock might push up the old rafters and catwalks.

Vladimir suggested wrapping a rope around the mid-section of the balloon, pulling it one way, and driving the Green Machine the opposite direction, all while inside the airdock. Attempting this procedure on Monday afternoon, the top of the balloon scraped a rafter. Within 10 seconds the balloon fluttered to the floor. Larry missed its demise; he was on the phone in his airdock office putting his creation on hold.

Tim cut test panels from the bottom fitting and saved the valves. Larry offered the spent plastic to The Lighter-Than-Air Society, whose members had helped sell his souvenirs. They clipped some sections from it, and left the rest. Bob Downing, the Akron Beacon Journal reporter, asked Larry for the rest of it. Downing persuaded some junior high school students to cut the balloon into 4x4 inch squares and mount them on a memento card. The Beacon Journal sold the souvenirs for $3 apiece, raising more than $9,000 for charities helping Akron's homeless.

Fewer bucks…

Postponing the flight cost the project more than $250,000. Some equipment had only been intended for one-time use. Scrubbing also involved transportation and storage of the remaining equipment, and travel home for key personnel. Some costs were saved, such as the launch master's bonus. Some costs were recovered, such as unused liquid helium returned to the supplier.

A lot of income was deferred: speaking fees, honoraria and endorsements. The National Geographic would have paid $40,000 for the crew's personal story, but only after a successful flight.

It would have been worth $35,000 apiece to emerge from the capsule after landing and answer the question 'Larry, Don and Vladimir, you've just circled the world in a balloon; where are you going now?' by saying 'We're going to Disney World.'

Hilton's $450,000 wouldn't move until *Earthwinds* reached 18,000 feet; Virgin held back its final $150,000; Canon's sponsorship was written so that $100,000 was paid up front, another $100,000 when the flight was completed; Sector's $50,000 would move on liftoff.

Wilcox had recruited Peter Benchley (of 'Jaws' fame) to narrate his film. Now he quickly re-scripted a film about the attempted launch, telescoping all the details of preparation and work in Akron into a 30-minute show ESPN eventually aired opposite the NCAA basketball finals.

Some of the contributing sponsors had nagging doubts. Loral Corp. had done far more for Larry Newman than they had ever planned to do. Little did Chairman Bernard Schwartz know back in 1990 that by assenting to the simple request for floor space in the airdock he would be committing his company for more than a quarter of a million dollars worth of involuntary sponsorship. The overtime for security guards, the long distance phone calls, media credentials, the heavy use of the parachute shop, photo lab, the tools and incidental materials all contributed to *Earthwinds*' preparedness—but without result. Schwartz commissioned a study to learn what Loral had gained from its act of corporate goodwill.

America West Airlines withdrew as a contributing sponsor, and refused outright to provide space-available travel to *Earthwinds*, a bad omen for Larry.

◆   ◆   ◆

Vladimir left the hibernation of Akron and returned to Star City, where he would try to bring order to a space program being squeezed by budget constraints. He faced a tough task: laying off 40 percent of his staff of 300 at the Cosmonaut Training Center.

Over the spring and summer months, he would train crews for the Mir station, search for new Intercosmos customers, and celebrate the joint agreement that would send U.S. crews to the Mir station and cosmonauts aboard the Space Shuttle.

Furthermore, he had been asked by his native Uzbekistan, now emerging as an independent Islamic republic in central Asia, to serve as a minister-at-large for economic development. In his homeland, years of environmental neglect had left Uzbekistan ravaged with disease, the Aral Sea drying up, fishing villages disappearing, crops failing, and resentment growing toward Moscow and Westerners. He knew the cultural, economic and political instability of the new republic would take years to sort out.

Drawing an ace

Larry quickly abandoned Akron as a launch site.

Bob Rice favored Moffett Field, or the Marine Corps hangar at Tustin, California. Tillamook, Oregon, was a candidate. Some looked into the availability of the Strato-Bowl in Rapid City, South Dakota. Another possibility was Moses Lake, Washington, near where the *Earthwinds* test flight had landed; Boeing Aircraft Co. maintained a runway there.

But Barron Hilton had other plans. He had just purchased the old MGM Grand/Bally's Casino in Reno, Nevada, near his beloved 650,000-acre Flying M ranch.

Reno sits in an open, flat, desert on the lee side of the Sierra Nevada Mountains, its location providing a natural shelter from winds. Stead Airport, a former Air Force Base just north of the city, offered a measure of security.

From its new base at the new hotel in Reno, *Earthwinds* would become a worldwide corporate promotion for his company, even in European capitals, boosting the company's visibility as it expanded its gaming ventures in Nevada and elsewhere. Hilton promised Larry one million dollars, and directed his marketing staff to begin looking for additional sponsors. From then on, it would be a Hilton project all the way, renamed the *Earthwinds* Hilton. Money problems would virtually dissolve.

The first task was to reduce Virgin Atlantic's role. Initially, Michael Kendrick tried to assert Virgin's claim on the capsule, the project's only tangible asset. Hilton sent his emissaries to meet with Branson and discuss buying him out.

They argued that with more than 350 million print media impressions tabulated—and uncounted millions more in airtime—*Earthwinds* had given Virgin Atlantic and the other sponsors oceans of publicity.

Finally, a contract was signed. Hilton credited Virgin for $800,000 worth of sponsorship—and bought out the remainder of Branson's interest for $550,000. Hilton Hotels Corp. formally took over the project. Virgin Atlantic would remain as a named sponsor—with its logo on the anchor balloon skirt.

Richard Branson's pledge of $1.5 million had allowed the project to attain critical mass. Barron Hilton thought his money could put it over the top.

As the person who had introduced Hilton to the project, Erin Porter sought a continuing role. At Hilton's personal request, she took a leave of absence from America West Airlines to coordinate the administrative and marketing workload for *Earthwinds* at Hilton headquarters. Her only misgiving, she told friends, was that she would have to put up with more idiosyncrasies from Larry and Lynne.

Neil Cohen left the pr firm he had co-founded less than a year earlier, and joined Hilton's staff as a vice president, with one key responsibility: coordinating Hilton's involvement in *Earthwinds*. Cohen was vested with authority to hire staff, find the new sponsors, and throttle up the publicity machine to maximum rpms. He would control the project's $3.6 million purse for the year and provide staff help for the Newmans.

The Hilton marketing people planned on recouping all of the company's direct investment. Cohen retained a consulting firm to develop souvenir products. Their budget had three scenarios: an unsuccessful launch; a partial success and, optimistically, a completely successful flight.

Merchandise would feature a stylized "H" as the *Earthwinds* Hilton logo; public calls to a 900-number would be narrated by actor Cliff Robertson at 95 cents per minute; signed posters, philatelic flight covers, and photographs would be sold. Altogether, a successful flight might bring in $4.5 million; an unsuccessful launch would result in a loss of $200,000 (primarily from the cost of leftover merchandise).

The new arrangement did little for John Wilcox. He was tired of *Earthwinds* and just wanted it to be over. He had invested hundreds of thousands of his company's dollars in a project that still dragged on! He was bitter at the way Larry embarrassed sponsors and alienated friends. Wilcox talked of writing a slam-dunk book he would call 'How to Piss off a Billionaire.'

Lachenmeier and Barrow also reconsidered whether a simpler design function better. They sketched out some ideas and took them to Barron Hilton. But Hilton, convinced of the efficacy of the unique system and wary of making changes before they were fairly tried, rejected their ideas.

The summer of '92

It took Lynne Newman two months to decompress. The tension of the build-up for the attempted launch, and her personal struggle with Carol Hart, left her in an emotional heap. Her doctor extended the Prozac prescription, put her on Flexeril, and told her to stay medicated until *Earthwinds* ended.

Larry returned to America West and requalified for his 757 captain's seat.

But hurt feelings continued. Don Moses' relationship with Larry was deteriorating.

The Sunday New York Times' final story from Akron was matched with a wire service photo of the project spokesman briefing reporters at 2 a.m. Saturday while the balloon was being moved back into the airdock. Larry seethed for a week. Where was HIS picture?

Larry and Lynne held several long heart-to-heart talks about who should stay in the project. Carol had to go, Lynne insisted. Larry would have to tell Don that Carol couldn't have any further role in the project. It was Lynne's ultimatum.

Larry brooded about making personnel changes. He came close to making a substitution in the flight crew, perhaps dropping Don Moses because of Carol's cold relationship with Lynne. He considered inviting Gene Cernan, or Mike Emich, or Tim Lachenmeier.

Meanwhile, Don and Carol rented a summer house on Kauai, taking Vern and Darlene Rich to Hawaii with them. They stayed busy repairing engines, fiberglassing boats, working hard until Hurricane Iniki virtually halted tourism there in mid-September. None communicated with Larry.

Larry had doubts about Bob Rice. He began blaming Rice for selecting Akron as the launch site. Rice hadn't been forceful enough in advising him to stay away from Akron, Larry complained; Rice knew that there less than a one percent chance of suitable weather forming during the winter launch window in Ohio. Vitriolic letters were exchanged.

Rice concluded that he 'didn't want to get involved in a shit-fight'. So the thoroughbred who had guided balloon pilots across the world's oceans and vast tracts of land, whose forecasts had opened the golden era of ballooning, was fired from 'the last great adventure in aviation.' With Rice gone, Larry also lost the services of Doc Wiley, the search-and-rescue partner on so many long-distance balloon flights.

In casting about for a new meteorologist, Larry sounded out a commercial service or two before offering the job to Len Snellman, the retired chief scientist for the western region of the National Weather Service. Snellman was perhaps best known for having provided the global weather for the Voyager airplane.

Unfortunately, Snellman had no ballooning experience. His special interest was the 'belt of the westerlies'—he never used the term jet stream. Snellman set limits on his job. If Rice's role was to present thoughtful, narrative options for discussion, Snellman's role simply was to interpret the data for upper air currents and pass them to the pilot.

'I told Larry and Barron Hilton at our first meeting how slim their chances were for launch and flight weather to occur at the same time: maybe only three times in a whole winter season. They didn't like that very much.'

Snellman was chagrined when he heard that his opinions were being second-guessed behind his back, and he promptly quit.

'Then Larry put on his good Jewish hat and gave me a great sales pitch on how important weather was to his operation. I stayed in.'

◆ ◆ ◆

Barron Hilton invited his long-time friend, the former FAA Administrator Donald D. Engen, to serve as director of operations. A former member of the National Transportation Safety Board and retired Vice Admiral, Engen had a distinguished a record as a naval aviator, with combat experience in Korea, Vietnam, as well as Washington's bureaucratic wars. By his own admission, he knew nothing about ballooning.

◆ ◆ ◆

Tom Barrow, the scholarly launchmaster whose composure and presence of mind served as a soothing tonic for everybody, decided it was time to investigate the numbing sensation in his extremities and his periodic inability to form certain words. When he finally saw a doctor, he was diagnosed with a malignant encapsulated brain tumor. Following emergency surgery, Tom began a long period of radiation therapy after which he had to learn how to walk all over again.

Other arrangements were also unraveling. Vladimir had found when he returned to Moscow that the deputy director of PHOTON—the defense agency that served as the financial conduit for the ASBV contribution—had mistaken the meaning of 'privatization'. Alexander Martinov, reportedly had begun selling state assets and retaining the proceeds. When this corruption was uncovered, he was tried and found to be 'an enemy of the people'. A new Russian sponsor, Tsnimash, fostered commercialization of Russian space projects and provided international contacts to stimulate investment.

While all the political and financial intrigue was developing, Vladimir's report about *Earthwinds* sent Russian scientists digging. They questioned many of Larry's assumptions. They worked through formulas and equations so Vladimir would become absolutely knowledgeable about how *Earthwinds* flew, even if Larry did not train him.

The Russians also made a number of safety suggestions based on their concern over the effect of wind shear as the balloon rose. They feared that the top of the balloon rising into a swift current of wind could tip at a sharp angle, causing the freely suspended helium dewars and gasoline tanks to swing like a pendulum and bang into the capsule. It invited catastrophic rupture of the liquid vessels. The Russian scientists recommended 'slap straps' under the capsule, tying the suspended tanks to one another.

Back in the U.S., Admiral Richard Truly had resigned as NASA Administrator, and his successor was looking for programs to cut. One line item in the budget without internal backing was the *Earthwinds* experiment. None of NASA's scientific balloon people had been involved in the project, and there was no clear need for basic research into jet stream wind particles; it would have cost $100,000 to analyze the raw data. The NASA science package was dropped, and with it went the project's original appeal to the cosmonaut.

By September, Larry had taken another unpaid leave from America West. Once again, his high-wire act was being performed over a financial safety net: Hilton paid him and Lynne a combined salary of $8,000 per month while they prepared for the flight. Larry parked the capsule under the porte cochere at the entrance to the Reno Hilton casino and worked on it in plain view of the arriving guests.

Don and Carol planned to come to Reno for the National Air Races but Larry told them there was no room in the Hilton hotel. They came anyway and stayed with friends, but Larry made no attempt to contact them. Even right at the airport, where Don and Carol joined Barron Hilton for lunch, Larry avoided Don and declined an invitation to join them.

A few days later, Don was back in his trailer next to his parents' home in Trona, California, when Larry called him to explain the new realities. Carol Hart would not be welcome in Reno, Larry told him. Neither would Vern Rich. Both of them should stay home, he said. Don, certain that Larry was trying to get him to withdraw from the flight, retained an attorney to ensure his position in the flight crew.

Weeks later, Don went back on the payroll as a crewmember. But he was bitter and seldom missed an opportunity to explain to whomever would listen how Larry was making mistakes.

◆   ◆   ◆

A trans-Atlantic balloon race in September 1992 heightened public awareness of long-distance ballooning. The pair who flew the longest distance included Richard Abruzzo, the 29-year old son of Ben Abruzzo. Richard had been just 15 when his father, Maxie Anderson and Larry Newman crossed the Atlantic. Their endurance record in the Double Eagle had stood 14 years. Richard Abruzzo and his co-pilot Troy Bradley broke it by staying up 146 hours, landing near Casablanca, Morocco.

Larry called to congratulate Richard and invited him to Reno—prompting speculation that Richard Abruzzo would be invited to join the *Earthwinds* crew.

'Ben was like a father to me, the father I never had. You know, he was 16 years older than me,' Larry told friends, 'and I am 16 years older than Richard.' He stopped tantalizingly short of finishing his thought '…and Richard can be like the son I never had.'

8
Sagebrush and Pogonip

The family reunion

The advance party assembled in October at the Reno Hilton. A hangar at Stead Airport became the workplace. Technicians streamed in to reinstall the high frequency radios, Global Position System navigational aids, avionics, Inmarsat satellite telephones, fiber optics laser cutters, computers, faxes, antennas and other paraphernalia.

The three Amigos, the electrical heroes from the Akron days—Gene Kemmerline, Dick Paige and E. J. Hendricks—were on hand to ensure each component's correct installation and wiring. Gene's cheerful wife Emma worked in the hangar answering phones.

Just as in Akron, the people and the business community of Reno offered generous assistance. One firm donated a Ku-band satellite receiver and antenna for the weather/operations center.

Another donated a large crane. Yet another, three winch trucks.

By the end of October, the list of volunteers totaled 250 names, many of which were painted on a banner to be hung from the helium dewars.

By early November, prompted by Erin Porter's weekly faxed updates, the *Earthwinds* kollectif grew in size and buzzed with intensity. John Ackroyd observed that it was a more mature, disciplined team, a team that knew each individual's strengths and weaknesses.

There was a sense of relief that the mission had not flown the previous February from Akron, when it was only hours from launch.

'We thought we were ready then, but we weren't,' Ackroyd said. 'We learned so much about the capsule, the engines, the communication systems, that this year's version of the procedures and systems is vastly superior.'

◆ ◆ ◆

Outside the hangar doors, the sweet smell of sagebrush wafted in the air. A remote, barren location, Stead had a special place in the annals of aerospace history. It was where NASA had sent the Gemini and Apollo astronauts for desert survival training, releasing them into the wild with a .22-cal. rifle and a machete to find edible animals and snakes.

Nature had provided Reno with mountainous shelter that made the site a good one for aviation year-round. The high desert usually enjoyed clear days, and the Sierra Nevada Mountains to the west kept the surface wind to a minimum. Winter days were marked with light wind as the cold air was sealed in by temperature inversions.

◆ ◆ ◆

George Saad from Ohio, an old Electra Flyer factory hand who had helped in Akron, and Tom Police from NASA's Lewis Research Center, who had been bitten by the *Earthwinds* bug a year earlier, took their accumulated personal leave and drove to Reno.

Special guests showed up. Richard Abruzzo and Troy Bradley came in fresh from their record-shattering Maine-to-Morocco flight.

John Ackroyd had brought Michelle Evans, whom he had met at the Quaker Square Hilton in Akron. She pitched in on the phones at the office at Stead Airport.

Vladimir arrived November 3, met with warm hugs and high-fives. It was a family reunion!

Tom Barrow, the launch master, was now recovering from his brain surgery. He had been through debilitating, humiliating and painful chemotherapy, had learned to walk again, but still relied on a cane for support.

A new spirit pervaded the camp. Much of it seemed to derive from Larry's "new" personality. For much of his life, friends and visitors never knew which Larry Newman would open the door when they knocked. Would it be Scary Larry, with the withdrawn look and bulging eyes? Schmoozing Larry, the confident, focused, eloquent aviator with the velvet voice? or Snarling Larry, distracted, insulting and impatient?

With financial concerns in someone else's hands, he relaxed. He delighted in showing off new gadgets. 'What's your home address?' he would ask visitors who stood inside the capsule with him. Larry would run the Street Address CD in the on-board computer, linked to the GPS satellite navigation system. He could show you the precise coordinates of your home or office, or whatever school or intersection was below the capsule in flight, in eight levels of magnitude. In flight, he explained, it would a moving map display, his balloon's location always pinpointed.

He had recruited another colleague from the old ultralight company, Frank Toney, to administer the budget. Toney was ferociously, unquestionably loyal to Larry, whose word on anything was final.

Larry had asked that no vehicles be allowed near the launch site 'because they create dust.' Well, if that was what Larry wanted, that was it! The rule was inviolable! Never mind that Barron Hilton had arranged three luxury coaches for his VIPs, that ESPN needed three 30-foot tall light towers to illuminate the site for its broadcast, that the media needed satellite trucks, that the volunteers would have to be shuttled to the work area, that the fire department and other emergency vehicles required access, etc. Unfortunately, Toney had never managed a large-scale public event. He would declare that something was one way, then forget what he had said, and reverse himself, or would simply pump out erroneous, sometimes ludicrous information. Toney had been told (in error) that unexploded Air Force ordnance remained out near the *Earthwinds* runways.

'We have to warn the public that they can't stand out in the desert to watch the launch,' he'd say. 'There are too many hazards out there: deadly snakes, blister bombs, pucker brush and dust.'

The more experienced hands soon learned to work around him.

Until Tom Barrow arrived on the scene to reclaim his role as the launch master, Toney was planning to manage that, too. He would say about Barrow, for instance, who still walked with a cane to steady himself after months of radiation, that everyone had to stand up on their own two feet. The cut was so unfair that no one could repeat it to Barrow.

Barrow drew his own conclusions about Toney, and ignored him.

Beginning around 7 a.m. each day, the staff would assemble for breakfast in the Grapevine, the hotel employee cafeteria in the basement, surrounded by cleaning ladies on one side and nubile casino attendants in tight, revealing costumes on the other. The Earthworms would traipse across the colorful, cacophonic casino floor and head out to the airport, where Larry conducted a daily 9 a.m. staff meeting.

♦   ♦   ♦

Cohen had the marketing engine humming, too. After one day of intense video media training (how to field questions, how to gain control of interviews), Larry, Don and Vladimir sat in their capsule for three hours while a link-up of 14 consecutive local news anchors took turns asking questions. The satellite media tour, an expensive favorite of Hollywood celebrities, reached into every major local media market in the country without requiring guests to travel a mile.

Pressure!

There still had not been a full run-up pressure test of the capsule. Modifications made over the summer had to be evaluated. Larry had hoped to take the capsule back to McDonnell Douglas' Space Systems Center in Huntington Beach, and conduct a manned pressure test. The engineers there had never performed such a test with pilots inside; *Earthwinds* would be the first. There had been time available in the chamber in May, and they scheduled the test—but Larry fretted that he couldn't afford to drive the capsule there—each highway trip required a special $15,000 insurance policy on the capsule. He cancelled the test and looked for an alternative.

He found the solution in Reno. One morning he and Don Moses trailered the capsule to the 8,900-foot summit of Mount Rose along the road to Lake Tahoe. Up in the mountain, he thought, temperature and pressure conditions would approximate those found early in flight.

Larry and Don sealed themselves inside the capsule. The engine started gulping air, which decreased interior pressure and simulated an altitude climb. As that was happening, they dialed in the desired interior pressure and turned on the screw compressor.

'When the screw compressor was engaged, we experienced a dramatic pressure bump on our ears as the cabin 'descended' down to 8,200 feet, which is the altitude the automatic cabin controller will maintain during our flight,' Larry reported.

Next, they turned on the second engine, which powered the electrical fan for the anchor balloon. If that worked without causing a loss of cabin pressure, it would be possible to make altitude changes without venting away helium from the lift balloon. If the second engine didn't engage, the only way to descend would be to vent gas, which would reduce the number of altitude adjustments they could make.

Everything worked as planned. Irritable and tense when the test-run began, an hour later, Schmoozing Larry emerged from the capsule, all smiles. After that, he turned his attention to the new launch method.

Operation Desert Storm

One thing lacking in Reno was a hangar large enough to contain the 100-foot anchor balloon prior to launch. There was no Loral Airdock or Tillamook blimp hangar in the desert.

Larry raised the idea of building a temporary hangar—an inflatable structure

Barron Hilton didn't like it. What if it collapsed and blew away? he asked. John Wilcox's didn't like it, either.

What if it gives way and kills somebody? he asked.

Larry stuck by his idea, explaining that he needed a large workspace for staging the launch equipment, and to inflate and pressure-test the anchor balloon slowly; a leak in the anchor balloon at launch would cause delay or even a scrub. The anchor balloon had to be checked. He would rip it open just before launch.

Tim Lachenmeier wanted nothing to do with the dome; Raven refused to bid on it. Tom Barrow thought it was cumbersome; he disavowed interest in it.

Larry said he would personally supervise its erection and deflation. He surveyed four manufacturers and came back with a bargain price. For $85,000, ThermoFlex, a company in Salina, Kan., could produce what he wanted: an air-filled temporary building, a hemisphere 240-feet across and 110 feet tall. After the flight, well, Barron Hilton could have the dome to cover the hotel swimming pool!

Despite the skepticism of sponsors and staff, the building was commissioned.

The monstrous dome was test-inflated on November 1 at the corner of two abandoned runways on Stead field. The white hemisphere stood like a visiting alien craft, starkly defying the reds and browns of the desert with its smooth white curves. A pedestrian access through a revolving door and a vehicular access through an airlock were the only egress points.

Earthwinds' dome was guaranteed to withstand 80-knot winds for 15 years. Its distinguishing feature was the requirement that it could be split open before launch. That accounted for the Velcro panel running over the top.

Opening it required volunteers to grab lines connected to the two halves of the hemisphere, and tug them apart. Larry scheduled a practice rip-out session to learn what unique wind forces would be created by the flapping fabric.

One morning two hot air balloonists inflated their craft inside the dome. On Larry's command, volunteers tugged their lines and ran into the desert. The top separated cleanly, and one hot air balloon ascended, while the other simulated a tied-down anchor balloon. The lesson learned was that the collapsing building did create turbulence; the anchor balloon would have to be tied down securely. Extra eyebolt tie-downs were cemented into the runway surface.

A few days later, while reinflating the dome, wind picked up and a section of the fabric tore. Larry blamed ThermoFlex workers, who had stitched it together too tight. Don Moses, quick to criticize, charged that Larry had panicked and caused the tear himself.

ThermoFlex fixed the tear, and the dome was ready again five days later. It meant that instead of being launch-ready by Nov. 15, they would be ready by Nov. 20. Although it was a minor setback, the delay would have catastrophic consequences.

On Saturday, November 14, 50 volunteers helped to uncrate the anchor balloon, inserted the electrical valve, wedged the capsule through the airlock, powered up the engines and started the anchor balloon's axial fans. They slowly inflated and pressurized the anchor balloon, which looked as proud and strong as the one inside the Akron airdock.

The next day, the wooden shipping crate containing the helium balloon came through the airlock.

Inside the inflatable dome at Reno's Stead Airport, the capsule and the anchor balloon are prepared for flight.

The mid-November weather looked hopeful. Each morning, team members would part the curtains in their Reno Hilton rooms to observe chimney smoke rising straight up. It was calm on the surface, good ballooning weather. Even the upper atmosphere track looked good. A sense of optimism surged.

Final experiments were installed. Larry declared that the capsule would be flight-ready by Friday, November 20. The mission could begin within days.

Larry studied the heavily laden capsule as Lynne helped load aboard the water and food and crew's personal gear. The weight worried him. A heavy balloon would have trouble ascending.

Suddenly, he delved into the food stocks, and began removing things. Keenly conscious of his lactose intolerance, he decided that all the cheese, butter and chocolate had to go. That reduced the weight but increased the tension: Larry had taken this step without consulting Vladimir, whose Central Asian and Russian diet consisted primarily of such staples. Learning of Larry's tinkering with his diet, Vladimir's face contorted in anger. A confrontation with Larry did not reverse the decision.

Staff attention turned to the forecast. A strong jet stream pattern—*no! a belt of westerlies!*—was swooping in at 150 mph from the northern Pacific Ocean; it would head straight east across northern Nevada. Upper air currents moving that rapidly were bound to produce strong surface winds at 6,000 feet, the elevation at Stead Airport. Steve Brown, the local National Weather Service meteorologist, warned that this condition often caused wind of 40 to 60 miles per hour. Normal Reno weather would follow: clear skies, calm wind. Launch by Thanksgiving morning looked probable.

'If we're not out of here by the end of the week,' Larry told the staff, 'I will be really surprised.'

Bill Swersey, the Gamma photographer, formed a dollar-per-person pool to guess the hour and date of takeoff.

◆ ◆ ◆

But as the final details of launch were firming up, another drama was forming. The field rep from ThermoFlex who had been camping out in his 'tent', was having second thoughts.

'We were crazy to take on this project,' Vic Bryant said. Too many little problems were happening. Bryant had been tightening a cable when fabric near one of the cables gave way, and the dome began to lose pressure. He patched it quickly, but told Frank Toney: 'I'm losing confidence in this building by the hour.'

Larry noticed a problem, too. The dome seemed to be getting taller! He suspected that the structural load tapes were stretching. If they expanded too much, the load would shift to the fabric...

On Tuesday night, Nov. 17, Vic Bryant was alone in the dome when a circuit breaker tripped. One of the generators shut down. When the back-up generator failed to kick in immediately, Bryant called for help on the cellular phone, and the word spread quickly to Larry and Barron at a dinner meeting of the Hilton board. All imagined the dome collapsing on the equipment in the middle of the night. There were some tense moments but the fear was greater than the reality. The back-up generator finally came on and the dome repressurized, but the net effect was erosion of Hilton's remaining confidence in the inflatable structure.

The following day, a very agitated Barron Hilton demanded a contingency plan. Steve Brown's big wind was about to blow through town. Hilton was deathly afraid the dome would be damaged. He quizzed Lachenmeier about how quickly the anchor balloon could be deflated, how long it would take to get the dome down.

Lachenmeier said it might take eight hours to deflate the anchor balloon, and cautioned against it. But he also warned that if it broke free, it could do serious damage. The contingency plan was to tie things down and ride out the storm.

◆ ◆ ◆

More members of the support team arrived Wednesday. Mike Schein delivered the liquid helium dewars to the airport; Vern Rich drove up from Phoenix; last year's hard feelings gone, Larry gave him a big welcome. Mike Emich flew in from Akron as the flight's Official Observer. Fred Gorrell and Don Campbell came to assist Tom Barrow with the launch.

Thursday morning I had planned a walk-through of the dome to familiarize the local media with their viewing areas on launch night. By 10 a.m., I had escorted two television camera crews, an AP reporter and photographer, a radio reporter and a local photographer through the revolving door into the dome. Outside, the wind was whistling along about 30 mph, and the sky was overcast.

Barrow, Gorrell and Campbell were conferring in a mobile home inside the dome.

Bill Swersey was taking pictures inside the capsule.

Larry was working on the liquid helium dewars with Mike Schein.

Vern Rich and George Saad, having spent the night in one of the three trailer homes parked inside the dome, were heading back to the hotel. They glanced over their shoulder for one last look.

There were two loud cracks. Harsh retorts echoed like gunfire. The dome had burst at the top! Daylight was streaming in! Dust was falling on upturned faces.

My first priority was to evacuate the photographers and reporters to a safe viewing area alongside the dome where they could document 'the breaking story.'

When Vern Rich saw the dome go slack, he wheeled his car around and sped back.

Larry hopped down off the dewars' trailer and went outside to implement the plan that he and Frank Toney had worked up that morning.

Mike Emich found himself instinctively going into his life-property-equipment saving mode.

'Ka-riste! We have cryogenics in here. Jesus God! Gasoline!...and the electrical generators are running! We need to evacuate everyone now!'

As the wind had its way with the dome, huge rents appeared in the vinyl fabric. Sections flapped violently in the wind. Larry shouted for people to drive their automobiles onto the slack part of the dome, hoping that their weight on the dome fabric might protect the anchor balloon from harm.

John Ackroyd cut load tapes on one panel so the vehicles trapped inside could be wheeled out.

The wind turned rough. Cars parked on the collapsing building rocked up and down, back and forth, like toys on a fireman's blanket.

Emich found himself tossed five feet into the air, and came down hard on his knees. He saw Tom Barrow lying nearby, knocked back by the flapping building. They saw Ackroyd go down and get up again.

Larry was in constant motion. The capsule! He had to save the capsule! If the anchor balloon pulled away and tipped over the capsule, *Earthwinds* might be delayed years! He raced back inside the wild, undulating building. Drawing his knife, he fought his way under the fabric and crawled forward until he found the capsule. He emerged astride the top of the capsule, slashing away at the fabric before it could drag the capsule off its pedestals. Antennas were being torn off the capsule. The satellite dish was blown away. Vladimir stood below, pulling material away until the capsule stood in the clear.

The howling wind whipped through the remaining structure, now pressing hard against the anchor balloon.

Vern Rich's first thought—like Emich's—was that they had to get the liquids out. The fully loaded liquid helium dewars and gasoline tanks were on the downwind side. The anchor balloon was about to smash into them!

'If the fuel tanks had gotten knocked over,' Vern said, 'and the fitting knocked off the bottom of the tank, we'd have had 800 gallons of gasoline on the carpet.

'So I just jumped on the forklift and drove it into the dome. When I got the forklift inside, the fuel tanks and the helium dewars were all clumped up together, right where the anchor balloon would conceivably go. So I picked up the fuel tanks that were full of gas.

Emich guided Vern as he backed the dewars out.

'I drove them outside,' Vern said, 'where, if they tipped over, it wouldn't be a problem. When I went back inside, Mike was at the trailer trying to figure out what to do. So we just picked up the front of the trailer, put the chain on them and pulled the dewars out through the airlock.'

'The biggest problem,' Schein said, 'was when Vern was turning this thing around we came real close to where the anchor balloon was. And you could feel that anchor balloon—you could feel it wanted to separate. It was almost gone already. And so we ran back in and got the fuel tanks which were on the pallet and we just took 'em on out.'

'We were saying 'Whew!' and all of a sudden WHOP! BAM!'

With an eruption of popping noises, the anchor balloon ripped loose from its moorings. The two-ton, 100-foot tall beast crashed into the new mobile home that had been Vern's bedroom hours before, and rolled it over. A leg from the inverted vehicle pierced the underside of the anchor balloon and there was more ripping and roaring. The anchor balloon bounced and took flight!

Propelled by the 35-mph winds, it bounded down the runway, bounced over several cars, and tumbled into the desert. As it rolled and bounced, the wound spread the length of the balloon, ripping along a seam.

The balloon disappeared over a sagebrush knoll, tumbled a mile into the desert, exhaled and gave up its shape. The dome collapsed and the horrible sound stopped. It was all over in 18 minutes.

Destruction of the inflatable dome and the dangerous escape of the anchor balloon across the desert delayed the first flight by several months.

As the desert wind blew, a light rain fell, then snow and hail. Within minutes, a rainbow appeared over the desert where the anchor balloon had died.

Vladimir was choked up, too emotional to speak. Don Moses declared sadly that the mission was over for a year: the capsule was too badly damaged, and the heat exchangers on top were bent beyond repair.

Larry strode through the sagebrush to supervise the clean-up. He removed the valves from the anchor balloon, which was then loaded onto a flatbed truck and taken back to the hangar. The Nevada Air National Guard came by with a deuce-and-a-half, and volunteers helped load loose equipment into it. Later that day, the capsule was rolled back into the National Air Races hangar.

Larry assessed the damage, and found that he had been lucky. No one had been injured. There had been no fire or explosion. The helium balloon remained safely in its shipping crate. The capsule had lost some antennas, but nothing else. The anchor balloon was recovered, albeit with a large tear. Larry conferred with Hilton officials and then put out a statement about this 'setback' and affirming that the project would continue within a few weeks.

ThermoFlex had promised that the dome would stand up to 80 mph but the wind hadn't topped 37 mph that day. Larry believed that the dome had not been made to specifications. He persuaded ThermoFlex to make a new one, even convincing them to allow six Reno area volunteers to go to Salina, Kansas, and help measure, cut and sew the new structure.

Larry shipped the anchor balloon back to Raven, but it was beyond repair. Construction of a new one began within days, at a cost of more than $211,000.

The *Earthwinds* family broke camp, planning to reconvene after Christmas.

Crew dynamics

By then, Don Moses could no longer suppress his doubts. He had lost confidence in Larry's judgment, health and stamina. His favorite pastime—and Carol's—became Larry-bashing. Don's earnest appearance made his attitude infectious: others picked up on the too-easy sport as well, such as Erin Porter and the Hilton marketing team who had peripheral dealings with Larry. Newman had committed ultimate sin: he had embarrassed Mr. Hilton in public! They believed the worst, and they talked.

Their differences politicized the camp into Larry's friends and Don's friends.

Mike Emich sensed this awkwardness when Larry invited him to a dinner party, and then Don asked him to a different event. Emich felt that he was being disloyal to one if he accepted the other's invitation.

Some worried that the tension would erupt in the capsule during flight. Ackroyd, the prototypical Project Man, recalled that his speed car team had come to America as disorganized greenhorns, and after a series of setbacks and weather delays, returned three years later as a disciplined professional racing team who helped one another. Years after setting the speed record, they still held annual reunions. Ackroyd believed that the *Earthwinds* team was congealing, too, and predicted that one day it would hold reunions and rejoice in its own success.

Despite Ackroyd's assessment, some people had gotten burned emotionally, victims of careless manners or hasty anger. Erin Porter, suffering emotionally from being wire-brushed too many times, sat back one day and sighed, 'There's just so much scar tissue that it will never heal.'

Only time would tell. But at this stage, the three crewmembers were not working as a team. The pilot paid them, and they did their jobs. Larry held the information; information was power, and power was control.

◆   ◆   ◆

Don Engen went to Reno and listened. It didn't take him long to identify some of the problems.

'The modus operandi had been so ingrained into {Larry Newman's and Frank Toney's} daily lives that they could not let go of the most minute detail,' he later recalled.

'Preoccupation with detail was clouding the larger picture.

While {Toney} listened to suggested changes in procedures, in fact nothing was changed. Administratively, the tight administrative control of the staff at the hangar kept both the Pilot and {Lynne} immersed in the smallest detail.'

Engen tried talking about these concerns with Larry.

'When challenged to bring more order into the daily preparations, he stated that the *Earthwinds* Project had thrived on individuality. This individuality lent an entrepreneurial free spirit to the project and was the reason that the project had come so far.'

That was fine early in the project, Engen said, 'but when things had to be done in sequence and within time constraints, that was the time when project order and discipline was needed. Our conversation led nowhere.'

Don Moses and Larry hadn't been real companions—Larry had been keeping a distance between Don and himself—and the bitterness between their women only exacerbated the tension. Larry had finally had told Carol Hart straight out that he didn't like her, and that she was not allowed to step foot into the hangar, use the phone or any office, collect any pay or have any role in the project.

Don was bitter because there was hardly any information flowing to him, there had been no in-capsule training, and he felt that he hadn't been taught how to fly.

Don had talked for a year about getting himself a balloon license for his own job protection. Yet his logbook showed only three hours of instruction in a hot air balloon; he needed a minimum of five more hours, an FAA check-ride and a written exam. He vowed again to get at least enough hours for a private license.

'Larry hasn't given us any training,' Don complained over a leisurely breakfast one morning near Lake Tahoe. 'Even our weather briefings come via Frank Toney. Larry himself never tells us what's going on.'

Don worried about what would happen on the flight, when Larry became exhausted by all the chores he had assigned himself. Don said he and Vladimir talked privately about how to deal with Larry, whom both feared would be prone to bad judgment when deprived of sleep.

'Will he be able to handle emergencies in flight?' Don asked Vladimir.

'Larry will have a problem,' Vladimir answered.

'Once we leave the ground, he's not going to pull any of his shit on us,' Don said.

Don and Vladimir fantasized about their course of action, what Don called the 'zip-lock solution':

'As soon as we take off, we're going to lace Larry's lips together with electrical ties and tell him: Fuck you! Go sit in the corner and stay there!'

Don never smiled when he said that. And it wasn't his only complaint.

'Larry's not healthy, and he knows it,' Don continued. 'He won't even get a First Class medical examination. He is losing weight steadily, his stomach bothers him all night long, and he has ulcers. Every morning at breakfast I watch him gulp down a fistful of pills.'

Don also said that Larry's insistence on controlling and managing everything—even things he didn't know anything about—led to burning out one of the engines. The story was that Don had thought he could improve engine performance.

'I spent months learning about nitrous oxide. I read books about it, studied it, and watched it being done. You have to add it when the engines are at a certain rpm. Larry and I were in the capsule with the engines screaming and he insisted on pushing the button himself. I shouted at him—NOW! He didn't do it. He waited. Then he pushed it.

'Now we have a severe knock in one engine and we have to replace it. That was the third engine he ruined!'

Don continued venting:

'We have no idea if these heat exchangers are going to work. We have tested them under cold and under pressure, but never together. If they don't work, we may have to come down in 12 or 18 hours.'

But on the question of adding nitrous oxide to the engine fuel, there was no agreement either. Larry believed that technique only worked on high-performance racecar engines, not the delicate machines installed in his capsule.

◆ ◆ ◆

The replacement anchor balloon arrived by truck on Christmas morning. For want of a photo-op, the shipping crate was wrapped with a huge red ribbon. While Christmas was a day of rest, Larry asked the volunteers to report on the 26th to erect the new dome. By Sunday morning, December 27, the dome was up and pressurized. Larry and Frank Toney were working inside, ready to move the capsule into place. Suddenly, a circumferential cable snapped, the bottom of the hemisphere lifted off the ground, and the new dome began collapsing! All they could do was watch. This time, Larry agreed that the dome had to go. He reverted to Plan B: an open-air launch.

Just for the record

Aviators intending to set records must meet certain criteria (such as membership in their country's aero club), follow certain procedures, and pay a fee to the National Aeronautic Association, which in turn processes the paperwork, assigns an official to monitor the flight, and reserves a period for the exclusive use of a record candidate. A staggering amount of paperwork is required, along with fees of $10,000 paid in advance.

Back in Akron, Larry had asked Mike Emich to handle this function.

Watching and recording the takeoff was the easy part; the difficulty came in tracking it and ensuring independently that it did not land. That required Emich to learn all of the ARGOS satellite tracking data, the NASA science package and other means of altitude and position verification. He spent weeks studying these systems until he mastered them.

A record attempter must belong to the organization sanctioning his attempt, but Larry, ever the outsider, had refused to join the Balloon Federation of America, the aeronauts' division of the NAA. To avoid embarrassment, one of the organization's officers paid Larry's $35 membership fee.

The rules forbid an official observer from receiving pay for his services, and while the project was Akron-based that was no problem. When it moved to Reno, Emich paid his own airfare, only to find upon arrival that there was no room at the Reno Hilton for him. He bought a room himself, expecting reimbursement.

Mike mentioned the room situation to Larry, who said he couldn't reimburse him since Mike hadn't gone through Lynne, the room coordinator. All this took place the day after the dome collapsed in November. Mike wound up eating his travel costs, but bitterly.

During the break before Christmas, Larry called Emich to say he wanted him back for the launch. Emich explained that he needed airfare and a room. Larry wouldn't spring for the airfare so if Mike wanted to be the Official Observer, he would have to do so at his own expense. After the hundreds of hours of effort he had invested in Akron, the donations he had arranged, the endless phone calls spent setting up his assignment; he could hardly believe that Larry would drop him over the cost of a few airline tickets. But this was the final straw. Emich withdrew as observer.

That put the NAA in a quandary. They appointed a California balloonist, Roger Barker, who then called Emich and asked for his help in figuring out the on-board tracking devices. Mike declined the honor and joined the *Earthwinds* alumni association, where he found himself in the company of Bob Rice, Doc Wiley, Richard Branson, Maj. Gen. Phil Conley, the president of Loral, the hierarchy of NASA and others.

'Tim finally told me how it works!'

Never completely at ease explaining how the anchor balloon actually worked, Larry kept pressuring Lachenmeier for performance data on the anchor balloon fans, the relationships of pressure and weight to altitude, for some simple charts and graphs that would unlock the mysteries. Lachenmeier sat down one morning, punched out all the formulas on his spreadsheet and handed the data to Larry. The new understanding stimulated the pilot.

That very night, December 30, Larry convened an all-hands lecture in his suite to share his newfound knowledge—except that Don and Vladimir didn't attend.

'For a year I've looked at this and I've been completely wrong about these numbers, and so now that it's been clarified, that's what I'll try to show you,' Larry explained.

'The important thing for us is the ability of the balloon to descend,' he said. 'We don't have a problem with this thing going up,' Larry said, 'it wants to go up. In fact, you could just whack the anchor balloon off and it'd go way up. The key for us is to keep it down...'

'We kept saying, "*Earthwinds* is controllable", but in the back of my mind I kept going: "How controllable is it? How do we know?"'

'Tim came up with a figure that said if we ran the fan for approximately 13 minutes it would generate 53 pounds of additional mass inside the anchor balloon, pumping four pounds per minute...'

'Fan performance is the key to the way the craft flies because those two fans are essentially downward ballast.

Larry talked to the fascinating numbers on his new charts for an hour and a half. Thirty staff members sprawled around the suite listening and asking questions. Nobody asked why this lesson was being learned so late in the game.

Meanwhile, down at the bar on the casino floor night after night, Tim Lachenmeier and Tom Barrow were expressing their grave doubts about the mission. The crew would be lucky if the flight got as far as the east coast, they agreed. The huge number of variables, from the heat exchangers to the anchor balloon to the unknowns of launch—and the real wild card: the ability and stamina of the pilot—produced profound doubt in the two men.

Simulated flight and survival training

Don Engen sensed the crew's pre-flight jitters. He spotted gaps in communication between crewmembers and other key members of the project. He scheduled a flight simulation, hoping to feed sample scenarios, in-flight emergencies, altitude changes, communication failures and radio checks into the capsule and evaluate the interplay.

Engen and Gene Cernan, both distinguished aviators whom Hilton had brought to the project, believed that the simulation should be written and managed by a 'trusted agent'.

Len Snellman, the new meteorologist, was excited about the simulations.

'In Voyager, we ran a lot of simulations,' Snellman said, 'and by the time Dick Rutan and Jeana Yeager took off, weather, operations and the flight crew all knew what we were doing. You only get that from practice.'

Larry wanted none of that, and he especially didn't want that 'washed-up astronaut' looking over his shoulder. If NASA put astronauts through their flights 100 times before they flew, that was fine for the folks at the Manned Spacecraft Center in Houston. The astronauts didn't build their own spacecraft, did they? They just sat there and pushed buttons.

When Larry directed Lynne and Frank Toney to plan the simulation, it became clear that he had turned the tables on everyone: the simulation would become his full-scale test of the people on the ground: the operations center, the weather center and the media center. Lynne and Frank developed two scenarios consisting of 3-hour blocks: the first was a simulated lift-off and climb-out to altitude; the second, an emergency landing in eastern Asia.

On the day before the big 'sim', Reno was savaged by its worst snowstorm in 25 years. The airport closed, and none of the key players got to town: Engen, Snellman, Dick Blosser of the communications team, or the media staff. The test was postponed.

Two days later, on New Year's Eve, the team got organized.

Larry, Don and Vladimir inside the capsule turned up all their radio equipment and evaluated each system. The Inmarsat-A voice system worked well. The Inmarsat-C system, a data link to the fax machine on board, worked great. The HF radio link through Rockwell Flight Test in Cedar Rapids, Iowa, worked, the amateur radio experiment worked, VHF worked. Only the Motorola radio hesitated and went down.

Sitting outside in bright sun, the closed capsule got warm. The inside temperature rose to 80, 85, then 90 degrees. The heat tired the crew, made their heads ache and made them hungry.

Although they had 40 days worth of food and water tucked away in corners of the capsule, none of them opened a candy bar, snack or hot meal.

Larry attributed the high temperature to having all of the equipment on. He started shutting things down and making a list of what he would do without.

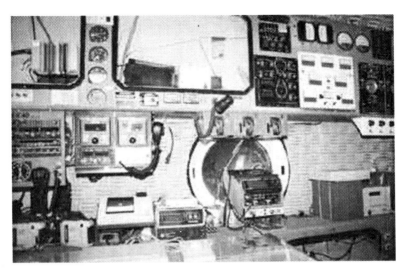

On the flight deck inside the Earthwinds capsule. Larry Newman said it was more complicated to fly than the Space Shuttle.

Other problems appeared. Vladimir and Larry kept bumping into one another; the shoot-edit-transmit workstation was too close to Larry's communications set-up. That would have to be moved.

That evening—New Year's Eve—there was another all-hands session in Larry's suite, during which the tedious lessons learned in the simulation were exchanged.

Larry asked Don Engen to take Vladimir aside and teach him radio etiquette; he complained that the Russian didn't seem to know how to begin and end his transmissions.

Don Engen considered safety of the crew of paramount importance.

Because Engen had come into the project relatively late, there was a flurry of last-minute activity over the weekend. Engen had set aside his lucrative international aviation consultancy.

Barron Hilton believed he had chosen the right man for this assignment, since Engen had served as President Reagan's FAA administrator, and a member of the National Transportation Safety Board—all after a career as a distinguished naval aviator.

Fire in the capsule, an ever-present danger, terrified Engen. 750 gallons of gasoline, fumes from the engine compartment, oilcans, oxygen bottles, engines operating at high temperatures, electrical equipment and a cosmonaut who chain-smoked could give rise to an inflammatory situation. Five halon fire extinguishers were placed within the capsule. Two were dedicated to the engine compartment and electronically armed to go off when heat reached a certain level; three were hung within easy reach of the crew.

When Engen learned that the sound baffling cones Larry had glued to the walls were not only flammable but also emitted cyanide gas when burned, he shuddered.

Russian space scientists had been just as concerned. The four oxygen bottles stored below the floorboard were in just the place where a fuel spill would run. Ackroyd, Engen and Dzhanibekov insisted that the oxygen be moved up to the flight deck. Larry relented, but thought that looked pretty crowded, so he deleted two oxygen bottles. Engen pleaded to reverse his decision:

'Larry, I implore you: take as much oxygen as possible. Oxygen is life itself, and you won't be able to come back for more.'

Larry took the message to heart, restored the two bottles and added a fifth and a sixth.

As Engen became acquainted with the capsule, he formulated an intense survival-training program. He borrowed Crew Resource Management videotapes from an airline friend, trying to teach crew interaction in a crisis, i.e., how to tactfully help the pilot-in-command steer clear of catastrophic errors, and how a pilot should solicit help from his crew during a crisis. While snowstorms pelted Reno, Engen pressed ahead with cram-session training from military survival experts. Two officers from Fallon Naval Air Station came over to teach capsule egress procedures and desert survival.

Two Air Force tech sergeants from Headquarters, Air Rescue Service at McClellan AFB in Sacramento spent a whole morning reviewing bailout procedures, survival equipment and the use of one-man rafts. The Nevada Air National Guard donated three of them.

'Be aware that things in the water will come up and bump you at night,' warned Tech Sgt. David Bradshaw as Larry's eyes bulged. 'They won't hurt you, Larry, they just want to know what you are.'

They showed an Air Force training film in which two pilots eject from a plane over a remote part of the ocean; one pilot dies and the other, to survive, must bury his friend at sea. How would the *Earthwinds* crew handle that situation? How would they get into a raft? How would they use their immersion suits? What should they carry in the survival pack? How should they use the equipment already stowed? Which end of a flare do you pull at night?

'Wherever you land, stay together,' Sgt. Bradshaw advised. 'Work as a team. Relax. Find an inner calm and be at peace. Slow down your heart rate. Stay hydrated.'

Engen booked the crew into one additional session—at the Mountain Warfare Training Center in Bridgeport, Calif., near Yosemite National Park. One of the Marine Corps trainers there took a special interest in the challenge of *Earthwinds*. A combat helicopter pilot named Captain Kerry Bartlett took the crew under his wing. He taught the crew to trap rabbits and deer, to use the .357 Magnums they carried, how to stay mentally clear, and how to bail out. Bartlett alleviated Larry's continuing concerns over dealing with polar bears, and the Marine said he was impressed with the amount of gear aboard the capsule.

'If anything,' Bartlett told Larry, 'you guys are over-equipped.'

Larry, Don and Vladimir, had only a few hours to absorb these principles of survival and establish a mind-set to go with the behavioral science lessons. Within a week, they would violate all the major precepts regarding crew resource management, working as a team and staying together after landing.

◆ ◆ ◆

As 1992 concluded, the *Earthwinds* team sat poised in Reno, still having doubts, still learning, still growing, nearly four years after the project began. All it needed now was a weather window.

Belts of westerlies, bolts of Stonehenge

Len Snellman, the retired chief scientist for the western region of the National Weather Service, was revered in aviation circles for having forecast the weather for the 11-day non-stop Voyager airplane global flight. A few veterans from the Voyager expedition joined him in Reno hoping for another miracle performance.

Now 72, he was eager to apply his special knowledge of the 'belt of the westerlies', popularly known as the jet stream.

New to ballooning, Snellman acknowledged his limitations and restricted himself to forecasting and reporting the movement of upper atmosphere winds. In fact, when he had agreed to take the job, Snellman startled some project staff by declaring that there were three things he would not do: 1) takeoff forecasts, 2) in-flight emergencies or 3) landing forecasts. (Some snickered that's all there was to a balloon flight).

Because Snellman had not been briefed on the detailed requirements for the *Earthwinds* flight or launch, he had to grope his way along. In early December, for instance, he had declared that the upper track would straighten out by the 28th or 29th to permit a launch. He had cast aside prudent day-by-day caution in order to produce what he unabashedly called 'sponsor's weather'. (As things turned out, Reno found itself paralyzed under the "snowstorm of the century" on Dec. 29). Another time, he innocently had asked how long a calm period was needed for launch. Such basic information was well known to everyone except, it seemed, the man responsible for forecasting it.

Despite all that, Snellman plunged into his work with the excitement of a kid eager to make the team. He met with Tom Barrow and learned all he could about the experience in Akron, and the desired flight weather. He longed to sit down with Tim Lachenmeier, who seemed to know a lot about how the balloon performed, but the balloon designer always seemed too busy.

In Snellman's weather center was a battery of computers and map-printers, with satellite photos of the world taped to the walls.

Every day promptly at noon, the old professor would don his characteristic professional garb: a white bib, proudly stained with grease pencils of various colors protruding from all the pockets. The aging grease marks reflected his accumulated wisdom. In a western nasal twang about an octave higher than one expected, he would conduct a 30-minute weather lesson and interpret nature's clues. He and his assistants would stand before their charts while their 'students' filled every seat in the classroom and the overflow crowd stood around the perimeter. Three seats in the front center were permanently reserved for the flight crew.

When Snellman posted a Red Flag, it meant no launch in the foreseeable future; a Yellow Flag meant possible launch conditions within five days, and a Green Flag meant probable launch within five days. At the end of each briefing, Snellman took great satisfaction in unveiling the current flag color.

It had been a tough winter in Reno. More snow already had fallen than in a quarter of a century. Ski resorts were reporting 17-foot bases. The cause of the snowstorms was a "blockage" in the upper atmosphere that brought cold moisture down the Pacific coastline, carried it over the mountains, where it chilled and turned into heavy snow.

'I'm old-fashioned,' Snellman would say. 'I look at the computer models, but they don't show us everything. I study the history of weather masses and I can spot things in the atmosphere.'

By Thursday, Jan. 7, Snellman could see these pretzel-shaped blockages over the eastern Pacific and over Europe were dissipating.

Sharing the weather office was Dan Gudgel, a crisp, crew-cut local weather specialist on a fast-track career with the National Weather Service. A cold dome settled in over the Reno area and would keep the winds down.

Remember what happened in Akron last year! Keep those winds down! A cold dome would do just that—and the colder the better.

Snellman, using his models, his instinct and a dose of courage, was encouraged by what he saw developing for next Tuesday morning, five days hence.

'I was watching a storm coming off the coast of Japan. Now, a computer model can't show how that will affect local weather in Reno, Nevada, five days later, but I knew how it would move, so five days out, I made the luckiest forecast of my life. I predicted 15 hours of essentially calm wind, and an upper track that would get them around the world in 12 days.'

It was the only viable pattern for at least two more weeks.

Unfortunately, that high cold dome would be immediately preceded by yet another large snowfall in the Truckee Valley, which would cripple Stead airport. Hilton had been hiring snowplows overtime after each big storm to clear the remote runways leading to the launch staging area. It cost $5,000 each time a new snow fell.

Snellman and Gudgel would have to make a decision by Saturday to set things in motion for a Tuesday launch.

With launch staring him right in the face, Tom Barrow had his own critical path agenda, and it wasn't going smoothly.

He and Lachenmeier had chosen a complicated procedure. Resembling its namesake in England, the "Stonehenge" launch technique required sinking a ring of industrial eyebolts, called earth anchors, into the pavement in a large circle around a payload. Their purpose was to restrain the helium balloon. During the staging for release, the lift balloon gradually would translate over the 'payload', i.e., the capsule. NASA had invented the procedure for launching high-altitude research balloons.

It had been Frank Toney's task to obtain the earth anchors from a construction contractor and see that they were planted where Barrow needed them. He did that, but after the second dome collapsed, Toney abandoned the original launch site and selected a new site about 100 yards south without telling Barrow. There were already earth anchors around the old dome that Barrow had counted on using. When Toney casually mentioned the new launch site during a general staff meeting early in January, Barrow's face turned red.

'I need that site cleaned up, and I need to use the earth anchors already in place there,' Barrow informed him. 'If you can't do it, you'll either have to find a new launch master, or serve in that role yourself.'

Toney assured Barrow that he could find replacement earth anchors and get them sunk into the runway concrete within a day or two.

As Toney went off to find them, he suggested that Barrow develop a different launch plan.

The level of unresolved detail was astonishing.

It's not easy being green

The senior staff crowded into Larry's office at Stead for Saturday's weather briefing. It was decision time.

Snellman reviewed all the influences in the eastern Pacific. With a flourish he removed the Yellow Flag and put up the Green Flag. He was calling for launch on Tuesday morning! Snellman looked right into Larry's eyes as he finished, waiting for a flicker of excitement, a surge of energy, an endorsement, a reaction, for God's sake! The eyes that met Len's contained...a vacuous gaze.

Larry had The Look again.

People who knew him understood that The Look would thaw in a few days, and that Larry would return to his jocular, boyish self. Snellman didn't know Larry, and he noticed this look immediately. When the pilot should have been able to unwind, relax, reflect on the flight plan and let people work for him, he couldn't.

Larry's mood change bothered Snellman.

'Have you noticed that Larry's eyes have been different since the minute we put up the Green flag?' he asked a confidante.

Communications director Dick Blosser observed something similar.

'Larry is operating in overload,' he said.

Don Engen—circumspect, respectful and publicly supportive of the project leader—expressed amazement at the range of minutia over which Larry asserted claimancy.

'He just tries to control every detail,' Engen said in amazement, shaking his head.

Even the normally placid, self-contained Vladimir was becoming openly critical and a bit withdrawn. He was deeply disturbed when Larry told him how often he felt ill, and that if he became ill during the flight they would have to land.

'He is keeping too many things to himself,' Vladimir said. 'I am not satisfied with Larry's health statement.'

On Sunday at breakfast in the Grapevine cafeteria, Larry remained quiet. Few of the excited staff knew how concerned he was about Lynne's back—her sciatica nerve was acting up, and she had been up two or three times during the night in acute pain. For another, Larry's stomach acid was depriving him of rest again.

Finally, he expressed doubts about Tom Barrow's stamina and acuity. He was disappointed, too, in Don Moses, who, it seemed to Larry, would go off skiing at all the wrong times…days before launch! Larry confided these doubts in his brother Ross, who was sleeping in the parlor outside Larry's room.

◆ ◆ ◆

A thick fog settled over the Truckee Meadows Valley on Sunday morning. As it lifted, tiny crystalline ice flakes appeared in the air, a phenomenon the local Indians called pogonip, the word for 'white death'. Breathing in the ice dust caused pneumonia, for which the Indians had no cure.

The fog in the valley created a new worry: what if there was fog on the morning of takeoff?

'If it's cloudy on launch morning,' Larry said, 'call Henderson's flying service over in Sacramento. They do cloud seeding. They'll get rid of the moisture by dropping dry ice particles in the fog.'

The 48-hour countdown began on Sunday morning with movement of equipment to the launch site from the National Air Races hangar.

A Keystone Kops routine took place at the launch site. It seemed that someone had walked off with the keys to the huge crane parked at the site. The crane was the only way to raise the capsule off its trailer, so it could be lowered onto wooden blocks. The trailer would then be used for transporting the helium dewars and gasoline tanks from the hangar to the launch site. When the keys were found, the crane's battery was found to have run down. And the engine was cold. It took an hour to warm the engine enough to charge the batteries to move the crane to pick up the capsule to use the trailer to move the dewars and pick up the tanks. The schedule fell two hours behind—for want of a key!

The shipping crates containing the helium balloon and the anchor balloon were brought out. The flight train suspension was attached to the crane and raised over the capsule. Antennas were bolted onto the capsule, camera pylons assembled, gasoline tanks and helium dewars nestled alongside the capsule, the slap straps fitted, fuel lines connected, fiber optic laser cutters plugged in.

'Get off at first light!'

Len Snellman still had the Green Flag up when he and Dan Gudgel began their last formal pre-flight map talk at noon on Monday. They had one main concern: a fast-approaching ridge line accompanied by clouds. To stay ahead of it, *Earthwinds* had to maintain a strict and timely launch schedule.

'That ridge will be right on our doorstep,' Snellman said, 'so I urge everybody involved with this launch, please let's not have any delays. We need to get off as soon as we can.

'Larry, you want to be off at first light, but I'd want you off at 4 a.m. This is a small window.'

Snellman reported more data, accompanied by a warning:

'Air Research Labs sent me a trajectory just a few minutes ago and the trajectory had us moving to the north! Well, the only way you have 'em moving to the north is if the ridge has gone by, and by then we'd be in a cloud problem.

'I didn't even bother to print it because their timing assumed a launch at 8 or 9 o'clock in the morning. It's a touch-and-go thing with regards to the clouds and maybe to the wind. Both of them are involved with that ridge.

'I can't emphasize any more strongly: you gotta get off at first light. Anything you can do to make it before first light would be helpful.'

The roomful of technicians and launch crew listened raptly.

Barrow and Lachenmeier arrived at the briefing just as Snellman's portion of the briefing concluded, missing his stern warning!

Gudgel took the floor to discuss the local weather at the launch site—stressing the good news about the light wind due to the cold dome and warning about the high clouds coming in.

'About 3 a.m., we think we're going to see some cirrus, some high clouds, and then within a couple of hours those high clouds are going to thicken up a bit. So about oh-five-hundred tomorrow, you may very well have high cloud cover overcast. That's basically no concern to us because the cold dome will have already established, with nine hours of radiational cooling.'

He went on to offer reassurance about the light wind.

'As long as the air comes from the north like this, there will be speeds of one, two or three knots, and any kind of moisture influence will be minimized.

'I don't look for the cold dome to break. I look for winds to be light and variable at the surface all day long today, plunging right back down in temperature after sunset and really establishing this inversion. So you'll be dealing with light winds in the basin over this snowfield.

'The concern for us going into tomorrow is that as this ridge moves by, we're going to be coming under the influence of a little trough approaching the coast, and we're looking for an increase in southerly wind—so it's important that we maintain the time schedule you have established for the launch—that you are off in the early morning hours.'

Gudgel acknowledged the difficult challenge the weather team faced:

'Out there on the launch field, we're going to be more nervous than a bunch of long-tail cats in a room full of rocking chairs.'

Gudgel made one more small observation that he thought useful.

'When the balloon does rise, it is going to go into warmer air.'

Lachenmeier said that if the temperature were close to the dew point, frost would form on the balloon cap, adding weight.

Somebody else questioned the strength of the inversion. Gudgel replied that there had been 'a good one the other day: it was 30 degrees difference at 400 feet above the ground.'

Barrow asked about possible increase in surface wind speed after sunrise. Gudgel said 'The cold dome is gonna hold. The inversion is set. I look for winds to hold at the surface.'

18 below

By Monday night, bitter cold had indeed settled into the valley. At dusk Tom Barrow's crew uncrated the poly balloon and connected the bottom fitting to a crane, which raised it out of the crate and over the capsule. There, John Ackroyd, Vern Rich Jr., and Tim Lachenmeier made the fitting to the top of the flight train. The remainder of the balloon was lifted out of the box and stretched down the south runway.

There was a breeze on launch field, however, and Tom Barrow delayed starting the flow of helium until it was down to two knots only 50 feet above the deck. It was the very flow that Dan Gudgel had illustrated on a topographical map a few days earlier.

With the temperature plunging, each breath exhaled produced ice on beards and moustaches. The moment of truth was at hand. At 8:35 p.m., Barrow signaled to open the diffuser valve. A rush of gas filled the tube, working its way forward to the crown of the balloon.

Soon both tubes were taking gas, and the graceful long inflation sleeves arched over the field.

◆ ◆ ◆

John Wilcox had lived through three years of this project, and was anxious to get on with the rest of his life. Now, however, the launch of this balloon was colliding head-on with his personal life. While the staff scrambled for last-minute details, his wife Juliette went into labor and John rushed her out of the Reno Hilton and right to the hospital. As the action was unfolding at Stead, John was coaching the birth of his first child. John had started this project (he had started both of them) and now he was missing the launch of the *Earthwinds* balloon because he was taking LaMoz breaths with his wife. At 11:30 p.m. on January 11, as 150 volunteers struggled outside to stage the global balloon flight, Juliette delivered John III.

◆ ◆ ◆

Besides the intense cold, another acute discomfort facing the field volunteers was that the fumes and exhaust from the diesel-powered cranes and trucks remained right in the bowl where the work was taking place; no wind carried away the noxious odors.

The bubble of helium in the balloon swelled and tugged the bag upward. At midnight, the balloon rose up over the capsule, and they continued shooting helium.

John Ackroyd had been working outside all Monday, with no opportunity for a break before the overnight shift. No one knew his job the way he did. Ackroyd's hands were numb from the cold; he already felt the onset of frozen tendons in his left hand. He would feel pain for several days until his hand thawed and circulation returned. Ackroyd's surges of energy belied his 55 years; he was midway through what became an outdoor work period of 28 consecutive hours.

The anchor balloon was unfolded carefully, unwrapped from its plastic shipping sheath, fans attached to the top and bottom valves. Huge fans were pumping air into it through both the top valve opening and the bottom valve.

The bottom of the anchor balloon was fitted with a 30-inch inflation plastic tube.

Condensation began to line the cylindrical walls of the bottom tube. It became obvious to Tim that this slowed the inflation rate a lot.

By midnight, the cold dome had set up sharply; the temperature just 400 feet above the surface was 20 degrees warmer. To Lachenmeier, Gudgel and Snellman, this was reassurance that the wind would remain light.

The wind was a far more important consideration than the Delta-T.

Barrow and Tim watched the wind carefully. They conferred every half-hour with the meteorological people.

◆ ◆ ◆

Night inflation of the 1.1 million cubic foot helium balloon in the desert at Reno.

The helium balloon stood over the capsule in absolutely still night air. The twin inflations were proceeding as smoothly as could be expected in cold air that now reached 18 degrees below zero.

Cold helium screeched from the huge red cylinders nestled on three flatbed trailers. Both long inflation sleeves hanging from the balloon fluttered and rippled as they carried the lifting gas into the 1.1-million cubic foot bag.

In the general confusion on the field, someone temporarily unplugged the extension cord that supplied electrical power to the capsule, and reconnected it to an outlet on a lamppost.

Although no one knew it at the time, that outlet was dead. Slowly, the amperage began to drain from the on-board batteries, which had absorbed the electrical load.

Only a few more hours to go until sunrise, and no more delays could be tolerated. Once the wind picked up, middle clouds would move in, and there would be a disaster on the field.

Lachenmeier and Barrow agreed that it was going to be close.

'By the morning,' Barrow said, 'there will either be a launch or a dramatic, dangerous abort.'

Every 30 minutes Dan Gudgel would bring them the latest soundings. The wind was averaging three to five mph...well within tolerances.

Several hundred well-heeled dignitaries, celebrities, personal friends and business affiliates of Hilton huddled together in VIP tent, cozy in their Sorrels and Patagonias and warmed by platters of catered hot food and bowls of three-alarm chili. Neil Cohen, the corporate pr man, finger-painted a frosty sign on the VIP's warm-up tent: 'Welcome to the Polar Hilton.'

At 2:30 a.m. it was time to wake up the crew. Tom Barrow pulled out his cellular phone and punched in the numbers to the Operations Center back at the Hilton, where Don Engen was waiting. Engen called Larry Newman.

Larry had hardly slept at all—his third consecutive night filled with pre-flight anxiety, stomach acid, insomnia and worry about Lynne's discomfort. Larry phoned Len Snellman, and then he and Lynne dressed.

Engen then dialed Don Moses' room. Don called his friend Vladimir. They rode out together with Carol Hart.

The inflation continued.

◆ ◆ ◆

Shortly after Larry, Don and Vladimir left the hotel one of the ground crew spotted a one-inch hole in the anchor balloon fabric! Lachenmeier examined the wound and found a clean, oval-shaped hole. He was baffled. Certainly that didn't happen at the Raven factory in Sioux Falls...such a hole could never have passed the Quality Control inspectors. How did it get there? Lachenmeier had no idea. But he knew for certain that this would stop the flight. The anchor balloon had to be absolutely airtight.

He and Barrow conferred in a nearby trailer. Rumors spread across the launch site like wildfire...to the press, to the VIPs, to the 150 volunteers and workers.

Tim had to repair the hole. Fortunately, he had packed a swatch of Spectra fabric, some Spectra thread, and a few needles.

At 3 a.m. he called Clive Blincoe, the parachute rigger whose shop was right there at Stead. If his bare hands could stand the exposure to the raw air, Blincoe could do it. Lachenmeier drove back to the hangar, retrieved his kit, picked up Blincoe at his house and went to work.

That's when Larry appeared at the bottom of the capsule ramp, dressed in his bright orange arctic overalls and jacket. He walked up the ramp and sat down inside his capsule.

Making some quick checks, he discovered that the capsule batteries were draining power fast. He needed the batteries for starting the engine. To preserve what was left of them, he shut down as much equipment as he could. If the engines didn't start aloft, the anchor balloon wouldn't pressurize, the screw compressor wouldn't turn, there would be no oxygen, the electric valves in the helium balloon wouldn't work, and they couldn't communicate! Only one thing was important: leave those batteries with enough juice to start the engines.

No one noticed the extension cord plugged into the dead outlet.

Exiting the capsule, he walked solemnly over to look at the hole in the anchor balloon. Then he stepped up into the launch master's trailer. Barrow quietly recounted the status: the poly balloon inflation had been slowed; the anchor balloon problem was being fixed. There would be about a three-hour delay. Snellman was reporting that the mid-level clouds were approaching more slowly than anticipated, but it remained a race against the clock. As Larry listened, every muscle in his face pulled tight.

Barrow floated an idea. If the hole could not be field-repaired, would Larry consider flying without the anchor balloon? *Earthwinds* had been conceived to use either the anchor balloon or cryogenic replenishment for altitude control. One was redundant. Larry stared back silently at Barrow, giving his suggestion a pocket veto. He wanted the repairs to go forth, and he wanted to fly with a fully functioning system.

◆   ◆   ◆

Vladimir lumbered into the capsule and sat down at the video-editing table. He turned on the editing machine, but it wouldn't work. He checked the connections and the plugs. He had memorized each wire and knew where things were supposed to go. Nothing happened. Vladimir was puzzled and distressed.

Maybe it was the bitter cold. He pulled out the manuals and began reading through them. After an hour, he gave up. The editing machine was kaput; he would have to shoot raw footage and save it. He knew that meant there could be no transmission of edited tape from the balloon to the chase plane, no need for Wilcox's crew to be on the chase plane. He also knew this would disappoint Canon, who had loaned all this equipment.

♦ ♦ ♦

About 3 a.m., the driver of one of the two winch trucks, believing that his job was done for the night, drove off into the darkness and went home. He had not been told that his continued service was crucial for the launch! By the time Barrow discovered the driver was missing, it was too late. Koh Murai, a local balloonist, loaned his pickup truck that happened to be equipped with a winch cable.

The five percent solution

In the frigid desert air, the helium balloon glimmered spectacularly under the halogen lights, shrouded in a misty vapor from the dewar's vapor and the exhaust chugging forth from the heavy diesel machinery and the remaining winch truck.

Directly below, the capsule rested on wooden blocks.

Larry and Barrow conferred in the trailer over a final piece of business. For three days the launch master had been requesting a total weight of all the capsule equipment. Now needed the figure so he could calculate how much helium to shoot into the poly balloon to lift it all up with a good margin of safety. The quantity of helium in the balloon at liftoff would determine the initial rate of ascent, as well as the altitude ceiling.

'A lot of last-minute decisions were being made relative to determining the gross weight,' Barrow later recalled. 'In the last few days, 600 pounds of lead shot ballast in small canvas bags had been added, then 100 pounds taken off.' Barrow needed the final number now. Larry and Lachenmeier had calculated exactly what they wanted for free lift, the excess over the gross weight. Too rapid a rate of climb might send the delicate balloon crashing through wind shear higher up. Neither knew how much stress the balloon could withstand. Lachenmeier mentioned without emphasis the temperature aloft data.

Larry gave Barrow a number. He wanted five percent free lift…19,500 pounds of lift. Barrow repeated the crucial number back, and Larry confirmed it.

The team continued shooting helium, pausing only long enough to change helpers in the bucket truck.

At daybreak, John Wilcox rushed in from the hospital. Acknowledging the congratulations of his friends, he then began directing his video crew.

By 8:00 a.m., the capsule began to float, having reached Barrow's magic "EQ" (equilibrium number). It was time to board the crew.

Barrow summoned Don and Vladimir from the VIP tent, where they had been drinking hot coffee, eating chili and mingling with Barron Hilton's guests.

The three flyers walked up the ramp one final time and stepped inside. When the blocks were pulled from under the capsule, the crew grinned broadly and leaned out the window—the quintessential photo opportunity. They spent 15 minutes waving and exchanging farewells while the anchor balloon team made the umbilical connection, and the final restraints were rigged into position.

Field security was non-existent. Every volunteer who showed up had been given a large green jacket printed with sponsors' names. Indistinguishable from one another although they had different functions, all freely roamed the launch site. VIPs who chose to walk into the preparation area did so freely. Media were escorted back and forth.

Gas inflation stopped when Larry reported that the upper load cell read 19,500 pounds.

'We were getting gas in at a good rate,' Barrow said. When he signaled the end of the gas inflation, enough helium remained in the truck for another 2,000 pounds of lift.

Tom Barrow had two face-to-face talks with Larry before he would let the capsule rise up to the end of its restraint lines over the anchor balloon.

First, he handed Larry a four-by-six-inch metal box containing electronic connections that, activated from the capsule, would sever the last lines holding the balloon. When Larry fired the device, the flight would begin.

Second, Barrow asked Larry to put the 'Launch Abort' procedures page in front of him. Larry couldn't find it. Barrow handed Larry a second laminated copy. They reviewed the procedures before the capsule was winched up.

The data streaming into the Operations/Weather Center profiled the inversion. The staff waited for Larry to check in with them and request their report. No one had told Ops that radios in the capsule had been shut off to preserve power.

On the field, the crew waived out the open door, then put on their parachutes. The winch-up procedure would take 45 minutes, during which time the anchor balloon would roll underneath. The launch area was cleared of vehicles and spectators. Barrow moved judiciously.

The weight of the anchor balloon was absorbed slowly as a single cable rolled it upright. When the Stonehenge maneuver concluded, the capsule was positioned over the center of the anchor balloon.

◆ ◆ ◆

By 10 a.m. Pacific time, with the capsule raised over the anchor balloon, Col. Doc Wiley was watching the live coverage on ESPN from the comfort of his living room in Albuquerque. He telephoned Bob Rice, who was at work in Bedford, Mass.

'What do you think, Bob?' Wiley asked.

Unable to view the launch on television, Rice had only his computer and his charts in front of him. He studied the data for a moment.

Rice knew balloons. He knew weather, and he knew how they interacted. Although he was still bitter at how Larry had treated him last year, he followed *Earthwinds*' progress with detached amusement. He saw the cold air on the surface and the air twenty degrees warmer just a few hundred feet overhead. It was a classic temperature inversion in a place notorious for them. He wondered how much free lift was designed into this takeoff. In Akron, he knew, the plan had been to climb out with 10 percent free lift. Rice watched his data and listened as Doc Wiley described what he saw on TV.

He spotted a disaster-in-the-making.

'The goddammned thing is gonna fall out of the sky like a rock if they launch into this,' Rice told Wiley in a matter-of-fact voice.

Back at the Operations/Weather Center, Engen, Snellman and their deputies were also watching the impending launch live on ESPN. The technicians sat by their finely honed, sophisticated array of radiotelephone equipment. They didn't know why Larry hadn't yet called them to perform the agreed-upon radio checks. It had been 72 hours since a single communications device had been tested. Dick Blosser, the facile operator and veteran of the Voyager aircraft global project, was chomping at the bit to get on the air. He broadcast the balloon's call sign into the blind, but there was no reply.

The Ops Department watched on TV. The ridge was overhead and the wind had already shifted.

9
Analysis and Rebuilding

Dirty linen

The dramatic start and sudden end of *Earthwinds*' flight received national attention. The three television networks highlighted it on Tuesday evening's news broadcast, using John Wilcox's video. The corporate marketing staff buzzed to Barron Hilton how many millions of media impressions the Hilton name was receiving. From the marketing standpoint, the event was a great success!

But after the big build-up about the longest flight in history, the five-mile flight looked, well…ridiculous!

The project's credibility had been badly damaged. The first to weigh in with conclusions was late night television talk show host David Letterman who explained the Top Ten Problems That Doomed the Round the World Balloon Flight:

10. Right before lift-off the fat guy from 'Cheers' snuck on.

9. First mate wouldn't quit with the 'Up, Up and Away' routine.

8. Nobody could drive a stick

7. Navigator insisted on bringing along his collection of good-luck anvils

6. Balloon built by G.E.

5. Those morons at Jiffy Lube

4. Shouldn't have agreed to deliver huge overflowing box of hatpins

3. Collided with DHL truck

2. Wasted all the helium doing Sally Struthers imitations

1. Someone had their tray table down

Larry, who always enjoyed a good laugh, giggled as I read him the list. Larry wasn't the only one giggling, though. *Earthwinds* became the laughing stock of the country. And that was the good news. The bad news was that the story of the personal relationship between the flight crew was a ticking time bomb.

Malcolm Browne was on to the story, and he pushed the detonator. The Science News section of The New York Times carried his story on page one under the banner: 'Recriminations Follow Debacle of Short First Flight of *Earthwinds*.'

Scanning the story, key words popped out:

'Bitter recriminations...most expensive...crash offers painful lesson...scarcely covered five miles...crash-landing...frantic effort...bad luck...ripped as it dragged...nearly catastrophic failure...dashed by the bitter accusations...he was critical...Newman had abandoned him in a dangerous situation...for both personal and professional reasons...Newman had ignored requests...badly designed and too heavily loaded with complicated and unnecessary equipment...without adequate engineering...key members said they were leaving the project...'

There it was: all the dirty laundry out on the line: Moses and Dzhanibekov turning on Newman; Newman attacking their inexperience. The story stung. It was the first really adverse story ever written about *Earthwinds*—ironically written by one of its earliest champions. Readers concluded that the project was over.

'On the back of an envelope...'

But why had the flight failed? Don Engen called on his experience as a former member of the National Transportation Safety Board, the federal agency that investigates aircraft incidents. He interviewed the pilots and collected data from the meteorologists, engineers, the launch master, the balloon designer and anyone else who cared to write. He returned home to Alexandria, Va., to prepare a 24-page summary.

Tim Lachenmeier calculated that the inversion caused a loss of lift in the gas equivalent to 998 pounds. To ascend through the warmer air above, the free lift, he now believed, should have been more than 10 percent.

In a separate report, Tom Barrow made clear that he thought Larry 'incompetent as a pilot' and as a leader, and told Baron Hilton so in plain language.

John Ackroyd lamented that the crew hadn't chosen to ascend up to 18,000 feet after the anchor balloon broke. Knowing that no laboratory could duplicate the flight conditions, he believed that Larry had missed a significant opportunity to evaluate critical equipment. The heat exchangers and screw compressor remained untested under actual conditions of cold, thin air.

Other report-writers took a different tack. Erin Porter took the opportunity to write as the chance to turn the tables on the Newmans for what she perceived as their abuse of her good humor.

'I dug up all the dirt I could find about them,' she boasted bitterly.

In his summary report, Engen reviewed the preparations and team interaction since November, recounting his own efforts to instill discipline into the management. His report contained no surprises as to the cause of the short flight: the temperature inversion had prevented the balloon from rising because the balloon 'lacked sufficient lift for its total weight for the conditions of flight at its lift off.

'The amount of lift necessary,' Engen wrote, 'had been agreed upon by Larry Newman and Tim Lachenmeier as 19,500 pounds. They provided this figure to the Launch Master Tom Barrow, as his goal for launch. The Launch Master met this goal.'

Engen then focused on Larry's personal management style and preparedness:

> The pressures on the pilot were immense. He assumed responsibility for everything and as the time for launch approached he could not accomplish all the things for which he felt responsible. He did not trust the Launch Master's health and reasoning. As a result he tried to lessen the Launch Master's absolute control of the launch.
>
> As the time for the launch drew closer, the pilot became overly calm and seemed to mentally withdraw. It was obvious that he felt the mounting pressure prior to launch. Because he had failed to delegate responsibility, many volunteer workers continued to bring detailed items to his attention at the last minute, using up more of his time.
>
> The mounting pressure seemed to adversely affect his ability to provide overall leadership for the project. He was overworked and showed the effect of this at a time that he should have been concentrating on the task of preparing to fly the balloon.

Engen had hoped for more crew preparation and training, and had tried to affect this during his first trip to Reno, at which time he had found other shortcomings:

> There were no standard checklists for complex procedures. Team training was missing. Only one person, the pilot, knew how to fly the balloon. He did not seem to share this knowledge nor encourage another crewmember to learn this as his backup.

Engen concluded that one 'skilled and knowledgeable manager' should run the project. That person 'should have good team building and communications skills and should be the ultimate authority for all major decisions. This person should not be double hatted, i.e., also pilot, engineer, financial administrator, etc.'

What Engen's report did not address were the central mysteries of launch night: how the hole got in the anchor balloon, and why Lachenmeier's erroneous calculations for free lift had gone unchallenged.

The mystery about the anchor balloon hole presented all sorts of potential intrigue on the spectrum from quality control issues to sabotage. It was never investigated. It was a fatal flaw: the delay caused by fixing that quarter-inch hole encompassed more than two hours, during which time the ridge passed overhead, the wind direction shifted, and the flight took off in an unfavorable direction: toward the nearest and lowest mountains in the vicinity.

What could be investigated and analyzed was the amount of free lift in the helium balloon. A fresh look was provided by Don Overs, the engineer whose advice Larry and Tim had spurned in Akron more than a year before.

Using temperature data gleaned from his local newspaper, Overs wrote out on the back of an envelope a formula showing that the air in the anchor balloon, when carried into the inversion, reduced the free lift by 1,443 pounds. In addition, the loss of lift attributed to carrying the mass of cold helium into warm air came to 865 pounds. The total, 2,308 pounds, was the amount of lift lost when *Earthwinds'* double balloon entered the inversion. No amount of lead shot dribbling could have compensated for that, Overs knew. Instead, an additional 35,000 cubic feet of helium should have been shot into the poly balloon, his figures showed.

Shooting extremely cold helium from the liquid dewars was futile at low altitude, Overs said, because liquid helium cannot be vaporized sufficiently fast to correct any immediate lift problem. Even in its cold state, it displaces more than its own weight but there would be no immediate noticeable effect.

'This is physics that any high school senior or first-year college physics student would have known,' he said. His formulas told how much, and for those less facile with a pencil and the back of an envelope, the numbers could easily be run on a computer spreadsheet.

Sponsor control

Upon reading Engen's report, Larry began calling his confidantes. Who should run the project? he asked. And who should fly with him? Under pressure to make a report to Barron Hilton and assemble a new crew, Larry called Tim Lachenmeier and Richard Abruzzo and even considered adding a fourth man as a back-up pilot-in-training. All should be gas-rated balloonists, he believed.

Abruzzo, who had observed the pre-flight activities and watched the Jan. 12 flight, hesitated when Larry called him. Don Moses had been working on him, and Abruzzo wanted to let the dust settle before he jumped aboard the wrong bandwagon. Privately, he told friends he didn't want to fly with Larry. In addition, he and Troy Bradley had already spent considerable effort planning their own global balloon flight attempt.

Larry wanted to clear the air with Mike Emich, still bewildered and hurt over how he was dropped as the NAA Observer. He called Emich and discussed not only the Jan. 12 flight but also the awkward circumstances that kept Emich from witnessing the launch, and then about the selection criteria for a new crew. Larry said he wanted someone with a background of a few long flights, medical training, and current aeronautical experience.

'Who do you have in mind?' Emich finally asked, taking nothing for granted.

'I'm thinking of a tall, balding gas balloon pilot,' Larry said, laughing, '...you!'

Larry told him that a special committee would convene to select the next flight crew. He wanted Mike to be in the running, along with Fred Gorrell, Richard Abruzzo and Tim Lachenmeier.

Emich cautiously considered the prospect of joining the world flight. He had doubts about whether he really should participate in a project with so much uncertainty. Where would his old *Earthwinds* friends be? How would the sponsors react? Would this jeopardize his job? his relationships at home?

Emich knew that if he joined the crew and made the flight, it would change his life, affect his reputation as a pilot, and could result in a significant financial gain. On the other hand, he believed that Larry's reputation and personality would make success difficult to attain and share.

◆   ◆   ◆

Back in Beverly Hills, Barron Hilton had finally decided to dismiss Larry from the project, but hadn't worked out how to tell Larry. Erin Porter and others lobbied mightily for getting rid of Larry. Hilton hesitated, and then decided to keep an open mind until he met with Newman.

Hilton was conducting his own investigation. He called Bob Rice and asked 'Who should have known about that inversion?'

'If I had been there, it would have been my responsibility,' Rice replied.

Irrespective of personal relations, the questions remained: 'Who could best run the project? If *Earthwinds* were to continue, who could fly the mission? Was it necessary for the pilot to be well-liked?'

'Was Magellan loved by his crew?' asked a senior Hilton executive. 'Was Arctic explorer Richard E. Byrd loved by his crew?'

Larry made his appeal in person. He met in Los Angeles Feb. 1 with Barron Hilton.

Hilton was reminded again of Larry's genuine eloquence, in person and in public. He realized that however abruptly Larry sometimes treated people, only one person was knowledgeable enough to fly this balloon.

But if Larry stayed, the rules had to change. Barron Hilton and his marketing staff, determined to salvage their investment, would have to assume complete responsibility for *Earthwinds*.

Hilton informed Larry that his role was limited to being pilot and trainer; he would report to a project manager, for whom a search would begin at once. To Larry, that was a relief: he remained as pilot in command but without paperwork and administrative headaches.

The Newmans adopted an attitude of meekness and contrition that was almost persuasive—they even enrolled in a Dale Carnegie course of self-improvement.

As to his physical health, Larry said that his stomach ailment cleared up as soon as he left Reno; he attributed it to tension associated with proximity to Don Moses.

To round out the crew, Barron Hilton still desperately wanted an international figure on board—perhaps Sabu Ichyoshi, a Japanese balloonist Larry had rejected two years earlier. The man Hilton really wanted was Vladimir Dzhanibekov.

◆ ◆ ◆

Barron Hilton applied tremendous pressure to convince Engen to accept the job of project director, but Engen demurred.

Devoting his time to *Earthwinds* would cut deeply into his lucrative international aviation consultancy, he told the hotelier. Hilton sweetened the offer with a $100,000 salary and a six-figure bonus if the balloon completed an orbit.

When he agreed to take the helm as *Earthwinds* project director, Engen insisted on complete authority over spending, acquisitions and hiring.

The endeavor that Larry had undertaken four years previously now overtook him.

He knew the dangers inherent in sponsor control—for while the Hilton people may have mastered marketing and public relations (more than a billion media impressions!), no one on the staff understood gas ballooning, much less atmospheric physics or the thermodynamic behavior of this particular balloon. Nor did they understand crew interaction inside the capsule. Even Engen, the decorated Naval aviator, National Transportation Safety Board chairman, and Administrator of the FAA, had never flown in a simple hot air balloon: he considered it too dangerous.

Larry would be required to train two other pilots, who would be selected 'by committee.' All would have to pass physical and mental examinations. Five would be trained; three selected as primary crew, two as backup. All would be required to carry gas balloon licenses.

The marketing staff quietly put out the word that Newman would be merely one of the candidates for the flight, and would have to be screened mentally and physically just like the others. Larry would be kept off the flight, they insisted, if he didn't perform or pass all the 'tests'. Engen knew that was nonsense.

◆ ◆ ◆

When Don Moses learned of the new management and other arrangements—and realized that his own fiery mutiny had fizzled—he quietly passed the word through Erin Porter, who had Barron Hilton's ear—and then directly to Don Engen—that he would be available to rejoin the crew. But Don's sharp words were in print around the world. There was no way Larry would allow him back in. And there was still the secret of Don's past, and the documentation Larry had purchased, which he believed held Don Moses in check.

Don laid elaborate plans for a global flight with Dzhanibekov and Lachenmeier. He had told people that Larry would be kicked out of *Earthwinds*. Carol Hart worked the phones trying to gather information from the old *Earthwinds* support team.

Carol and Don were awaiting word from Russia of a sponsorship commitment. Under their plan, Vladimir would oversee construction of a capsule in his country—they would convert a pressurized fighter plane cockpit and then ship it to the U.S. Lachenmeier would serve as the balloon designer and pilot. They named Tom Barrow as operations director, and approached Canon about picking up the sponsorship.

Moses pursued a Texas oilman for sponsorship.

Hilton wanted Vladimir back. Vladimir declared that he would fly only if Don Moses flew. The marketing staff insisted that getting Vladimir back was a priority. They wanted resume luster in the crew. Barron Hilton knew that this would require his personal salesmanship.

◆ ◆ ◆

Larry solicited resumes from potential crewmembers. Engen held a peremptory challenge on each choice. Lachenmeier asked not to be considered.

Larry continued calling Richard Abruzzo, who was managing the Sandia Peak Tramway in Santa Fe that he had inherited from his father. In mid-February, Larry and Richard spent three days together…fishing, comparing notes on their respective flying experiences, and remembering Ben, the father to one and the father figure to the other.

They discovered that Larry soon would be the same age as Ben when Double Eagle II flew across the Atlantic, and Richard, at 30, the same age as Larry had been on that flight. Sentiment bonded them. Larry offered Richard the newly created title co-captain.

Engen concurred. There was one more seat to fill, and the two back-up slots.

◆ ◆ ◆

Larry asked Mike Emich if he would consider the stand-by position. Emich could see that this would involve a leave of absence from his civil service job, a major disruption to his household routine. If he accepted, it meant he would be on call to conduct more training in survival, in medicine, in flying, for the primary crew.

In early March, Emich flew to Scottsdale for a long weekend of fishing, canoeing and talking. When he arrived, he also found Richard Abruzzo and Dave Melton, Abruzzo's back-up pilot from the trans-Atlantic flight. There was much talk about Abruzzo's six-day Atlantic flight, and warm remembrances of Ben Abruzzo.

Emich, the embodiment of quiet confidence, laid on the table his 22 years of flying experience, ratings as a multi-engine instrument pilot, gas balloon pilot, builder of four hot air balloons, training as a paramedic and wide knowledge of the *Earthwinds* system.

Melton, who had begun ballooning three years earlier, recently had built from a kit a balloon that could be filled with anhydrous ammonia—the newest fad in gas ballooning. Melton, a technician at the Los Alamos National Laboratory in New Mexico, also had a fair knowledge of automobile engines.

Larry had no illusions about the pedestal on which Hilton executives had placed Vladimir. 'The money wants Vladimir back,' he explained to the crew candidates. 'The money is making all the decisions about the project. If we have to take Vladimir, we will do our thing and we will let him do his thing.'

Emich and Newman frankly discussed Vladimir's lack of ballooning experience, and agreed that if the sponsors started placing people in the capsule who couldn't contribute to the mission, it would impair the flight.

As they were meeting, Engen and Gene Cernan telephoned Vladimir. The rules had changed, they explained. Everyone on board would receive training, and Vladimir was the key to a successful international mission. The three-star American admiral and The Last Man on the Moon persuaded the Russian general to keep an open mind about rejoining the crew.

Within days, Engen met with Hilton, and then called each of the contenders. He left a message on Emich's answering machine saying that he and Melton had been selected as back-up crewmembers. The primary flight crew would consist of Larry Newman, captain, Richard Abruzzo, co-captain…and Vladimir Dzhanibekov, pilot!

The back-up pilots were not ranked first or second, and did not back up any particular member of the primary flight crew. Who slipped into a vacant seat 'would depend on circumstances,' Engen told Emich. To induce each of them to accept, they would be paid, on a pro-rata basis, $3,000 per month during training and preparation. There was a performance bonus if the team succeeded: $10,000 each for the flight crew for a new distance record, and $15,000 each for the flight crew for a new endurance record, and $25,000 if they made it all around the world. Backup pilots would each receive one-half.

As Emich was contemplating Engen's offer, Larry called.

'Hey, Mike, are you flying with me?' he asked, claiming not to know who had been selected for the flight crew.

Emich felt that he had just participated in a big charade. He believed that although he had much to contribute, the cards had been stacked from the beginning: the sponsors' marketing departments were now driving what started out as a scientific endeavor. Serving as a conditional alternate in a marketing ruse held little interest. He declined Engen's offer.

◆ ◆ ◆

For Vladimir, winning a seat on *Earthwinds* was no prize. He was burdened with other problems. First, the economy of Russia's emerging democracy had wreaked havoc on the space program budget. VIP perks were disappearing. The Russian space program had become a sideshow to his country's political difficulties. *Earthwinds* had become a high-risk, low-return venture and Larry Newman a distraction he didn't want to deal with.

Driving home in his little Yuri from Moscow to Star City one March night, with his scientist friend George Karabadzhak as a passenger, Vladimir was startled by a semi-trailer that suddenly cut across two lanes of traffic and into his path. On an icy road, faced with the choice of going under the truck, or into its rear wheels, he made a split-second decision, swerved sharply to the right and plunged into the wheels…

When the spinning stopped, Vladimir knew he was badly banged up—and lucky to be alive. The stabbing pang in his left leg was the result of a dislocated and multiply fractured knee. Then a second car smashed into the truck, jarring him again. His head banged against the steering wheel, opening a cut clear through his lower lip. With great effort, he jammed his knee back into its socket, and waited two hours for an ambulance. The injury would keep Vladimir in a leg cast for eight weeks and in rehabilitation therapy at a Black Sea sanitarium for three months.

Barron Hilton flew to Brussels and to Istanbul on business in April. He continued on to Moscow with Gene Cernan, where they called upon Vladimir in the sanitarium. As Cernan looked around, he was shocked.

'I didn't think he would ever walk again,' Cernan recalled. 'And that hospital was a frightening place!'

Rejoining the project would be a mutually beneficial opportunity, Hilton promised him—good for Russia, and good for him personally. Hilton dangled future employment opportunities and affiliations before the cosmonaut.

'Barron Hilton explained to me his ideas to improve things and get it more sophisticated, more reliable to some extent—and also his personal feeling and great wish to proceed with this project. It helped me explain to our Russian officials that I had to proceed,' said Vladimir later.

He liked the American hotelier immensely, he liked Cernan and he liked Don Engen.

He assured Hilton he would heal quickly and be ready to fly in November—but that this was his last time.

Engen's hand was now firmly on the helm.

He directed Larry to write a complete manual for each component aboard the complex capsule. That summer Larry produced detailed essays and flow charts describing the flight train suspension, capsule compressor, fuel and air distribution system, capsule coolant system, fiber optic laser cable cutters, communication and navigation equipment, operating procedures for ascent, level flight and descent.

Engen appointed John Ackroyd to head the capsule preparation team, told him to make the capsule as safe as possible, and gave him free reign. Somebody pointed out that the heat exchangers wouldn't work in their present configuration: the exhaust was on the wrong side, like a radiator that warmed pipes on one side but didn't circulate. Had a crew flown the capsule into the cold upper atmosphere, it would have been far too hot for comfort.

Ackroyd reversed the outflow position on the heat exchanger, and took much satisfaction in the throughput.

Ackroyd spent all summer at Reno modifying the capsule. Many radios were removed, and the Northstar V GPS system was replaced with three new hand-held GPS units.

Ackroyd removed the engines, built a fireproof case for the engine compartment, and then reinstalled them. He also built a 'trench' for the capsule's electrical wiring. That required longer wires from the equipment to the power source, and so the Three Amigos came back from Akron to rewire the capsule. In fact, E. J. Hendrix, Dick Paige and Gene Kemmerline, shuttled from Akron to Reno four times over the summer months removing old wiring and installing new equipment.

In place of the Canon still video transceiver, they installed an AT&T Picasso Still-Image Phone. It could store 32 images that could send a TV-quality image over the Inmarsat phone line in under 40 seconds.

They put in a Magnavox Inmarsat system.

An analysis of engine efficiency showed that sufficient duration could be obtained with only one gasoline fuel tank. Leaving behind one 450-gallon tank would lighten the load by more than a ton.

Vern Rich, Jr., briefly returned to repair the minor damage the heat exchangers suffered in the January 12 landing.

As for the launch team, Tom Barrow was gone by mutual agreement. Koh Murai, a Reno balloonist and engineer who had assisted Barrow, became launch master. He and Engen xeroxed Barrow's notes, edited the procedures, and visited NASA's scientific balloon facility at Palestine, Tex., to study launch techniques.

Tim Lachenmeier, alarmed that the anchor balloon ruptured when it scraped Mount Peterson, thought the Spectra fabric might not be as strong as once imagined. He deliberated long and hard about the anchor balloon. Was it of adequate size? What would be the effect of a larger anchor? He ran some numbers and recommended a larger anchor balloon. Adding ten feet of diameter would increase the volume by 175,000 cubic feet, carrying the same weight of air but under less pressure. That changed the relationship between the lift balloon and the anchor at float altitude, requiring a new set of charts and graphic references for the flight crew.

Lachenmeier also recommended building another poly balloon, although a back-up balloon remained crated in the basement of the Reno Hilton. He was concerned that the fill tubes had cracked so quickly in the cold weather. He won a contract to construct another 1.1-million cubic foot polyethylene balloon identical to the ones made before, with reinforced fill tubes.

When Engen called Len Snellman, he got a stunning surprise: Snellman was fed up. He spoke plainly:

'I never felt that the people running this project were really concerned about meteorology. The public relations aspects had a much higher priority. I wanted to run three or four seminars for the main players to show what I could do and see how we reacted to each other, but I only got part of one evening for that.

'That really ticked me off. And Lachenmeier never accepted me; he just wanted Bob Rice back.

'I wanted to run a lot of simulated missions, but in the only one we ran it was Frank Toney who put in the weather. I guess the Voyager project spoiled me. That was a scientific and organized project, but this whole operation was based on PR.'

Engen was in a quandary. He consulted Barron Hilton, and then took a calculated risk: he left an urgent message for Bob Rice to call him.

Rice was startled to hear from anyone in *Earthwinds*, but he curiously returned Engen's message.

'What would it take to get you back in this project?' Engen asked.

Rice paused.

'I don't think Newman even wants to be in the same state with me,' he said.

'Never mind that,' Engen told him. 'I am running *Earthwinds* now. Can you send me a proposal telling me what your requirements are—equipment, fees, and so on?'

Rice was dubious but amused.

'*Earthwinds* is the only game in town right now.' he reminded his colleagues at Weather Services Corp. 'Let's do it.'

They prepared a detailed proposal for Engen, who promptly called and warmly thanked Rice, telling him the committee he chaired would make its choice in a few days.

Two days later Rice got another message on his voice mail. It was Engen again, advising curtly that another meteorologist had been chosen. Rice was livid. He had eaten a lot of crow to present his proposal, had spent considerable effort putting it together for the one man who said he had the authority to decide these things, only to be given the heave-ho once again. Blistering mad, he called Engen.

'It looks like you don't have as much authority as you thought you had,' Rice said. 'Isn't there anyone in that goddam organization who can deal in good faith?'

The person chosen to make the vital *Earthwinds* forecast—and to step into the big shoes vacated by Bob Rice and Len Snellman—was retired American Airlines weatherman Harry Maybeck. Snellman met with him one afternoon and shared what he knew. After that, Maybeck was left to his own devices.

◆   ◆   ◆

The Hilton organization decided to rely exclusively on its own marketing firm for media work. No outside experts or balloon specialists would tell the story to the media. As a result, my service to *Earthwinds* ended. Henceforth, I would cover the story as a reporter, an activity that did not endear me to the new project management.

A race around the world?

Selection of the 'new' flight crew for *Earthwinds* firmly established the challenge of a flight around the world. Other teams pushed their preparations into high gear.

While the *Earthwinds* team waited out another season for the winter weather, no one could help but keep an eye on the other teams of balloonists were interested in the global flight, and who were capable of making it.

◆ ◆ ◆

Joe Kittinger, a retired Air Force colonel who once piloted a balloon to 102,000 feet, jumped out and free fell for 17 miles before opening his parachute, was known as a courageous pilot who could hang a balloon in the sky longer than anyone else. Shot down over North Vietnam in 1972, Kittinger kept himself sane as a prisoner of war in the Hanoi Hilton by planning long-distance balloon flights. When he came back, he became the best long-distance competitive balloonist in the U.S. In 1982, he took off from St. Louis in a conventional 35,000-cubic foot gas balloon and flew 1,348 miles to Quebec. Two years later, he proved his mettle with a solo flight across the Atlantic Ocean, departing from Caribou, Maine, and landing in Savonna, Italy, covering 3,535 miles in three and a half days.

Kittinger immediately declared his interest in flying the Pacific Ocean—and made plans for a world flight, again solo.

◆ ◆ ◆

In September 1986, three Dutch balloonists led by Henk Brink crossed the Atlantic from St. John's, Newfoundland, to Amsterdam, in a 200,000 cubic foot hybrid helium/hot air balloon in only three days. Upon their return, they, too, began thinking about a longer flight.

Sure enough, early in 1992 Brink and co-pilot Willem Hageman announced plans to fly a hybrid helium/hot air balloon from Amsterdam around the world. The National Research Laboratory in The Netherlands was supervising the design, construction and certification of the crew capsule. Brink and Hageman said they would go as late as December in their 210-foot tall system.

◆ ◆ ◆

Julian Nott, a Briton who set a hot air balloon altitude record of 55,134 feet, had unveiled in late 1986 a pressurized two-man gondola which he proposed to suspend beneath a superpressure helium balloon, inside of which was a smaller balloon, called a ballonet, filled with air. As the balloon rose and the gas expanded, the ballonet would shrink. To prevent further climbing, he would pressurize the ballonet with air. Nott proposed to fly from Australia and ascend into the Southern Hemisphere jet stream. He opened an office in New York City and raised $900,000 in grants from companies and foundations—about half his goal. That's where he hit the limit.

Privately, he complained that contributions began to dry up when Branson joined forces with Larry Newman in 1990. But he kept trying.

Nott renamed the balloon from Endeavor to Intrepid to Explorer (for the Explorers Club in New York), and announced that he would launch from Southern California. He announced the flight again, for a March 1989 start from California, if he could raise his goal of $1.5 million. Still later, he moved his equipment to Lakehurst, N.J., and secured permission to fly from the Navy base there.

◆ ◆ ◆

In 1988, John Petrehn of Kansas and Col. Towland Smith had come close to launching their round-the-world flight from Argentina. They used two government surplus polyethylene balloons filled with helium and another balloon with hot air. They had planned to circle the globe in the sub-tropical jet stream. One of the helium balloons ripped during takeoff preparations, which ended the attempt. Petrehn, a Kansas businessman, was planning to return to Argentina for another around-the-world attempt when he died of a heart attack.

Per Lindstrand, ousted two years previously as president of the balloon company that had built his and Richard Branson's Atlantic and Pacific balloons, emerged with a new factory and 24 employees. Over in England, he was planning a massive, solar-assisted hybrid helium and hot air balloon for a very long voyage.

Julian Nott, the erstwhile world balloon voyager, polished up a new and improved slick brochure describing his Explorer project, although his capsule and equipment remained locked in a Navy hangar at Lakehurst, awaiting ransom for payment of monthly storage fees.

Troy Bradley, Richard Abruzzo's trans-Atlantic partner, talked hopefully of a global balloon flight. His plan was to ascend far above the jet stream under a huge balloon, and make a slow, very-high-altitude orbit.

Joe Kittinger, the solo long distance flyer, conferred with Tim Lachenmeier about building a globally capable balloon. Kittinger had no trouble lining up a support staff—but sponsorship for a global flight was still out of reach, and several prospective donors told him they wanted to await the outcome of *Earthwinds*' next effort.

By early summer, 1993, as many as six balloon teams were preparing to fly around the world. It would be a very interesting flying season.

Dunking, jumping and keeping their spots

Hilton continued adding sponsors. Long negotiations with the Japan Travel Bureau produced a $200,000 contribution early in January, days before the disastrous flight. One condition, however, was that the chase plane would have to land in Tokyo for a press conference. Hilton began studying the cost of this sponsor's terms: landing fees for the BAC 1–11 at Tokyo's Haneda airport were staggering; VIP transportation downtown would cost a fortune; the room rental and a suitable banquet would be extravagant. Furthermore, that would take a whole day from the schedule at a time when Snellman said the balloon would be traveling at peak speed, perhaps more than 200 knots.

Other sponsor participation remained murky. Canon's contract with ESPN had expired at the end of December, and its contract to support 'Expedition Earth' on ESPN ended three months later. The company said it was disappointed in the quality of Wilcox's shows in the series.

Canon's support had been the key to Wilcox's made-for-TV-movie. That, in turn, gave the project visibility in the Far East and throughout Europe. But there was little sentiment on the part of Canon officials to pour additional money into *Earthwinds*. The loss of Canon meant the loss of much crucial equipment that had been loaned: the L-1 camcorders in the capsule, the still video imagery, the capability for compressed-motion video, and lots of office computer equipment.

Worse for Wilcox, ESPN decided not to renew its enormous news commitment.

'The failure at Reno was enough to push ESPN to the point of saying: we're not going to do this anymore' recalled production director Bill Shanahan. 'As a news event on our Sports Center, there was not a lot of interest there. At first it was exciting, then it was delayed because of the Gulf War, and then we had the Akron delays. After a while, people lost interest. Our viewers want sports news—and this was nothing like a Michael Jordan slam-dunk. We decided that it was best to let the air out of this one. Reno just pushed it over the edge.'

Hilton was determined make a profit on the next flight.

AT&T signed on as a sponsor, as did American Express and Nescafe. In a Faustian bargain, Miller Brewing Company also became a sponsor, busting the original Wilcox-Newman taboo against alcohol and tobacco advertising. Importantly, all put clauses in their contracts similar to Hilton's: that the flight had to reach 18,000 feet before major money would move. And the contracts would expire one year from the date of the first flight attempt.

Engen knew he had to launch the flight early in the season.

He emphasized flight simulation and survival training. He booked the crew into a rigorous two-week course at the Marine Corps Mountain Warfare Center in California, the team learned to survive in a snow cave and to exist with little food. In a four-day wilderness survival exercise, they ate exactly four power bars—and captured and cooked one rabbit. All three lost weight.

During the course, Larry became reacquainted with Marine Captain Kerry Bartlett, who listened intently to the account of the previous year's travails.

Engen scheduled Larry, Richard and Dave into the Naval Aviation Training School at Pensacola, where they learned techniques for survival at sea, and even rode the infamous Dilbert Dunker, which slams a cockpit into a pool, inverts it and evaluates a pilot's ability to emerge on top. He ordered skydiving sessions in Arizona so they could experience bailout phenomena.

He ended an old debate by ordering the installation of crew restraint belts on the floor of the capsule.

And while juggling all these projects and his aviation consultancy, Engen kept a wary Dutch uncle's eye on Larry.

'He has mended his ways, and has gone out of his way to be nice to everyone he talks to,' Engen said approvingly, but added, 'of course leopards don't change their spots, do they?'

Engen wanted all the outside training finished by the end of September, so the crew could begin an intense 30-day training period, including simulated launch and flight.

But back in Reno, gremlins remained. The amigos found during a test of the radios that when they keyed a microphone on a high-frequency receiver, an errant electrical impulse shut down the engines. Hendrix, Paige and Kemmerline added shielding to the wires.

The amigos were watching one afternoon early in October when a microphone was keyed. It produced an electrical charge that activated the halon fire suppressant, flooding the engine compartment. They consulted with fire suppression experts, and added more shielding to the wires.

◆　◆　◆

Abruzzo was hailed as the fair-haired boy. Towering over everyone else at 6-foot-3, he was reserved and kept to himself. People instinctively liked him.

Things slowly changed as people spoke behind Richard's back. Maybe that 'self-confident reserve' really meant 'smug'; Richard's ambivalence became a sign of his 'flakiness'; he was a non-working rich kid, a know-it-all; he wouldn't associate with the technicians or dirty his hands.

Engen, indisputably ensconced as the eminence grise, recruited retired military officers to fill in his operations staff and plan for battle on November 1. Because he ran it like a military operation, the pre-launch confusion and intensity of previous years was missing.

Engen pointedly told Larry and Lynne to stay at home until he called them to Reno during the first week of October. Vladimir returned to the States late in September, having made a robust recovery from his car crash, but Larry made no effort to contact him. Abruzzo kept his annual commitment to fly in the Albuquerque hot air balloon fiesta.

Lynne Newman found herself with far less to do than she had in years before. Thinking about how Engen and his cronies had taken over her jobs, and Larry's, she would flush and blink.

'Some people have other ways of doing things,' she would shrug as she bit her lip.

Lynne was reduced to being, well, just the wife of one of the pilots, and missed her role as a central organizer and administrator.

Tim Lachenmeier, despite his participation in the previous season's cabal, agreed wearily to return for another launch. Raven had built a new polyethylene balloon with reinforced fill tubes, and the new, larger anchor balloon. Lachenmeier would supervise their inflation.

'This is my last year on this project,' he confided to friends. 'Let's just get them launched and let them have a long flight across the U.S., across the Atlantic, and maybe into Russia. They can break all the records for distance and duration.'

He and Tom Barrow had lost hope of making a complete orbit.

Having said that, Lachenmeier would return to his new favorite subject: he and Barrow would lead a team that would fly a 'cocoon balloon' around the world. Their planning was in the advanced stages. Funding awaited an outcome of the *Earthwinds* flight.

Ups 'n' downs

As launch master, Tom Barrow had written a manual called, '81 Simple Steps to Launching the *Earthwinds* Balloon.' Engen and new launch master Koh Murai consulted that manual over the summer of '93, making additions and deletions to it.

The new weatherman, Harry Maybeck, had no such book from his predecessor. However, he had spent 37 years forecasting for American Airlines and now taught at Plymouth State College in Holderness, New Hampshire.

He arrived in Reno on the first of November. Tall, confident and lucky—Professor Maybeck quickly spotted the twin pattern that *Earthwinds* needed: it would occur on Saturday, Nov. 6.

'This looks better than it has for weeks,' he said. 'It's a perfect window for us.'

Launch preparations were set in motion.

Light surface wind would drop off to zero after sunset, and would stay calm with a very mild inversion—only eight degrees this time—through mid-morning Saturday. The upper track made a run toward Texas and Louisiana, then a gentle turn toward the Virginia shoreline.

'It goes north of the U.K. and into Scandinavia, then dips toward the western part of Russia, across the Caspian Sea, over the Japan home islands, and back to the U.S.'

Maybeck's trajectory showed an 18-day flight, but he kept his fingers crossed:

'As a meteorologist, I've always felt that any forecast longer than three or four days is risky,' Maybeck confessed. 'Now I've made one that goes almost three weeks.'

Maybeck's quick forecast sent the Earthworms scurrying back to Reno. Tom Barrow, working for Raven Industries, flew in to help Lachenmeier and Murai. Frank Toney, ousted as last year's project administrator, flew in from Phoenix just to watch. John Wilcox and his camera crews rushed in from Aspen. Photographer Bill Swersey came back from an assignment in Russia. Mike Emich flew in from Akron just to watch the drama play out.

Neil Cohen, the intensely focused Hilton marketing man, fretted over the political and military tensions in North Korea. If they invaded South Korea, he mused, fighting would displace the *Earthwinds* Hilton from the front pages and evening news broadcasts—and could sharply reducing revenue from the public 900-number.

◆ ◆ ◆

The surface wind on Friday night, November 5, remained restless until well after dark. It was 9 p.m. before Koh Murai passed the word to uncrate the helium balloon, install the top valve, and unroll the anchor balloon. That took three hours. The hoped-for 10 p.m. inflation time came and went as the wind settled.

At 1 a.m., the anchor balloon team began pumping air. Ten minutes later, helium squirted up the long inflation sleeves into the poly balloon. Lachenmeier, supervising the helium balloon, allowed the bubble of gas rise up fairly quickly over the capsule. When his crew let their hands off, there appeared to be just a tiny dollop of gas at the top, with long slender folds of polyethylene hanging below.

As the night hours passed, the balloon grew fatter. The ground crew made up for lost time by shooting helium faster.

◆   ◆   ◆

At 3 a.m., confirming that both balloons were being inflated, Don Engen called Larry's room. The pilots dressed quickly, and were driven to the launch site.

By 4:30 a.m., the capsule was floating off its blocks, restrained by a single strand of 1/2-inch Spectra rope running through a series of shackles and shives. The rope ran from a winch truck to an earth anchor bolt cemented into the pavement, then up to the balloon's bottom fitting, down again to another eyebolt, up to the capsule, and so forth, forming a pyramid around the capsule.

The pyramid gently restrained the capsule after the helium balloon raised it. Barrow's original notes, which Murai and Engen had edited, showed that the load on the pyramid should not exceed about 1,000 pounds of upward force—or about 250 pounds per anchor bolt. When the capsule began 'floating,' the load should be shifted to another set of long triangular tie-down lines, which had a break point of 88,000 pounds.

◆   ◆   ◆

The crew arrived at 5 a.m., glanced at the balloons, and then strode into the tent, where cheers from friends and family members greeted them. In a few moments, Larry, Vladimir and Richard strode toward the capsule. It was time to board.

Dave Melton, as back-up pilot, had been sitting in the capsule. An anomaly with engine number two worried him. A squeaky sound told him that the bearings were failing.

It was too late to pull the engine and replace the bearings, so he shut it down. The flight crew would have to run it intermittently and hope that it lasted. Its sole purpose was to power the fan to the anchor balloon.

He tested the radios, and watched the readings on the upper load cell. It was such routine work that his wife Shelley spent a few hours sitting in the capsule with him. She left when the flight crew showed up, and Tim Lachenmeier climbed in to verify the readings on free lift.

Mindful of the lessons of January, Lachenmeier had participated in a long afternoon meeting, calculating the temperature inversion and the all-up weight before finally fixing the desired free lift at 12 percent. That meant the upper balloon load cell would read 22,000 pounds at liftoff, nine percent more than on the January flight.

Lachenmeier noted that the upper balloon load cell already read more than 19,000 pounds. Overhead, they were still shooting helium into the balloon. It was more than 85 percent filled, two hours before sunrise.

No one noticed that a step was being overlooked. There was excessive tension on the pyramid lines. They now strained upward with a force of more than 4,000 pounds.

Larry and Vladimir now within 100 feet of the boarding ramp.

John Ackroyd, with nearly 20 continuous hours of work outdoors, leisurely walked up the ramp and exchanged a few pleasantries with Lachenmeier and Melton. He turned and started down the ramp.

Mike Schein, trim, short and lightweight, was good at handling a helium diffuser. Murai sent him back up in one cherry picker to accelerate the inflation. Schein located the reinflation sleeve and stuffed the helium diffuser hose into it. Now gas was flowing from two sources again. Schein rested his hands on the lip of the bucket truck.

In the other bucket truck a few feet away from him stood Dave Bussen, attaching the scat hose that led up from the liquid helium heat exchanger to the other reinflation sleeve.

Then came a horrible sound: a popping, a whoosh, and then a clanging collision of metal parts. The capsule was breaking free! It ascended straight up!

It halted as abruptly as it started. Overhead, the 180-foot tall helium balloon swayed and staggered with the sudden start and stop. Loose cables, wires, hoses and rope dangled below the capsule. Ackroyd instinctively raised his arms to cover his face, stepped off the ramp and looked up. The capsule had banged into the bucket trucks!

Mike Schein had watched in amazement as the capsule rushed up at him. A helium dewar crunched into his cherry picker, and broke his finger. He trampolined into the air and his feet came level with the handrail, but he landed inside.

The other side of the capsule crashed into the bottom of Bussen's cherry picker, sending it up another 10 feet in the air, where it stayed for a few seconds. Bussen didn't see it coming; he had been working with his back to the capsule. Now he was high in the air, and the bucket truck was sliding off. It lurched, and then swung wildly away before the position-holding hydraulics forced its return. Bussen's truck slammed into a helium dewar. His hard hat was knocked off, and he found himself akilter. A huge cloud of gasified helium seeped from the dewar, obscuring his view.

Underneath the capsule, a power cord had snapped free, leaving Lachenmeier and Melton in the dark. Ropes and wires flailed about wildly. The anchor balloon's skirt fouled in the tie-down lines.

Melton had been looking straight out the capsule port when the anchor gave way.

'All of a sudden I saw the horizon disappear. I knew we were going up, but I didn't know how far we had gone until I got to the side and looked down.'

Melton knew they had to prepare either to rise and then bail out, or try to get the capsule back on the ground with themselves in it. He helped Lachenmeier pull on a backpack parachute. Lachenmeier, over Larry's protests, had made a few training jumps prior to the Tillamook prototype flight. Melton had also done some mountain climbing, and quickly explained to Lachenmeier how the figure eight repelling rig worked.

A crowd quickly gathered near the perimeter. VIPs streamed from the tent and walked across the sagebrush to get a closer look.

For a moment it appeared that the balloon and capsule would separate from the remaining lines, and take off in an uncontrolled ascent.

Larry rushed forward, whipped out his two-way radio and called Melton. Having helped Lachenmeier with his parachute, Melton leaned out the port, conferring with Larry by radio. He unwrapped the rip line from where it was tied outside the capsule door, and pulled. That opened the panel at the top of the balloon, releasing $80,000 worth of helium into the atmosphere. With the helium seeping out, the capsule naturally descended. It crunched down abruptly on the runway.

But the drama wasn't over. Impact with the pavement ruptured the exterior fuel cylinder. Four hundred fifty gallons of gasoline began spilling as the unwilling passengers jumped clear.

Moments before the crew was to climb aboard, an anchor bolt holding the balloon to the ground gave way, and the capsule broke away, threatening an uncontrolled ascent.

Seeing the fuel spill, Vladimir grabbed a fire extinguisher from a nearby truck, inverted it, and prepared to put out a fire. He turned it on, but only drops of condensation fell from the nozzle. He looked for a shovel to scoop sand and dirt on the gasoline, but none was there. He looked for an ambulance, but found none.

Minutes later, the Stead Airport fire department arrived and secured the area.

'Had that gasoline ignited,' Barrow dryly recalled, 'we would have had a significant pyrotechnic display.'

Fearing the anchor balloon would be damaged if left inflated, Larry grabbed a knife and cut open one of its seams.

In less than 12 minutes, the scene on the field morphed from a proud, tall, system ready for the crew to embark, into a mass of spent plastic and synthetic fabric draped over an empty capsule.

◆ ◆ ◆

In the reception tent following the collapse, Larry startled guests when he told them that he looked upon *Earthwinds* 'as slightly more complex than the Space Shuttle. We don't get the huge resources that the government does and we are learning as we go.'

He turned to Dave Melton and observed wryly:

'Well, Dave, you and I have something else in common now. We're the only two people who have ever landed the *Earthwinds* capsule.'

Lachenmeier thought to himself that he was the only one who had ever flown *Earthwinds* in the right direction.

◆ ◆ ◆

Engen immediately concluded that the incident would cause a six to eight week delay.

Others expressed doubts whether the system could be made flyable again. All three of the Amigos believed the end had come.

'I didn't believe the capsule was salvageable,' said a visibly discouraged Gene Kemmerline. He stood in the warm-up tent and hugged his wife Emma, who had also just arrived that evening. E.J. Kendricks said simply, 'it can't be fixed.'

George Saad, a volunteer on leave from NASA Lewis Research Center in Cleveland, thought that the specially built $250,000 liquid helium flasks were extensively damaged in the accident.

Others adopted a philosophical attitude.

Stoically observing the latest ruins on the runway, Vladimir thought for a long while, then whispered sadly,

'There are no small details.'

Do svidaniya, Earthwinds

Miraculously, despite the calamitous event, *Earthwinds* had endured another industrial accident without major injury. How much longer could such luck hold?

After a day's rest, the team returned to Stead Airport to assess the status of the equipment, and to begin another clean-up operation.

The helium dewars' heat exchangers had to be re-aligned. There was a spare gas cylinder. Despite the jarring impact, the capsule looked as solid as the day it had left Burt Rutan's factory. The anchor balloon would have to be packed up and trucked to Sioux Falls, a new bladder inserted, and stitched up again. Most importantly, in a crate in the basement of the Reno Hilton sat the spare helium balloon—left over from the previous year's effort.

Having evaluated the hardware, the staff met in the now-familiar de-briefing session.

There, they concluded that the principal cause of the accident was that a 10-inch earth anchor bolt had failed along a hairline crack. It was a small detail.

'So many things went well on Friday night. We are fortunate no one was hurt, and we are not in a rush to make any decisions,' said Engen, still eager to continue.

Then Larry took the floor.

'I have a much better feeling this year than last year,' he began, looking around the room. 'This is such a family. When I arrived at the capsule, I really felt ready to fly. I felt the capsule was ready. It was the first time in the whole project I have felt that way.

'This really is a great family, not just a team. I love all you people. Last year there was so much bitterness, and all of that is gone now.'

Then he dropped his bombshell:

'My proposal is that we not scramble to do it again this winter. I'm not ready. January is not an ideal time for weather. January gets colder and the weather pattern is not as good.

'I called Barron today and told him this. The best thing is for everybody to take an emotional rest. The engineering team can get back to rebuilding the capsule after some rest.

'Finally,' he said, 'I beg all of you to stay with our family and don't give up on us.'

Engen ignored Newman's suggestion. He had a mission to complete. He scheduled a new launch-ready date of January 5.

♦ ♦ ♦

Vladimir's mood was ebullient. He had kept his end of the bargain—and now saw the perfect way out. In the months he had been away from Moscow, important things had been happening at home: the October revolution of the old apparatchiks, bloodletting in the street, and political turmoil. Vladimir was also leading a small think-tank of Russian scientists who were about to announce new findings in the field of cold fusion research. Most importantly, the Russian space program was about to be infused with new life.

In January, two American astronauts would arrive in Moscow to begin training for a 90-day life sciences and medical mission aboard the Mir station in June of 1995. It was exactly the kind of mission that excited Vladimir; he had begun his space career as a back-up commander for the first joint mission with the Americans. Now, exactly 20 years later, he was responsible for preparing the Russian and American crews for the second mission.

NASA would send up two cosmonauts on the Space Shuttle; the Mir crew would return on the Shuttle.

Moreover, Russia and the U.S. had just agreed that 10 space shuttle flights would be made to the Mir station. The U.S. would pay Russia $100 million a year for the next four years. The agreement poured badly needed money into the financially troubled program.

Vladimir told Engen of these developments, and recalled his pledge to Barron Hilton. They had no choice but to let him go.

With Vladimir gone, the project lost more than its most colorful and beloved character; it lost its last pretense of international cooperation and science.

In mid-November, Dave Melton, who had loyally served Richard Abruzzo as crew chief for the trans-Atlantic balloon race the year before, moved up and became a member of *Earthwinds'* All-American primary flight crew.

In the weeks following, analysis focused on comparisons with January's successful launch and November's failure. It was quietly concluded that the new launch master had failed to implement a significant step. When the capsule was barely floating, he should have boarded the crew, raised the capsule and shifted to the heavier tie-down lines. Instead, continuous helium inflation placed excessive pressure on the anchor bolts cemented into the old Stead Airport runway. They gave way under four times the force that had held them in place during January's successful launch.

Ackroyd was concerned over the stress on the capsule. He examined the four-eyebolt suspension points, and found that they had weakened. He called Burt Rutan, whose firm had designed and built the capsule. But when Rutan heard how much weight was now being carried onboard, he recommended a major overhaul that would involve shipping the capsule back to Mojave. There was no time for that kind of work if *Earthwinds* were going to fly this season.

Engen pressed Lachenmeier to rebuild the anchor balloon as soon as possible. He also wanted Lachenmeier to retrofit the back-up polyethylene balloon with reinforced fill tubes. But Lachenmeier was discouraged. Like most people associated with the project who also had other jobs, he was catching hell from his colleagues at work, and now he was also catching it from Engen.

His superiors at Raven Industries had always looked askance at his participation in the inflation and launch of *Earthwinds*' balloons. Raven wasn't in that business. Now they called him in again. This time, Tim was openly questioning the project's feasibility.

He had been the driving force behind the project within the conservatively managed company that designed and built the unique balloons. Now, without his advocacy, the firm's lawyers saw their chance to intervene.

Back in Reno, Lachenmeier had seen well-meaning volunteers walk on the anchor balloon to press out the last remaining air pockets. But what had been underneath the anchor balloon? Gravel? Rough concrete? A few abrasions or holes, and the airtight integrity of the Spectra would be gone. Loss of fabric integrity might lead to rupture under full pressure, and Raven could be held liable. An inch-by-inch inspection—the only sure way to guarantee quality control—would take weeks, if it were possible at all. Building a new anchor balloon would take longer.

Engen's demands for action landed on the lawyers' desks at Raven's Sioux Falls offices.

Showdown in Sioux Falls

Based on Lachenmeier's analysis, and their own concern, Raven's lawyers responded to Engen with a memorandum early in December stating that the company would no longer provide its product to *Earthwinds*. They would neither repair the anchor balloon nor upgrade the polyethylene balloon. It was not in Raven's best interests to continue supporting this project, they said. Although *Earthwinds* had been a steady customer, financial risks now far outweighed the reward. Chief executive Dave Christiensen would not bet the company on Larry Newman's performance in the air.

When Engen and Newman read Raven's response, they called out their heavy artillery to save the project: Barron Hilton.

Hilton, powerful, rich and confident, flew the next day to Sioux Falls, and with a phalanx of aides walked in to the office of Raven's chief executive, Dave Christiansen.

'What will it take for us to do business?' he demanded from Christiansen.

Flanked with ample representation of attorneys on both sides, the two men argued back and forth. Hilton was determined to strike a deal. Christiansen, a conservative manager, said Raven wanted nothing to do with *Earthwinds*. What he had learned about it convinced him that his firm's liability was too great.

'Tell me what you need,' Hilton persisted.

Christiansen said there were safety issues about the way the launch attempt in November had been managed. If there were a catastrophic accident that killed people, he could lose the entire company. Raven needed complete liability coverage.

Hilton dug in, working toward setting up whatever conditions would allow Raven to support one final launch attempt. He negotiated each point and promised that things would be different on the next try.

Raven's attorneys demanded redress of all their safety concerns:

- the balloons would be sold and delivered in 'as-in' condition, without warranty, disavowing its earlier consulting work, Raven stated that its studies 'merely represent an unskilled effort…based upon inconclusive, incomplete and inadequate information…and are not to be relied upon.'
- all members of the flight crew would have to sign a statement acknowledging that 'the extremely perilous and hazardous nature of the circumnavigation attempt creates an extremely great risk of accident, injury, death, property damage and financial loss…'
- the launch coordinator would have to be trained in abort procedures,
- the launch crew would be limited to 25 persons,
- the helium balloon inflation would be under the control of a professional,
- the crew chief for the anchor balloon would spend a day in Sioux Falls getting briefed on launch techniques,
- launch site security would have to be built up, with primary and secondary perimeters enforced by uniformed security officers,

- a four-foot chain link fence must mark the launch working area; a second, eight-foot chain link fence would enclose VIPs and media,
- emergency personnel such as fire fighters, medics, ambulance crew, and others, would have to remain on site during inflation and launch,
- a physically enclosed command and communication center would be established at the launch site, with a back-up mobile command center,
- the anchor balloon must be restrained during inflation by a large earth mover truck, to withstand up to 15 knots of wind, until the Stonehenge rotation maneuver,
- the flight crew must be boarded before the capsule reached equilibrium, and must remain aboard until launch or abort,
- no one except the flight crew would be allowed above the capsule after the helium balloon came overhead,
- the entire cryogenic helium system would have to be tested just before launch, and
- Hilton would have to pay the premium for Raven's $50 million liability insurance policy.

The last point produced bitter contention. The insurance policy indemnifying Raven became a condition for shipment of the repaired anchor balloon and reinforced polyethylene balloon.

When the negotiations nearly collapsed, in a moment of braggadocio Hilton said he would pay that.

Everyone shook hands on the deal, and the Hilton party jetted back to Beverly Hills.

Hilton was confident that his aviation underwriter would include *Earthwinds'* two balloons in his policy. After all, he owned helicopters, corporate jets, hot air balloons and gliders.

But Hilton, unaccustomed to being told 'No', was stunned when his underwriter refused to cover *Earthwinds'* balloons and Raven on the policy.

He turned to Lloyd's underwriting syndicate in London—it, too, had been savaged in recent years, its partners' wealth stripped away by natural disasters, aviation and space mishaps, and worldwide terrorism. They wouldn't touch this one.

Hilton told Raven that insurance was unavailable. Was there another way? Raven's lawyers replied that a bond of $50 million would satisfy their concerns.

Hilton exploded. There was no way he would put up that kind of money just to protect Raven!

Meanwhile, Tim Lachenmeier didn't want to become known as the designer of the balloon that couldn't fly. His people were making the repairs and modifications that Engen wanted.

Repairing the anchor balloon was especially tedious and labor-intensive. Every inch of spectra fabric had to pass over a light-board for inspection. Just removing the stitches along the seam that Larry had ripped open took more than 30 minutes per foot.

When Lachenmeier's crew finished, they crated the balloons and sent them to the loading dock.

◆ ◆ ◆

By then, Engen and Newman had grown even more suspicious of Lachenmeier, doubting his math as well as his intentions. Why were his previous calculations so wrong? Why hadn't he factored in the temperature inversion last January? How could he and Barrow openly discuss their own plans for a global flight? Why wouldn't he prepare the operating graphs for the new anchor balloon? Why wouldn't Raven produce the complete engineering study they had promised?

Engen and Newman concluded that they would be better off without Lachenmeier. And Barron Hilton vowed he would never again do business with Raven Industries.

Engen and launch master Koh Murai had met a man at NASA's balloon facility in Palestine, Texas, who could supervise inflation of the poly balloon. Homer Woodie had inflated more than 600 poly balloons in his career, all unmanned. They hired him to come to Reno for *Earthwinds'* final attempt.

They also revised the launch procedure from an eight-hour drill to a more conservative and cautious 14-hour exercise. Inevitably, every action had a consequence. The longer time on the field required a longer period of absolute calm before launch.

Engen began comparing the successful launch of the previous year with the most recent procedure, and discovered that someone had overlooked the engineering field survey of Stead Airport. The old cement out there on the launch site was weak. Abandoning the old site, he shifted the launch to an area near the National Air Races grandstands. The tarmac was newer there, and security easier to manage.

Newman remained in Scottsdale, waiting for Engen's summons.

◆ ◆ ◆

Shortly before Christmas, Dave Melton and Richard Abruzzo drove up to Sioux Falls and met with Lachenmeier. *Earthwinds'* designer sat with them for hours, explaining the anchor balloon theory. Lachenmeier also reiterated the written warning he had given earlier.

'The circumnavigation attempt...creates an extremely great risk of accident, injury, property damage and financial loss,' he said.

Citing a nine percent failure rate in polyethylene balloons over the past seven years—and two within the past 12 months—Lachenmeier reminded them that the any failure of the *Earthwinds* balloon 'would most likely result in the death or serious physical injury of those in the capsule and possibly people on the ground. We strongly recommend that you seriously consider the potential for such a catastrophic deflation of the helium balloon in determining whether to proceed with the Circumnavigation Attempt.'

Abruzzo grew restless. One person at the meeting described him as 'scattered and flighty, and not overly attentive to detail.' On the long drive back to Albuquerque with Melton, he had second thoughts.

The complexity of the craft and the possibilities for error and consequent catastrophe were enough to try anyone's nerve. On the day after Christmas, he called Engen, and then Newman, to tell them that he was withdrawing from the project.

Engen was furious, Newman embarrassed. Engen had seen failures of nerve before; in the Navy, he had more than once taken back the wings of aviators who no longer could mentally or emotionally face the hazards of flight. Abruzzo, son of the conqueror of the Atlantic and Pacific, an Atlantic conqueror himself, had seen his father and mother die because of a single mistake.

He allowed himself to be "unwinged" on New Year's Eve, 1993, five days before the new launch-ready date.

Earthwinds entered its fifth year.

10

Into Thin Air

> *A good pilot is compelled always to evaluate what's happened so he can apply what he's learned. Up there, we have to push it. That's our job.*
>
> —'Viper', Commanding Officer, Top Gun

The open seat

It was New Year's Eve. Mike Emich had just settled in for a quiet night at home in Akron with his girlfriend.

An urgent phone call shattered their serenity at 10 p.m.

'Are you still interested in *Earthwinds*?' Larry Newman wanted to know.

'Yeah, Larry. Why are you asking?'

'Well, it looks like Richard Abruzzo won't be flying with us. We're ready to fly. Raven has finished the work on the balloons. This is our best chance, and our last launch attempt. I want you to be on the crew.'

Emich disguised his flabbergast while Larry talked for half an hour, using all his persuasive tools of salesmanship.

'You can be part of history. This is the opportunity of a lifetime,' Larry pressed him. 'When can you come to Reno?'

Emich felt that he was getting a complete treatment from the Sultan of Schmooze, and told Larry he needed time to think things over and gather more information.

'Larry, I've been out of the loop on *Earthwinds* since last spring. I need to get up to speed on the changes you've made.'

He would also have to get approval from his chain of command in the Fire Department for a leave of absence. He would have to talk with his family. And he wanted to collect some independent data.

Don Engen, vacationing at Lake Tahoe, called Emich three times the next day and urged him to accept the offer. Abruzzo had experienced a failure of nerve, he said.

Larry called again and put Lynne on the phone. She needed Mike's measurements for his flight suit.

'We never really liked Richard anyway,' she told him. 'Hilton wanted him. You're the one Larry wanted to fly with all along.'

While Emich's fire station lieutenant arranged a month of trades for his work shifts, Mike conferred with his father, and reviewed the opportunity. He also called Dave Melton and talked for an hour. He called John Ackroyd, who knew none of this intrigue, but said he was not fond of Abruzzo's work habits or attitude.

Given the information he had and the limited time, Emich evaluated the risks. He had niggling doubts, but was confident he could take care of himself.

He made his decision and called Engen to say he was in.

Engen thanked him and said he would call back in two hours…after he talked with Abruzzo again.

Moments later, Larry called Mike and asked for the decision.

'I'm in, but I am wondering about Richard,' Mike said.

'Let's get this straight. I am the captain and I will say who's flying with me. I don't want Richard. I have already told Richard he's the back-up and you're the primar—oops, there's my other line. Can you hold, Mike?'

It was Richard Abruzzo on Larry's other line. He had just finished a long talk with Gene Cernan, who pumped him up with Moon landing stories, NASA training, Naval aviation training, and how to recognize butterflies. Cernan did a great sales job—now Abruzzo wanted back in.

'Mike, you'll never guess who that was,' Larry said. 'Richard wants to come back. But as far as I'm concerned, you're in the crew. Don Engen is going to talk to Richard. I've got to go fly a charter right now. Just remember one thing: there's no way Richard is coming back…unless he calls Barron Hilton personally.'

The words stung Mike. He had activated his entire chain of command to arrange his leave, and had made an intellectual decision. He had to pack to leave the next morning to get to Reno for the Jan. 5 launch-ready date. And now he could be acutely embarrassed if Richard Abruzzo called Hilton!

Engen told Abruzzo that he was out. Emich would fly. Richard said he would support Mike in any way he could, and would assist with the launch.

The Hilton marketing organization insisted on secrecy. Mike was ordered to tell no one about the crew change until Hilton made the announcement.

Emich found a first class ticket was waiting for him at Cleveland Hopkins Airport. Upon arrival in Reno, he was ensconced in a high-roller suite at the Hilton, 'with more square footage than my house.'

Indoctrination began the next morning with a three-hour simulation in the capsule, classroom exercises, and Engen's Crew Resource Management training.

A flight plan described responses to possible emergencies. One that caught Emich's eye right away was the procedure for dealing with anchor balloon failure. If there were a catastrophic failure or if the anchor balloon failed to pressurize for any reason, the crew would continue the flight anyway. They would fly on to establish a new distance record, using the liquid helium to restore altitude as needed. The flight crew agreed on that without question. It was a lesson from the previous year: if they were fortunate enough to get launched safely, they would keep going!

Emich watched Abruzzo in class, and thought his behavior was 'scatterbrained': he was doodling, and juggling oranges.

Emich made calls privately from his spacious room, reaching out for reassurance that the mathematics and physics—still largely the work of Newman and Lachenmeier—were correct, that the anchor balloon wouldn't explode when it pressurized, that sufficient ballast was being carried, and so on.

Without the company of independent gas balloon pilots to help him re-prove the numbers generated by people with a financial stake in flying, Emich spent hours on the phone reviewing numbers for free lift, the operating procedures for the anchor balloon fan, for climbing capability, for altitude maintenance. He evaluated Newman's Dec. 22 memo to Engen line-by-line, and asked his trusted advisor Don Overs to do the same.

Overs, already familiar with the theoretical requirements, tested every number on his personal computer.

Deadline weather

Weatherman Maybeck called the pattern virtually the day Emich arrived in Reno. The high-pressure dome would yield light winds over northern Nevada by Tuesday or Wednesday, January 11 or 12.

A pattern was forming for a big dome of high pressure over the western United States. The ground in Reno was free of snow, so the inversion would not be acute. The surface pattern showed calm wind and clear skies: perfect for launch.

The appearance of a usable weather pattern increased the urgency of getting the balloons off Raven's loading dock, 1,200 miles away. The risk of public embarrassment—disclosure that *Earthwinds* had no balloons!—led Engen to impose a gag order on the team. The whereabouts of the balloons would remain a secret while teams of corporate lawyers squabbled over how and whether to release them.

Engen set a deadline of 4 p.m. Friday. If the balloons were in transit by that time, they would arrive in Reno in time for the launch team to rig them for a Tuesday morning liftoff. Any later than that, and the window would be missed.

There was a separate urgency in the negotiations, known to only a few decision-makers. The contracts with the major sub-sponsors were due to expire on Wednesday, January 12—one year from the date of the previous year's flight. Each sponsor's contract contained a flight performance clause: the money would flow when *Earthwinds* reached 18,000 feet. Hundreds of thousands of dollars in sponsorship money would flow into Hilton's account, and into the Wilcox-Newman partnership.

Barron Hilton intensified his search for an underwriter who could handle the $50 million policy protecting Raven Industries. With the clock running out late Friday, Hilton struck a deal for a $56,250 premium with a syndicate led by AIG. The insurance giant faxed the letter of intent to Raven and Hilton demanded that Raven ship the balloons.

In Sioux Falls, chief executive Dave Christensen insisted that his lawyers review the policy first. It protected the whole project and named Raven as an additional insured party. Hilton sent a flatbed truck to park outside the Raven plant. Late that night, after the lawyers satisfied themselves that Raven was indemnified, Lachenmeier and Barrow dragged themselves to work, started up the forklift trucks and loaded the two crates onto Hilton's truck. At midnight, the truck sped away into the darkness.

A huge party ensued at the Reno Hilton, with the beer taps wide open. They had launch weather! The balloons were in transit!

◆ ◆ ◆

But there was another item of business for the support team in Reno. Everyone who would be in proximity to the launch site, including the flight crew, was asked to sign a long waiver stating that they would never sue anyone if something went wrong. The waiver was attached to a memo spelling out Raven's failure rate and several disaster scenarios.

A notary public was brought in, and 'we had a signing party,' one participant recalled.

The next day at the airport, Emich noticed something new: two wide Kevlar straps wrapped around the capsule. He asked Ackroyd about them. To climb through an inversion, Ackroyd said, the crew would carry extra ballast in the form of biodegradable glass beads, known as bismuth. This last-minute addition placed additional strain on the capsule suspension points.

'The capsule is now severely overweight due to the extra ballast being carried.' Ackroyd told him. 'Right now it's 4,000 pounds over the load that Burt Rutan designed it to carry.'

Ackroyd explained that the 'lifting eyes' built into the capsule 'were reputedly designed to an ultimate load of 14,000 pounds, but have not been tested and their integrity is unknown.'

The factor of safety for the critical suspension components was down to 1.4—far below the intended safety factor of 5.0. Don Overs had voiced the same concern two years earlier.

Emich discovered that this debate had been raging internally for more than a month. In December, Ackroyd had written a memo warning about overloading the capsule:

'It is easy to imagine a launch situation where the dynamic snatch load would reach or exceed a factor of 2,' Ackroyd said. 'Failure at this stage would be catastrophic, with no time to escape...'

'Increasing capsule weight to 10,000 pounds could be the straw that breaks the camel's back, reducing an already marginal safety factor from hazardous to foolhardy.'

The loaded capsule already weighed 10,138 pounds.

Ackroyd told Emich he had wrapped the straps around the capsule 'in case those eyes break.'

◆ ◆ ◆

In private discussions with his Akron colleagues, the Three Amigos, Emich learned more unsettling news.

E. J. Hendrix had been uncomfortable with the radios. Connections were still shorting out wires and creating interference. The video cameras, Hendrix told him, sometimes shut off when the crew keyed the HF radio. And when the crew keyed the mike during simulated flight they sometimes felt a small shock in their feet.

Hendrix believed the antennas were too close to the capsule. His worst fear was that the high frequency radios might inadvertently activate the laser cutters.

The electronics data and the capsule stress weren't the only things troubling Emich. Melton had 'I-wanna-fly-itis,' and would do anything to protect his hard-won seat in the flight crew. Unfortunately, Melton had developed an acute ear infection. His Eustachian tubes were blocked so badly that any pressure change caused him to cringe; Larry and Mike halted a pressure-test of the capsule because Melton was in such pain. Even though he looked sick, Abruzzo encouraged him to stay with it.

◆ ◆ ◆

By the end of the weekend, with the balloon crates on the highway, the weather settling in for Tuesday morning, Hilton was eager to get things in motion. Sunday morning, Ackroyd rolled the capsule into place and his crew began prepping it for flight.

On Sunday Maybeck predicted a 10-degree temperature inversion at the surface, an isothermal condition above that, and a second six-degree inversion at the top of the surrounding Sierra Nevada Mountains.

Then Maybeck mentioned that the crew should expect scattered clouds at 18,000 feet. Newman stopped him.

'High scattered clouds? We're going to have to look at this,' he said. Newman was worrying not only about picking up moisture on the envelopes (adding weight), but also a new concern: loss of superheat.

Newman's flight profile memo to Engen had declared that 'superheat will be regarded as a non-factor during climb-out.' Now, however, he said he was depending on superheat to keep the balloon climbing. Sun warms the gas and allows the gas to expand, giving added lift. However, atmospheric physics are such that gas in a swiftly rising balloon cools, slowing the rate of ascent. With ballast and free lift critically short, superheat would provide Earthwind's necessary edge.

Don Flood, the new operations director, a fixed-wing aviator whom Engen had hired, told Newman:

'You'll get plenty of superheat through the high clouds!'

Newman's principal experience flying a gas balloon in sunlight was 15 years earlier, aboard Double Eagle II, which went to France in fair weather. Double

Eagle V, the Pacific flight, flew in clouds all the way from Japan to California—without superheat.

Unaware that he was presenting a physical paradox, Maybeck told the crew to climb as rapidly as possible to 34,000 feet. If they failed to climb quickly, they would be stuck in a trough, a large U-shaped windflow that would send the balloon far south. But the recommendation regarding rapid ascent contradicted the flight plan, which called for a slow climb-out to avoid rupturing the anchor balloon.

Emich argued against a rapid climb-out because of adiabatic cooling. He knew the helium temperature would drop quickly if the balloon rose quickly—and that would reduce the lift.

'We're marginal on free lift now,' he said. 'Climbing out fast will take us into a negative lift.'

Emich observed that the long-range weather pattern into which he was supposed to fly did not resemble the guidelines of previous years: a swift straight track in the jet stream. Why should they accept a pattern that obviously would not work?

'This is the best you're going to get this time of year,' Maybeck said. The flight would start by going the wrong direction: southwest. Over the Pacific Ocean, well off the coast of Los Angeles, it would trace a large circular pattern for a few days before the upper wind changed and brought it back over southern California. From there, upper winds would carry it along the southern tier of the U.S., up to the Carolinas, then rapidly toward Greenland, where another trough went rushing south toward Africa, then another up toward Siberia. It looked to Emich like a perilous, high-amplitude course.

The sponsors and flight managers were more concerned about launching than about succeeding in a global flight, he thought. They had a do-or-die attitude.

The January 12 deadline remained a secret from Newman's crewmates.

Group Think

Emich's mind buzzed with uncertainty on Monday morning as the clock moved ahead. Inflation might begin within 15 hours.

He cut through the trappings of luxury and potential fame ('You can become a part of history!') to focus simply on the physics of flight. After all, *his gonads* were on the line here...not Hilton's, not Engen's, not Maybeck's or the sponsors' or the paid staff hustling around, and certainly none of the fixed-wing crowd making decisions. Virtually everyone around him stood to gain some corporate, political, monetary or marketing advantage from the flight.

He worked the phones aggressively and discretely, phoning me and Overs with more numbers to crunch, formulas to compare. He re-read the Raven memo he and the others had been required to sign. Reviewing the stern language, he ate breakfast with Tim Lachenmeier and quizzed him about Raven's disclaimer. Lachenmeier waived off his concerns.

'Don't worry about that memo, Mike,' the designer said, 'This balloon is okay.'

Emich was unconvinced.

'The thing that bothers me,' Emich said to me on Monday morning, 'is that all the decision-makers here are being paid by Hilton to get this balloon launched. They are getting bonuses for a flight that reaches 18,000 feet. The sponsors are applying tremendous pressure to fly. But none of the decision-makers have flown in a gas balloon. It's a classic exercise in "Group Think." Mass psychology is taking over.

'You've got to what-if everything, and that's not being done,' he said. 'We've got a sick crewman whose back-up wants him to fly, no gas pilots in the decision-making loop, tremendous pressure from sponsors, a capsule that is severely overweight, people flying in from all over to launch this thing, and others going through the mechanical motions here. Nobody is thinking about the basic question, Should we fly or not?'

◆ ◆ ◆

As the pilots and senior staff convened at Stead that Monday morning, Maybeck prepared his weather briefing. Suddenly the silence of the desert airport was broken with the wailing of police sirens, sounds that moved closer and closer.

The staff peered through the windows as two Nevada Highway Patrol cars pulled in behind Richard Abruzzo's car and ordered him to stand spread-eagle and put his hands on top of the car while they patted him down.

Sensing what was happening, Lynne Newman rolled up two *Earthwinds* color posters (the ones featuring Abruzzo, Newman, Dzhanibekov and Melton), took them out to the police officers, and introduced herself.

The officers charged Abruzzo with going more than 100 mph (76 through a school zone), ignoring five stop signs, veering left of center, and evading a police officer. Somehow, Lynne persuaded them to let Abruzzo finish his business at the airport.

◆ ◆ ◆

Emich ignored the distraction and studied Maybeck's briefing. To Mike, the upper pattern looked unacceptable, and the wind above the peaks wouldn't settle. Steve Brown, the local forecaster, made a convincing case for waiting until Tuesday night/Wednesday morning. But the decision had been made: they would fly on the morning of January 12.

After the briefing, Emich asked the flight crew to remain in the room for a private meeting. Everyone needed to have the utmost confidence in the systems and in one another, he told Larry, Dave and Richard. But having evaluated the available data with outside consultants, Emich said he found the personal risk far greater than anticipated. He asked to be excused from the flight.

'This is the hardest decision I've ever had to make,' Emich told his crewmates.

Larry was sympathetic. Melton was troubled. Abruzzo was undecided; he knew that now he had to rejoin the flight crew.

That night at a previously scheduled send-off dinner for the whole *Earthwinds* entourage in a private room at the Reno Hilton, Engen announced the crew change. Richard Abruzzo was welcomed back into the crew. As for Mike Emich, Admiral Engen said, well, it was a complicated project and Mike was having trouble adjusting to the complexity of the capsule, the computers and GPS tracking devices aboard. It was better that Emich was withdrawing.

Emich couldn't believe what he was hearing!

Engen already had warned everyone against giving press interviews, and Mike had intended to keep his safety concerns private. But now he decided that the only way to defend this attack on his intelligence was to tell the truth in public.

The next day, he gave a long interview to the Akron Beacon Journal, handing reporter Bob Downing Raven's warning memo.

About the same time, Engen put his version in writing as guidance for the media office, which began reciting it to reporters. Barron Hilton also tried to manage the message.

He asked his friend the actor Cliff Robertson to talk with Emich.

'Barron and I are very concerned about you,' the actor said, putting his arm around Emich, 'and we want you to come out of this looking like a hero. We're going to say that Richard had a serious family problem and that's why he temporarily withdrew. You held his place for him. When the family problem was resolved, you graciously agreed to step aside so he could take his rightful place in the crew.'

'Cliff, that's not true!' Emich protested.

'Well, that's what we're saying,' Robertson replied coldly.

The aging actor, who had built his reputation for honesty by exposing a major Hollywood studio's check-writing scam, now called media with his version of the story. When reporters called to clear up the confusion, Emich realized he would be fighting the entire Hilton/Hollywood publicity machine: it would be his word against theirs. He told the reporters to find out the truth for themselves.

Flight II: Crossing the wire-transfer threshold

The crew change was mostly a sideshow to the main event, of course, and only a handful of reporters (outside of Emich's hometown of Akron) took note of it. The sponsors didn't care who flew with Newman. And out at the airport, there was work to do. VIPs would soon be arriving, the caterer had to be called, buses arranged, food ordered. The 900-number had to be updated, media kits updated with the new bios, and Fed-Ex'd. The balloon was going up again, and preparations were in high gear all day Tuesday.

The now-familiar inflation process began at 9 p.m. on Tuesday night, and this time it went flawlessly. Kleig lights played on the balloon as it stood up in the night sky.

The inflation team squirted 16,200 pounds of lift into the helium balloon before pausing at midnight. The wind remained calm. With the helium inflation having proceeded so well, Engen woke up Larry at five minutes after midnight, then each of the other two pilots.

They were escorted to the airport, and inside the capsule by 1 a.m.

Engen assured the party of Hilton well-wishers that the crew was inside the capsule for the duration—that they would not come out to greet the guests. The wives and families had already said their goodbyes at the foot of the capsule.

Thirty minutes after the crew boarded, a light zephyr blew across the desert, and the capsule stirred a bit. It moved just enough to rise off the wooden blocks it was resting on—and to come down and crush a pipe connected to a heat exchanger.

John Ackroyd evaluated the damage, at first calling it 'a potential show-stopper', and then concluding it simply a broken pipe. He and Gary Palmer crawled underneath to weld a repair, using up one hour of a built-in hold.

When the repairs were complete at 2:30 a.m., Lachenmeier's team received permission to begin inflating the anchor balloon. The air was cold and saturated, normal for winter nights in the desert. The National Weather Service recorded the relative humidity and the dew point on the field as 80 percent.

Beyond the double security fences, VIPs assembled inside the Ponderosa House, downing soft drinks and munching on a stew made from Vladimir's plov recipe. They watched the launch-field proceedings on closed circuit TV.

Abruzzo's sister Mary Pat sat nervously, occasionally weeping, and seeking comfort from an older brother.

Suddenly, Larry Newman hopped out of the capsule and walked 100 yards over to the VIP area. He made a head call, and then found Lynne inside the lounge area. He chatted amiably as he greeted a few guests. Then, arm around his wife, he walked back out to the capsule.

The anchor balloon filled slowly with the heavy air.

The capsule crew, the launch team and the VIPs waited for sunrise.

Just before dawn, a hot air balloon took off from the tarmac nearby. The balloonist let his craft ascend at 250 feet per minute up to 10,000 feet, showing *Earthwinds*' crew the early route they'd travel.

One more helium shoot took the reading on the load cell up to 22,550 pounds of lift. Larry called out to stop the fill. His helium balloon now had more than 12 percent free lift. At sunrise, he knew there would be a bit of wind on the field, and he was worrying about its effect.

Larry and Koh Murai had a short discussion about whether to try a 'dynamic launch'—releasing *Earthwinds* for flight before executing the Stonehenge rotation of the anchor balloon—but Larry decided that was too risky.

At 7:00 a.m., he flipped a switch that closed the anchor balloon valve. That would help the anchor balloon keep its shape during the rotation maneuver.

As the launch crew raised the capsule and began the Stonehenge maneuver, the anchor balloon slowly rotated and rolled west, twisting two full turns. That much wind on the field meant trouble.

The pre-flight checklist now called for a pause to open the anchor balloon's bottom valve and decompress the balloon to 80 percent of capacity. That would ensure a rapid climb to at least mountain peak level.

But with fresh evidence of the wind picking up, Larry decided to dispense with the decompression. He'd take off with a full anchor balloon and ballast his way to altitude.

The checklist also required turning on the Inmarsat Standard-C computer linked to the laptop computer and the GPS, which would automatically report *Earthwinds*' position to the Operations Center and allow Engen's staff to communicate with the crew during climb-out. In the haste to depart, the computer was left off.

The Stonehenge maneuver was completed moments before official sunrise. *Earthwinds* stretched to its full height, held to the ground by four tether lines.

The sun would be on the horizon at 7:15 a.m. and Larry wanted to be off the ground by that moment.

Standing in the capsule more than 125 feet above the ground, Larry directed Dave Melton to throw the switch that opened the anchor balloon's bottom valve.

Suddenly, streaks of golden light played on the folds in the translucent poly balloon. Time to go!

Richard Abruzzo went to the hatch and looked out, holding the fire-cutter device in his hand. On Larry's signal, he flipped it open and pushed the buttons. A laser cable cutter severed the last ties to the ground. One year from its first flight, *Earthwinds* leapt cleanly away at 7:15 a.m.

◆ ◆ ◆

Earthwinds' second flight from Reno began exactly one year after its first, but insiders knew it wasn't going anywhere.

At the moment of liftoff, waiters in tuxedos stepped forward with silver trays loaded with full champagne glasses for all 250 of Hilton's guests in the security pen.

Among them were members of the company's board of directors, suppliers, family and friends of the crew, reporters and the entire executive staff from Winzen International, Inc., Raven's competitor in the scientific balloon business.

Harry Combs, whose introduction to Barron Hilton had enabled the project to continue, huddled with Erin Porter as they watched the fruits of their introduction rise from the ground.

Applause broke out, and then whistles. Tears of joy and fear flowed from many faces.

◆ ◆ ◆

Richard and Dave were momentarily startled as the capsule began to twist and rotate. Creaks and groans came from the hull. The capsule countered its first rotation, and then untwisted yet again.

One thousand feet up, it encountered a six-degree temperature inversion, and stopped climbing.

Abruzzo was ready. He cut open ballast bags. Melton poured the contents out the hatch. Twenty-five pound bursts of Bismuth beads hit the anchor balloon skirt, bounced off and dispersed. Larry told them to keep ballasting. They did, and the climb resumed.

In the cold morning air, a narrow vapor trail vented from the bottom of anchor balloon.

◆ ◆ ◆

As *Earthwinds* climbed and drifted away, helicopters carrying video cameramen followed, sending back live imagery of the balloon over the stark landscape.

Don Flood called out the altitudes and distance to the senior staff who listened on two-way radios.

Back in the Operations Center, Dick Blosser waited again—exactly as he had the previous year—for some communication from the balloon. Flood called Reno Stead departure control to report the takeoff. No communication came from the capsule.

Larry, remembering the criticism directed at him the previous year, had prepared the Operations Department for this.

'The takeoff phase of the flight will be the most demanding,' he had written in a memo. 'While it is vital that the support team on the ground knows the status of the flight, the liftoff is a phase when communicating is a major distraction.

'The balance between capsule communications with the ground and precise control of the balloon at lower altitudes must be weighed carefully. Evaluating the forces on the system requires extreme concentration during the climbout and any conversation will most likely be initiated by a crewmember in the capsule when there is a break in the action.'

The Operations Center staff waited.

◆ ◆ ◆

Stead Airport is 5,000 feet above sea level. The capsule had to be closed and pressurized at eight thousand feet. After they had ballasted through the inversion and were confident of sustaining a good rate of climb, Richard and Dave dogged down the three handles on both doors. They verified the setting on the automatic cabin controller—8,200 feet—and turned on the screw compressor. It came to life with a slight 'thunk', and then yielded to a high hum as the machinery compressed the increasingly thin outside air into breathable air for the flight crew.

They sealed the doors and pressurized the capsule at 9,600 feet. All ballasting now would have to be made through the airlock on the capsule floor.

Faces of the ground crew relaxed when the balloon reached 10,000 feet—clearing the nearest peaks—and kept climbing at a rate of ascent about 200 feet per minute.

The anchor balloon, already full, prevented a more rapid climb. Through the small valve at its bottom, it was exhaling warm air.

The flight crew had on its check list a requirement to 'cycle' the valve on the way up; in theory the opening-and-closing action would prevent locking or freezing up. The crew ignored the checklist, and the valve remained open.

Lachenmeier wished for a faster rate of climb, and radioed a question up to three pilots: 'How much ballast are you using for the ascent?'

There was no reply.

'They aren't talking to us,' Lachenmeier frowned.

He could have used the figure to calculate options later in the flight. Lachenmeier only knew that the balloon was flying through an isothermal condition, a low-grade inversion—and that much he had learned from Maybeck's briefing.

♦ ♦ ♦

Earthwinds was now climbing through 12,000 feet at 400 feet per minute. The crew sat in simple folding aluminum lawn chairs; the only concession to comfort was to exchange the web strapping with padding in *Earthwinds* Hilton colors.

As the climb continued, the big countdown started. Those in the know huddled around radios as Operations Director Flood called out the altitudes.

'Only 3,000 feet more,' someone said at 8:00 a.m. as the balloon passed through 15,000 feet, now 12 miles south of Reno.

'Oh, they've got it now!' replied another veteran launch assistant.

At 8:12 a.m., nearly an hour after leaving the ground, *Earthwinds* passed through 18,000 feet. Smiles broke out among the cognoscenti.

Barron Hilton, chasing in a helicopter, was immensely relieved.

At that moment, Neil Cohen, Hilton's marketing vice-president, ordered that a wire be sent to all the sponsors advising that the 18,000-foot threshold had been crossed. To meet their legal requirement, executives at American Express, AT&T, Miller Brewing Company and Nescafe should immediately wire-transfer the balance of their sponsorship funds.

Within minutes, tidy sums totaling more than $700,000 flowed into the *Earthwinds* Hilton account at a Beverly Hills bank.

♦ ♦ ♦

At that same moment, John Ackroyd had been eating breakfast with Malcolm Browne. The New York Times science writer, having brought the adventure to the public's attention, was still following the story in earnest. He had made friends with many of the project's workers. But he was astonished when Ackroyd rose to leave.

'If you'll excuse me, I have to go to California now,' the engineer said.

Why, asked Browne, are you going to California?

'Because that's where they are going to land,' Ackroyd declared matter-of-factly.

Browne didn't know whether he should believe Ackroyd, but the comment troubled him. How could Ackroyd know that? What was going on?

◆ ◆ ◆

At 18,000, Larry turned on his aircraft radio and advised Oakland Center on 128.8 MHz that the balloon was now in Positive Controlled Airspace. From then on, as the transponder squawked, Air Traffic Control knew *Earthwinds*' position and altitude—but the operations center still did not. The laptop computer in the capsule, linked to the GPS and to the Operations Center by Inmarsat Standard C, remained off.

ATC called *Earthwinds* by its call sign, 'N92VH' (for the year of its intended flight from Akron and the names of the two principal sponsors, Virgin and Hilton.)

Inside the capsule, little anomalies appeared. The windows began to fog up from the moisture inside. A tube from the engine compartment pumped fresh air into the thermal space between the double glass. Richard and Dave opened the floorboard, checked the connections, and found a disconnected hose in the engine bay. When they reinserted it, the window fog disappeared.

The crew tried to read the temperature outside, but discovered that an external thermistor had come off during the launch.

The climb continued with little conversation among the crew, or contact with the ground. The helium balloon swelled from 100 feet in diameter to its design size of 140 feet in diameter as it approached its full volume.

Clay Lacey, one of the legends of aeronautical photography, roared aloft from Reno Canon Airport in his Learjet and began chasing the balloon. He ran his first intercept at 9:24 a.m.—more than two hours into the balloon flight. He made a long arc, approaching the hourglass shape from the south, and his contrail roared past *Earthwinds*' capsule at more than 400 mph.

'Hey, Clay,' Larry called on the radio. 'You're dropping snowflakes on my windows!'

Four minutes later, he arced back and made another pass, then another, shooting still and video pictures for John Wilcox.

Over Yosemite National Park, Richard Abruzzo looked down through the bubble window in the bottom of the capsule and saw El Capitan to one side of the anchor balloon. He had climbed mountains in that park, and recognized the terrain. Abruzzo photographed the breathtaking sight.

Then he turned on the video cameras to record some of the scenes inside the capsule, but whenever he cued the camera, the radios cut out.

The achy-breaky anchor balloon

At 33,000 feet above the ground, the helium balloon overhead had expanded to its maximum volume. The thin air outside was minus 55 degrees F. A little more than two hours after takeoff, the critical ascent stage of the flight was nearly over—or so the crew thought.

The new anchor balloon was about to be pressurized for the first time. Three primary electrical connections led to it: two dropped into the top, and one carried power to the valve at the bottom.

A 150-volt, three-phase Bendix alternator powered a large electric fan at the crown, which would only be used to alter the altitude. By increasing air pressure in the anchor balloon, the crew could descend slowly, losing perhaps 1,000 feet per hour. To descend more quickly, they would have to valve helium from the upper balloon.

No test on the ground with the fully inflated anchor balloon had exceeded the pressures that would be encountered in flight.

Theoretical calculations showed that a rupture of the anchor balloon in daylight—and the loss of its restraining ballast—would send the balloon up 2,500 feet higher.

Larry reviewed the procedures. Closing the bottom valve would pressurize the anchor balloon; they would climb a bit higher, then the added weight would arrest their ascent. If he timed it just right, the anchor valves would be closed at 33,000 feet, and when the pressure inside the anchor balloon reached .67 psi. Ideally, the balloon would stop climbing and level off at 35,000 feet.

He asked Dave Melton to flick the switches that closed both valves.

No indicator light came on.

Larry thought at first that the light was broken. But without the added weight to arrest its climb, the balloon continued ascending. In a few minutes it had climbed right up to 37,000 feet and was still gaining altitude.

The crew could look out the windows and see that the poly balloon's overflow tubes were exhaling helium. The balloon had risen through 'pressure height' and was still climbing and gaining superheat. But if it went much higher, the cabin's screw compressor would lose efficiency, and begin to deprive the flight crew of oxygen.

In a gas balloon, it takes a few moments to reverse momentum. A pilot must valve and wait, or ballast and wait. A balloon in free ascent will rise through pressure height, then become slightly heavy. Judicious ballasting stabilizes the altitude. That's the art of ballooning.

Now, however, Larry felt he had to intervene. He electrically opened the helium valves to arrest the ascent—and when he did, one of the three helium valves stuck in the open position.

He reported the failure to the operations office by voice radio.

Larry's transmission was brief.

'It's not working,' he said. 'I don't have time to talk now.'

'What's not working?' Flood asked. 'Turn on the computer so we can talk on that.'

'The anchor balloon valve isn't closing. I'm busy working on it.'

The brief transmission startled the operators in the center at the Reno Hilton; they went into a crisis strategy session.

Former astronaut Gene Cernan suggested sending up a list of yes-or-no questions. They did that, but Larry came back with short, unhelpful answers.

One problem was that nobody in operations knew exactly where the balloon was at this point. Dick Blosser set up a land-line phone patch through the Oakland Air Traffic Control.

The radio silence caused great frustration in the Operations Center. Everyone knew that the capsule was equipped with a diverse array of electronic equipment for communicating.

'The primary long distance communications tool in the capsule is not voice, but data transmission called Standard C,' Larry had written in pre-flight memo to Engen.

The Inmarsat Standard C, a laptop computer using a geosynchronous satellite as its modem, could send data to computers in the operations center in Reno and in the chase plane.

Each Standard C message was transmitted with the balloon's precise location, course and speed over the ground. It only required 12 volts of DC power to operate.

While they waited for a fax via the Inmarsat Standard-C, or a voice transmission describing the problem, Dick Blosser played back Larry's initial reports on a tape recorder, looking for some clue to the problem.

'With Larry, you never know...' he said. 'He just doesn't talk when there's a problem.'

Engen summoned the three amigos to the Operations Center with all their manuals and paperwork, but since Larry wouldn't answer questions from the ground, they had little information to go on.

They waited, but got no solid information.

Gene Cernan had been standing in the Operations Center. He had seen a lot in his career, having space-walked as a Gemini astronaut and having been to the Moon twice and driven a buggy on the Moon's surface. And he had stood around the Flight Director's console at the Manned Spacecraft Center in Houston enough times to know how pilots and controllers should deal with crises. Frustrated, he now left the Operations Center and slowly walked down the hotel hallway.

Shaking his head sadly, he muttered:

'How can you help a guy when he doesn't communicate?

'There is a way to handle it from both ends very professionally,' Cernan said, 'but we can't get the other side to do anything except say 'Yeah, I tried that but it didn't work'. How the hell do you know?

'You can't trouble-shoot, bring in the world of experts to solve your problems, if you can't answer some specific questions.

'These poor guys (in the operations center) don't know how to help somebody because everything down there is still What-If. They can't get a straight answer from up there.

'I've been in those situations,' said Cernan. 'Maybe we didn't ask the questions forcefully enough, but there are guys down here who are smarter…that's why they're down here…and they want to help. They're experts. They're valve makers. They're balloon makers. They're engineers and technicians.

'We don't know what the problem is, whether the valve is frozen or what. We may not know but we can start eliminating things.'

◆ ◆ ◆

About 10:00 a.m., Burt Rutan, whose company had built the capsule, called Engen to get a briefing on how the launch had gone. Rutan had just spoken with Don Moses, who had not been informed that the flight was starting. Engen was aware that Moses knew a lot about the valve, and he wanted expert advice quickly. Could Rutan ask Don Moses to call Engen immediately? Engen gave Rutan his cellular number.

Rutan called Moses, but remembering how badly Newman had treated him, Moses wasn't about to lift a finger to help now.

◆   ◆   ◆

Up in the capsule, Larry had to make a decision quickly. If *Earthwinds* continued drifting in this direction at this speed, it would be out over the Pacific Ocean and the Los Angeles area within a few hours. Without a functioning anchor balloon valve, and now with a leaking helium balloon valve, they might descend at sunset right into the ocean.

Larry, Dave and Richard speculated that the bottom valve was frozen. Perhaps they should descend to a lower altitude, where the warmer temperature would thaw it.

They opened the remaining two helium valves and let some gas out. It took continuous valving to bring the balloon down in the mid-day heat.

As *Earthwinds* descended, the anchor balloon began twisting again, making as many as two revolutions, like winding a rubber band. The capsule, in turn, unwound first, turning as it had on takeoff. As air rushed past the anchor balloon, the cycle repeated.

The delicate fiber optic cables that controlled the cut-away mechanism began to degrade. The uncontrolled twisting and turning concerned the junior crewmembers.

'Richard and I were a bit nervous watching this twisting,' Melton wrote later, 'and we looked at each other and then at Larry, who was sitting in a chair, calm as can be, enjoying a sandwich.'

They descended to lower air, and opened the hatch at 16,000 feet. They tried cycling the valve several times without result.

'We continued to try to close the valve every ten minutes or so without success,' Melton said. 'At this point we knew our flight was over and a landing inevitable.'

No amount of switch-throwing would close the anchor balloon valve. The lower balloon was unpressurized, and would not work.

There was no discussion of continuing on. They discarded the plan to fly a long distance even without the anchor balloon.

Hovering over the San Joaquin Valley, the crew packed away loose items and prepared to land. They radioed their intention to the ground.

Engen summoned the three women most concerned about the flight crew. Telling them to pack quickly, he dispatched Lynne Newman, Shelley Melton and Abruzzo's girlfriend Nancy in a plane bound for Fresno.

Engen radioed up one final point, reminding Larry not to touch anything in the capsule or on the balloons after landing. He would send a team to evaluate why the equipment failed. Engen then immediately dispatched E.J. Hendricks in Barron Hilton's executive jet, the Cessna Citation, to Fresno. It would be Hendricks' job to be first on the scene, to recover the valve and evaluate what led to its failure.

Near noon, Engen notified the Fresno County, Calif., emergency services department that the balloon was descending near them. He scrounged a search-and-rescue operation from Lemore Naval Air Station south of Fresno. A squadron of SH3 helicopters operated from the base where Engen himself once served. The Lemore tower homed in on *Earthwinds'* signal. The balloon was at 4,000 feet and sinking slowly.

Engen chartered a helicopter and dispatched the project's flight surgeon, along with Mike Emich, since Mike was a trained paramedic. The helo clattered off toward Fresno, and came in sight of the towering balloons. It was bright, hazy and hard to see. The doctor was eager to talk with the crew, but Emich advised him to wait: it was more important to let the crew concentrate on landing safely, he said. The medical helo turned away to refuel.

Joy over Fresno

In the fields below, bright haze obscured visibility beyond more than four miles. Peering through the haze, Larry Newman relaxed when he saw that he was over familiar terrain.

He pushed the throttle forward with his left hand, revving the engine to maximum rpms. Then he took the stick in his right hand, wiggled it left and right to level the horizon, and thrust it toward the instruments. He nosed over into a steep dive.

Within seconds, he was flying at a 30-degree angle, plunging right toward the ground! Airspeed increased quickly—100, 110, 120 miles per hour. Slowly, he eased back on the stick and the nose started coming up. Back, back, back, hold it there. Now the cowling came racing past the horizon, airspeed bleeding off. Ugh. Straight up!

Steady back, all blue sky now, airspeed dropping off to 80. There's the horizon again, coming down from the top of the window. Hey, dad, we're upside down! His fingers were wrapped tightly around the stick. When the ground half covered his field of vision, he pulled the stick hard to left. The right wing went up and the plane rolled over into straight and level flight again. There, he had done it by himself—his first Immelmann. He was seven years old!

It was his defining moment. He was an aerial acrobat! Sitting on his father's lap in the cockpit, he had done what no other boy could do.

He learned the trick by watching and imitating Herb Newman, an amateur airman and Brooklyn-born knockabout who went by the moniker Speedy. A rough-hewn gambler, a hustler with street smarts, an unrefined intelligence and a passion for aviation that matched his passion for racy women, Speedy had accepted the plane to settle a gin-rummy debt, and taught himself to fly.

Father and son went flying every weekend over these planted fields of central California and through the mountain passes into the desert of Nevada. Speedy sometimes flew loops, just for the hell of it, and his boy took to the air as if he owned the sky.

Every morning during the picking season, having scouted by air the farms that needed harvesting, he would drive around in an old bus, pick up unemployed migrant workers and deliver them to the lush fields in the Valley, where they worked as day laborers harvesting cotton, cantaloupes, peaches, grapes and vegetables. As Larry got older, sometimes he'd go out into the fields and pick cotton, too.

But Larry loved flying more than anything else. He and Speedy would fly from farm to farm in the San Joaquin Valley, landing on dirt roads and ploughed fields to set up business with farmers. In a family whose parents were breaking up, flying gave Larry his identity, and a freedom beyond which other boys could barely imagine.

Sometimes he'd sit up on phone books or pillows and steer while his dad read the newspaper. It was a welcome respite from an otherwise dreary life in Fresno.

Larry went to school in Fresno until age 10, when his parents separated and his mother took him, his little brother Ross, age 4, and their baby sister to Los Angeles. She established an interior design business and eventually remarried, but Larry rebelled against the devoutly Jewish side of his family. He did not like school or Temple, but learned enough Hebrew to be bar mitzvahed. After that, he disavowed any interest in religion. The son of a Hungarian Jewish mother and a Russian Jewish father, he would go through life with the ethnicity but not the practice of a faith.

In Fresno, his father practically lived out of an airport office, finally getting himself a decent business plane, a four-place Piper. Once while the Tripacer was parked nearby, Speedy bet a Baja farmer $100 that his 12-year-old son could solo the plane. Larry jumped in the plane, started it himself, and made a couple of passes around the field before landing—his first solo. It was another seminal event for this boy, an achievement that set him apart from all other youths.

Talkative and engaging, Speedy worked all the angles, living on the edge of the law. He loved taking risks. Once he had smuggled goods into Mexico, risking jail and life and limb. He couldn't resist taking chances for a buck. Sometimes he'd fly off to Las Vegas and leave his son outside a casino for a whole day. Inside, Speedy gambled away, or won, money for food, fuel and rent.

'You could say,' Speedy would laugh years later when asked about his profession, 'that I make investments on the outcomes of sporting events.'

He took Larry on a few special trips; they preceded the train of Queen Elizabeth and Prince Philip across Canada in October 1957 and sold souvenir photos, badges and buttons. A born haggler, Speedy tried passing on to his son the tricks of working a crowd, of making a dollar by 'talking faster than your ice cream will melt'.

Larry became a smooth talker, too, inheriting the useful techniques of schmoozing and oozing sincerity when it suited his purpose. With his boyish enthusiasm and cocky self-confidence, he quickly surpassed his father in these skills. It was a gift, this knack for stories, jokes and persuasive explanations. But if the business side of his father's character lacked meaning, Larry made up for it with his single-minded love of flying.

Life above that Valley set him apart from other kids. It had shaped his character and given him a mask of brassy self-assurance. In high school, his attention wavered. Teachers couldn't fly airplanes.

'They tried to teach me about places like Canada, but I had already flown there and back,' Larry once scoffed.

He had done an Immelmann at seven! Soloed at twelve! This was the stuff of legends! He earned his license as soon as he was legally eligible, at 17. It was all he wanted to do.

After graduating from high school in Los Angeles near the bottom of his class in 1965—by his own admission a bit of a clown, and socially a loner—he went back to Fresno and started hanging around Chandler downtown airport.

◆ ◆ ◆

The old memories flashed by in a nanosecond, but they reconnected Larry to his roots as his $7 million craft sank toward these familiar fields of his boyhood.

At 2:09 p.m., *Earthwinds* gently touched a soft, furrowed cotton field in a place called Tranquility, 202 miles south-southwest of Reno.

They recognized Larry in the valley.

People who hadn't seen him for 20 years came up to him. They knew his father! They remembered him!

11

Around the World or Bust

'He got it up, but he couldn't sustain it.'
—Pam, cocktail waitress at the Reno Hilton Casino

Sunset in the cotton fields

A freshly plowed field welcomed the capsule back to earth, as gentle a landing as could be made in a balloon. The climate in central California was shirtsleeve warm.

Upon landing, Larry had tried to release the anchor balloon. He had plugged in the fiber optic cable cutters, which would sever the anchor balloon and the poly balloon. At the moment of impact, he plunged the cutter device—but the Holex cutters failed again!

Fortunately, with the wind calm, the helium balloon stood straight overhead, a magnet for curious townsfolk.

Abruzzo and Melton exited the capsule and hopped into the soft brown soil. Larry called Don Engen on the Inmarsat telephone to give a quick status report; Engen asked Larry not to touch anything.

◆   ◆   ◆

Admiral Engen then dispatched Ackroyd and the Three Amigos to a private terminal at Reno Canon airport, where Hilton's Citation jet rushed them to the Fresno airport. Ackroyd and the Amigos jumped on a chartered helicopter shuttling to the cotton field.

They arrived too late to do what Engen wanted them to do.

Ignoring Engen's dictum not to touch anything, Larry had walked around to the bottom of the anchor balloon. Finding the valve motor still whirring, he turned it off, unbolted the valve and removed it. Examining what he held in his hands, he quickly diagnosed the failure: the shaft pin had sheared off the valve.

◆   ◆   ◆

Deflation of the helium balloon was taking a long time. After an hour or so, Richard and Larry pulled the manual rip panel, releasing the helium and collapsing the spent plastic balloon.

To deflate the anchor balloon rapidly, Larry opened a hunting knife, and walked the length of a seam, allowing the air to billow forth from the dying behemoth.

◆   ◆   ◆

Larry relaxed by eating an apple, chatting with the migrant workers and a few residents who remembered him as a boy.

TV camera crews and reporters trudged into the cotton field and The Fresno Bee newspaper sent out a photographer. That afternoon, an enterprising editor called Larry's father, who maintained a home in Fresno. Speedy kept up a brave front about being the proud father, and told a few old-days stories, but his son remained estranged from him, and they did not get together.

As the sun was setting, Larry, Richard, Dave and Emich left the landing site. Pointing out scenes from his boyhood in Fresno—his home over there, his high school down that street, the airport where he learned to fly, Larry seemed in a relaxed, serene mood.

They joined their women at Fresno Airport, and flew back to Reno late that night in Hilton's Citation. There was little talk during the flight home, but all the pilots were grateful for one thing: they had survived!

At a news conference the next day, Larry proclaimed the flight a success. He stated his intention to continue, tacitly acknowledging the ire that some of the sponsors were feeling.

'…Even if we lose all of our sponsors, we will continue. My wife and I, we're not swayed by anything…'

Spin control and the 5th great Diaspora

Three days later, the capsule, the crated anchor balloon, the huge gasoline tank and the liquid helium dewars were loaded onto a flatbed truck and driven back to Reno.

The second flight flight had spotlighted old problems, and identified new ones. Why had the cable cutters failed again? What prevented Larry from communicating when he most needed help? Were they still having communication problems, and if so, why?

What had caused the anchor balloon to revolve so much during descent? How much did that damage the fiber optic cables? How could the spinning be prevented?

Many questions focused on the valve. Had it been made correctly? had it been altered? had it been tested? Raven people believed that Larry had 'cheaped out' on the valve. They had given him a bid for a valve that Larry thought was too high. He found another source, and purchased the valve directly from a Canadian supplier who had tested it using dry gas—but not freezing, water-saturated air.

The case for using a dry gas such as nitrogen in the anchor balloon had been presented two years earlier by Don Overs. Larry had rejected it.

In addition, Larry had the roll-pin of the valve drilled out and replaced with a shear pin. Raven engineers expressed doubts about it at the time, but did not intervene.

In his analysis on the landing field, Gene Hendrix found water inside the anchor balloon—a sure sign that ice had formed inside, freezing and disabling the valve. Ackroyd was keenly disappointed that on this second flight the crew had recorded no engineering data. Had they stayed longer at altitude, the capsule pressure system, the screw compressor, engine performance, life-support, communication and living arrangements might have been evaluated. Ackroyd now seriously considered leaving the project. He had other offers. Julian Nott's balloon project in Australia needed a pressurized capsule, and the sponsors had contacted him. There was also a new challenge to the motorcar speed record, which involved a lucrative offer.

◆ ◆ ◆

The remainder of the staff dispersed with the four winds, some to await another call, some not.

Don Engen had given his best—but realized he would never be able to 'manage' Larry Newman. He wrote gracious thank-you letters, closed out the administrative files and packed up his office. Now 76 years old and still vigorous, he moved on to his next project—helping to start an airline.

John Wilcox had virtually bankrupted his Adventure World Productions. Once again, he began taking steps to dissolve the American Soviet Balloon Venture and to end his long, strained partnership with Larry Newman. The only thing of value for Wilcox now was the possibility, however slim, of a film about the *Earthwinds* story. He had cabinets full of videotape, but until a successful flight, there was nowhere to market such a film.

Wilcox, always slightly star-struck, moved to Hollywood to produce a film about panda bears for Paramount Studios. His staff, who had watched over the management of the Expedition Earth series, joined other firms. Attorney Millard Zimet joined a Denver law firm. Leisl Clark produced an African safari film, and kept track of the *Earthwinds* videotape, and eventually joined pubic broadcasting's Nova in Boston. Others were unemployed.

The Three Amigos said they wouldn't go back if Larry alone were in charge. They wanted a buffer from his tinkering and meddling.

◆ ◆ ◆

The corporate sponsors learned of the flight's abrupt end just after their money hit the bank at Beverly Hills.

It was a potential embarrassment to Hilton, and unfair to the sponsors—most of whom had long-term business relationships with the hotel company. Their money was returned. Neil Cohen had been in charge of the sponsorship program; he had sent the telegram demanding the wire transfer when the balloon reached 18,000 feet. Within a month, he left Hilton and took a marketing job with a hamburger chain in Florida.

◆ ◆ ◆

Larry met in mid-February with Barron Hilton at the Flying M ranch, eager to convince his patron to let him try it again. But Hilton delivered more bad news. His board of directors, in a movement led by Mike Ribero, had put their feet down. No more of the shareholders' money must be spent on the balloon project. That wasn't Hilton's line of business, they argued, and the public failure and ridicule did nothing for the firm.

Of course, Barron Hilton was free to spend his own fortune to see *Earthwinds* fly one more time. And, in fact, he was hooked; he couldn't let go of Larry's dream. Larry bargained for one more try, a project in which he alone would be the leader.

From Hilton's personal perspective, the only value in the *Earthwinds* Hilton was the marketing exposure a successful flight would bring. It would be measured by the number of times the news media mentioned the 'H-word.' Barron Hilton made a commitment to support one more launch—but told Larry that *Earthwinds* would become a bare-bones, low-budget operation. There would be significant reductions in expenditures, and none of the big-company perquisites that they enjoyed.

And once again, as in the Akron days and during the first year in Reno, Larry Newman would manage it all.

Back in Scottsdale, Larry directed his lawyer Michael Widener to accept Wilcox's offer to dissolve the now doubly outdated American Soviet Balloon Venture (there was no 'Soviet Union' and there was no 'Soviet' balloonist involved. Larry incorporated a new business, *Earthwinds*, Inc., which became the shell for continuing the project.

Within that charter, the project remained alive, however tenuously.

◆   ◆   ◆

Larry exerted his personal efforts at pr damage control.

He and his two crewmates wrote personal stories for a national ballloonists' magazine. '*Earthwinds* Hilton—we know it will work,' Larry began. 'After the longest flight to date…'

He saw to it that Abruzzo's and Melton's stories praised his skill as the pilot. He called up newspaper reporters and quizzed them about stories they had written about the flight, going over their stories line-by-line. He denounced those in the news business who 'know all the negatives' about his project.

◆   ◆   ◆

But some influential reporters thought that *Earthwinds* had completely lost its credibility.

'I became dismayed at the utter lack of candor on the part of the people running the project, including Larry himself,' Malcolm Browne told me. The New York Times reporter, who had enthusiastically followed the project for two years and had traveled to Reno to watch the latest launch, now derided 'the whole charade' of the January flight. 'They knew 15 minutes after they took off that they were going to land in California that afternoon,' Browne said.

◆ ◆ ◆

Larry complained about the pictures Clay Lacey had made from the Lear that flew so close to *Earthwinds* at its highest altitude. They weren't of print quality, he said.

He told Gamma to assign another photographer. What had Bill Swersey done wrong? Gamma editors asked. His camera had distracted Harry Maybeck during a weather briefing.

For his part, Swersey, like many others, was tiring of *Earthwinds*, and stung from the repeated barbs. He was splitting costs 50/50 with Gamma, and had invested nearly $10,000 of his own money in film, lodging and travel, now with dubious prospects of ever recovering his investment. He was ambivalent about returning for another series of attempts—but had sufficient professional pride to defend adamantly his right to do so.

'I've been meaning to give Larry an earful,' he wrote months later, 'and am still burning at his latest criticism of me. All I can do now is wish him the worst.'

◆ ◆ ◆

Erin Porter remained with the Hilton organization. She had brought the project to Barron Hilton's attention and felt responsible for the relationship. Her personal loyalty remained with Barron Hilton.

Over the coming months, she would meet quietly with reporters and supporters, as Barron Hilton's personal emissary. The effervescent former flight attendant did her best to project an atmosphere of normalcy within the troubled project.

With the Hilton Hotel serving as the host hotel for the popular Albuquerque Balloon Fiesta, Porter managed an *Earthwinds* exhibit, where most of the balloonists called it 'a laughing stock'.

Quoth the Raven, 'Nevermore'

After the bickering with Raven, Larry knew he had to find another balloon builder. He went back to Winzen, the firm he had approached five years earlier.

By March, Larry was meeting with Raven's sole competitor in the plastic balloon industry. Winzen's liability concerns were allayed by the fact that Hilton's blanket insurance policy could also cover them (as it had covered Raven) against product liability claims.

They began a complete engineering study. Led by Larry Eppley, an engineering manager at Winzen, they wanted to refit the anchor balloon, build a new polyethylene balloon for *Earthwinds*, and undertake a top-to-bottom review of the assumptions and the hardware already in use. Winzen's researchers looked at the valves and their venting capability, which on first analysis had seemed inadequate.

The engineering study focused on the construction as well as the dynamic response of the balloon. Previous assumptions had assumed a stable, floating craft. The flight had demonstrated that the anchor balloon turned and twisted, and risked fouling the suspension and electrical lines.

They looked at the weight situation, too. Why was it necessary to carry 4,000 pounds of bismuth glass bead ballast when one had an anchor balloon? Winzen's engineers recommended increasing the pressure in the anchor balloon from 1.1 atmospheres to 1.5 atmospheres—a dramatic increase in tension on the Spectra fabric.

Winzen engineers also looked at the cumbersome, complicated procedure for carrying liquid helium. Was that necessary? would it really be effective in prolonging a flight?

'We knew what they were trying to do—top off the balloon—but the question was how fast can they boil off the liquid helium,' Eppley said. 'Our studies showed that you need considerably more heat than you can get from the ambient air at high altitude.'

Finally, the new engineers wanted to evaluate the entire capsule, the life-support equipment and power sources. While they were going over his invention, Larry wrote an article he called *Earthwinds*—Never Give Up, in which he defended the decision to dump Raven (because of the 'eleven catastrophic failures in the preceding five years') and his selection of Winzen.

'Dr. James Rand, president of Winzen, informed us that they had zero failures of their balloons during the same period. Winzen's engineering, manufacturing and support staff appears to be top notch.'

Larry met with Winzen's team several times during the summer, reviewing their changes. The polyethylene balloon was made of stronger material, and featured three fill tubes instead of two.

Winzen removed the upper high-pressure fan from the anchor balloon and replaced it with a flapper mechanism in addition to a low-pressure fan. That simplified the wiring on board and reduced the power requirement.

Winzen's senior engineer, John Crenshaw, was concerned that the new team was 'constrained by the budget from making major revisions.'

'We took a preliminary look, and concluded that *Earthwinds* had a reasonably good chance of success if certain things happened,' Crenshaw said. 'But we made clear that we would not be involved in flight management procedures. *Earthwinds* would provide their own people for that.'

'Our goal was to deliver the polyethylene balloon and the anchor balloon refurbished with a new plastic liner to Stead Airport in Reno by the end of October.'

Crenshaw met with Larry in August and warned him:

'The thing that this system requires is a great amount of anticipatory flight management. It requires anticipating actions not just by a few minutes, but in some cases by several hours.

'This vehicle exemplifies the Pilot's First Commandment: Thou shalt never, ever, let this vehicle get ahead of you.'

'Yeah,' Larry smiled, 'I learned that with my first pair of roller skates.'

The sincerest form of flattery

Earthwinds' fifth failure had increased doubts in many people that the earth could be navigated in a balloon of that design. Had *Earthwinds* even come close to its goal, or stayed up longer, the dream might have looked realistic. Now, prospective sponsors held back.

However, failure didn't stop the dreaming. Those who had been awaiting the outcome of *Earthwinds*' final attempt now found new vigor in their own plans.

'Larry Newman has proven that it takes more than money alone to make a global balloon flight,' said Troy Bradley, Abruzzo's old partner.

Buoyed by his success in the trans-Atlantic race, Bradley began a public subscription campaign to raise $2 million for a high-altitude flight. He proposed using an off-the-shelf scientific balloon made by Raven, flying at 100,000 feet altitude. At such a high altitude, he would drift west rather than east. Bradley's team asked an Albuquerque oil rig firm to build their capsule. The crew would attempt to purchase pressure suits left over from the Russian space program—and remain in their bulky suits for the entire flight.

Tim Lachenmeier, the designer and inventor of *Earthwinds*' hourglass-shaped, two-balloon idea, who four years earlier had persuaded Larry Newman that this system could fly around the world, now turned his attention to the global flight he wanted to make. Raven would build a "cocoon balloon"—the pressure vessel inside the helium envelope. Joining him as co-pilots would be Tom Barrow and Col. Joe Kittinger, the ex-Air Force balloonist. When The New York Times called for a comment in mid-summer, Lachenmeier volunteered that Richard Branson would likely be a sponsor and that the Russians might loan a cosmonaut to the effort.

A surprise entrant in the global flight sweepstakes was Dick Rutan. Employees at his brother's Rutan Aircraft Factory down the road from Edwards Air Force Base experimented on the leading edge of aviation technology. Recently, they had built the Delta Clipper, a reusable rocket that would take off and land vertically. Now, for Dick, they had also outlined a small, lightweight, one-man balloon capsule. Rutan went to Cameron Balloons in England, to discuss purchasing a 250,000 cubic foot hybrid helium-and-hot air balloon. He would fly below the altitude where he'd need a pressurized cabin.

But the competitor considered most-likely-to-succeed remained the one who said the least. The Flying Dutchman Henk Brink, through his Global Adventures Foundation, commissioned a Dutch submarine manufacturer to finish his pressurized capsule, and Cameron Balloons to deliver a 700,000 cubic foot helium/ hot air balloon. By early autumn Brink and his wife/co-pilot were sitting in The Netherlands waiting for weather. They were committed to flying by December—but the Dutchmen never announced their plans in advance. Their operations center at Schipol Airport in Amsterdam would come alive only six hours before launch, giving competitors little to go on.

The number one question on the minds of the *Earthwinds* camp was: What's Brink up to?

Barebones

Attempting to rebuild his project, Larry and Lynne met with Jim and Laura Kitchell for dinner at their sizable modern house. The Kitchells, leading citizens of Reno, were members of the local balloon club. Jim Kitchell was a prosperous business executive and chairman of the Reno Airport Authority, which had approved Larry's use of Stead Airport.

The Newmans mentioned that they were thinking about asking some of members of the local balloon club to host the *Earthwinds* volunteers during the next launch attempt. The Kitchells nodded and said that would be nice. Nothing more was said—until the next morning.

'Larry and I were thinking about our conversation about the volunteers last night,' Lynne told Mrs. Kitchell in a phone call, 'and we decided to take you up on your offer. We're going to move in with you!'

That specific prospect hadn't been discussed, of course. The Kitchells did some thinking about the housing plan, and thought less of it than their polite smiles had earlier indicated. The Newmans would not move in with them, after all.

◆ ◆ ◆

The project desperately needed money and management.

Long ago, when the anchor balloon was added to the design, Richard Branson had negotiated a permanent presence for Virgin Atlantic Airways' logo. As long as there was an anchor balloon skirt, it would prominently bear the airline's logo. Now, with the anchor balloon being rebuilt, *Earthwinds* needed money to carry on. Hilton approached Virgin, and Branson's company put in an additional $250,000 to keep the project alive for one more attempt.

◆ ◆ ◆

Tony Hesch, a Reno area volunteer, would serve as project coordinator and liaison to Weather, Operations, Engineering, and Launch.

Hesch put together an organization filled with familiar faces: Dan Gudgel and Steve Brown would assist Maybeck at launch. In Operations, Dave Bussen would operate the computers and Dick Blosser would try again to serve as the radio communicator.

In the engineering department, John Ackroyd would serve as chief, assisted by the Three Amigos as electricians, and Mike Schein as the cryogenic helium handler.

Launch master Koh Murai held his job, with Homer Woodie, the retired NASA balloon man on the poly, and Tony Rivera, who would manage the anchor.

But there was no mistaking who really was in charge. The names at the top of the pyramid were Larry Newman, Pilot-in-Command; Lynne Newman, Project Administrator.

And since Larry was in a position to demand total loyalty, he asked everyone on the staff to sign a statement promising that they would not write or speak about the project unless they had his prior written approval.

Not everyone agreed. Co-captains Richard Abruzzo and Dave Melton had arranged their contract with Hilton the previous fall under which they were free to write about their adventure with *Earthwinds*. Now, when Larry pressed for the new loyalty statement, Melton went along with it, but Abruzzo did not. The tension between him and Newman quickly boiled over into anger.

Richard remembered hearing about some of the disagreements his late father had had with Larry Newman. Twice on the Double Eagle V flight across the Pacific, Ben had to physically restrain Larry from premature ballasting that would have doomed the flight. On the ground and in the air, Larry was prone to hot-headedness, rash action, and questionable judgment, and Abruzzo remained concerned about his own safety.

In early summer, Ben Abruzzo's son resigned from the crew a second and final time, ending the storybook relationship that never was, the poetic symmetry of the surrogate father-to-son-of-father.

◆ ◆ ◆

The opening in the crew gave Larry a chance to make a key move. Who could help the project the most? He needed a survivor, a pilot with courage, and someone who could look up to him. He thought back to his friend Kerry Bartlett, the Marine Corps helicopter pilot from the Mountain Warfare School.

Bartlett held a fixed-wing rating. He could bring knowledge of survival, medicine, aviation and adventure to the team. Bartlett had left the Marine Corps and when he qualified for a pilot certificate in hot air balloons, Larry named him to the flight crew.

Meanwhile, Melton, at age 35, was emerging as a serious, intelligent partner. He radiated confident enthusiasm. His friendly personality and fresh approach to problem solving won him the respect of the support staff.

He arranged another leave of absence from his job at the Los Alamos National Laboratory in New Mexico, where he was working on developing a solid waste incinerator.

Melton was a natural adventurer. Before he discovered ballooning he had raced on the NASCAR Dirt Track Race Car Circuit. He knew engines, the life-supporting component of *Earthwinds*.

◆ ◆ ◆

John Ackroyd remained, working directly for Larry, preparing the capsule and the suspension system, and consulting on the launch. The regular team members—the Amigos, in particular—wouldn't have returned without Ackroyd's leadership.

Gene Kemmerline's expertise was high tech electrical wiring. Called to Reno in September to ready the capsule, he literally had his work cut out for him.

With diminished sponsorship and the new engineering study in hand, Larry had gone through the capsule removing equipment that was not mission-critical. He took out the fax machine that had been linked to the Inmarsat-C, and he removed the Inmarsat satellite telephone.

He removed the three custom-built Russian atmospheric and environmental experiments on which Vladimir and the scientists at Moscow State University had spent so many months.

The loss of Hilton's corporate sponsorship meant that the corporate business jet that had been gloriously re-painted and trumpeted as the "*Earthwinds* Hilton Chase Plane", could not be used for chasing a balloon around the world. There would be no VIP entourage—no Astronaut Gene Cernan, no Richard Branson, none of Barron Hilton's cigar-chomping cronies, no Hollywood celebrities, no wives or girlfriends, no official photographer. Nor would there be extravagantly staged promotional appearances enroute at strategic business sites or at Hilton or Conrad hotels around the world. Instead, a small jet would carry a camera crew for Wilcox's tenuous movie.

Without a television audience on the ground, there was no need for the live video or the digital still photography for which Canon and Codek had developed special software and hardware. The only video of the flight would be shot with standard video cameras, and released after landing.

Kemmerline pulled out the now-unnecessary cable that had made *Earthwinds* such a marvel, and lightened the load by hundreds of pounds.

The fiber optic cable cutters were another story. Although Larry had survived without using them on *Earthwinds*' first two flights, inevitably there would come a time when the cutters would save the life of his crew. Their purpose was a quick jettisoning of the balloons at the moment of touch down. If the balloons couldn't be cut away from the capsule in a high-wind landing, the capsule would drag across the terrain, into rocks, crevasses, buildings, power lines or other obstacles.

Kemmerline remained baffled by their continuing failure and set about making them work right. They still balked. Hoping to save the cost of a full-factory repair job, Larry found a retired Holex technician in Florida, to whom he sent his vital cutters. The retiree worked on them and sent them back—but they were still not functioning. Returned, installed and tested, they failed again. So back they went to the factory for overhaul.

Then another serious equipment problem cropped up. When Larry dispatched the two liquid helium dewars to be refilled in mid-October, he found that one could not hold pressure. Over the years, the fragile dewars had taken a lot of abuse for which they were never intended. Custom-crafted at a cost of $250,000, they were designed for one-time use in a stable aircraft and not for over-the-road transport or rough handling. Yet they had been trucked from Boulder, Colo. to Middletown, Ohio, (where they were filled), then to Akron. After the two aborted launch tries from Akron, they had been trucked back to Scottsdale, and finally to Reno. Twice they had been trucked over the mountains into California to be filled with the precious liquid. They had been crash-landed in the Sierra Nevada Mountains, in January 1993; banged into the tarmac during the launch field accident in November 1993, carried up to 37,000 feet and then dropped into the dirt in Tranquility, Calif. on the January 1994 flight.

The dewars made *Earthwinds* unique: if used correctly, their contents gave the crew the opportunity for in-flight refueling—a back-up to the anchor balloon—and Larry had tried gasifying helium on each flight.

The loss of one dewar would not only reduce the potential duration, but would have a domino effect on all other calculations: all calculations for helium balloon volume and anchor balloon pressure were based on carrying a fixed amount of weight aloft. Leaving behind a dewar weighing 1,500 pounds, or seven percent of the gross weight, meant putting in less helium at liftoff. But then, the balloon would rise higher—well above the jet stream, and the flight would go off course. One could compensate by over pressurizing the anchor balloon, but that could become an explosive solution.

Larry knew he had little choice but to send the crippled dewar back to Cryogenic Technical Services in Boulder, where technicians could try to repair it. It would be a month before they knew if it could be fixed.

Closing in / closing out

Winzen's new helium balloon and the refurbished anchor balloon arrived in Reno on Oct. 18. Erin Porter mailed hundreds of VIP invitations, promising to call or fax everyone within two days of the flight, a chore she performed for Barron Hilton before every flight.

Hilton still entertained two hopes of recovering his investment. In the most optimistic scenario, stamp collectors would buy signed covers that had flown around the world. That plan necessitated having the Reno post office cancel thousands of pieces of mail each day of a flight; the envelopes would be signed by the flight crew, and cancelled again at the landing site.

The second chance for recouping was through calls to the 900-number: 1-900-93-EARTH. What did callers get for $2 per minute? They heard a scratchy, 3-minute narrative by actor Cliff Robertson, with music in the background; it was harder to understand than a cheap home answering machine. Complaints poured in. When the flight began, the plan was to have Larry's voice follow Robertson's on the long and expensive message.

◆　◆　◆

Hilton Hotels Corp. surprised the investment world in mid-November by announcing that it had hired an investment bank to study 'strategic alternatives to enhance shareholder value.' Barron Hilton, now 67, was putting his company on the auction block. The stock jumped 10 points in one day. Senior Hilton executives, quietly acknowledging boardroom tension, had already begun leaving the company.

Larry Newman's chief patron was disengaging from the business. If *Earthwinds* didn't fly before the company was sold, it probably never would fly under any company's sponsorship.

Barron Hilton was not the only business executive capable of surprises. In Sioux Falls, Raven chairman Dave Christiansen announced that his company was acquiring for $1.1 million in cash the balloon-manufacturing plant of Winzen, Intl.—his only competitor, and the only other supplier of high-altitude research balloons.

The announcement meant that *Earthwinds* could never acquire another balloon.

◆　◆　◆

Neither the weather in northwest Nevada nor the jet stream pattern offered an immediate opportunity to fly, but that was academic anyway: key equipment remained out for repair, and new distractions came along.

In early December, Winzen engineers began expressing second thoughts about the anchor balloon. Now they 'de-rated' the allowable maximum pressure. They now believed that the anchor would be less effective a ballast-maker than previously thought.

As wind and snowstorms plagued Reno, the publicity machine announced that the team was ready.

Almost at once, a weather opportunity appeared—on the weekend before Christmas. The announcement went out on the wire services, and plans were put in motion. They would launch on Wright Brothers Day, Dec. 17. They'd be in the air during the Winter solstice, and back on the ground before New Year's Eve.

For this attempt, a weak high-pressure system would prevail over the western U.S., accompanied by valley fog. In the upper atmosphere, a high-amplitude track led up toward Montana, swooped southeast toward the Gulf Coast, and up sharply over Jacksonville, Fla.

Preparations went forward. Tanks were topped off, volunteers and media contacted, launch equipment moved into place. In an unopened shipping crate sat the repaired anchor balloon. Winzen's new helium balloon was fitted with its valve, hooked to the crane, and lifted above the capsule.

The decision about whether to send this flight into Saturday's marginal weather went right down to the wire. By 2 p.m., Maybeck, Hesch and Newman convened to find high wind moving across the desert, a storm brewing on the Pacific coast, a storm building on the east coast from the Carolinas to Newfoundland, and a meandering jet stream pattern. With the noose drawing tighter, they closed that launch window.

Nothing else looked suitable for at least two weeks. The camp adjourned for Christmas.

Flight III: Fallin' into Fallon

The day after Christmas, the team reassembled. During the lull, Larry had reconsidered his relationship with Kerry Bartlett. The ex-Marine Corps pilot was insisting on checklists, going by the book. It contrasted with Larry's personal freewheeling approach. Bartlett had begun to speak up. The staff sensed tension brewing. Soon, the Marine Corps pilot whose heroism and Arctic survival skills had so impressed Larry, was dumped on the pretense that he 'wanted to spend more time with his family.'

To fill Bartlett's seat, Larry turned to George Saad, the 35-year-old mechanical engineering technician from NASA in Cleveland who had been with the project for more than three years as a volunteer. Saad, who spent ten years in the Air Force, had been responsible for connecting and monitoring instruments in the capsule.

'George's knowledge and expertise in the on-board electrical and mechanical system provides an extra measure of confidence to the flight crew,' Newman announced in a formal statement. 'He has been with the *Earthwinds* Hilton project longer than most of our project team members, and has undergone in-depth pre-flight training. He brings with him survival skills honed during his 10 years in the Air Force, and has completed the two-week skydiving course required for each member of our flight crew.'

In the game of musical chairs, Saad thus became the 10th *Earthwinds* crew-member, filling the highly volatile third seat.

◆ ◆ ◆

Facing an impending launch window, the new crew swung into readiness.

On Thursday, Dec. 29, the sub-tropical jet stream was moving north to mid-Nevada. If they caught it just right, a large high-pressure system to the west of Reno would send the balloon south, where it might intercept the sub-tropical jet. The preparations once again went forward full-tilt, with publicity alerts, volunteers scrambling, sleep cycles disturbed.

The surface conditions, however, were deteriorating. By 9 p.m., the wind was 20 knots on Stead field, and the sky was overcast—not launch weather. The media, inevitably, recounted the project's history of failed flights, launch field incidents and bad weather.

The whole procedure rolled over into the next day, where it was repeated. This time the countdown went right down to the moment before the helium shoot. At 11 p.m., the soundings from the Dessert Research Institute indicated that the wind would remain testy throughout the night, and launch was postponed.

On Friday, Dec. 30, there was another 2 p.m. briefing. The crew had been told to expect only a one-in-five chance of flying, but they had to go through the motions anyway. This time, Steve Brown and Harry Maybeck delivered good news: the surface weather would be perfect: calm, clear and not too cold. In the upper atmosphere, the jet stream core was already east by a few hundred miles, but they could catch it if they left by sunrise. This looked real.

The launch team went right to work. But first, Larry warned the ground crew that no one could bring a camera or take a picture without his permission. Only his personal photographer recorded the proceedings.

Helium inflation began at 10 p.m. The team knew their assignments—this was the fourth inflation in Nevada—and it went faster with Winzen's third fill tube.

The first surprise of the evening came upon opening the anchor balloon. It had been packed differently than Raven used to pack it, and as a result, when laid out it was turned upside down. That would complicate the launch in unexpected ways.

Annoying handling problems plagued the process. By 2 a.m., when inflation of the re-built anchor balloon began, workers could see some brown stains and splotches on it. Gene Kemmerline recognized dirt from the cotton field at Fresno where the once-pristine white balloon touched down in January.

In the 22-degree cold night air, as it always does in the desert, the humidity began to climb. By 5 a.m., the air was saturated with 84 percent humidity.

And during the Stonehenge maneuver, when the helium balloon was raised to allow the anchor balloon to come into place directly below the capsule, the anchor balloon turned again. The umbilical lines from the capsule to the anchor had become twisted. In response, the capsule and helium balloon counter-rotated, and fouled the four restraint lines.

As the sun came up over the mountains, light shined through the translucent balloon and the thin skirt above the anchor balloon.

The load cell reading told the crew that the all-up weight was 24,700 pounds, including 1,600 pounds of ballast—far less than the 4,000 pounds carried on the earlier flights.

The launch procedure once again called for backing off some of the pressure in the anchor balloon. Again Larry waived it off. He wanted to ascend with the anchor balloon full. The valve was opened, and the anchor balloon breathed out some air.

There was a chance the pyramid lines could foul the umbilical lines leading to the anchor balloon, and that would disable the anchor altogether. At this point, the launch procedure called for firing the explosive squibs holding the balloon down, to begin the flight.

Rather than attempt that, however, Koh Murai and Larry decided it was best to use a bolt cutter and manually chop the restraint lines. The procedure had not been practiced before. Murai's team brought out new cutters and severed the restrain lines.

At 6:45 a.m. on December 31, 1994, *Earthwinds* left the ground for the third time. Larry Newman, Dave Melton, 36, and rookie balloonist George Saad, 35, climbed into a clear blue sky.

With the balloon moving slowly to the east, John Ackroyd cracked to a reporter:

"We've actually got the balloon away. We got it away very cleanly…it's actually going in the right direction for the first time."

The craft climbed swiftly, 800 feet per minute, and ballasting was hardly necessary because of the mild inversion at 500 feet. The big Winzen helium balloon carried the craft upward faster.

Earthwinds passed the now-familiar milestones: over Pea Vine, the highest mountain; above the last inversion layer; to 8,000 feet, where the doors were closed and sealed; the start of the screaming screw compressor making oxygen. Inside the capsule, the crew wore Bose noise cancellation headsets to suppress the engine sounds.

Climbing steadily, a little faster now, *Earthwinds* entered a wind stream at 24,000 feet, carrying it along at 25 knots, a little south of east. The temperature outside was minus 33 degrees F.

Two hours into the flight, it was time to close the valve on the anchor balloon, to slow down *Earthwinds'* ascent so it could park at its intended float altitude.

Here was the moment of truth for the Winzen engineering team. They had rated the Spectra anchor balloon far stronger than Raven had—with a bigger lift balloon, you needed more ballast, and the only source of that was the anchor balloon. Lachenmeier's engineering team had come to the opposite conclusion after the first flight: keep the helium balloon at 1.1 million cubic feet, and enlarge the anchor balloon to 100-foot diameter. One of the engineering teams was wrong.

Monitoring the pressure in the anchor balloon on the Magnahelic instruments, Larry radioed down that the anchor balloon reading was .73 psi. Already, the anchor balloon was pressurizing, and reducing the rate of ascent. It was still well below the rated design capability that Winzen's engineers had ascribed to it—but now more than 12 percent over the maximum limit that Tim Lachenmeier had recommended.

The balloon ascended through 28,000 feet.

In the thin morning air, there was a loud explosion, then a physical jolt. The capsule rocked violently, and Larry, Dave and George hit the deck. Glaring through the bubble-shaped window in the floor of the capsule, George Saad could see what had happened:

The anchor balloon had exploded!

Part of the upper valve had blasted toward the pressurized capsule, careening into it. The fabric shredded from seam to seam, from gore to gore, vertically and horizontally. The anchor balloon emptied itself in seconds and Saad could see it hanging below like a limp dishrag.

Moments later, the rate of climb indicator showed a rapid rate of ascent as *Earthwinds'* giant poly balloon, relieved of considerable weight, raced upward. The dynamic pressure on the helium balloon in such a rapid climb was enormous. Within moments, it might rupture. With the balloon already at 100 percent of its helium capacity, gas now flowed out the three overflow tubes.

Larry radioed a Mayday to the ground as the balloon climbed higher, out of control now. He opened the electrical valves on the helium balloon—yet the system, now freed of hundreds of pounds of weight, continued soaring skyward.

As it climbed and climbed, the crew feared for their lives. Overpressurization of the helium balloon was one huge risk—if it split, they would fall seven miles to their death—but the crew also wondered whether the capsule pressure would hold. It reached 38,000 feet before the helium valving had the intended effect.

Then the crippled *Earthwinds* balloon began its long descent into oblivion, slowly but very surely.

Far below them, the crew could see a thick cloud deck where the air was misty and warm. The valleys were filled with fog as the cold air trapped in them was warmed by the sunshine. The ground was nearly obscured, and the conditions dropped to IFR—Instrument Flight Rules—as the balloon descended.

Somewhere over Fallon Naval Air Station, the balloon entered a deck of soupy clouds and disappeared below the horizon. In the Operations Center back at the Reno Hilton, tracking was lost.

Over a remote valley in a test range at Fallon Naval Air Station, 80 miles east of Reno, and three hours after reaching peak altitude, the long, useless remains of the anchor balloon bumped the ground, and arrested the descent. It was rough, desolate terrain, and the wind was picking up.

The Spectra remnants dragged through the rocky desolation. Larry knew that he had to get rid of the helium balloon, or risk being dragged into more treacherous areas.

As the capsule itself touched down at 11:34 a.m., Larry fired the fiber optic cutters to release the helium balloon.

But the cutters failed again! They had never worked right! Now the balloon was dragging through this ordnance test range. He tried to rip it out manually, but couldn't. There was no choice but to continue valving helium out the top—an agonizingly slow process. Eventually, the weight of the Spectra, the capsule and the gasoline tank and helium dewars became too much for the exhaling helium balloon, and the rough drag across the desert came to an end.

Eventually it would take 12 men pulling on the manual destruct line to open the helium balloon.

◆ ◆ ◆

But it did not take that many men to pull the destruct line on financing. Barron Hilton held that line firmly in his grasp, and he had been embarrassed for the last time. After a short grace period of letting the dust settle, he had concluded that he would let this project expire.

Long ago, Speedy Newman had taught Larry one secret of salesmanship: you gotta talk faster than the ice cream melts.

This time, the words fell on deaf ears. The ice cream had melted.

Newman announced in March that Hilton would no longer sponsor his flights. Events were overtaking him, sponsors had abandoned him, and the dream that he had inherited from Ben Abruzzo now belonged to others.

Epilogue

The global flight

The world was circumnavigated by balloon during the first 21 days of March 1999, by the Swiss adventurer and psychiatrist Dr. Bertrand Piccard and Brian Jones. They flew from Chateau d'Oex, Switzerland, and landed in Egypt. It was Piccard's third try. American Steve Fossett made the flight solo in 2001, flying in the Southern Hemisphere. It was his seventh attempt.

Where are they now?

Larry Newman and Lynne Newman divorced a few years after *Earthwinds* ended. Larry left America West Airlines. In 1997, he suffered multiple broken bones and nearly lost his eyesight in a skydiving accident after colliding in mid-air with another jumper while approaching a landing zone.

Richard Abruzzo continues flying hot air and gas balloons and has set national and world records, some surpassing feats of his late father, Ben Abruzzo. He operates a business in Albuquerque NM.

John Ackroyd continues supporting adventure projects, and played a leading role in the Brandon-Lindstrand global flight attempts, as well as supporting new efforts to surpass the land speed record.

Tom Barrow died in April 2000 of complications from brain cancer. He spent his last years as a design engineer with Raven Industries' Aerostar Division, and remained cheerful and helpful to the end.

Richard Branson was knighted by Queen Elizabeth II, and made three unsuccessful attempts to fly around the world by balloon with Per Linstrand. He continues to operate the Virgin Group of companies and make piles of money.

Henk Brink abandoned his global flight without ever ascending.

Malcolm Browne continued reporting for The New York Times until after Bertrand Piccard's successful flight. Browne retired to a small town in Vermont with his wife Leilu. He still regrets being misled by Larry Newman and remains keenly interested in balloon flight.

Liesl Clark lives near Boston and works as a producer for Nova, where she chases adventure stories and was a member of the Everest IMAX film team. She has written, directed and produced television documentaries since 1992, including the Emmy-nominated films "Everest-the Death Zone" and "Lost on Everest," which documents the 1999 discovery of the body of George Leigh Mallory.

Neil Cohen sells billboard space online for a San Francisco company.

Vladimir Dzhanibekov retired from the Russian space program, served for a while as director of the Cosmonaut Museum near Moscow, and now works for a wireless communication company in Russia.

Mike Emich continues flying balloons and multi-engine fixed-wing aircraft. He was promoted to Lieutenant in the Akron Fire Department.

Vice Admiral Donald D. Engen was killed on July 13, 1998 when a motorized glider he was flying came apart in the skies over Nevada. At the time of his death he was the Director of the Smithsonian's National Air & Space Museum in Washington DC.

Barron Hilton remains one of the richest men in America as chairman of Hilton Hotels Corp.

Tim Lachenmeier left Raven Industries and joined GSSL Inc. near his native Tillamook, Oregon, where he builds and operates super-pressure scientific high-altitude balloons. Koh Murai works with him.

Dave Melton joined up with Dick Rutan and obtained Hilton sponsorship for their global balloon attempt in 1998, which ended with both pilots bailing out when their balloon ruptured. Melton suffered a severe hip injury on landing, but recovered and returned to work at Los Alamos National Laboratory in New Mexico. The balloon capsule was destroyed by fire hours later when it struck powerlines in Louisiana.

Don Moses married Carol Hart and returned to Kauai, Hawaii and their boat business, HiTech Fiberglasss Inc., where they build and sell the SeaCat, a highly regarded twin-hulled catamaran.

Erin Porter remained active in supporting around-the-world ballooning projects, helping Dick Rutan, then Richard Branson and Per Lindstrand. In 2003 she moved to the Outer Banks of North Carolina to market the Centennial of Flight for the National Parks Service.

Vernon Rich continues his adventurous life, participating in the attempt to rescue and fly away the B-29 KeeBird that crashed on the ice in northern Greenland in 1947, as recounted in the book, "Hunting Warbirds." He supported jet car driver Craig Breedlove's Spirit of America. Between adventures he and his wife Darlene live in Phoenix.

Bob Rice made forecasts that led the Team New Zealand sailing syndicate to victory in the America's Cup in 1994 and its defense in 1998; he continues forecasting for global sailing events. After directing 27 long-distance balloon flights and three Everest climbs, he keeps trying to retire, but occasionally accepts special projects such as assisting Steve Fossett in his global flights. He lives in Wolfboro, New Hampshire.

George Saad still works at NASA in Cleveland.

Leonard Snellman, meteorologist, died in 1999 from congestive heart failure following a battle with cancer. He had spent 39 years as a meteorologist for the U.S. government.

Bill Swersey contributed photos to this book. He works for a multi-media company in New York City.

John Wilcox, President of American Adventure Productions Inc., in Aspen, Colorado, continues producing documentary series programming for network broadcast and has won 24 National Emmy Awards for documentary programming. He also wrote and produced a feature film for Warner Brothers, The Amazing Panda Adventure, the first American feature film shot entirely in China.

0-595-28705-0